A SOURCE BOOK OF

MEDIÆVAL HISTORY

DOCUMENTS ILLUSTRATIVE OF EUROPEAN LIFE AND
INSTITUTIONS FROM THE GERMAN INVASIONS
TO THE RENAISSANCE

EDITED BY

FREDERIC AUSTIN OGG, A. M.

ASSISTANT IN HISTORY IN HARVARD UNIVERSITY
AND INSTRUCTOR IN SIMMONS COLLEGE

NEW YORK ·:· CINCINNATI ·:· CHICAGO

AMERICAN BOOK COMPANY

COPYRIGHT, 1907, BY

FREDERIC AUSTIN OGG

ENTERED AT STATIONERS' HALL, LONDON

W. P. 2

PREFACE

THIS book has been prepared in consequence of a conviction, derived from some years of teaching experience, (1) that sources, of proper kind and in carefully regulated amount, can profitably be made use of by teachers and students of history in elementary college classes, in academies and preparatory schools, and in the more advanced years of the average high school, and (2) that for mediæval history there exists no published collection which is clearly adapted to practical conditions of work in such classes and schools.

It has seemed to me that a source book designed to meet the requirements of teachers and classes in the better grade of secondary schools, and perhaps in the freshman year of college work, ought to comprise certain distinctive features, first, with respect to the character of the selections presented, and, secondly, in regard to general arrangement and accompanying explanatory matter. In the choice of extracts I have sought to be guided by the following considerations: (1) that in all cases the materials presented should be of real value, either for the historical information contained in them or for the more or less indirect light they throw upon mediæval life or conditions; (2) that, for the sake of younger students, a relatively large proportion of narrative (annals, chronicles, and biography) be introduced and the purely documentary material be slightly subordinated; (3) that, despite this principle, documents of vital importance, such as *Magna Charta* and *Unam Sanctam*, which cannot be ignored in even the most hasty or elementary study, be presented with some fulness; and (4) that, in general, the rule should be to give longer passages from fewer sources, rather than more fragmentary ones from a wider range.

With respect to the manner of presenting the selections, I have sought: (1) to offer careful translations—some made afresh from the printed originals, others adapted from good translations already available—but with as much simplification and modernization of language as close adherence to the sense will permit. Literal, or nearly literal,

3

translations are obviously desirable for maturer students, but, because of the involved character of mediæval writings, are rarely readable, and are as a rule positively repellent to the young mind; (2) to provide each selection, or group of selections, with an introductory explanation, containing the historical setting of the extract, with perhaps some comment on its general significance, and also a brief sketch of the writer, particularly when he is an authority of exceptional importance, as Einhard, Joinville, or Froissart; and (3) to supply, in footnotes, somewhat detailed aid to the understanding of obscure allusions, omitted passages, and especially place names and technical terms.

For permission to reprint various translations, occasionally verbatim but usually in adapted form, I am under obligation to the following: Messrs. Houghton, Mifflin and Co., publishers of Miss Henry's translation of Dante's *De Monarchia;* Messrs. Henry Holt and Co., publishers of Lee's *Source Book of English History;* Messrs. Ginn and Co., publishers of Robinson's *Readings in European History;* Messrs. Charles Scribner's Sons, publishers of Thatcher and McNeal's *Source Book for Mediæval History;* Messrs. G. P. Putnam's Sons, publishers of Robinson and Rolfe's *Petrarch;* and Professor W. E. Lingelbach, of the University of Pennsylvania, representing the University of Pennsylvania *Translations and Reprints from the Original Sources of European History.*

In the preparation of the book I have received invaluable assistance from numerous persons, among whom the following, at least, should be named: Professor Samuel B. Harding, of the University of Indiana, who read the entire work in manuscript and has followed its progress from the first with discerning criticism; Professor Charles H. Haskins, of Harvard University, who has read most of the proof-sheets, and whose scholarship and intimate acquaintance with the problems of history teaching have contributed a larger proportion of whatever merits the book possesses than I dare attempt to reckon up; and Professors Charles Gross and Ephraim Emerton, likewise of Harvard, whose instruction and counsel have helped me over many hard places.

The final word must be reserved for my wife, who, as careful amanuensis, has shared the burden of a not altogether easy task.

FREDERIC AUSTIN OGG

CAMBRIDGE, MASS.

INTRODUCTION

THE NATURE AND USE OF HISTORICAL SOURCES

IF one proposes to write a history of the times of Abraham Lincoln, how shall one begin, and how proceed? Obviously, the first thing needed is information, and as much of it as can be had. But how shall information, accurate and trustworthy, be obtained? Of course there are plenty of books on Lincoln, and histories enough covering the period of his career to fill shelf upon shelf. It would be quite possible to spread some dozens of these before one's self and, drawing simply from them, work out a history that would read well and perhaps have a wide sale. And such a book might conceivably be worth while. But if you were reading it, and were a bit disposed to query into the accuracy of the statements made, you would probably find yourself wondering before long just where the writer got his authority for this or that assertion; and if, in foot-note or appendix, he should seem to satisfy your curiosity by citing some other biography or history, you would be quite justified in feeling that, after all, your inquiry remained unanswered,—for whence did this second writer get *his* authority? If you were thus persistent you would probably get hold of the volume **The question** referred to and verify, as we say, the statements of fact **of authority** or opinion attributed to it. When you came upon them **in a book** **of history** you might find it there stated that the point in question is clearly established from certain of Lincoln's own letters or speeches, which are thereupon cited, and perhaps quoted in part. At last you would be satisfied that the thing must very probably be true, for there you would have the words of Lincoln himself upon it; or, on the other hand, you might discover that your first writer had merely adopted an opinion of somebody else which did not have behind it the warrant of any first-hand authority. In either case you might well wonder why, instead of using and referring only to books of other later authors like himself, he did not go directly to Lincoln's own works, get his facts from them, and give authority for his statements at first hand. And if you pushed the matter farther it would very soon occur to you that there are some books on Lincoln and his period which are not carefully written, and therefore not trustworthy, and that your author may very well have used some of these, falling blindly into their errors and at times wholly escaping the correct interpretation of things which could be had, in incontrovertible form, from Lincoln's own pen, or from the testimony of his contemporaries. In other words, you would begin to distrust him because he had failed to go to the "sources" for his materials, or at least for a verification of them.

How, then, shall one proceed in the writing of history in order to make sure of the indispensable quality of accuracy? Clearly, the first thing to be borne in mind is the necessity of getting information through channels which are as direct and immediate as possible. Just as in ascertaining the facts regarding an event of to-day it would be desirable to get the testimony of an eye-witness rather than an account after it had passed from one person to another, suffering more or less distortion at every step, so, in seeking a trustworthy description of the **The superiority of direct sources of knowledge** battle of Salamis or of the personal habits of Charlemagne, the proper course would be to lay hold first of all of whatever evidence concerning these things has come down from Xerxes's or Charlemagne's day to our own, and to put larger trust in this than in more recent accounts which have been played upon by the imagination of their authors and perhaps rendered wholly misleading by errors consciously or unconsciously injected into them. The writer of history must completely divest himself of the notion that a thing is true simply because he finds it in print. He may, and should, read and consider well what others like himself have written upon his subject, but he should be wary of accepting what he finds in such books without himself going to the materials to which these writers have resorted and ascertaining whether they have been used with patience and discrimination. If his subject is Lincoln, he should, for example, make sure above everything else, of reading exhaustively the letters, speeches, and state papers which have been preserved, in print or in manuscript, from Lincoln's pen. Similarly, he should examine with care all letters and communications of every kind transmitted to Lincoln. Then he should familiarize himself with the writings of the leading men of Lincoln's day, whether in the form of letters, diaries, newspaper and magazine articles, or books. The files, indeed, of all the principal periodicals of the time should be gone through in quest of information or suggestions not to be found in other places. And, of course, the vast mass of public and official records would be invaluable—the journals of the two houses of Congress, the dispatches, orders, and accounts of the great executive departments, the arguments before the courts, with the resulting decisions, and the all but numberless other papers which throw light upon the practical conditions and achievements of the governing powers, national, state, and local. However much one may be able to acquire from the reading of later biographies and histories, he ought not to set about the writing of a new book of the sort unless he is willing to toil patiently through all these first-hand, contemporary materials and get some warrant from them, as being nearest the events themselves, for everything of importance that he proposes to say. This rule is equally applicable and urgent whatever the subject in hand—whether the age of Pericles, the Roman Empire, the Norman conquest of England, the French Revolution, or the administrations of George Washington—though, obviously, the character and amount of the contemporary materials of which one can avail himself varies enormously from people to people and from period to period.

History is unlike many other subjects of study in that our knowledge of it, at best, must come to us almost wholly through indirect means. That is to say, all our information regarding the past, and most of it regarding our own day, has to be obtained, in one form or another, through other people, or the remains that they have left behind them. No one of us can know much about even so recent an event as the

Indirect character of all historical knowledge Spanish-American War, except by reading newspapers, magazines and books, talking with men who had part in it, or listening to public addresses concerning it—all indirect means. And, of course, when we go back of the memory of men now living, say to the American Revolution, nobody can lay claim to an iota of knowledge which he has not acquired through indirect channels. In physics or chemistry, if a student desires, he can reproduce in the laboratory practically any phenomenon which he finds described in his books; he need not accept the mere word of his text or of his teacher, but can actually behold the thing with his own eyes. Such experimentation, however, has no place in the study of history, for by no sort of art can a Roman legion or a German comitatus or the battle of Hastings be reproduced before mortal eye.

For our knowledge of history we are therefore obliged to rely absolutely upon human testimony, in one form or another, the value of such testimony depending principally upon the directness with which it comes to us from the men and the times under consideration. If it reaches us with reasonable directness, and represents a well authenticated means of studying the period in question from the writings or other

An "historical source" defined traces left by that period, it is properly to be included in the great body of materials which we have come to call historical sources. An historical source may be defined as any product of human activity or existence that can be used as direct evidence in the study of man's past life and institutions. A moment's thought will suggest that there are "sources" of numerous and widely differing kinds. Roughly speaking, at least, they fall into two great groups: (1) those in writing and (2) those in some form other than writing. The first group is by far the larger and more important. Foremost in it stand annals, chronicles, and histories, written from time to time all along the line of human history, on the cuneiform tablets of the Assyrians or the parchment rolls of the mediæval monks, in the polished Latin of a Livy or the sprightly French of a Froissart. Works of pure literature also—epics, lyrics, dramas, essays—because of the light that they often throw upon the times in which they were written, possess a large value of the same general character. Of nearly equal importance is the great class of materials which may be called documentary—laws, charters, formulæ, accounts, treaties, and official

Written sources orders or instructions. These last are obviously of largest value in the study of social customs, land tenures, systems of government, the workings of courts, ecclesiastical organizations, and political agencies—in other words, of *institutions*— just as chronicles and histories are of greatest service in unraveling the *narrative* side of human affairs.

Of sources which are not in the form of writing, the most important are: (1) implements of warfare, agriculture, household economy, and the chase, large quantities of which have been brought to light in various parts of the world, and which bear witness to the manner of life prevailing among the peoples who produced and used them; (2) coins, hoarded up in treasuries or buried in tombs or ruins of one sort or another, frequently preserving likenesses of important sovereigns, with

Sources other than in writing dates and other materials of use especially in fixing chronology; (3) works of art, surviving intact or with losses or changes inflicted by the ravages of weather and human abuse—the tombs of the Egyptians, the sculpture of the Greeks, the architecture of the Middle Ages, or the paintings of the Renaissance; (4) other constructions of a more practical character, particularly dwelling-houses, roads, bridges, aqueducts, walls, gates, fortresses, and ships,—some well preserved and surviving as they were first fashioned, others in ruins, and still others built over and more or less obscured by modern improvement or adaptation.

These are some of the things to which the writer of history must go for his facts and for his inspiration, and it is to these that the student, whose business is to learn and not to write, ought occasionally to resort to enliven and supplement what he finds in the books. As there are many kinds of sources, so there are many ways in which such materials may be utilized. If, for example, you are studying the life of the Greeks and in that connection pay a visit to a museum of fine arts and scrutinize Greek statuary, Greek vases, and Greek coins, you are very clearly using sources. If your subject is the church life of the later Middle Ages and you journey to Rheims or Amiens or Paris to contemplate the splendid cathedrals in these cities, with their spires

Various ways of using sources and arches and ornamentation, you are, in every proper sense, using sources. You are doing the same thing if you make an observation trip to the Egyptian pyramids, or to the excavated Roman forum, or if you traverse the line of old Watling Street—nay, if you but visit Faneuil Hall, or tramp over the battlefield of Gettysburg. Many of these more purely "material" sources can be made use of only after long and sometimes arduous journeys, or through the valuable, but somewhat less satisfactory, medium of pictures and descriptions. Happily, however, the art of printing and the practice of accumulating enormous libraries have made possible the indefinite duplication of *written* sources, and consequently the use of them at almost any time and in almost any place. There is but one Sphinx, one Parthenon, one Sistine Chapel; there are not many Roman roads, feudal castles, or Gothic cathedrals; but scarcely a library in any civilized country is without a considerable number of the monumental *documents* of human history —the funeral oration of Pericles, the laws of Tiberius Gracchus, Magna Charta, the theses of Luther, the Bill of Rights, the Constitution of the United States—not to mention the all but limitless masses of histories, biographies, poems, letters, essays, memoirs, legal codes, and official records of every variety which are available for any one who seriously desires to make use of them.

But why should the younger student trouble himself, or be troubled, with any of these things? Might he not get all the history he can be expected to know from books written by scholars who have given their lives to exploring, organizing, and sifting just such sources? There can be no question that schools and colleges to-day have the use of better text-books in history than have ever before been available, and that truer notions of the subject in its various relations can be had from even the most narrow devotion to these texts than could be had from the study of their predecessors a generation ago. If the object of studying history were solely to acquire facts, it would, generally speaking, be a waste of time for high school or younger college students to wander far from text-books. But, assuming that history is studied not alone for the mastery of facts but also for the broadening of culture, and for certain kinds of mental training, the properly regulated use of sources by the student himself is to be justified on at least three grounds: (1) Sources

The value of sources to the student help to an understanding of the point of view of the men, and the spirit of the age under consideration. The ability to dissociate one's self from his own surroundings and habits of thinking and to put himself in the company of Cæsar, of Frederick Barbarossa, or of Innocent III., as the occasion may require, is the hardest, but perhaps the most valuable, thing that the student of history can hope to get. (2) Sources add appreciably to the vividness and reality of history. However well-written the modern description of Charlemagne, for example, the student ought to find a somewhat different flavor in the account by the great Emperor's own friend and secretary, Einhard; and, similarly, Matthew Paris's picture of

the raving and fuming of Frederick II. at his excommunication by
Pope Gregory ought to bring the reader into a somewhat more intimate
appreciation of the character of the proud German-Sicilian emperor.
(3) The use of sources, in connection with the reading of secondary
works, may be expected to train the student, to some extent at least,
in methods of testing the accuracy of modern writers, especially when
the subject in hand is one that lends itself to a variety of interpreta-
tions.   In the sources the makers of history, or those who stood close
to them, are allowed to speak for themselves, or for their times, and the
study of such materials not only helps plant in the student's mind the
conception of fairness and impartiality in judging historical characters,
but also cultivates the habit of tracing things back to their origins and
verifying what others have asserted about them. So far as practicable
the student of history, from the age of fourteen and onwards, should be
encouraged to develop the critical or judicial temperament along with
the purely acquisitive.

In preparing a source book, such as the present one, the purpose is to
further the study of the most profitable sources by removing some of
the greater difficulties, particularly those of accessibility and language.
Clearly impracticable as anything like historical "research" undoubtedly is for younger students, it is none the less believed that there are
abundant first-hand materials in the range of history which such students will not only find profitable but actually enjoy, and that any
Simplicity   acquaintance with these things that may be acquired
of many   in earlier studies will be of inestimable advantage sub-
mediæval
sources   sequently. It is furthermore believed, contrary to the
assertions that one sometimes hears, that the history of the Middle
Ages lends itself to this sort of treatment with scarcely, if any, less
facility than that of other periods.   Certainly Gregory's Clovis, Asser's
Alfred, Einhard's Charlemagne, and Joinville's St. Louis are living per-
sonalities, no less vividly portrayed than the heroes of a boy's story-
book. Tacitus's description of the early Germans, Ammianus's account
of the crossing of the Danube by the Visigoths and his pictures of the
Huns, Bede's narrative of the Saxon invasion of Britain, the affectionate letter Stephen of Blois to his wife and children, the portrayal
of the sweet-spirited St. Francis by the Three Companions, and Froissart's free and easy sketch of the battle of Crécy are all interesting, easily

comprehended, and even adapted to whet the appetite for a larger acquaintance with these various people and events. Even solid documents, like the Salic law, the Benedictine Rule, the Peace of Constance, and the Golden Bull, if not in themselves exactly attractive, may be made to have a certain interest for the younger student when he realizes that to know mediæval history at all he is under the imperative necessity of getting much of the framework of things either from such materials or from text-books which essentially reproduce them. It is hoped that at least a reasonable proportion of the selections herewith presented may serve in some measure to overcome for the student the remote and intangible character which the Middle Ages have much too commonly, though perhaps not unnaturally, been felt to possess.

CONTENTS

A SOURCE BOOK OF MEDIÆVAL HISTORY

CHAPTER I.

THE EARLY GERMANS

1. A Sketch by Cæsar

ONE of the most important steps in the expansion of the Roman Republic was the conquest of Gaul by Julius Cæsar just before the middle of the first century B.C. Through this conquest Rome entered deliberately upon the policy of extending her dominion northward from the Mediterranean and the Alps into the regions of western and central Europe known to us to-day as France and Germany. By their wars in this direction the Romans were brought into contact with peoples concerning whose manner of life they had hitherto known very little. There were two great groups of these peoples—the Gauls and the Germans—each divided and subdivided into numerous tribes and clans. In general it may be said that the Gauls occupied what we now call France and the Germans what we know as Belgium, Holland, Denmark, Germany, and Austria. The Rhine marked a pretty clear boundary between them.

During the years 58–50 B.C., Julius Cæsar, who had risen to the proconsulship through a long series of offices and honors at Rome, served the state as leader of five distinct military expeditions in this country of the northern barbarians. The primary object of these campaigns was to establish order among the turbulent tribes of Gauls and to prepare the way for the extension of Roman rule over them. This great task was performed very successfully, but in accomplishing it Cæsar found it necessary to go somewhat farther than had at first been intended. In the years 55 and 54 B.C., he made two expeditions to Britain to punish the natives for giving aid to their Celtic kinsfolk in Gaul, and in 55 and 53 he crossed the Rhine to compel the Germans to remain on their own side of the river and to cease troubling the Gauls by raids and invasions, as they had recently been doing. When (about 51 B.C.) he came to write his *Commentaries on the Gallic War*, it is very natural that he should have taken care to give a brief sketch of the leading peoples whom he had been fighting, that is, the Gauls, the Britons, and the Germans. There are two places in the *Commentaries* where the Germans are described at some length. At the beginning of Book IV. there is an account of the particular tribe known as the Suevi, and in the middle of Book VI. there is a longer sketch of the Germans in general. This latter is the passage translated below. Of course we are not to suppose that Cæsar's knowledge of the Germans was in any sense thorough. At no time did he get far into their country, and the people whose manners and customs he had an opportunity to observe were only those who were pressing down upon, and occasionally across, the Rhine boundary—a mere fringe of the great race stretching back to the Baltic and, at that time, far eastward into modern Russia. We may be sure that many of the more remote German tribes lived after a fashion quite different from that which Cæsar and his legions had an opportunity to observe on the Rhine-Danube frontier. Still, Cæsar's account, vague and brief as it is, has an importance that can hardly be exaggerated. These early Germans had no written literature and but for the descriptions of them left by a few Roman writers, such as Cæsar, we should know almost nothing about them. If we bear in mind that the account in the *Commentaries* was based upon very keen, though limited, observation, we can get out of it a good deal of interesting information concerning the early ancestors of the great Teutonic peoples of the world to-day.

Source —Julius Cæsar, *De Bello Gallico* ["The Gallic War"], Bk. VI., Chaps. 21–23.

21. The customs of the Germans differ widely from those of the Gauls; [1] for neither have they Druids to preside over religious

[1] In chapters 11–20, immediately preceding the present passage, Cæsar gives a comparatively full and minute description of Gallic life and institutions. He knew more about the Gauls than about the Germans, and, besides, it was his experiences among them that he was writing about primarily.

services,[1] nor do they give much attention to sacrifices. They count in the number of their gods those only whom they can **Their religion** see, and by whose favors they are clearly aided; that is to say, the Sun, Vulcan,[2] and the Moon. Of other deities they have never even heard. Their whole life is spent in hunting and in war. From childhood they are trained in labor and hardship. . . .

22. They are not devoted to agriculture, and the greater portion of their food consists of milk, cheese, and flesh. No one **Their system of land tenure** owns a particular piece of land, with fixed limits, but each year the magistrates and the chiefs assign to the clans and the bands of kinsmen who have assembled together as much land as they think proper, and in whatever place they desire, and the next year compel them to move to some other place. They give many reasons for this custom— that the people may not lose their zeal for war through habits established by prolonged attention to the cultivation of the soil; that they may not be eager to acquire large possessions, and that the stronger may not drive the weaker from their property; that they may not build too carefully, in order to avoid cold and heat; that the love of money may not spring up, from which arise quarrels and dissensions; and, finally, that the common people may live in contentment, since each person sees that his wealth is kept equal to that of the most powerful.

23. It is a matter of the greatest glory to the tribes to lay waste, as widely as possible, the lands bordering their territory, thus making them uninhabitable.[3] They regard it as the best

[1] The Druids were priests who formed a distinct and very influential class among the Gauls. They ascertained and revealed the will of the gods and were supreme in the government of the tribes. Druids existed also among the Britons.

[2] By Vulcan Cæsar means the German god of fire.

[3] Of the Suevi, a German tribe living along the upper course of the Danube, Cæsar says: "They consider it their greatest glory as a nation that the lands about their territories lie unoccupied to a very great extent, for they think that by this it is shown that a great number of nations cannot withstand their power; and thus on one side of the Suevi the lands are said to lie desolate for about six hundred miles."—*Gallic War*, Bk. IV., Chap. 3.

proof of their valor that their neighbors are forced to withdraw from those lands and hardly any one dares set foot there; at the same time they think that they will thus be more secure, since the fear of a sudden invasion is removed. When a tribe is either repelling an invasion or attacking an outside people, magistrates

Leaders and officers in war and peace are chosen to lead in the war, and these are given the power of life and death. In times of peace there is no general magistrate, but the chiefs of the districts and cantons render justice among their own people and settle disputes.[1] Robbery, if committed beyond the borders of the tribe, is not regarded as disgraceful, and they say that it is practised for the sake of training the youth and preventing idleness. When any one of the chiefs has declared in an assembly that he is going to be the leader of an expedition, and that those who wish to follow him should give in their names, they who approve of the undertaking, and of the man, stand up and promise their assistance, and are applauded by the people. Such of these as do not then follow him are looked upon as deserters and traitors, and from that day no one has any faith in them.

To mistreat a guest they consider to be a crime. They protect **German hospitality** from injury those who have come among them for any purpose whatever, and regard them as sacred. To them the houses of all are open and food is freely supplied.

---

[1] This statement is an instance of Cæsar's vagueness, due possibly to haste in writing, but more likely to lack of definite information. How large these districts and cantons were, whether they had fixed boundaries, and how the chiefs rendered justice in them are things we should like to know but are not told.

2. A Description by Tacitus

TACITUS (54–119),[1] who is sometimes credited with being the greatest of Roman historians, published his treatise on the *Origin, Location, Manners, and Inhabitants of Germany* in the year 98. This was about a century and a half after Cæsar wrote his *Commentaries*. During this long interval we have almost no information as to how the Germans were living or what they were doing. There is much uncertainty as to the means by which Tacitus got his knowledge of them. We may be reasonably sure that he did not travel extensively through the country north of the Rhine; there is, in fact, not a shred of evidence that he ever visited it at all. He tells us that he made use of Cæsar's account, but this was very meager and could not have been of much service. We are left to surmise that he drew most of his information from books then existing but since lost, such as the writings of Posidonius of Rhodes (136–51 B.C.) and Pliny the Elder (23–79). These sources were doubtless supplemented by the stories of officials and traders who had been among the Germans and were afterwards interviewed by the historian. Tacitus's essay, therefore, while written with a desire to tell the truth, was apparently not based on first-hand information. The author nowhere says that he had *seen* this or that feature of German life. We may suppose that what he really did was to gather up all the stories and reports regarding the German barbarians which were already known to Roman traders, travelers, and soldiers, sift the true from the false as well as he could, and write out in first class Latin the little book which we know as the *Germania*. The theory that the work was intended as a satire, or sermon in morals, for the benefit of a corrupt Roman people has been quite generally abandoned, and this for the very good reason that there is nothing in either the treatise's contents or style to warrant such a belief. Tacitus wrote the book because of his general interest in historical and geographical subjects, and also, perhaps, because it afforded him an excellent opportunity to display a literary skill in which he took no small degree of pride. That it was published separately instead of in one of his larger histories may have been due to public interest in the subject during Trajan's wars in the Rhine country in the years 98 and 99. The first twenty-seven

---

[1] All dates from this point, unless otherwise indicated, are A.D.

chapters, from which the selections below are taken, treat of the Germans in general—their origin, religion, family life, occupations, military tactics, amusements, land system, government, and social classes; the last nineteen deal with individual tribes and are not so accurate or so valuable. It will be found interesting to compare what Tacitus says with what Cæsar says when both touch upon the same topic. In doing so it should be borne in mind that there was a difference in time of a century and a half between the two writers, and also that while Tacitus probably did not write from experience among the Germans, as Cæsar did, he nevertheless had given the subject a larger amount of deliberate study.

Source — C. Cornelius Tacitus, *De Origine, Situ, Moribus, ac Populis Germanorum* [known commonly as the "Germania"], Chaps. 4–24, *passim*. Adapted from translation by Alfred J. Church and William J. Brodribb (London, 1868), pp. 1–16. Text in numerous editions, as that of William F. Allen (Boston, 1882) and that of Henry Furneau (Oxford, 1894).

4. For my own part, I agree with those who think that the tribes of Germany are free from all trace of intermarriage with **Physical characteristics** foreign nations, and that they appear as a distinct, unmixed race, like none but themselves. Hence it is that the same physical features are to be observed throughout so vast a population. All have fierce blue eyes, reddish hair, and huge bodies fit only for sudden exertion. They are not very able to endure labor that is exhausting. Heat and thirst they cannot withstand at all, though to cold and hunger their climate and soil have hardened them.

6. Iron is not plentiful among them, as may be inferred from the nature of their weapons.[1] Only a few make use of swords or long lances. Ordinarily they carry a spear (which they call a *framea*), with a short and narrow head, but so sharp and easy to handle that the same weapon serves, according to circumstances, for close or distant conflict. As for the horse-soldier, he is satisfied with a shield and a spear. The foot-soldiers also scatter

---

[1] In reality iron ore was abundant in the Germans' territory, but it was not until long after the time of Tacitus that much use began to be made of it. By the fifth century iron swords were common.

showers of missiles, each man having several and hurling them to an immense distance, and being naked or lightly clad with a little cloak. They make no display in their equipment. Their shields alone are marked with fancy colors. Only a few have corselets,[1] and just one or two here and there a metal or leather helmet.[2] Their horses are neither beautiful nor swift; nor are they taught various wheeling movements after the Roman fashion, but are driven straight forward so as to make one turn to the right in such a compact body that none may be left behind another. On the whole, one would say that the Germans' chief strength is in their infantry. It fights along with the cavalry, and admirably adapted to the movements of the latter is the swiftness of certain foot-soldiers, who are picked from the entire youth of their country and placed in front of the battle line.[3] The number of these is fixed, being a hundred from each *pagus*,[4] and from this they take their name among their countrymen, so that what was at the outset a mere number has now become a title of honor. Their line of battle is drawn up in the shape of a wedge. To yield ground, provided they return to the attack, is regarded as prudence rather than cowardice. The bodies of their slain they carry off, even when the battle has been indecisive. To abandon one's shield is the basest of crimes. A man thus disgraced is not allowed to be present at the religious ceremonies, or to enter the council. Many, indeed, after making a cowardly escape from battle put an end to their infamy by hanging themselves.[5]

Their weapons and mode of fighting

1 Coats of mail.

2 Defensive armor for the head and neck.

3 See Cæsar's description of this mode of fighting.—*Gallic War*, Bk. I., Chap. 48.

4 The canton was known to the Romans as a *pagus* and to the Germans themselves as a *gau*. It was made up of a number of districts, or townships (Latin *vicus*, German *dorf*), and was itself a division of a tribe or nation.

5 A later law of the Salian Franks imposed a fine of 120 *denarii* upon any man who should accuse another of throwing down his shield and running away, without being able to prove it" [see p. 64].

7. They choose their kings[1] by reason of their birth, but their generals on the ground of merit. The kings do not enjoy unlimited or despotic power, and even the generals command more by example than by authority. If they are energetic, if they take a prominent part; if they fight in the front, they lead because they are admired. But to rebuke, to imprison, even to flog, is allowed to the priests alone, and this not as a punishment, or at the general's bidding, but by the command of the god whom they believe to inspire the warrior. They also carry with them **The Germans in battle** into battle certain figures and images taken from their sacred groves.[2] The thing that most strengthens their courage is the fact that their troops are not made up of bodies of men chosen by mere chance, but are arranged by families and kindreds. Close by them, too, are those dearest to them, so that in the midst of the fight they can hear the shrieks of women and the cries of children. These loved ones are to every man the most valued witnesses of his valor, and at the same time his most generous applauders. The soldier brings his wounds to mother or wife, who shrinks not from counting them, or even demanding to see them, and who provides food for the warriors and gives them encouragement.

11. About matters of small importance the chiefs alone take counsel, but the larger questions are considered by the entire tribe. Yet even when the final decision rests with the people the affair is always thoroughly discussed by the chiefs. Except in the case of a sudden emergency, the people hold their assemblies on certain fixed days, either at the new or the full moon;

---

[1] Many of the western tribes at the time Tacitus wrote did not have kings, though in eastern Germany the institution of kingship seems to have been quite general. The office, where it existed, was elective, but the people rarely chose a king outside of a privileged family, assumed to be of divine origin.

[2] Evidently these were not images of their gods, for in another place (Chap. 9) Tacitus tells us that the Germans deemed it a dishonor to their deities to represent them in human form. The images were probably those of wild beasts, as the wolf of Woden (or Odin), or the ram of Tyr, and were national standards preserved with religious care in the sacred groves, whence they were brought forth when the tribe was on the point of going to war.

for these they consider the most suitable times for the transaction

Their popular assemblies of business. Instead of counting by days, as we do, they count by nights, and in this way designate both their ordinary and their legal engagements. They regard the night as bringing on the day. Their freedom has one disadvantage, in that they do not all come together at the same time, or as they are commanded, but two or three days are wasted in the delay of assembling. When the people present think proper, they sit down armed. Silence is proclaimed by the priests who, on these occasions, are charged with the duty of keeping order. The king or the leader speaks first, and then others in order, as age, or rank, or reputation in war, or eloquence, give them right. The speakers are heard more because of their ability to persuade than because of their power to command. If the speeches are displeasing to the people, they reject them with murmurs; if they are pleasing, they applaud by clashing their weapons together, which is the kind of applause most highly esteemed.[1]

13. They transact no public or private business without being armed, but it is not allowable for any one to bear arms until he has satisfied the tribe that he is fit to do so. Then, in the presence of the assembly, one of the chiefs, or the young man's father, or some kinsman, equips him with a shield and a spear. These arms are what the toga is with the Romans, the first honor with which a youth is invested. Up to this time he is regarded as merely a member of a household, but afterwards as a member of the state. Very noble birth, or important service rendered by the father, secures for a youth the rank of chief, and such lads attach them-

---

[1] The German popular assembly was simply the periodical gathering of free men in arms for the discussion and decision of important points of tribal policy. It was not a legislative body in the modern sense. Law among the Germans was immemorial custom, which, like religion, could be changed only by a gradual shifting of popular belief and practice. It was not "made" by any process of deliberate and immediate choice. Nevertheless, the assembly constituted an important democratic element in the government, which operated in a measure to offset the aristocratic element represented by the *principes* and *comitatus* [see p. 28]. Its principal functions were the declaring of war and peace, the election of the kings, and, apparently, the hearing and deciding of graver cases at law.

selves to men of mature strength and of fully tested valor.   It is no
shame to be numbered among a chief's companions.[1]   The com-

The chiefs and their compan- ions   panions have different ranks in the band, according to the will of the chief; and there is great
rivalry among the companions for first place in
the chief's favor, as there is among the chiefs for the possession
of the largest and bravest throng of followers.   It is an honor, as
well as a source of strength, to be thus always surrounded by a
large body of picked youths, who uphold the rank of the chief in
peace and defend him in war.   The fame of such a chief and his
band is not confined to their own tribe, but is spread among
foreign peoples; they are sought out and honored with gifts in
order to secure their alliance, for the reputation of such a band
may decide a whole war.

14. In battle it is considered shameful for the chief to allow
any of his followers to excel him in valor, and for the followers
not to equal their chief in deeds of bravery.   To survive the chief
and return from the field is a disgrace and a reproach for life.
To defend and protect him, and to add to his renown by courageous fighting is the height of loyalty.   The chief fights for
victory; the companions must fight for the chief.   If their native
state sinks into the sloth of peace and quiet, many noble youths

The German love of war   voluntarily seek those tribes which are waging
some war, both because inaction is disliked by
their race and because it is in war that they win renown most
readily; besides, a chief can maintain a band only by war, for
the men expect to receive their war-horse and their arms from
their leader.   Feasts and entertainments, though not elegant, are
plentifully provided and constitute their only pay.   The means of
such liberality are best obtained from the booty of war.   Nor
are they as easily persuaded to plow the earth and to wait for the
year's produce as to challenge an enemy and earn the glory of

[1] This relation of *principes* (chiefs) and *comites* (companions) is mentioned
by Cæsar [see p. 22].   The name by which the Romans designated the band
of companions, or followers, of a German chieftain was *comitatus*.

wounds. Indeed, they actually think it tame and stupid to acquire by the sweat of toil what they may win by their blood.[1]

15. When not engaged in war they pass much of their time in the chase, and still more in idleness, giving themselves up to sleep and feasting. The bravest and most warlike do no work; they give over the management of the household, of the home, and of the land to the women, the old men, and the weaker

Life in times of peace members of the family, while they themselves remain in the most sluggish inactivity. It is strange that the same men should be so fond of idleness and yet so averse to peace.[2] It is the custom of the tribes to make their chiefs presents of cattle and grain, and thus to give them the means of support.[3] The chiefs are especially pleased with gifts from neighboring tribes, which are sent not only by individuals, but also by the state, such as choice steeds, heavy armor, trappings, and neck-chains. The Romans have now taught them to accept money also.

16. It is a well-known fact that the peoples of Germany have no cities, and that they do not even allow buildings to be erected close together.[4] They live scattered about, wherever a spring, or

[1] Apparently the Germans did not now care much more for agriculture than in the time of Cæsar. The women, slaves, and old men sowed some seeds and gathered small harvests, but the warrior class held itself above such humble and unexciting employment. The raising of cattle afforded a principal means of subsistence, though hunting and fishing contributed considerably.

[2] Compare the Germans and the North American Indians in this respect. The great contrast between these two peoples lay in the capacity of the one and the comparative incapacity of the other for development.

[3] The Germans had no system of taxation on land or other property, such as the Romans had and such as we have to-day. It was not until well toward the close of the Middle Ages that the governments of kingdoms built up by Germanic peoples in western Europe came to be maintained by anything like what we would call taxes in the modern sense.

[4] The lack of cities and city life among the Germans struck Tacitus with the greater force because of the complete dominance of city organization to which he, as a Roman, was accustomed. The Greek and Roman world was made up, in the last analysis, of an aggregation of *civitates*, or city states. Among the ancient Greeks these had usually been independent; among the Romans they were correlated under the greater or lesser control of a centralized government; but among the Germans of Tacitus's time, and long after, the mixed agricultural and nomadic character of the people effectually

a meadow, or a wood has attracted them. Their villages are not arranged in the Roman fashion, with the buildings connected and joined together, but every person surrounds his dwelling with an open space, either as a precaution against the disasters **Lack of cities** of fire, or because they do not know how to build. **and towns** They make no use of stone or brick, but employ wood for all purposes. Their buildings are mere rude masses, without ornament or attractiveness, although occasionally they are stained in part with a kind of clay which is so clear and bright that it resembles painting, or a colored design. . . .

23. A liquor for drinking is made out of barley, or other grain, and fermented so as to be somewhat like wine. The dwellers **Their food** along the river-bank[1] also buy wine from traders. **and drink** Their food is of a simple variety, consisting of wild fruit, fresh game, and curdled milk. They satisfy their hunger without making much preparation of cooked dishes, and without the use of any delicacies at all. In quenching their thirst they are not so moderate. If they are supplied with as much as they desire to drink, they will be overcome by their own vices as easily as by the arms of an enemy.

24. At all their gatherings there is one and the same kind of amusement. This is the dancing of naked youths amid swords and **German** lances that all the time endanger their lives. Ex- **amusements** perience gives them skill, and skill in turn gives grace. They scorn to receive profit or pay, for, however reckless their pastime, its reward is only the pleasure of the spectators. Strangely enough, they make games of chance a serious employment, even when sober, and so venturesome are they about winning or losing that, when every other resource has failed, on the final throw of the dice they will stake even their own freedom.

---

prevented the development of anything even approaching urban organization. Their life was that of the forest and the pasture, not that of forum, theatre, and circus.

[1] That is, on the Rhine, where traders from the south brought in wines and other Roman products. The drink which the Germans themselves manufactured was, of course, a kind of beer.

He who loses goes into voluntary slavery and, though the younger and stronger of the players, allows himself to be bound and sold. Such is their stubborn persistency in a bad practice, though they themselves call it honor. Slaves thus acquired the owners trade off as speedily as possible to rid themselves of the scandal of such a victory.

CHAPTER II.

THE VISIGOTHIC INVASION

3. The Visigoths Cross the Danube (376)

THE earliest invasion of the Roman Empire which resulted in the permanent settlement of a large and united body of Germans on Roman soil was that of the Visigoths in the year 376. This invasion was very far, however, from marking the first important contact of the German and Roman peoples. As early as the end of the second century B.C. the incursions of the Cimbri and Teutones (113–101) into southern Gaul and northern Italy had given Rome a suggestion of the danger which threatened from the northern barbarians. Half a century later, the Gallic campaigns of Cæsar brought the two peoples into conflict for the first time in the region of the later Rhine boundary, and had the very important effect of preventing the impending Germanization of Gaul and substituting the extension of Roman power and civilization in that quarter. Roman imperial plans on the north then developed along ambitious lines until the year 9 A.D., when the legions of the Emperor Augustus, led by Varus, were defeated, and in large part annihilated, in the great battle of the Teutoberg Forest and the balance was turned forever against the Romanization of the Germanic countries. Thereafter for a long time a state of equilibrium was preserved along the Rhine-Danube frontier, though after the Marcomannic wars in the latter half of the second century the scale began to incline more and more against the Romans, who were gradually forced into the attitude of defense against a growing disposition of the restless Germans to push the boundary farther south.

During the more than three and a half centuries intervening between the battle of the Teutoberg and the crossing of the Danube by the Visigoths, the intermingling of the two peoples steadily increased. On the one hand were numerous Roman travelers and traders who visited the

Germans living along the frontier and learned what sort of people they were. The soldiers of the legions stationed on the Rhine and Danube also added materially to Roman knowledge in this direction. But much more important was the influx of Germans into the Empire to serve as soldiers or to settle on lands allotted to them by the government. Owing to a general decline of population, and especially to the lack of a sturdy middle class, Rome found it necessary to fill up her army with foreigners and to reward them with lands lying mainly near the frontiers, but often in the very heart of the Empire. The over-population of Germany furnished a large class of excellent soldiers who were ready enough to accept the pay of the Roman emperor for service in the legions, even if rendered, as it often was, against their kinsmen who were menacing the weakened frontier. From this source the Empire had long been receiving a large infusion of German blood before any considerable tribe came within its bounds to settle in a body. Indeed, if there had occurred no sudden and startling overflows of population from the Germanic countries, such as the Visigothic invasion, it is quite possible that the Roman Empire might yet have fallen completely into the hands of the Germans by the quiet and gradual processes just indicated. As it was, the pressure from advancing Asiatic peoples on the east was too great to be withstood, and there resulted, between the fourth and sixth centuries, a series of notable invasions which left almost the entire Western Empire parceled out among new Germanic kingdoms established by force on the ruins of the once invincible Roman power. The breaking of the frontier by the West Goths (to whom the Emperor Aurelian, in 270, had abandoned the rich province of Dacia), during the reign of Gratian in the West and of Valens in the East, was the first conspicuous step in this great transforming movement.

The ferocious people to whose incursions Ammianus refers as the cause of the Visigothic invasion were the Huns [see p. 42], who had but lately made their first appearance in Europe. Already by 376 the Ostrogothic kingdom of Hermaneric, to the north of the Black Sea, had fallen before their onslaught, and the wave of conquest was spreading rapidly westward toward Dacia and the neighboring lands inhabited by the Visigoths. The latter people were even less able to make effectual resistance than their eastern brethren had been. Part of them had become Christians and were recognizing Fridigern as their leader, while the remaining pagan element acknowledged the sway of Athanaric. On the arrival of the Huns, Athanaric led his portion of the people into the Carpathian Mountains and began to prepare for resistance, while the Christians, led by Fridigern and Alaf (or Alavivus), gathered on the Danube and begged permission to take refuge across the river in Roman territory. Athanaric and his division of the Visigoths, having become Christians, entered the Empire a few years later and settled in Moesia.

Ammianus Marcellinus, author of the account of the Visigothic invasion given below, was a native of Antioch, a soldier of Greek ancestry and apparently of noble birth, and a member of the Eastern emperor's bodyguard. Beyond these facts, gleaned from his *Roman History*, we have almost no knowledge of the man. The date of his birth is unknown, likewise that of his death, though from his writings it appears that he lived well toward the close of the fourth century. His *History* began with the accession of Nerva, 96 A.D., approximately where the accounts by Tacitus and Suetonius end, and continued to the death of his master Valens in the battle of Adrianople in 378. It was divided into thirty-one books; but of these thirteen have been lost, and some of those which survive are imperfect. Although the narrative is broken into rather provokingly here and there by digressions on earthquakes and eclipses and speculations on such utterly foreign topics as the theory of the destruction of lions by mosquitoes, it nevertheless constitutes an invaluable source of information on the men and events of the era which it covers. Its value is greatest, naturally, on the period of the Visigothic invasion, for in dealing with these years the author could describe events about which he had direct and personal knowledge. Ammianus is to be thought of as the last of the old Roman school of historians.

Source—Ammianus Marcellinus, *Rerum Gestarum Libri qui Supersunt*, Bk. XXXI., Chaps. 3–4. Translated by Charles D. Yonge under the title of *Roman History during the Reigns of the Emperors Constantius, Julian, Jovianus, Valentinian, and Valens* (London, 1862), pp. 584–586. Text in edition of Victor Gardthausen (Leipzig, 1875), Vol. II., pp. 239–240.

In the meantime a report spread extensively through the other nations of the Goths [i.e., the Visigoths], that a race of men, hitherto unknown, had suddenly descended like a whirlwind from the lofty mountains, as if they had risen from some secret recess of the earth, and were ravaging and destroying everything that came in their way. Then the greater part of the population (which, because of their lack of necessities, had deserted Athanaric), resolved to flee and to seek a home remote from all knowledge of the barbarians; and after a long deliberation as to where to fix their abode, they resolved that a retreat into Thrace

Visigoths ask permission to settle within the Empire was the most suitable, for these two reasons: first of all, because it is a district most abundant in grass; and in the second place, because, by the great breadth of the Danube, it is wholly separated from the barbarians [i.e, the Goths], who were already exposed to the thunderbolts of foreign warfare. And the whole population of the tribe adopted this resolution unanimously. Accordingly, under the command of their leader Alavivus, they occupied the banks of the Danube; and having sent ambassadors to Valens,[1] they humbly entreated that they might be received by him as his subjects, promising to live peaceably and to furnish a body of auxiliary troops, if any necessity for such a force should arise.

While these events were passing in foreign countries, a terrible rumor arose that the tribes of the north were planning new and

Rumors of Gothic movements reach Rome unprecedented attacks upon us,[2] and that over the whole region which extends from the country of the Marcomanni and Quadi to Pontus,[3] a barbarian host composed of various distant nations which had suddenly been driven by force from their own country, was now, with all their families, wandering about in different directions on the banks of the river Danube.

At first this intelligence was treated lightly by our people, be-

[1] Valens was the Eastern emperor from 364 until his death in the battle of Adrianople in 378. His brother Valentinian was emperor in the West from 364 to 375. Gratian, son of Valentinian, was the real sovereign in the West when the Visigoths crossed the Danube.

[2] That is, upon the writer's people, the Romans.

[3] The Marcomanni and Quadi occupied a broad stretch of territory along the upper Danube in what is now the northernmost part of Austria-Hungary. Pontus was a province in northern Asia Minor.

cause they were not in the habit of hearing of any wars in those remote regions until after they had been terminated either by victory or by treaty.　But presently the belief in these occurrences grew stronger, being confirmed, moreover, by the arrival of the foreign ambassadors who, with prayers and earnest en-
Their coming represented as a blessing to the Empire treaties, begged that the people thus driven from their homes and now encamped on the other side of the river might be kindly received by us. The affair seemed a cause of joy rather than of fear, according to the skilful flatterers who were always extolling and exaggerating the good fortune of the Emperor; congratulating him that an embassy had come from the farthest corners of the earth unexpectedly, offering him a large body of recruits, and that, by combining the strength of his own nation with these foreign forces, he would have an army absolutely invincible; observing farther that, by the payment for military reinforcements which came in every year from the provinces, a vast treasure of gold might be accumulated in his coffers.

Full of this hope, he sent several officers to bring this ferocious people and their wagons into our territory.　And such great
The crossing of the Danube pains were taken to gratify this nation, which was destined to overthrow the empire of Rome, that not one was left behind, not even of those who were stricken with mortal disease.　Moreover, having obtained permission of the Emperor to cross the Danube and to cultivate some districts in Thrace, they crossed the stream day and night, without ceasing, embarking in troops on board ships and rafts, and canoes made of the hollow trunks of trees.　In this enterprise, since the Danube is the most difficult of all rivers to navigate, and was at that time swollen with continual rains, a great many were drowned, who, because they were too numerous for the vessels, tried to swim across, and in spite of all their exertions were swept away by the stream.

In this way, through the turbulent zeal of violent people, the ruin of the Roman Empire was brought on. This, at all events, is neither obscure nor uncertain, that the unhappy officers who **Number of the** were intrusted with the charge of conducting **invaders** the multitude of the barbarians across the river, though they repeatedly endeavored to calculate their numbers, at last abandoned the attempt as useless; and the man who would wish to ascertain the number might as well attempt to count the waves in the African sea, or the grains of sand tossed about by the zephyr.[1]

4. The Battle of Adrianople (378)

Before crossing the Danube the Visigoths had been required by the Romans to give up their arms, and also a number of their children to be held as hostages. In return it was understood that the Romans would equip them afresh with arms sufficient for their defense and with food supplies to maintain them until they should become settled in their new homes. So far as our information goes, it appears that the Goths fulfilled their part of the contract, or at least were willing to do so. But the Roman officers in Thrace saw an opportunity to enrich themselves by selling food to the famished barbarians at extortionate prices, and a few months of such practices sufficed to arouse all the rage and resentment of which the untamed Teuton was capable. In the summer of 378 the Goths broke out in open revolt and began to avenge themselves by laying waste the Roman lands along the lower Danube frontier. The Eastern emperor, Valens, hastened to the scene of insurrection, but only to lose the great battle of Adrianople, August 9, 378, and to meet his own death. "The battle of Adrianople," says Professor Emerton, "was one

---

[1] Mœller (*Histoire du Moyen Age*, p. 58), estimates that the Goths who now entered Thrace numbered not fewer than 200,000 grown men, accompanied by their wives and children. The Italian Villari, in his *Barbarian Invasions of Italy*, Vol. I., p. 49, gives the same estimate. The tendency of contemporary chroniclers to exaggerate numbers has misled many older writers. Even Mœller's and Villari's estimate would mean a total of upwards of a million people. That there were so many may well be doubted. The Vandals played practically as important a part in the history of their times as did the Visigoths; yet it is known that when the Vandals passed through Spain, in the first half of the fifth century, they numbered not more than 20,000 fighting men, with their wives and children.

of the decisive battles of the world. It taught the Germans that they could beat the legions in open fight and that henceforth it was for them to name the price of peace. It broke once for all the Rhine-Danube frontier." Many times thereafter German armies, and whole tribes, were to play the rôle of allies of Rome; but neither German nor Roman could be blinded to the fact that the decadent empire of the south lay at the mercy of the stalwart sons of the northern wilderness.

Source —Ammianus Marcellinus, *Rerum Gestarum Libri qui Supersunt*, Bk. XXXI., Chaps. 12–14. Translated by Charles D. Yonge [see p. 34], pp. 608–615 *passim*. Text in edition of Victor Gardthausen (Leipzig, 1875), Vol. II., pp. 261–269.

He [Valens] was at the head of a numerous force, neither un-warlike nor contemptible, and had united with them many

The Goths approach the Roman army veteran bands, among whom were several officers of high rank—especially Trajan, who a little while before had been commander of the forces.

And as, by means of spies and observation, it was ascertained that the enemy was intending to blockade with strong divisions the different roads by which the necessary supplies must come, he sent a sufficient force to prevent this, dispatching a body of the archers of the infantry and a squadron of cavalry with all speed to occupy the narrow passes in the neighborhood. Three days afterwards, when the barbarians, who were advancing slowly because they feared an attack in the unfavorable ground which they were traversing, arrived within fifteen miles from the station of Nice[1] (which was the aim of their march), the Emperor, with wanton impetuosity, resolved on attacking them instantly, because those who had been sent forward to reconnoitre (what led to such a mistake is unknown) affirmed that the entire body of the Goths did not exceed ten thousand men. . . .[2]

[1] Nice was about thirty miles east of Adrianople.
[2] The Visigoths under Fridigern finally took their position near Adrianople and Valens led his army into that vicinity and pitched his camp, fortifying it with a rampart of palisades. From the Western emperor, Gratian, a messenger came asking that open conflict be postponed until the army from

When the day broke which the annals mark as the fifth of the Ides of August [Aug. 9] the Roman standards were advanced with haste. The baggage had been placed close to the walls of Adrianople, under a sufficient guard of soldiers of the legions. The treasures and the chief insignia of the Emperor's rank were within the walls, with the prefect and the principal members of **The battle begins** the council.[1] Then, having traversed the broken ground which divided the two armies, as the burning day was progressing towards noon, at last, after marching eight miles, our men came in sight of the wagons of the enemy, which had been reported by the scouts to be all arranged in a circle. According to their custom, the barbarian host raised a fierce and hideous yell, while the Roman generals marshalled their line of battle. The right wing of the cavalry was placed in front; the chief portion of the infantry was kept in reserve. . . .[2]

And while arms and missiles of all kinds were meeting in fierce conflict, and Bellona,[3] blowing her mournful trumpet, was raging more fiercely than usual, to inflict disaster on the Romans, our men began to retreat; but presently, aroused by the reproaches of their officers, they made a fresh stand, and the battle increased like a conflagration, terrifying our soldiers, numbers of whom were pierced by strokes of the javelins hurled at them, and by arrows.

Rome could join that from Constantinople. But Valens, easily flattered by some of his over-confident generals, foolishly decided to bring on a battle at once. Apparently he did not dream that defeat was possible.

[1] After the battle here described, which occurred in the open plain, the victorious Goths proceeded to the siege of the city itself, in which, however, they were unsuccessful. The taking of fortified towns was an art in which the Germans were not skilled.

[2] When both armies were in position Fridigern, "being skilful in divining the future," says Ammianus, "and fearing a doubtful struggle," sent a herald to Valens with the promise that if the Romans would give hostages to the Goths the latter would cease their depredations and even aid the Romans in their wars. Richomeres, the Roman cavalry leader, was chosen by Valens to serve as a hostage; but as he was proceeding to the Gothic camp the soldiers who accompanied him made a rash attack upon a division of the enemy and precipitated a battle which soon spread to the whole army.

[3] The goddess of war, regarded in Roman mythology as the sister of Mars.

Then the two lines of battle dashed against each other, like the beaks of ships and, thrusting with all their might, were tossed to and fro like the waves of the sea. Our left wing had advanced actually up to the wagons, with the intent to push on still farther if properly supported; but they were deserted by the rest of the cavalry, and so pressed upon by the superior numbers of the enemy that they were overwhelmed and beaten down like **The fury of** the ruin of a vast rampart. Presently our in- **the conflict** fantry also was left unsupported, while the various companies became so huddled together that a soldier could hardly draw his sword, or withdraw his hand after he had once stretched it out. And by this time such clouds of dust arose that it was scarcely possible to see the sky, which resounded with horrible cries; and in consequence the darts, which were bearing death on every side, reached their mark and fell with deadly effect, because no one could see them beforehand so as to guard against them. The barbarians, rushing on with their enormous host, beat down our horses and men and left no spot to which our ranks could fall back to operate. They were so closely packed that it was impossible to escape by forcing a way through them, and our men at last began to despise death and again taking to their swords, slew all they encountered, while with mutual blows of battle-axes, helmets and breastplates were dashed in pieces.

Then you might see the barbarian, towering in his fierceness, hissing or shouting, fall with his legs pierced through, or his right hand cut off, sword and all, or his side transfixed, and still, in the last gasp of life, casting around him defiant glances. The plain was covered with corpses, showing the mutual ruin of the combatants; while the groans of the dying, or of men fearfully wounded, were intense and caused much dismay on all sides. Amid all this great tumult and confusion our infantry were exhausted by toil and danger, until at last they had neither strength left to fight nor spirits to plan anything. Their spears were broken by the frequent collisions, so that they were forced to content themselves with their drawn swords, which they thrust into the **The Romans put to flight** dense battalions of the enemy, disregarding their own safety, and seeing that every possibility of escape was cut off from them. . . . The sun, now high in the heavens (having traversed the sign of Leo and reached the abode of the heavenly Virgo[1]) scorched the Romans, who were emaciated by hunger, worn out with toil, and scarcely able to support even the weight of their armor. At last our columns were entirely beaten back by the overpowering weight of the barbarians, and so they took to disorderly flight, which is the only resource in extremity, each man trying to save himself as best he could. . . .

Scarcely one third of the whole army escaped. Nor, except the battle of Cannæ, is so destructive a slaughter recorded in our annals;[2] though, even in the times of their prosperity, the Romans have more than once been called upon to deplore the uncertainty of war, and have for a time succumbed to evil Fortune.

[1] Signs of the zodiac, sometimes employed by the Romans to give figurative expression to the time of day.

[2] The number of Romans killed at Cannæ (216 B.C.) is variously estimated, but it can hardly have been under 50,000.

CHAPTER III.

THE HUNS

5. Descriptions by a Graeco-Roman Poet and a Roman Historian

THE Huns, a people of Turanian stock, were closely related to the ancestors of the Magyars, or the modern Hungarians. Their original home was in central Asia, beyond the great wall of China, and they were in every sense a people of the plains rather than of the forest or of the sea. From the region of modern Siberia they swept westward in successive waves, beginning about the middle of the fourth century, traversed the "gateway of the nations" between the Caspian Sea and the Ural Mountains, and fell with fury upon the German tribes (mainly the Goths) settled in eastern and southern Europe. The descriptions of them given by Claudius Claudianus and Ammianus Marcellinus set forth their characteristics as understood by the Romans a half-century or more before the invasion of the Empire by Attila. There is no reason to suppose that either of these authors had ever seen a Hun, or had his information at first hand. When both wrote the Huns were yet far outside the Empire's bounds. Tales of soldiers and travelers, which doubtless grew as they were told, must have supplied both the poet and the historian with all that they knew regarding the strange Turanian invaders. This being the case, we are not to accept all that they say as the literal truth. Nevertheless the general impressions which one gets from their pictures cannot be far wrong.

Claudius Claudianus, commonly regarded as the last of the Latin classic poets, was a native of Alexandria who settled at Rome about 395. For ten years after that date he occupied a position at the court of the Emperor Honorius somewhat akin to that of poet-laureate. Much of his writing was of a very poor quality, but his descriptions were sometimes striking, as in the stanza given below. On Ammianus Marcellinus see p. 34.

Sources — (a) Claudius Claudianus, *In Rufinum* ["Against Rufinus"], Bk. I.,
323–331.   Text in *Monumenta Germaniæ Historica, Auctores
Antiquissimi*, Vol. X., pp. 30–31. Translated in Thomas Hodgkin, *Italy and Her Invaders* (Oxford, 1880), Vol. II., p. 2.

(b) Ammianus Marcellinus, *Rerum Gestarum Libri qui Supersunt*,
Bk. XXXI., Chaps. 2–4 [see p. 34].   Translated in Hodgkin,
ibid., pp. 34–38.

(a)

There is a race on Scythia's [1] verge extreme

Eastward, beyond the Tanais' [2] chilly stream.

The Northern Bear [3] looks on no uglier crew:

Base is their garb, their bodies foul to view;

Their souls are ne'er subdued to sturdy toil

Or Ceres' arts: [4] their sustenance is spoil.

With horrid wounds they gash their brutal brows,

And o'er their murdered parents bind their vows.

Not e'en the Centaur-offspring of the Cloud [5]

Were horsed more firmly than this savage crowd.

Brisk, lithe, in loose array they first come on,

Fly, turn, attack the foe who deems them gone.

(b)

The nation of the Huns, little known to ancient records, but
spreading from the marshes of Azof to the Icy Sea,[6] surpasses
all other barbarians in wildness of life. In the first days of infancy, deep incisions are made in the cheeks of their boys, in order
that when the time comes for whiskers to grow there, the sprout-
ing hairs may be kept back by the furrowed scars; and hence

[1] A somewhat indefinite region north and east of the Caspian Sea.

[2] The modern Don, flowing into the Sea of Azof.

[3] One of two constellations in the northern hemisphere, called respectively
the Great Bear and the Lesser Bear, or *Ursa Major* and *Ursa Minor*. The
Great Bear is commonly known as the Dipper.

[4] That is, agriculture. The Huns were even less settled in their mode of
life than were the early Germans described by Tacitus.

[5] A strange creature of classical mythology, represented as half man and
half horse.

[6] The White Sea. It is hardly to be believed that the Huns dwelt so far
north. This was, of course, a matter of sheer speculation with the Romans.

they grow to maturity and to old age beardless. They all, however, have strong, well-knit limbs and fine necks. Yet they

Physical ap-
pearance of the
Huns

are of portentous ugliness and so crook-backed that you would take them for some sort of two-footed beasts, or for the roughly-chipped stakes which are used for the railings of a bridge. And though they do just bear the likeness of men (of a very ugly type), they are so little advanced in civilization that they make no use of fire, nor of any kind of relish, in the preparation of their food, but feed upon the roots which they find in the fields, and the half-raw flesh of any sort of animal. I say half-raw, because they give it a kind of cooking by placing it between their own thighs and the backs of their horses. They never seek the shelter of houses, which they look upon as little better than tombs, and will enter only upon the direst necessity; nor would one be able to find among them even a cottage of wattled rushes; but, wandering at large over mountain and through forest, they are trained to endure from infancy all the extremes of cold, of hunger, and of thirst.

They are clad in linen raiment, or in the skins of field-mice sewed together, and the same suit serves them for use in-doors **Their dress** and out. However dingy the color of it may become, the tunic which has once been hung around their necks is never laid aside nor changed until through long decay the rags of it will no longer hold together. Their heads are covered with bent caps, their hairy legs with the skins of goats; their shoes, never having been fashioned on a last, are so clumsy that they cannot walk comfortably. On this account they are not well adapted to encounters on foot; but on the other hand they are almost welded to their horses, which are hardy, though of ugly shape, and on which they sometimes ride woman's fashion. On horseback every man of that nation lives night and day; on horseback he buys and sells; on horseback he takes his meat and drink, and when night comes on he leans forward upon the narrow neck of his horse and there falls into a deep sleep, or wanders into the varied fantasies of dreams.

When a discussion arises upon any matter of importance they come on horseback to the place of meeting. No kingly sternness overawes their deliberations, but being, on the whole, well-contented with the disorderly guidance of their chiefs, they do not scruple to interrupt the debates with anything that comes into their heads. When attacked, they will sometimes engage in regular battle. Then, going into the fight in order of columns, **Their mode** they fill the air with varied and discordant cries. **of fighting** More often, however, they fight in no regular order of battle, but being extremely swift and sudden in their movements, they disperse, and then rapidly come together again in loose array, spread havoc over vast plains and, flying over the rampart, pillage the camp of their enemy almost before he has become aware of their approach. It must be granted that they are the nimblest of warriors. The missile weapons which they use at a distance are pointed with sharpened bones admirably fastened to the shaft. When in close combat they fight without regard to their own safety, and while the enemy is intent upon parrying the thrusts of their swords they throw a net over him and so entangle his limbs that he loses all power of walking or riding.

Not one among them cultivates the ground, or ever touches a plow-handle. All wander abroad without fixed abodes, without **Their nomadic** home, or law, or settled customs, like perpetual **character** fugitives, with their wagons for their only habitations. If you ask them, not one can tell you what is his place of origin. They are ruthless truce-breakers, fickle, always ready to be swayed by the first breath of a new desire, abandoning themselves without restraint to the most ungovernable rage.

Finally, like animals devoid of reason, they are utterly ignorant of what is proper and what is not. They are tricksters with words and full of dark sayings. They are never moved by either religious or superstitious awe. They burn with unquenchable thirst for gold; and they are so changeable and so easily moved to wrath that many times in the day they will quarrel with their comrades on no provocation, and be reconciled, having received no satisfaction.

CHAPTER IV.

THE EARLY FRANKS

6. The Deeds of Clovis as Related by Gregory of Tours

THE most important historical writer among the early Franks was a bishop whose full name was Georgius Florentius Gregorius, but who has commonly been known ever since his day as Gregory of Tours. The date of his birth is uncertain, but it was probably either 539 or 540. He was not a Frank, but a man of mixed Roman and Gallic descent, his parentage being such as to rank him among the nobility of his native district, Auvergne. At the age of thirty-four he was elected bishop of Tours, and this important office he held until his death in 594. During this long period of service he won distinction as an able church official, as an alert man of affairs, and as a prolific writer on ecclesiastical subjects. Among his writings, some of which have been lost, were a book on the Christian martyrs, biographies of several holy men of the Church, a commentary on the Psalms, and a treatise on the officers of the Church and their duties.

But by far his largest and most important work was his *Ecclesiastical History of the Franks*, in ten books, written well toward the end of his life. It is indeed to be regarded as one of the most interesting pieces of literature produced in any country during the Middle Ages. For his starting point Gregory went back to the Garden of Eden, and what he gives us in his first book is only an amusing but practically worthless account of the history of the world from Adam to St. Martin of Tours, who died probably in 397. In the second book, however, he comes more within the range of reasonable tradition, if not of actual information, and brings the story down to the death of Clovis in 511. In the succeeding eight books he reaches the year 591, though it is thought by some that the last four were put together after the author's death by some of his associates. However that may be, we may rest assured that the history grows in accuracy as it approaches the period in which it was written. Naturally it is at its best in the later books, where events are described that happened within the writer's lifetime, and with many of which he had a close connection. Gregory was a man of unusual activity and of wide acquaintance among the influential people of his day. He served as a counselor of several Frankish kings and was a prominent figure at their courts. The shrine of St. Martin of Tours[1] was visited by pilgrims from all parts of the Christian world and by conversation with them Gregory had an excellent opportunity to keep informed as to what was going on among the Franks, and among more distant peoples as well. He was thus fortunately situated for one who proposed to write the history of his times. As a bishop of the orthodox Church he had small regard for Arians and other heretics, and so was in some ways less broad-minded than we could wish; and of course he shared the superstition and ignorance of his age, as will appear in some of the selections below. Still, without his extensive history we should know far less than we now do concerning the Frankish people before the seventh century. He mixes legend with fact in a most confusing manner, but with no intention whatever to deceive. The men of the earlier Middle Ages knew no other way of writing history and their readers were not critical as we are to-day. The passages quoted below from Gregory's history give some interesting information concerning the Frankish conquerors of Gaul, and at the same time show something of the spirit of Gregory himself and of the people of his times.

Particularly interesting is the account of the conversion of Clovis and of the Franks to Christianity. When the Visigoths, Ostrogoths, Vandals, Lombards, and Burgundians crossed the Roman frontiers and settled within the bounds of the old Empire they were all Christians in name, however much their conduct might be at variance with

---

[1] St. Martin was born in Pannonia somewhat before the middle of the fourth century. For a time he followed his father's profession as a soldier in the service of the Roman emperor, but later he went to Gaul with the purpose of aiding in the establishment of the Christian Church in that quarter. In 372 he was elected bishop of Tours and shortly afterwards he founded the monastery with which his name was destined to be associated throughout the Middle Ages. This monastery, which was one of the earliest in western Europe, became a very important factor in the prolonged combat with Gallic paganism, and subsequently a leading center of ecclesiastical learning.

their profession. The Franks, on the other hand, established themselves in northern Gaul, as did the Saxons in Britain, while they were yet pagans, worshipping Woden and Thor and the other strange deities of the Germans. It was about the middle of the reign of King Clovis, or, more definitely, in the year 496, that the change came. In his *Ecclesiastical History* Gregory tells us how up to this time all the influence of the Christian queen, Clotilde, had been exerted in vain to bring her husband to the point of renouncing his old gods. In his wars and conquests the king had been very successful and apparently he was pretty well satisfied with the favors these old gods had showered upon him and was unwilling to turn his back upon such generous patrons. But there came a time, in 496, in the course of the war with the Alemanni, when the tide of fortune seemed to be turning against the Frankish king. In the great battle of Strassburg the Franks were on the point of being beaten by their foe, and Clovis in desperation made a vow, as the story goes, that if Clotilde's God would grant him a victory he would immediately become a Christian. Whatever may have been the reason, the victory was won and the king, with characteristic German fidelity to his word, proceeded to fulfill his pledge. Amid great ceremony he was baptized, and with him three thousand of his soldiers the same day. The great majority of Franks lost little time in following the royal example.

Two important facts should be emphasized in connection with this famous incident. The first is the peculiar character of the so-called "conversion" of Clovis and his Franks. We to-day look upon religious conversion as an inner experience of the individual, apt to be brought about by personal contact between a Christian and the person who is converted. It was in no such sense as this, however, that the Franks—or any of the early Germans, for that matter—were made Christian. They looked upon Christianity as a mere portion of Roman civilization to be adopted or let alone as seemed best; but if it were adopted, it must be by the whole tribe or nation, not by individuals here and there. In general, the German peoples took up Christianity, not because they became convinced that their old religions were false, but simply because they were led to believe that the Christian faith was in some ways better than their own and so might profitably be taken advantage of by them. Clovis believed he had won the battle

Med. Hist.—4

of Strassburg with the aid of the Christian God when Woden and
Thor were about to fail him; therefore he reasoned that it would be a
good thing in the future to make sure that the God of Clotilde should
always be on his side, and obviously the way to do this was to become
himself a Christian. He did not wholly abandon the old gods, but
merely considered that he had found a new one of superior power.
Hence he enjoined on all his people that they become Christians; and
for the most part they did so, though of course we are not to suppose
that there was any very noticeable change in their actual conduct and
mode of life, at least for several generations.

The second important point to observe is that, whereas all of the other
Germanic peoples on the continent had become Christians of the
Arian type, the Franks accepted Christianity in its orthodox form such
as was adhered to by the papacy. This was sheer accident. The
Franks took the orthodox rather than the heretical religion simply
because it was the kind that was carried to them by the missionaries,
not at all because they were able, or had the desire, to weigh the two
creeds and choose the one they liked the better. But though they
became orthodox Christians by accident, the fact that they became
such is of the utmost importance in mediæval history, for by being
what the papacy regarded as true Christians rather than heretics they
began from the start to be looked to by the popes for support. Their
kings in time became the greatest secular champions of papal interests,
though relations were sometimes far from harmonious. This virtual
alliance of the popes and the Frankish kings is a subject which will
repay careful study.

Source—Gregorius Episcopus Turonensis, *Historia Ecclesiastica Francorum*
[Gregory of Tours, "Ecclesiastical History of the Franks"], Bk. II.,
Chaps. 27–43 *passim*. Text in *Monumenta Germaniæ Historica,
Scriptores Rerum Merovingicarum*, Vol. I., Part 1, pp. 88–89, 90–
95, 98–100, 158–159.

27. After all these things Childeric[1] died and his son Clovis ruled
in his stead. In the fifth year of the new reign Syagrius, son of
Ægidius, was governing as king of the Romans in the town of

[1] Childeric I., son of the more or less mythical Merovius, was king from 457
to 481. Clovis became ruler of the Salian branch of the Franks in this latter
year. The tomb of Childeric was discovered at Tournai in 1653.

Soissons, where his father had held sway before him.[1] Clovis now advanced against him with his kinsman Ragnachar, who also held a kingdom, and gave him an opportunity to select a field of battle. Syagrius did not hesitate, for he was not at all afraid to risk an encounter. In the conflict which followed, however, the Roman soon saw that his army was doomed to destruction; so, turning and fleeing from the field, he made all

The battle of Soissons (486) haste to take refuge with King Alaric at Toulouse.[2] Clovis then sent word to Alaric that he must hand over the defeated king at once if he did not wish to bring on war against himself. Fearing the anger of the Franks, therefore, as the Goths continually do, Alaric bound Syagrius with chains and delivered him to the messengers of King Clovis. As soon as the latter had the prisoner in his possession he put him under safe guard and, after seizing his kingdom, had him secretly slain.[3]

At this time the army of Clovis plundered many churches, for the king was still sunk in the errors of idolatry. Upon one occasion the soldiers carried away from a church, along with other ornaments of the sacred place, a remarkably large and beautiful vase. The bishop of that church sent messengers to the king to

The story of the broken vase ask that, even if none of the other holy vessels might be restored, this precious vase at least might be sent back. To the messengers Clovis could only reply: "Come with us to Soissons, for there all the booty is to be divided. If when we cast lots the vase shall fall to me, I will return it as the bishop desires."

When they had reached Soissons and all the booty had been

---

[1] Ægidius and his son Syagrius were the last official representatives of the Roman imperial power in Gaul; and since the fall of the Empire in the West even they had taken the title of "king of the Romans" and had been practically independent sovereigns in the territory between the Somme and the Loire, with their capital at Soissons, northeast of Paris.

[2] Alaric II., king of the Visigoths, 485–507.

[3] The battle of Soissons in 486, with the defeat and death of Syagrius, insured for the Franks undisputed possession southward to the Loire, which was the northern frontier of the Visigothic kingdom.

brought together in the midst of the army the king called attention to the vase and said, "I ask you, most valiant warriors, to
allow me to have the vase in addition to my rightful share."
Then even those of his men who were most self-willed answered:
"O glorious king, all things before us are thine, and we ourselves
are subject to thy control. Do, therefore, what pleases thee best,
for no one is able to resist thee." But when they had thus
spoken, one of the warriors, an impetuous, jealous, and vain man,
raised his battle-ax aloft and broke the vase in pieces, crying as
he did so, "Thou shalt receive no part of this booty unless it fall
to you by a fair lot." And at such a rash act they were all
astounded.

The king pretended not to be angry and seemed to take no
notice of the incident, and when it happened that the broken
vase fell to him by lot he gave the fragments to the bishop's
messengers; nevertheless he cherished a secret indignation in
his heart. A year later he summoned all his soldiers to come
fully armed to the Campus Martius, so that he might make an
Clovis's inspection of his troops.[1] After he had reviewed
revenge the whole army he finally came across the very
man who had broken the vase at Soissons. "No one," cried out
the king to him, "carries his arms so awkwardly as thou; for
neither thy spear nor thy sword nor thy ax is ready for use," and
he struck the ax out of the soldier's hands so that it fell to the
ground. Then when the man bent forward to pick it up the
king raised his own ax and struck him on the head, saying,
"Thus thou didst to the vase at Soissons." Having slain him,
he dismissed the others, filled with great fear.[2] . . .

[1] The Campus Martius was the "March-field," i. e., the assembling place
of the Frankish army. It was not regularly in any one locality but wherever
the king might call the soldiers together, as he did every spring for purposes
of review. In the eighth century the month of May was substituted for
March as the time for the meeting.

[2] In the words of Hodgkin (*Charles the Great*, p. 12), "the well-known
story of the vase of Soissons illustrates at once the German memories of
freedom and the Merovingian mode of establishing a despotism. As a battle
comrade the Frankish warrior protests against Clovis receiving an ounce

30. The queen did not cease urging the king to acknowledge the true God and forsake idols, but all her efforts failed until at length a war broke out with the Alemanni.[1] Then of necessity he was compelled to confess what hitherto he had wilfully denied. It happened that the two armies were in battle and there was great slaughter.[2] The army of Clovis seemed about to be cut in pieces. Then the king raised his hands fervently toward the heavens and, breaking into tears, cried: "Jesus Christ, who Clotilde declares to be the son of the living God, who it is said givest help to the oppressed and victory to those who put their trust in thee, I invoke thy marvellous help. If thou wilt give me victory over my enemies and I prove that power which thy followers say they have proved concerning thee, I will believe in thee and will be baptized in thy name; for I have called upon my own gods and it is clear that they have neglected to give me aid. Therefore I am convinced that they have no power, for they do not help those

Clovis decides to become a Christian (496) who serve them. I now call upon thee, and I wish to believe in thee, especially that I may escape from my enemies." When he had offered this prayer the Alemanni turned their backs and began to flee. And when they learned that their king had been slain, they submitted at once to Clovis, saying, "Let no more of our people perish, for we now belong to you." When he had stopped the battle and praised his soldiers for their good work, Clovis returned in peace to his kingdom and told the queen how he had won the victory by calling on the name of Christ. These events took place in the fifteenth year of his reign.[3]

beyond his due share of the spoils. As a battle leader Clovis rebukes his henchman for the dirtiness of his accoutrements, and cleaves his skull to punish him for his independence."

[1] The Alemanni were a German people occupying a vast region about the upper waters of the Rhine and Danube. They had been making repeated efforts to acquire territory west of the Rhine—an encroachment which Clovis resolved not to tolerate.

[2] The battle was fought near Strassburg, in the upper Rhine valley.

[3] The ultimate result of the defeat of the Alemanni was that the Frankish kingdom was enlarged by the annexation of the great region known in the later Middle Ages as Suabia, comprising modern Alsace, Baden,

31. Then the queen sent secretly to the blessed Remigius, bishop of Rheims, and asked him to bring to the king the gospel of salvation. The bishop came to the court where, little by little, he led Clovis to believe in the true God, maker of heaven and earth, and to forsake the idols which could help neither him nor any one else. "Willingly will I hear thee, O holy father," declared the king at last, "but the people who are under my authority are not ready to give up their gods. I will go and consult them about the religion concerning which you speak." When he had come among them, and before he had spoken a word, all the people, through the influence of the divine power, cried out with one voice: "O righteous king, we cast off our mortal gods and we are ready to serve the God who Remigius tells us is immortal."

When this was reported to the bishop he was beside himself with joy, and he at once ordered the baptismal font to be prepared. The streets were shaded with embroidered hangings; the churches were adorned with white tapestries, exhaling sweet odors; perfumed tapers gleamed; and all the temple of the

The baptism of Clovis and his warriors baptistry was filled with a heavenly odor, so that the people might well have believed that God in His graciousness showered upon them the perfumes of Paradise. Then Clovis, having confessed that the God of the Trinity was all-powerful, was baptized in the name of the Father, and of the Son, and of the Holy Ghost, and was anointed with the holy oil with the sign of the cross. More than three thousand of his soldiers were baptized with him. . . .

35. Now when Alaric, king of the Goths, saw that Clovis was conquering many nations, he sent messengers to him, saying, "If it please my brother, let us, with the favor of God, enter into an alliance." Clovis at once declared his willingness to do as Alaric

Würtemberg, the western part of Bavaria, and the northern part of Switzerland. The Alemanni as a people disappeared speedily from history, being absorbed by their more powerful neighbors. Their only monument to-day is the name by which the French have always known the people of Germany —*Allemands.*

suggested and the two kings met on an island in the Loire, near
the town of Amboise in the vicinity of Tours.[1] There they talked,
ate, and drank together, and after making mutual promises of
friendship they departed in peace.

37. But Clovis said to his soldiers: "It is with regret that I see
the Arian heretics in possession of any part of Gaul. Let us,
with the help of God, march against them and, after having conquered them, bring their country under our own control." This
proposal was received with favor by all the warriors and the
army started on the campaign, going towards Poitiers, where

**Clovis resolves
to take the
Visigoths'
lands in Gaul**
Alaric was then staying. As a portion of the
troops passed through the territory about Tours,
Clovis, out of respect for the holy St. Martin,
forbade his soldiers to take anything from the country except
grass for the horses. One soldier, having come across some hay
which belonged to a poor man said, "Has, then, the king given us
permission to take only grass? O well! hay is grass. To take it
would not be to violate the command." And by force he took
the hay away from the poor man. When, however, the matter
was brought to the king's attention he struck the offender with
his sword and killed him, saying, "How, indeed, may we hope
for victory if we give offense to St. Martin?" This was enough
thereafter to prevent the army from plundering in that country.

When Clovis arrived with his forces at the banks of the Vienne
he was at a loss to know where to cross, because the heavy rains

**Miraculous in-
cidents of the
campaign**
had swollen the stream. During the night he
prayed that the Lord would reveal to him a
passage. The following morning, under the
guidance of God, a doe of wondrous size entered the river in

[1] The Loire was the boundary between the dominions of the two kings.
There have been many famous instances in history of two sovereigns coming
together to confer at some point on the common border of the territories
controlled by them, notably the interview of Napoleon and Tsar Alexander I.
on the Niemen River in 1807. The Franks and the Visigoths had been
enemies ever since by Clovis's defeat of Syagrius their dominions had been
brought into contact (486), and the present jovial interview of the two kings
did not long keep them at peace with each other.

plain sight of the army and crossed by a ford, thus pointing out
the way for the soldiers to get over. When they were in the
neighborhood of Poitiers the king saw at some distance from his
tent a ball of fire, which proceeded from the steeple of the church
of St. Hilary[1] and seemed to him to advance in his direction, as
if to show that by the aid of the light of the holy St. Hilary he
would triumph the more easily over the heretics against whom
the pious priest had himself often fought for the faith. Clovis
then forbade his army to molest any one or to pillage any property in that part of the country.

Clovis at length engaged in battle with Alaric, king of the
Goths, in the plain of Vouillé at the tenth mile-stone from
Poitiers.[2] The Goths fought with javelins, but the Franks
charged upon them with lances. Then the Goths took to flight,
as is their custom,[3] and the victory, with the aid of God, fell to
Clovis. He had put the Goths to flight and killed their king,
The Visigoths Alaric, when all at once two soldiers bore down
defeated by upon him and struck him with lances on both
Clovis (507) sides at once; but, owing to the strength of his
armor and the swiftness of his horse, he escaped death. After
the battle Amalaric, son of Alaric, took refuge in Spain and ruled
wisely over the kingdom of his father.[4] Alaric had reigned
twenty-two years. Clovis, after spending the winter at Bor-
deaux and carrying from Toulouse all the treasure of the king,
advanced on Angoulême. There the Lord showed him such
favor that at his very approach the walls of the city fell down of

[1] St. Hilary was bishop of Poitiers in the later fourth century. He was a
contemporary of St. Martin of Tours and a co-worker with him in the organization of Gallic Christianity.

[2] The plain of Vouillé was ten miles west of Poitiers.

[3] This amusing comment of Gregory was due largely to his prejudice in
favor of the Franks and against the heretical Visigoths.

[4] The Visigothic kingdom in Spain, with its capital at Toledo, endured
until the Saracen conquest of that country in 711 and the years immediately
following, but it did not give evidence of much strength. It stood so long
only because the Pyrenees made a natural boundary against the Franks and
because, after Clovis, for two hundred years the Franks produced no great
conqueror who cared to crowd the Visigoths into still closer quarters.

their own accord.[1] After driving out the Goths he brought the place under his own authority. Thus, crowned with victory, he returned to Tours and bestowed a great number of presents upon the holy church of the blessed Martin.[2]

40. Now while Clovis was living at Paris he sent secretly to the son of Sigibert,[3] saying: "Behold now your father is old and lame. If he should die his kingdom would come to you and my friendship with it." So the son of Sigibert, impelled by his ambition, planned to slay his father. And when Sigibert set out from Cologne and crossed the Rhine to go through the Buchonian forest,[4] his son had him slain by assassins while he was sleeping in his tent, in order that he might gain the kingdom for himself. But by the judgment of God he fell into the pit which he had digged for his father. He sent messengers to Clovis to announce the death of his father and to say: "My father is dead and I have his treasures, and likewise the kingdom. Now send trusted men to me, that I may give them for you whatever you would like out of his treasury." Clovis replied: "I thank you for your kindness and will ask you merely to show my messengers all your treasures, after which you may keep them yourself." And when the messengers of Clovis came, the son of Sigibert showed them the treasures which his father had collected.

[1] Clovis, particularly after his conversion to Christianity in 496, was the hero of Gregory's history and apparently the enthusiastic old bishop did not lose an opportunity to glorify his career. At any rate it would certainly be difficult to relate anything more remarkable about him than this legend of the walls of Angoulême falling down before him at his mere approach.

[2] This notable campaign had advanced Frankish territory to the Pyrenees, except for the strip between these mountains and the Rhone, known as Septimania, which the Visigoths were able to retain by the aid of the Ostrogoths from Italy. No great number of Franks settled in this broad territory south of the Loire, and to this day the inhabitants of south France show a much larger measure of Roman descent than do those of the north. It may be added that Septimania was conquered by Clovis's son Childebert in 531, and thus the last bit of old Gaul—practically modern France—was brought under Frankish control.

[3] This was Cloderic, son of Sigibert the Lame, king of a tribe of Franks living along the middle Rhine. Sigibert was one of the numerous independent and rival princes whom Clovis used every expedient to put out of the way.

[4] Along the Upper Weser, near the monastery of Fulda.

And while they were looking at various things, he said: "My father used to keep his gold coins in this little chest." And they said, "Put your hand down to the bottom, that you may show us everything." But when he stooped to do this, one of the messengers struck him on the head with his battle-ax, and thus he met the fate which he had visited upon his father.

Other means by which Clovis extended his power

Now when Clovis heard that both Sigibert and his son were dead, he came to that place and called the people together and said to them: "Hear what has happened. While I was sailing on the Scheldt River, Cloderic, son of Sigibert, my relative, attacked his father, pretending that I had wished him to slay him. And so when his father fled through the Buchonian forest, the assassins of Cloderic set upon him and slew him. But while Cloderic was opening his father's treasure chest, some man unknown to me struck him down. I am in no way guilty of these things, for I could not shed the blood of my relatives, which is very wicked. But since these things have happened, if it seems best to you, I advise you to unite with me and come under my protection." And those who heard him applauded his speech, and, raising him on a shield, acknowledged him as their king. Thus Clovis gained the kingdom of Sigibert and his treasures, and won over his subjects to his own rule. For God daily confounded his enemies and increased his kingdom, because he walked uprightly before Him and did that which was pleasing in His sight.

42. Then Clovis made war on his relative Ragnachar.[1] And when the latter saw that his army was defeated, he attempted to flee; but his own men seized him and his brother Richar and brought them bound before Clovis. Then Clovis said: "Why have you disgraced our family by allowing yourself to be taken prisoner? It would have been better for you had you been slain." And, raising his battle-ax,

The removal of remaining rivals

[1] Ragnachar's kingdom was in the region about Cambrai.

he slew him. Then, turning to Richar, he said, "If you had aided your brother he would not have been taken;" and he slew him with the ax also. Thus by their death Clovis took their kingdom and treasures. And many other kings and relatives of his, who he feared might take his kingdom from him, were slain, and his dominion was extended over all Gaul.

43. And after these things he died at Paris and was buried in the basilica of the holy saints which he and his queen, Clotilde,

The death of Clovis (511) had built. He passed away in the fifth year after the battle of Vouillé, and all the days of his reign were thirty years.

7. The Law of the Salian Franks

WHEN the Visigoths, Lombards, and other Germanic peoples settled within the bounds of the Roman Empire they had no such thing as written law. They had laws, and a goodly number of them, but these laws were handed down from generation to generation orally, having never been enacted by a legislative body or decreed by a monarch in the way that laws are generally made among the civilized peoples of to-day. In other words, early Germanic law consisted simply of an accumulation of the immemorial custom of the tribe. When, for example, a certain penalty had been paid on several occasions by persons who had committed a particular crime, men came naturally to regard that penalty as the one regularly to be paid by *any one* proved guilty of the same offense; so that what was at first only habit gradually became hardened into law—unwritten indeed, but none the less binding. The law thus made up, moreover, was personal rather than territorial like that of the Romans and like ours to-day. That is, the same laws did not apply to all the people throughout any particular country or region. If a man were born a Visigoth he would be subject to Visigothic law throughout life, no matter where he might go to live. So the Burgundian would always have the right to be judged by Burgundian law, and the Lombard by the Lombard law. Obviously, in regions where several peoples dwelt side by side, as in large portions of Gaul, Spain, and northern Italy, there was no small amount of confusion and the courts had to be conducted in a good many different ways.

After the Germans had been for some time in contact with the Romans they began to be considerably influenced by the customs and ways of doing things which they found among the more civilized people. They tried to master the Latin language, though, on the whole, they succeeded only so well as to create the new "Romance" tongues which we know as French, Spanish, Portuguese, and Italian. They adopted the Roman religion, i. e., Christianity. And, among the most important things of all, they took up the Roman idea of having their law written out rather than in the uncertain shape of mere tradition. In this work of putting the old customary law in written form the way was led by the Salian branch of the Franks. Just when the Salic code was drawn up is not known, but the work was certainly done at some time during the reign of Clovis, probably about the year 496. The portions of this code which are given below will serve to show the general character of all the early Germanic systems of law—Visigothic, Lombard, Burgundian, and Frisian, as well as Frankish; for among them all there was much uniformity in principles, though considerable variation in matters of detail. Like the rest, the Salic law was fragmentary. The codes were not intended to embrace the entire law of the tribe, but simply to bring together in convenient form those portions which were most difficult to remember and which were most useful for ready reference. In the Salic code, for instance, we find a large amount of criminal law and of the law of procedure, but only a few touches of the law of property, or indeed of civil law of any sort. There is practically nothing in the way of public or administrative law. Many things are not mentioned which we should expect to find treated and, on the other hand, some things are there which we should not look for ordinarily in a code of law. The greater portion is taken up with an enumeration of penalties for various crimes and wrongful acts. These are often detailed so minutely as to be rather amusing from our modern point of view. Yet every one of the sixty-five chapters of the code has its significance and from the whole law can be gleaned an immense amount of information concerning the manner of life which prevailed in early Frankish Gaul. For the Merovingian period in general the Salic law is our most valuable documentary source of knowledge, just as for the same epoch the *Ecclesiastical History* of Gregory of Tours is our most important narrative source.

Source—Text in Heinrich Geffcken, *Lex Salica* ["The Salic Law"], Leipzig, 1898; also Heinrich Gottfried Gengler, *Germanische Rechtsdenkmäler* ["Monuments of German Law"], Erlangen, 1875, pp. 267–303. Adapted from translation in Ernest F. Henderson, *Select Historical Documents of the Middle Ages* (London, 1896), pp. 176–189.

I.

1. If any one be summoned before the *mallus* [1] by the king's law, and do not come, he shall be sentenced to 600 *denarii*, which make 15 *solidi*. [2]

2. But he who summons another, and does not come himself, if a lawful impediment have not delayed him, shall be **Summonses to** sentenced to 15 *solidi*, to be paid to him whom **the meetings** he summoned.
of the local
courts 3. And he who summons another shall go with witnesses to the home of that man, and, if he be not at home, shall enjoin the wife, or any one of the family, to make known to him that he has been summoned to court.

4. But if he be occupied in the king's service he cannot summon him.

---

[1] The *mallus* was the local court held about every six weeks in each community or hundred. In early German law the state has small place and the principle of self-help by the individual is very prominent. To bring a suit one summons his opponent himself and gets him to appear at court if he can. Ordinarily the court merely determines the method by which the guilt or innocence of the accused may be tested. Execution of the sentence rests again with the plaintiff, or with his family or clan group.

[2] "The monetary system of the Salic law was taken from the Romans. The basis was the gold *solidus* of Constantine, $\frac{1}{72}$ of a pound of gold. The small coin was the silver *denarius*, forty of which made a *solidus*. This system was adopted as a monetary reform by Clovis, and the statement of the sum in terms of both coins is probably due to the newness of the system at the time of the appearance of the law."—Thatcher and McNeal, *Source Book for Mediæval History*, p. 17. The gold *solidus* was worth somewhere from two and a half to three dollars, but its purchasing power was perhaps equal to that of twenty dollars to-day, because gold and silver were then so much scarcer and more valuable. Such estimates of purchasing power, however, involve so great uncertainty as to be practically worthless.

5. And if he shall be inside the hundred attending to his own affairs, he can summon him in the manner just explained.

XI.

1. If any freeman steal, outside of a house, something worth 2 *denarii*, he shall be sentenced to 600 *denarii*, which make 15 *solidi*.

2. But if he steal, outside of a house, something worth 40

Theft by a freeman *denarii*, and it be proved on him, he shall be sentenced, besides the amount and the fines for delay, to 1,400 *denarii*, which make 35 *solidi*.

3. If a freeman break into a house and steal something worth 2 *denarii*, and it be proved on him, he shall be sentenced to 15 *solidi*.

4. But if he shall have stolen something worth more than 5 *denarii*, and it be proved on him, he shall be sentenced, besides the value of the object and the fines for delay, to 1,400 *denarii*, which make 35 *solidi*.

5. But if he shall have broken, or tampered with, the lock, and thus have entered the house and stolen anything from it, he shall be sentenced, besides the value of the object and the fines for delay, to 1,800 *denarii*, which make 45 *solidi*.

6. And if he shall have taken nothing, or have escaped by flight, he shall, for the housebreaking alone, be sentenced to 1,200 *denarii*, which make 30 *solidi*.

XII.

1. If a slave steal, outside of a house, something worth 2

Theft by a slave *denarii*, besides paying the value of the object and the fines for delay, he shall be stretched out and receive 120 blows.

2. But if he steal something worth 40 *denarii*, he shall pay 6 *solidi*. The lord of the slave who committed the theft shall restore to the plaintiff the value of the object and the fines for delay.

XIV.

Robbery with assault

1. If any one shall have assaulted and robbed a freeman, and it be proved on him, he shall be sentenced to 2,500 *denarii*, which make 63 *solidi*.

2. If a Roman shall have robbed a Salian Frank, the above law shall be observed.

3. But if a Frank shall have robbed a Roman, he shall be sentenced to 35 *solidi*.

XV.

The crime of incendiarism

1. If any one shall set fire to a house in which people were sleeping, as many freemen as were in it can make complaint before the *mallus;* and if any one shall have been burned in it, the incendiary shall be sentenced to 2,500 *denarii*, which make 63 *solidi*.[1]

XVII.

Various deeds of violence

1. If any one shall have sought to kill another person, and the blow shall have missed, he on whom it was proved shall be sentenced to 2,500 *denarii*, which make 63 *solidi*.

2. If any person shall have sought to shoot another with a poisoned arrow, and the arrow has glanced aside, and it shall be proved on him, he shall be sentenced to 2,500 *denarii*, which make 63 *solidi*.

5. If any one shall have struck a man so that blood falls to the floor, and it be proved on him, he shall be sentenced to 600 *denarii*, which make 15 *solidi*.

6. But if a freeman strike a freeman with his fist so that blood does not flow, he shall be sentenced for each blow—up to 3 blows—to 120 *denarii*, which make 3 *solidi*.[2]

[1] The Burgundian law (Chap. 41) contained a provision that if a man made a fire on his own premises and it spread to fences or crops belonging to another person, and did damage, the man who made the fire should recompense his neighbor for his loss, provided it could be shown that there was no wind to drive the fire beyond control. If there was such a wind, no penalty was to be exacted.

[2] The law of the Lombards had a more elaborate system of fines for wounds

XIX.

1. If any one shall have given herbs to another, so that he die, he shall be sentenced to 200 *solidi*, or shall surely be given over to fire.

Use of poison or witchcraft

2. If any person shall have bewitched another, and he who was thus treated shall escape, the author of the crime, having been proved guilty of it, shall be sentenced to 2,500 *denarii*, which make 63 *solidi*.

XXX.

6. If any man shall have brought it up against another that he has thrown away his shield, and shall not have been able to prove it, he shall be sentenced to 120 *denarii*, which make 3 *solidi*.[1]

Punishment for slander

7. If any man shall have called another "gossip" or "perjurer," and shall not have been able to prove it, he shall be sentenced to 600 *denarii*, which make 15 *solidi*.

XXXIV.

1. If any man shall have cut 3 staves by which a fence is bound or held together, or shall have stolen or cut the heads of 3 stakes, he shall be sentenced to 600 *denarii*, which make 15 *solidi*.

2. If any one shall have drawn a harrow through another's

than did the Salic code. For example, knocking out a man's front teeth was to be paid for at the rate of sixteen *solidi* per tooth; knocking out back teeth at the rate of eight *solidi* per tooth; fracturing an arm, sixteen *solidi*; cutting off a second finger, seventeen *solidi*; cutting off a great toe, six *solidi*; cutting off a little toe, two *solidi*; giving a blow with the fist, three *solidi*; with the palm of the hand, six *solidi*; and striking a person on the head so as to break bones, twelve *solidi* per bone. In the latter case the broken bones were to be counted "on this principle, that one bone shall be found large enough to make an audible sound when thrown against a shield at twelve feet distance on the road; the said feet to be measured from the foot of a man of moderate stature."

[1] The man who had "thrown away his shield" was the coward who had fled from the field of battle. How the Germans universally regarded such a person appears in the *Germania* of Tacitus, Chap. 6 (see p. 25). To impute this ignominy to a man was a serious matter.

field of grain after the seed has sprouted, or shall have gone

The offense of trespass through it with a wagon where there was no road, he shall be sentenced to 120 *denarii*, which make 3 *solidi*.

3. If any one shall have gone, where there is no road or path, through another's field after the grain has grown tall, he shall be sentenced to 600 *denarii*, which make 15 *solidi*.

XLI.

1. If any one shall have killed a free Frank, or a barbarian living under the Salic law, and it shall have been proved on him, he shall be sentenced to 8,000 *denarii*.

2. But if he shall have thrown him into a well or into the

Punishments for homicide water, or shall have covered him with branches or anything else, to conceal him, he shall be sentenced to 24,000 *denarii*, which make 600 *solidi*.

3. If any one shall have slain a man who is in the service of the king, he shall be sentenced to 24,000 *denarii*, which make 600 *solidi*.[1]

4. But if he shall have put him in the water, or in a well, and covered him with anything to conceal him, he shall be sentenced to 72,000 *denarii*, which make 1,800 *solidi*.

5. If any one shall have slain a Roman who eats in the king's palace, and it shall have been proved on him, he shall be sentenced to 12,000 *denarii*, which make 300 *solidi*.[2]

6. But if the Roman shall not have been a landed proprietor and table companion of the king, he who killed him shall be sentenced to 4,000 *denarii*, which make 100 *solidi*.

[1] This was the so-called "triple wergeld." That is, the lives of men in the service of the king were rated three times as high as those of ordinary free persons.

[2] Here is an illustration of the personal character of Germanic law. There is one law for the Frank and another for the Roman, though both peoples were now living side by side in Gaul. The price put upon the life of the Frankish noble who was in the king's service was 600 *solidi* (§ 3), but that on the life of the Roman noble in the same service was but half that amount. The same proportion held for the ordinary freemen, as will be seen by comparing §§ 1 and 6.

7. If he shall have killed a Roman who was obliged to pay tribute, he shall be sentenced to 63 *solidi*.

9. If any one shall have thrown a freeman into a well, and he has escaped alive, he [the criminal] shall be sentenced to 4,000 *denarii*, which make 100 *solidi*.

XLV.

1. If any one desires to migrate to another village, and if one or more who live in that village do not wish to receive him— **Right of migration** even if there be only one who objects—he shall not have the right to move there.

3. But if any one shall have moved there, and within 12 months no one has given him warning, he shall remain as secure as the other neighbors.

L.

1. If any freeman or leet[1] shall have made to another a promise to pay, then he to whom the promise was made shall, within 40 **Enforcement of debt** days, or within such time as was agreed upon when he made the promise, go to the house of that man with witnesses, or with appraisers. And if he [the debtor] be unwilling to make the promised payment, he shall be sentenced to 15 *solidi* above the debt which he had promised.

LIX.

1. If any man die and leave no sons, the father and mother shall inherit, if they survive.

Rights of inheritance **2.** If the father and mother do not survive, and he leave brothers or sisters, they shall inherit.

3. But if there are none, the sisters of the father shall inherit.

4. But if there are no sisters of the father, the sisters of the mother shall claim the inheritance.

[1] A leet was such a person as we in modern times commonly designate as a serf—a man only partially free.

5. If there are none of these, the nearest relatives on the father's side shall succeed to the inheritance.

6. Of Salic land no portion of the inheritance shall go to a woman; but the whole inheritance of the land shall belong to the male sex.[1]

LXII.

1. If any one's father shall have been slain, the sons shall have half the compounding money [wergeld]; and the other half, the

Payment of wergeld

nearest relatives, as well on the mother's as on the father's side, shall divide among themselves.[2]

2. But if there are no relatives, paternal or maternal, that portion shall go to the fisc.[3]

---

[1] This has been alleged to be the basis of the misnamed "Salic Law" by virtue of which no woman, in the days of the French monarchy, was permitted to inherit the throne. As a matter of fact, however, the exclusion of women from the French throne was due, not to this or to any other early Frankish principle, but to later circumstances which called for stronger monarchs in France than women have ordinarily been expected to be. The history of the modern "Salic Law" does not go back of the resolution of the French nobles in 1317 against the general political expediency of female sovereigns [see p. 420].

[2] The wergeld was the value put by the law upon every man's life. Its amount varied according to the rank of the person in question. The present section specifies how the wergeld paid by a murderer should be divided among the relatives of the slain man.

[3] That is, to the king's treasury.

CHAPTER V.

THE ANGLES AND SAXONS IN BRITAIN

8. The Saxon Invasion (cir. 449)

THE Venerable Bede, the author of the passage given below, was born about 673 in Northumberland and spent most of his life in the Benedictine abbey of Jarrow on the Tyne, where he died in 735. He was a man of broad learning and untiring industry, famous in all parts of Christendom by reason of the numerous scholarly books that he wrote. The chief of these was his *Ecclesiastical History of the English People*, covering the period from the first invasion of Britain by Cæsar (B.C. 55) to the year 731. In this work Bede dealt with many matters lying properly outside the sphere of church history, so that it is exceedingly valuable for the light which it throws on both the military and political affairs of the early Anglo-Saxons in Britain. As an historian Bede was fair-minded and as accurate as his means of information permitted.

The Angle and Saxon seafarers from the region we now know as Denmark and Hanover had infested the shores of Britain for two centuries or more before the coming of Hengist and Horsa which Bede here describes. The withdrawal of the Roman garrisons about the year 410 left the Britons at the mercy of the wilder Picts and Scots of the north and west, and as a last resort King Vortigern decided to call in the Saxons to aid in his campaign of defense. Such, at least, is the story related by Gildas, a Romanized British chronicler who wrote about the year 560, and this was the view adopted by Bede. Recent writers, as Mr. James H. Ramsay in his *Foundations of England*, are inclined to cast serious doubts upon the story because it seems hardly probable that any king would have taken so foolish a step as that attributed to Vortigern.[1] At any rate, whether by invitation or for pure love

[1] James H. Ramsay, *The Foundations of England* (London, 1898), I., p. 121.

of seafaring adventure, certain it is that the Saxons and Angles made
their appearance at the little island of Thanet, on the coast of Kent,
and found the country so much to their liking that they chose to remain rather than return to the over-populated shores of the Baltic.
There are many reasons for believing that people of Germanic stock
had been settled more or less permanently in Britain long before the
traditional invasion of Hengist and Horsa. Yet we are justified in
thinking of this interesting expedition as, for all practical purposes, the
beginning of the long and stubborn struggle of Germans to possess the
fruitful British isle. While Visigoths and Ostrogoths, Vandals and
Lombards were breaking across the Rhine-Danube frontier and finding new homes in the territories of the Roman Empire, the Angles,
Saxons, and Jutes from the farther north were led by their seafaring
instincts to make their great movement, not by land, but by water,
and into a country which the Romans had a good while before been
obliged to abandon. There they were free to develop their own peculiar
Germanic life and institutions, for the most part without undergoing
the changes which settlement among the Romans produced in the case
of the tribes whose migrations were towards the Mediterranean.

Source—Bæda, *Historia Ecclesiastica Gentis Anglorum* [Bede, "Ecclesiastical
History of the English People"], Bk. I., Chaps. 14–15. Translated
by J. A. Giles (London, 1847), pp. 23–25.

They consulted what was to be done,[1] and where they should
seek assistance to prevent or repel the cruel and frequent incur-
The Britons   sions of the northern nations. And they all
decide to call   agreed with their king, Vortigern, to call over to
in the Saxons   their aid, from the parts beyond the sea, the
Saxon nation; which, as the outcome still more plainly showed,
appears to have been done by the inspiration of our Lord Himself, that evil might fall upon them for their wicked deeds.

In the year of our Lord 449,[2] Martian, being made emperor

[1] Bede has just been describing a plague which rendered the Britons at
this time even more unable than usual to withstand the fierce invaders from
the north; also lamenting the luxury and crime which a few years of relief
from war had produced among his people.
[2] This date is evidently incorrect. Martian and Valentinian III. became

with Valentinian, the forty-sixth from Augustus, ruled the Empire seven years. Then the nation of the Angles, or Saxons, being invited by the aforesaid king, arrived in Britain with three long ships, and had a place assigned them to reside in by the same king, in the eastern part of the island,[1] that they might thus appear to be fighting for their country, while their real intentions were to enslave it. Accordingly they engaged with the enemy, who were come from the north to give battle, and obtained the victory; which, being known at home in their own country, as also the fertility of the islands and the cowardice of the Britons, a larger fleet was quickly sent over, bringing a still greater number of men, who, being added to the former, made up an invincible army. The newcomers received from the Britons a place to dwell, upon condition that they should wage war against their enemies for the peace and security of the country, while the Britons agreed to furnish them with pay.

The Saxons settle in the island

Those who came over were of the three most powerful nations of Germany—Saxons, Angles, and Jutes. From the Jutes are descended the people of Kent and of the Isle of Wight, and those also in the province of the West Saxons who are to this day called Jutes, seated opposite to the Isle of Wight. From the Saxons, that is, the country which is now called Old Saxony, came the East Saxons, the South Saxons, and the West Saxons. From the Angles, that is, the country which is called Anglia, and which is said, from that time, to remain desert to this day, between the provinces of the Jutes and the Saxons, are descended the East Angles, the Midland Angles, Mercians, all the race of the Northumbrians, that is, of those nations that dwell on the

joint rulers of the Empire in 450; hence this is the year that Bede probably meant.

[1] That is, Thanet, which practically no longer exists as an island. In Bede's day it was separated from the rest of Kent by nearly half a mile of water, but since then the coast line has changed so that the land is cut through by only a tiny rill. The intervening ground, however, is marshy and only partially reclaimed.

north side of the River Humber, and the other nations of the English.

The first two commanders are said to have been Hengist and Horsa. Horsa, being afterwards slain in battle by the Britons,[1]

Hengist and Horsa was buried in the eastern part of Kent, where a monument bearing his name is still in existence. They were the sons of Victgilsus, whose father was Vecta, son of Woden; from whose stock the royal races of many provinces trace their descent. In a short time swarms of the aforesaid nations came over into the island, and they began to increase so much that they became a terror to the natives themselves who had invited them. Then, having on a sudden entered into a league with the Picts, whom they had by this time repelled by

The Saxons turn against the Britons the force of their arms, they began to turn their weapons against their confederates. At first they obliged them to furnish a greater quantity of provisions; and, seeking an occasion to quarrel, protested that unless more plentiful supplies were brought them they would break the confederacy and ravage all the island; nor were they backward in putting their threats in execution.

They plundered all the neighboring cities and country, spread the conflagration from the eastern to the western sea without any opposition, and covered almost every part of the island. Public as well as private structures were overturned;

Their devastation of the country the priests were everywhere slain before the altars; the prelates and the people, without any respect of persons, were destroyed with fire and sword; nor were there any to bury those who had been thus cruelly slaughtered. Some of the miserable remainder, being taken in the mountains, were butchered in heaps. Others, driven by hunger, came forth and submitted themselves to the enemy for food, being destined to undergo perpetual servitude, if they

---

[1] This battle was fought between Hengist and Vortimer, the eldest son of Vortigern, at Aylesford, in Kent.

were not killed upon the spot. Some, with sorrowful hearts, fled
beyond the seas. Others, continuing in their own country, led
a miserable life among the woods, rocks, and mountains, with
scarcely enough food to support life, and expecting every moment to be their last.[1]

9. The Mission of Augustine (597)

How or when the Christian religion was first introduced into Britain
cannot now be ascertained. As early as the beginning of the third
century the African church father Tertullian referred to the Britons
as a Christian people, and in 314 the British church was recognized
by the Council of Arles as an integral part of the church universal.
Throughout the period of Roman control in the island Christianity
continued to be the dominant religion. When, however, in the fifth
century and after, the Saxons and Angles invaded the country and
the native population was largely killed off or driven westward (though
not so completely as some books tell us), Christianity came to be pretty
much confined to the Celtic peoples of Ireland and Wales. The invaders were still pagans worshiping the old Teutonic deities Woden,
Thor, Freya, and the rest, and though an attempt at their conversion
was made by a succession of Irish monks, their pride as conquerors
seems to have kept them from being greatly influenced. At any rate,
the conversion of the Angles and Saxons was a task which called for
a special evangelistic movement from no less a source than the head
of the Church. This movement was set in operation by Pope Gregory I.
(Gregory the Great) near the close of the sixth century. It is reasona·
ble to suppose that the impulse came originally from Bertha, the
Frankish queen of King Ethelbert of Kent, who was an ardent Christian and very desirous of bringing about the conversion of her adopted
people. In 596 Augustine (not to be confused with the celebrated
bishop of Hippo in the fifth century) was sent by Pope Gregory at the
head of a band of monks to proclaim the religion of the cross to King

[1] It is by no means probable that the invasion of Britain by the Saxons was
followed by such wholesale extermination of the natives as is here represented,
though it is certain that everywhere, except in the far west (Wales) and
north (Scotland), the native population was reduced to complete subjection.

Ethelbert, and afterwards to all the Angles and Saxons and Jutes in the island. On Whitsunday, June 2, 597, Ethelbert renounced his old gods and was baptized into the Christian communion. The majority of his people soon followed his example and four years later Augustine was appointed "Bishop of the English." After this encouraging beginning the Christianizing of the East, West, and South Saxons went steadily forward.

Source—Bæda, *Historia Ecclesiastica Gentis Anglorum*, Bk. I., Chaps. 23, 25–26. Adapted from translation by J. A. Giles (London, 1847), pp. 34–40 *passim.*

In the year of our Lord 582, Maurice, the fifty-fourth from Augustus, ascended the throne,[1] and reigned twenty-one years. In the tenth year of his reign, Gregory, a man renowned for learning and piety, was elected to the apostolical see of Rome, and presided over it thirteen years, six months and ten days.[2] He,

Pope Gregory I. sends missionaries to Britain being moved by divine inspiration, in the fourteenth year of the same emperor, and about the one hundred and fiftieth after the coming of the English into Britain, sent the servant of God, Augustine,[3] and with him several other monks who feared the Lord, to preach the word of God to the English nation. They, in obedience to the Pope's commands, having undertaken that work, were on their journey seized with a sudden fear and began to think of returning home, rather than of proceeding to a barbarous, fierce, and unbelieving nation, to whose very language they

They become frightened at the outlook were strangers; and this they unanimously agreed was the safest course.[4] In short, they sent back Augustine, who had been appointed to be consecrated bishop in case they were received by the Eng-

[1] That is, the throne of the Eastern Empire at Constantinople.

[2] Gregory was a monk before he was elected pope. He held the papal office from 590 to 604 [see p. 90].

[3] Augustine at the time (596) was prior of a monastery dedicated to St. Andrew in Rome.

[4] The missionaries had apparently gone as far as Arles in southern Provence when they reached this decision.

lish, that he might, by humble entreaty, obtain consent of the holy Gregory, that they should not be compelled to undertake so dangerous, toilsome, and uncertain a journey. The Pope, in reply, sent them an encouraging letter, persuading them to proceed in the work of the divine word, and rely on the assistance of the Almighty. The substance of this letter was as follows:

"Gregory, the servant of the servants of God, to the servants of our Lord. Forasmuch as it had been better not to begin a good work than to think of abandoning that which has been begun, it behooves you, my beloved sons, to fulfill the good work which, by the help of our Lord, you have undertaken. Let not, therefore, the toil of the journey nor the tongues of evil-speaking men deter you. With all possible earnestness and zeal perform that which, by God's direction, you have undertaken; being assured that much labor is followed by an eternal reward. When Augustine, your chief, returns, whom we also constitute your abbot,[1] humbly obey him in all things; knowing that whatsoever you shall do by his direction will, in all respects, be helpful to your souls. Almighty God protect you with his grace, and grant that I, in the heavenly country, may see the fruits of your labor; inasmuch as, though I cannot labor with you, I shall partake in the joy of the reward, because I am willing to labor. God keep you in safety, my most beloved sons. Dated the 23rd of July, in the fourteenth year of the reign of our pious and most august lord, Mauritius Tiberius, the thirteenth year after the consulship of our said lord."

Augustine, thus strengthened by the confirmation of the blessed Father Gregory, returned to the work of the word of God, with the servants of Christ, and arrived in Britain. The powerful Ethelbert was at that time king of Kent. He had extended his dominions as far as the great River Humber, by which

Gregory's letter of encouragement

---

[1] An abbot was the head of a monastery. Should such an establishment be set up in Britain, Augustine was to be its presiding officer.

the Southern Saxons are divided from the Northern.[1] On the
east of Kent is the large isle of Thanet containing according to
Augustine the English reckoning 600 families, divided from
and his com- the other land by the River Wantsum, which is
panions arrive about three furlongs over and fordable only in
in Kent
two places, for both ends of it run into the sea.[2] In this island
landed the servant of our Lord, Augustine, and his companions,
being, as is reported, nearly forty men. By order of the blessed
Pope Gregory, they had taken interpreters of the nation of
the Franks,[3] and sending to Ethelbert, signified that they were
come from Rome and brought a joyful message, which most undoubtedly assured to all that took advantage of it everlasting
joys in heaven and a kingdom that would never end, with the
living and true God. The king, having heard this, ordered that
they stay in that island where they had landed, and that they
be furnished with all necessaries, until he should consider what
to do with them. For he had before heard of the Christian religion, having a Christian wife of the royal family of the Franks,
called Bertha;[4] whom he had received from her parents upon
condition that she should be permitted to practice her religion
with the Bishop Luidhard, who was sent with her to preserve
her faith.[5]

Some days after, the king came to the island, and sitting in
the open air, ordered Augustine and his companions to be brought

[1] The Germanic peoples north of the Humber were more properly Angles,
but of course they were in all essential respects like the Saxons. Ethelbert
was not actually king in that region, but was recognized as "bretwalda,"
or over-lord, by the other rulers.

[2] For later changes in this part of the coast line, see p. 70, note 1.

[3] This was possible because the Franks and Saxons, being both German,
as yet spoke languages so much alike that either people could understand
the other without much difficulty.

[4] Bertha was a daughter of the Frankish king Charibert. The Franks
had been nominally a Christian people since the conversion of Clovis in 496
[see p. 53]—just a hundred years before Augustine started on his mission
to the Angles and Saxons.

[5] Luidhard had been bishop of Senlis, a town not many miles northeast of
Paris. Probably Augustine and his companions profited not a little by the
influence which Luidhard had already exerted at the Kentish court.

into his presence. For he had taken precaution that they should not come to him in any house, lest, according to an ancient superstition, if they practised any magical arts, they might impose upon him, and so get the better of him. But they came furnished with divine, not with magic virtue, bearing a silver cross for their banner, and the image of our Lord and Savior painted on a board; and singing the litany, they offered up their prayers to the Lord for the eternal salvation both of themselves and of **Augustine** those to whom they were come. When Augustine **preaches to** had sat down, according to the king's commands, **King Ethel-** and preached to him and his attendants there **bert** present the word of life, the king answered thus: "Your words and promises are very fair, but as they are new to us, and of uncertain import, I cannot approve of them so far as to forsake that which I have so long followed with the whole English nation. But because you are come from afar into my kingdom, and, as I conceive, are desirous to impart to us those things which you believe to be true and most beneficial, we will not molest you, but give you favorable entertainment and take care to supply you with necessary sustenance; nor do we forbid you to preach and win as many as you can to your religion." Accordingly he permitted them to reside in the city of Canterbury, which was the metropolis of all his dominions, and, according to his promise, besides allowing them sustenance, did not refuse them liberty to preach. It is reported that, as they drew near to the city, after their manner, with the holy cross and the image of our sovereign Lord and King, Jesus Christ, they sang this litany together: "We beseech thee, O Lord, in all Thy mercy, that Thy anger and wrath be turned away from this city, and from Thy holy house, because we have sinned. Hallelujah."

As soon as they entered the dwelling-place assigned them, they began to imitate the course of life practised in the primitive Church; applying themselves to frequent prayer, watching, and fasting; preaching the word of life to as many as they could; despising all worldly things as not belonging to them; receiving only their necessary food from those they taught; living **The life of the** themselves in all respects in conformity with **missionaries at** what they prescribed for others, and being always **Canterbury** disposed to suffer any adversity, and even to die for that truth which they preached. In short, several believed and were baptized, admiring the simplicity of their innocent life, and the sweetness of their heavenly doctrine. There was, on the east side of the city, a church dedicated to the honor of St. Martin, built whilst the Romans were still in the island, wherein the queen, who, as has been said before, was a Christian, used to pray.[1] In this they first began to meet, to sing, to pray, to say mass, to preach, and to baptize, until the king, being converted to the faith, allowed them to preach openly, and build or repair churches in all places.

When he, among the rest, induced by the unspotted life of these holy men, and their pleasing promises, which by many **Ethelbert** miracles they proved to be most certain, believed **converted** and was baptized, greater numbers began daily to flock together to hear the word, and forsaking their heathen rites, to associate themselves, by believing, to the unity of the church of Christ. Their conversion the king encouraged in so far that he compelled none to embrace Christianity, but only showed more affection to the believers, as to his fellow-citizens in the heavenly kingdom. For he had learned from his instructors and guides to salvation that the service of Christ ought to be voluntary, not by compulsion. Nor was it long before he gave his teachers a settled residence in his metropolis of Canterbury, with such possessions of different kinds as were necessary for their subsistence.[2]

---

[1] "The present church of St. Martin near Canterbury is not the old one spoken of by Bede, as it is generally thought to be, but is a structure of the thirteenth century, though it is probable that the materials of the original church were worked up in the masonry in its reconstruction, the walls being still composed in part of Roman bricks."—J. A. Giles, *Bede's Ecclesiastical History*, p. 39.

[2] Thus was established the "primacy," or ecclesiastical leadership, of Canterbury, which has continued to this day.

CHAPTER VI.

THE DEVELOPMENT OF THE CHRISTIAN CHURCH

10. Pope Leo's Sermon on the Petrine Supremacy

In tracing the history of the great ecclesiastical institution known as the papacy, the first figure that stands out with considerable clearness is that of Leo I., or Leo the Great, who was elected bishop of Rome in the year 440. Leo is perhaps the first man who, all things considered, can be called "pope" in the modern sense of the term, although certain of his predecessors in the bishop's seat at the imperial capital had long claimed and exercised a peculiar measure of authority over their fellow bishops throughout the Empire. Almost from the earliest days of Christianity the word *papa* (pope) seems to have been in common use as an affectionate mode of addressing any bishop, but after the fourth century it came to be applied in a peculiar manner to the bishop of Rome, and in time this was the only usage, so far as western Europe was concerned, which survived. The causes of the special development of the Roman bishopric into the powerful papal office were numerous. Rome's importance as a city, and particularly as the political head of the Mediterranean world, made it natural that her bishop should have something of a special dignity and influence. Throughout western Europe the Roman church was regarded as a model and its bishop was frequently called upon for counsel and advice. Then, when the seat of the imperial government was removed to the East by Constantine, the Roman bishop naturally took up much of the leadership in the West which had been exercised by the emperor, and this added not a little in the way of prestige. On the whole the Roman bishops were moderate, liberal, and sensible in their attitude toward church questions, thereby commending themselves to the practical peoples of the West in a way that other bishops did not always do. The growth of temporal possessions, especially in the way of land, also made the Roman bishops more independent and able to hold their own. And the activity of such men as Leo the Great in warding off the attacks of the German barbarians, and in providing popular leadership in the absence of such leadership on the part of the imperial authorities, was a not unimportant item.

After all, however, these are matters which have always been regarded by the popes themselves as circumstances of a more or less transitory and accidental character. It is not upon any or all of them that the papacy from first to last has sought to base its high claims to authority. The fundamental explanation, from the papal standpoint, for the peculiar development of the papal power in the person of the bishops of Rome is contained in the so-called theory of the "Petrine Supremacy," which will be found set forth in Pope Leo's sermon reproduced in part below. The essential points in this theory are: (1) that to the apostle Peter, Christ committed the keys of the kingdom of heaven and the supremacy over all other apostles on earth; (2) that Peter, in the course of time, became the first bishop of Rome; and (3) that the superior authority given to Peter was transmitted to all his successors in the Roman bishopric. It was fundamentally on *these* grounds that the pope, to quote an able Catholic historian, was believed to be "the visible representative of ecclesiastical unity, the supreme teacher and custodian of the faith, the supreme legislator, the guardian and interpreter of the canons, the legitimate superior of all bishops, the final judge of councils—an office which he possessed in his own right, and which he actually exercised by presiding over all ecumenical synods, through his legates, and by confirming the acts of the councils as the Supreme Head of the Universal Catholic Church." [1] Modern Protestants discard certain of the tenets which go to make up the Petrine theory, but it is essential that the student of history bear in mind that the people of the Middle Ages never doubted its complete and literal authenticity, nor questioned that the authority of the papal office rested at bottom upon something far more fundamental than a mere fortunate combination of historical circumstances. Whatever one's personal opinions on the issues involved, the point to be insisted upon is that in studying mediæval church life and organization the universal acceptance of these beliefs and conclusions be never lost to view.

[1] John Alzog. *Manual of Universal Church History* (trans. by F. J. Pabisch and T. S. Byrne), Cincinnati, 1899, Vol. I., p. 668.

Leo was pope from 440 to 461 and it has been well maintained that he was the first occupant of the office to comprehend the wide possibilities of the papal dignity in the future. In his sermons and letters he vigorously asserted the sovereign authority of his position, and in his influence on the events of his time, as for example the Council of Chalcedon in 451, he sought with no little success to bring men to a general acknowledgment of this authority.

Source—Text in Jacques Paul Migne, *Patrologiæ Cursus Completus* ["Complete Collection of Patristic Literature"], First Series, Vol. LIV., cols. 144–148. Translated in Philip Schaff and Henry Wace, *Select Library of Nicene and Post-Nicene Fathers of the Christian Church* (New York, 1895), Second Series, Vol. XII., pp. 117–118.

Although, therefore, dearly beloved, we be found both weak and slothful in fulfilling the duties of our office, because, whatever devoted and vigorous action we desire to undertake, we are hindered in by the frailty of our nature, yet having the unceasing propitiation of the Almighty and perpetual Priest [Christ], who being like us and yet equal with the Father, brought down His Godhead even to things human, and raised His Manhood even to things Divine, we worthily and piously rejoice over His dispensation, whereby, though He has delegated the care of His sheep to many shepherds, yet He has not Himself abandoned the guardianship of His beloved flock. And from His overruling

The apostle Peter still with his Church and eternal protection we have received the support of the Apostle's aid also, which assuredly does not cease from its operation; and the strength of the foundation, on which the whole superstructure of the Church is reared, is not weakened by the weight of the temple that rests upon it. For the solidity of that faith which was praised in the chief of the Apostles is perpetual; and as that remains which Peter believed in Christ, so that remains which Christ instituted in Peter.

For when, as has been read in the Gospel lesson,[1] the Lord had asked the disciples whom they believed Him to be amid the

[1] That is, the passage of Scripture read just before the sermon.

various opinions that were held, and the blessed Peter had replied, saying, "Thou art the Christ, the Son of the living God,"
Christ's com-mission to Peter the Lord said, "Blessed art thou, Simon Bar-Jona, because flesh and blood hath not revealed it to thee, but My Father, which is in heaven. And I say to thee, that thou art Peter, and upon this rock will I build My church, and the gates of Hell shall not prevail against it. And I will give unto thee the keys of the kingdom of heaven. And whatsoever thou shalt bind on earth, shall be bound in heaven; and whatsoever thou shalt loose on earth, shall be loosed also in heaven." [Matt. xvi. 16–19.]

The dispensation of Truth therefore abides, and the blessed Peter persevering in the strength of the Rock, which he has received, has not abandoned the helm of the Church, which he undertook. For he was ordained before the rest in such a way that from his being called the Rock, from his being pronounced the Foundation, from his being constituted the Doorkeeper of the kingdom of heaven, from his being set as the Umpire to bind and to loose, whose judgments shall retain their validity in
Peter proper-ly rules the Church through his successors at Rome heaven—from all these mystical titles we might know the nature of his association with Christ. And still to-day he more fully and effectually performs what is intrusted to him, and carries out every part of his duty and charge in Him and with Him, through whom he has been glorified. And so if anything is rightly done and rightly decreed by us, if anything is won from the mercy of God by our daily supplications, it is of his work and merits whose power lives and whose authority prevails in his see.[1]   . . .

And so, dearly beloved, with becoming obedience we celebrate to-day's festival [2] by such methods, that in my humble person he

[1] "See" is a term employed to designate a bishop's jurisdiction. According to common belief Peter had been bishop of Rome; his see was therefore that which Leo now held.

[2] The anniversary of Leo's elevation to the papal office.

Med. Hist.—6

may be recognized and honored, in whom abides the care of all the shepherds, together with the charge of the sheep commended to him, and whose dignity is not belittled even in so unworthy an

Leo claims to be only Peter's representative

heir. And hence the presence of my venerable brothers and fellow-priests, so much desired and valued by me, will be the more sacred and precious, if they will transfer the chief honor of this service in which they have deigned to take part to him whom they know to be not only the patron of this see, but also the primate of all bishops. When therefore we utter our exhortations in your ears, holy brethren, believe that he is speaking whose representative we are. Because it is his warning that we give, and nothing else but his teaching that we preach, beseeching you to "gird up the loins of your mind," and lead a chaste and sober life in the fear of God, and not to let your mind forget his supremacy and consent to the lusts of the flesh.

Short and fleeting are the joys of this world's pleasures which endeavor to turn aside from the path of life those who are called to eternity. The faithful and religious spirit, therefore, must desire the things which are heavenly and, being eager for the

An exhortation to Christian constancy

divine promises, lift itself to the love of the incorruptible Good and the hope of the true Light. But be assured, dearly-beloved, that your labor, whereby you resist vices and fight against carnal desires, is pleasing and precious in God's sight, and in God's mercy will profit not only yourselves but me also, because the zealous pastor makes his boast of the progress of the Lord's flock. "For ye are my crown and joy," as the Apostle says, if your faith, which from the beginning of the Gospel has been preached in all

The peculiar privilege of the church at Rome

the world, has continued in love and holiness. For though the whole Church, which is in all the world, ought to abound in all virtues, yet you especially, above all people, it becomes to excel in deeds of piety, because, founded as you are on the very citadel of the Apostolic

Rock, not only has our Lord Jesus Christ redeemed you in common with all men, but the blessed Apostle Peter has instructed you far beyond all men.

11. The Rule of St. Benedict

A VERY important feature of the church life of the early Middle Ages was the tendency of devout men to withdraw from the active affairs of the world and give themselves up to careers of self-sacrificing piety. Sometimes such men went out to live alone in forests or other obscure places and for this reason were called anchorites or hermits; but more often they settled in groups and formed what came to be known as monasteries. The idea that seclusion is helpful to the religious life was not peculiar to Christianity, for from very early times Brahmins and Buddhists and other peoples of the Orient had cherished the same view; and in many cases they do so still. Monasticism among Christians began naturally in the East and at first took the form almost wholly of hermitage, just as it had done among the adherents of other Oriental religions, though by the fourth century the Christian monks of Syria and Egypt and Asia Minor had come in many cases to dwell in established communities. In general the Eastern monks were prone to extremes in the way of penance and self-torture which the more practical peoples of the West were not greatly disposed to imitate. Monasticism spread into the West, but not until comparatively late—beginning in the second half of the fourth century—and the character which it there assumed was quite unlike that prevailing in the East. The Eastern ideal was the life of meditation with as little activity as possible, except perhaps such as was necessary in order to impose hardships upon one's self. The Western ideal, on the other hand, while involving a good deal of meditation and prayer, put much emphasis on labor and did not call for so complete an abstention of the monk from the pursuits and pleasures of other men.

In the later fifth century, and earlier sixth, several monasteries of whose history we know little were established in southern Gaul, especially in the pleasant valley of the Rhone. Earliest of all, apparently, and destined to become the most influential was the abbey of St. Martin at Tours, founded soon after St. Martin was made bishop of Tours in 372.

But the development of Western monasticism is associated most of all with the work of St. Benedict of Nursia, who died in 543. Benedict was the founder of several monasteries in the vicinity of Rome, the most important being that of Monte Cassino, on the road from Rome to Naples, which exists to this day. One should guard, however, against the mistake of looking upon St. Benedict as the introducer of monasticism in the West, of even as the founder of a new monastic *order* in the strict sense of the word. The great service which he rendered to European monasticism consisted in his working out for his monasteries in Italy an elaborate system of government which was found so successful in practice that, in the form of the Benedictine Rule (*regula*), it came to be the constitution under which for many centuries practically all the monks of Western countries lived. That it was so widely adopted was due mainly to its definite, practical, common-sense character. Its chief injunctions upon the monks were poverty, chastity, obedience, piety, and labor. All these were to be attained by methods which, although they may seem strange to us to-day, were at least natural and wholesome when judged by the ideas and standards prevailing in early mediæval times. Granted the ascetic principle upon which the monastic system rested, the Rule of St. Benedict must be regarded as eminently moderate and sensible. It sprang from an acute perception of human nature and human needs no less than from a lofty ideal of religious perfection. The following extracts will serve to show its character.

Source—Text in Jacques Paul Migne, *Patrologiæ Cursus Completus*, First Series, Vol. LXVI., cols. 245–932 *passim*. Adapted from translation in Ernest F. Henderson, *Select Historical Documents of the Middle Ages* (London, 1896), pp. 274–314.

Prologue. . . . We are about to found, therefore, a school for the Lord's service, in the organization of which we trust that we shall ordain nothing severe and nothing burdensome. But even if, the demands of justice dictating it, something a trifle irksome shall be the result, for the purpose of amending vices or preserving charity, thou shalt not therefore, struck by fear, flee the way of salvation, which cannot be entered upon except through a narrow entrance.

2. *What the abbot should be like.* An abbot who is worthy to preside over a monastery ought always to remember what he is called, and carry out with his deeds the name of a Superior. For he is believed to be Christ's representative, since he is called by His name, the apostle saying: "Ye have received the spirit of adoption of sons, whereby we call Abba, Father" [Romans viii. 15]. And so the abbot should not (grant that he may not) teach, or decree, or order, anything apart from the precept of the Lord; but his order or teaching should be characterized by the marks of divine justice in the minds of his disciples. Let the abbot

Responsibility of the abbot for the character and deeds of the monks always be mindful that, at the terrible judgment of God, both things will be weighed in the balance, his teaching and the obedience of his disciples. And let the abbot know that whatever of uselessness the father of the family finds among the sheep is laid to the fault of the shepherd. Only in a case where the whole diligence of their pastor shall have been bestowed on an unruly and disobedient flock, and his whole care given to their wrongful actions, shall that pastor, absolved in the judgment of the Lord, be free to say to the Lord with the prophet: "I have not hid Thy righteousness within my heart; I have declared Thy faithfulness and Thy salvation, but they, despising, have scorned me" [Psalms xl. 10]. And then let the punishment for the disobedient sheep under his care be that death itself shall prevail against

He must teach by example as well as by precept them. Therefore, when any one receives the name of abbot, he ought to rule over his disciples with a double teaching; that is, let him show forth all good and holy things by deeds more than by words. So that to ready disciples he may set forth the commands of God in words; but to the hard-hearted and the more simple-minded, he may show forth the divine precepts by his deeds.

He shall make no distinction of persons in the monastery. One shall not be more cherished than another, unless it be the one whom he finds excelling in good works or in obedience. A free-born man shall not be preferred to one coming from servitude, unless there be some other reasonable cause. But if, by the demand of justice, it seems good to the abbot, he shall do this, no matter what the rank shall be. But otherwise they shall keep their own places. For whether we be bond or free, we are all **His duty to encourage, to admonish, and to punish** one in Christ; and, under one God, we perform an equal service of subjection. For God is no respecter of persons. Only in this way is a distinction made by Him concerning us, if we are found humble and surpassing others in good works. Therefore let him [the abbot] have equal charity for all. Let the same discipline be administered in all cases according to merit. . . . He should, that is, rebuke more severely the unruly and the turbulent. The obedient, moreover, and the gentle and the patient, he should exhort, that they may progress to higher things. But the negligent and scorners, we warn him to admonish and reprove. Nor let him conceal the sins of the erring; but, in order that he may prevail, let him pluck them out by the roots as soon as they begin to spring up.

And let him know what a difficult and arduous thing he has undertaken—to rule the souls and uplift the morals of many. And in one case indeed with blandishments, in another with rebukes, in another with persuasion—according to the quality or intelligence of each one—he shall so conform and adapt himself to all that not only shall he not allow injury to come to the flock committed to him, but he shall rejoice in the increase of a good flock. Above all things, let him not, deceiving himself or undervaluing the safety of the souls committed to him, give more heed to temporary and earthly and passing things; but let him always reflect that he has undertaken to rule souls for which he is to render account.

3. *About calling in the brethren to take counsel.* Whenever anything of importance is to be done in the monastery, the abbot shall call together the whole congregation,[1] and shall himself

[1] That is, the body of monks residing in the monastery.

explain the matter in question. And, having heard the advice of the brethren, he shall think it over by himself, and shall do

The monks to be consulted by the abbot what he considers most advantageous. And for this reason, moreover, we have said that all ought to be called to take counsel, because often it is to a younger person that God reveals what is best. The brethren, moreover, with all subjection of humility, ought so to give their advice that they do not presume boldly to defend what seems good to them; but it should rather depend on the judgment of the abbot, so that, whatever he decides to be best, they should all agree to it. But even as it behooves the disciples to obey the master, so it is fitting that he should arrange all matters with care and justice. In all things, indeed, let

The Rule to be followed by every one as a guide every one follow the Rule as his guide; and let no one rashly deviate from it. Let no one in the monastery follow the inclination of his own heart. And let no one boldly presume to dispute with his abbot, within or without the monastery. But, if he should so presume, let him be subject to the discipline of the Rule.

33. *Whether the monks should have anything of their own.* More than anything else is this special vice to be cut off root and

No property to be owned by the monks individually branch from the monastery, that one should presume to give or receive anything without the order of the abbot, or should have anything of his own. He should have absolutely not anything, neither a book, nor tablets, nor a pen—nothing at all. For indeed it is not allowed to the monks to have their own bodies or wills in their own power. But all things necessary they must expect from the Father of the monastery; nor is it allowable to have anything which the abbot has not given or permitted. All things shall be held in common; as it is written, "Let not any man presume to call anything his own." But if any one shall have been discovered delighting in this most evil vice, being warned once and again, if he do not amend, let him be subjected to punishment.[1]

48. *Concerning the daily manual labor.* Idleness is the enemy of the soul.[2] And therefore, at fixed times, the brothers ought to be occupied in manual labor; and again, at fixed times, in sacred reading.[3] Therefore we believe that both seasons ought to be arranged after this manner,—so that, from Easter until the Calends of October,[4] going out early, from the first until the fourth hour they shall do what labor may be necessary. From **Daily schedule for the summer season** the fourth hour until about the sixth, they shall be free for reading. After the meal of the sixth hour, rising from the table, they shall rest in their beds with all silence; or, perchance, he that wishes to read may read to himself in such a way as not to disturb another. And the *nona* [the second meal] shall be gone through with more moderately about the middle of the eighth hour; and again they shall work at what is to be done until Vespers.[5] But, if the emergency or poverty of the place demands that they be occupied in picking fruits, they shall not be grieved; for they are truly monks if they live by the labors of their hands, as did also our fathers and the apostles. Let all things be done with moderation, however, on account of the faint-hearted.

In days of Lent they shall all receive separate books from the library, which they shall read entirely through in order. These

---

[1] The vow of poverty which must be taken by every Benedictine monk meant only that he must not acquire property individually. By gifts of land and by their own labor the monks became in many cases immensely rich, but their wealth was required to be held in common. No one man could rightfully call any part of it his own.

[2] The converse of this principle was often affirmed by Benedictines in the saying, "To work is to pray."

[3] The Bible and the writings of such Church fathers as Lactantius, Tertullian, Origen, St. Augustine, St. Chrysostom, Eusebius, and St. Jerome.

[4] The first day of the month.

[5] Thus the ordinary daily programme during the spring and summer months would be: from six o'clock until ten, manual labor; from ten until twelve, reading; at twelve, the midday meal; after this meal until the second one about half past two, rest and reading; and from the second meal until evening, labor. Manual labor was principally agricultural.

books are to be given out on the first day of Lent. Above all there shall be appointed without fail one or two elders, who shall

Reading during Lent go round the monastery at the hours in which the brothers are engaged in reading, and see to it that no troublesome brother be found who is given to idleness and trifling, and is not intent on his reading, being not only of no use to himself, but also stirring up others. If such a one (may it not happen) be found, he shall be reproved once and a second time. If he do not amend, he shall be subject under the Rule to such punishment that the others may have fear. Nor shall brother join brother at unsuitable hours. Moreover, on Sunday all shall engage in reading, excepting those who are assigned to various duties. But if any one be so negligent and lazy that he will not or can not read, some task shall be imposed upon him which he can do, so that he be not idle. On feeble or delicate brothers such a task or art is to be imposed, that they shall neither be idle nor so oppressed by the violence of labor as to be driven to take flight. Their weakness is to be taken into consideration by the abbot.

53. *Concerning the reception of guests.* All guests who come shall be received as though they were Christ. For He Himself

Hospitality enjoined said, "I was a stranger and ye took me in" [Matt. xxv. 35]. And to all fitting honor shall be shown; but, most of all, to servants of the faith and to pilgrims. When, therefore, a guest is announced, the prior or the brothers shall run to meet him, with every token of love. And first they shall pray together, and thus they shall be joined together in peace.

54. *Whether a monk should be allowed to receive letters or anything.* By no means shall it be allowed to a monk—either from his relatives, or from any man, or from one of his fellows—to receive or to give, without order of the abbot, letters, presents, or any gift, however small. But even if, by his relatives, anything has been sent to him, he shall not presume to receive it, unless

it has first been shown to the abbot. But if the latter order
it to be received, it shall be in the power of the abbot to give it
Power of abbot to whomsoever he wishes. And the brother to
to dispose of
articles sent to whom it happened to have been sent shall not
the monks be displeased; that an opportunity be not given
to the devil. Whoever, moreover, presumes to do otherwise
shall be subject to the discipline of the Rule.

12. Gregory the Great on the Life of the Pastor

GREGORY THE GREAT, whose papacy extended from 590 to 604, was a
Roman of noble and wealthy family, and in many ways the ablest man
who had yet risen to the papal office. The date of his birth is not recorded, but it was probably about 540, some ten years after St. Benedict
of Nursia had established his monastery at Monte Cassino. He was
therefore a contemporary of the historian Gregory of Tours [see p. 47].
The education which he received was that which was usual with young
Romans of his rank in life, and it is said that in grammar, rhetoric, logic,
and law he became well versed, though without any claim to unusual
scholarship. He entered public life and in 570 was made prætor of the
city of Rome. All the time, however, he was struggling with the strange
attractiveness which the life of the monk had for him, and in the end,
upon the death of his father, he decided to forego the career to which his
wealth and rank entitled him and to seek the development of his higher
nature in seclusion. With the money obtained from the sale of his great
estates he established six monasteries in Sicily and that of St. Andrew
at Rome. In Gregory's case, however, retirement to monastic life did
not mean oblivion, for soon he was selected by Pope Pelagius II., as
resident minister (*apocrisiarius*) at Constantinople and in this important position he was maintained for five or six years. After returning
to Rome he became abbot of St. Andrews, and in 590, as the records
say, he was "demanded" as pope.

Gregory was a man of very unusual ability and the force of his strong
personality made his reign one of the great formative epochs in papal
history. Besides his activity in relation to the affairs of the world in
general, he has the distinction of being a literary pope. His letters
and treatises were numerous and possessed a quality of thought and

style which was exceedingly rare in his day. The most famous of his writings, and justly so, is the *Liber Regulæ Pastoralis*, known commonly to English readers as the "Pastoral Care," or the "Pastoral Rule." This book was written soon after its author became pope (590) and was addressed to John, bishop of Ravenna, in reply to inquiries received from him respecting the duties and obligations of the clergy. Though thus put into form for a special purpose, there can be no doubt that it was the product of long thought, and in fact in his *Magna Moralia*, or "Commentary on the Book of Job," written during his residence at Constantinople, Gregory declared his purpose some day to write just such a book. Everywhere throughout Europe the work was received with the favor it deserved, and in Spain, Gaul, and Italy its influence upon the life and manners of the clergy was beyond estimate. Even in Britain, after King Alfred's paraphrase of it in the Saxon tongue had been made, three hundred years later [see p. 193], it was a real power for good. The permanent value of Gregory's instructions regarding the life of the clergy arose not only from the lofty spirit in which they were conceived and the clear-cut manner in which they were expressed, but from their breadth and adaptation to all times and places. There are few books which the modern pastor can read with greater profit. The work is in four parts: (1) on the selection of men for the work of the Church; (2) on the sort of life the pastor ought to live; (3) on the best methods of dealing with the various types of people which every pastor will be likely to encounter; and (4) on the necessity that the pastor guard himself against egotism and personal ambition. The passages below are taken from the second and third parts.

Source—Gregorius Magnus, *Liber Regulæ Pastoralis* [Gregory the Great, "The Book of the Pastoral Rule"]. Text in Jacques Paul Migne, *Patrologiæ Cursus Completus*, First Series, Vol. LXXVII., cols. 12–127 *passim*. Adapted from translation in Philip Schaff and Henry Wace, *Select Library of Nicene and Post-Nicene Fathers of the Christian Church* (New York, 1895), Second Series, Vol. XII., pp. 9–71 *passim*.

The conduct of a prelate [1] ought so far to be superior to the conduct of the people as the life of a shepherd is accustomed to exalt him above the flock. For one whose position is such that

[1] Gregory's remarks and instructions in the *Pastoral Rule* were intended to apply primarily to the local priests—the humble pastors of whom we hear

the people are called his flock ought anxiously to consider how great a necessity is laid upon him to maintain uprightness. It **The qualities** is necessary, then, that in thought he should be **which ought to** pure, in action firm; discreet in keeping silence, **be united in** **the pastor** profitable in speech; a near neighbor to every one in sympathy, exalted above all in contemplation; a familiar friend of good livers through humility, unbending against the vices of evil-doers through zeal for righteousness; not relaxing in his care for what is inward by reason of being occupied in outward things, nor neglecting to provide for outward things in his anxiety for what is inward.

The ruler should always be pure in thought, inasmuch as no impurity ought to pollute him who has undertaken the office **Purity of heart** of wiping away the stains of pollution in the **essential** hearts of others also; for the hand that would cleanse from dirt must needs be clean, lest, being itself sordid with clinging mire, it soil all the more whatever it touches.

The ruler should always be a leader in action, that by his living he may point out the way of life to those who are put under him, **He must teach** and that the flock, which follows the voice and **by example** manners of the shepherd, may learn how to walk rather through example than through words. For he who is required by the necessity of his position to *speak* the highest things is compelled by the same necessity to *do* the highest things. For that voice more readily penetrates the hearer's heart, which the speaker's life commends, since what he commands by speaking he helps the doing by showing.

The ruler should be discreet in keeping silence, profitable in speech; lest he either utter what ought to be suppressed or suppress what he ought to utter. For, as incautious speaking leads into error, so indiscreet silence leaves in error those who might have been instructed.

little, but upon whose piety and diligence ultimately depended the whole influence of the Church upon the masses of the people. The general principles laid down, however, were applicable to all the clergy, of whatever rank.

The ruler ought also to understand how commonly vices pass themselves off as virtues. For often niggardliness excuses itself under the name of frugality, and on the other hand extravagance conceals itself under the name of liberality. Often inordinate carelessness is believed to be loving-kindness, and unbridled wrath is accounted the virtue of spiritual zeal. Often hasty action is taken for promptness, and tardiness for the deliberation **He must be able to distin guish virtues and vices** of seriousness. Whence it is necessary for the ruler of souls to distinguish with vigilant care between virtues and vices, lest stinginess get possession of his heart while he exults in seeming frugality in expenditure; or, while anything is recklessly wasted, he glory in being, as it were, compassionately liberal; or, in overlooking what he ought to have smitten, he draw on those that are under him to eternal punishment; or, in mercilessly smiting an offense, he himself offend more grievously; or, by rashly anticipating, mar what might have been done properly and gravely; or, by putting off the merit of a good action, change it to something worse.

Since, then, we have shown what manner of man the pastor ought to be, let us now set forth after what manner he should **No one kind of teaching adapted to all men** teach. For, as long before us Gregory Nazianzen,[1] of reverend memory, has taught, one and the same exhortation does not suit all, inasmuch as all are not bound together by similarity of character. For the things that profit some often hurt others; seeing that also, for the most part, herbs which nourish some animals are fatal to others; and the gentle hissing that quiets horses incites whelps; and the medicine which abates one disease aggravates another; and the food which invigorates the life of the strong kills little children. Therefore, according to the quality of the hearers ought the discourse of teachers to be fashioned, so as to suit all and each for their several needs, and yet never deviate from the

---

[1] Gregory, bishop of Nazianzus (in Cappadocia), was a noted churchman of the fourth century.

art of common edification. For what are the intent minds of hearers but, so to speak, a kind of harp, which the skilful player, in order to produce a tune possessing harmony, strikes in various ways? And for this reason the strings render back a melodious sound, because they are struck indeed with one quill, but not with one kind of stroke. Whence every teacher also, that he may edify all in the one virtue of charity, ought to touch the hearts of his hearers out of one doctrine, but not with one and the same exhortation.

Differently to be admonished are these that follow:

Men and women.

The poor and the rich.

The joyful and the sad.

Prelates and subordinates.

Servants and masters.

The wise of this world and the dull.

Various classes of hearers to be distinguished

The impudent and the bashful.

The forward and the faint-hearted.

The impatient and the patient.

The kindly disposed and the envious.

The simple and the insincere.

The whole and the sick.

Those who fear scourges, and therefore live innocently; and those who have grown so hard in iniquity as not to be corrected even by scourges.

The too silent, and those who spend time in much speaking.

The slothful and the hasty.

The meek and the passionate.

The humble and the haughty.

The obstinate and the fickle.

The gluttonous and the abstinent.

Those who mercifully give of their own, and those who would fain seize what belongs to others.

Those who neither seize the things of others nor are bountiful with their own; and those who both give away the things they have, and yet cease not to seize the things of others.

Those who are at variance, and those who are at peace.

Lovers of strife and peacemakers.

Those who understand not aright the words of sacred law; and those who understand them indeed aright, but speak them without humility.

Those who, though able to preach worthily, are afraid through excessive humility; and those whom imperfection or age debars from preaching, and yet rashness impels to it.

(Admonition 7).[1] Differently to be admonished are the wise of this world and the dull. For the wise are to be admonished that they leave off knowing what they know;[2] the dull also are to be admonished that they seek to know what they know not. In the former this thing first, that they think themselves wise, is to be overcome; in the latter, whatsoever is already known of

How the wise and the dull are to be admonished

heavenly wisdom is to be built up; since, being in no wise proud, they have, as it were, prepared their hearts for supporting a building. With those we should labor that they become more wisely foolish,[3] leave foolish wisdom, and learn the wise foolishness of God: to these we should preach that from what is accounted foolish-

---

[1] After enumerating quite a number of other contrasted groups in the foregoing fashion Gregory proceeds in a series of "admonitions" to take up each pair and tell how persons belonging to it should be dealt with by the pastor. One of these admonitions is here given as a specimen.

[2] Gregory's attitude toward the "learning of the world," especially the classical languages and literatures, was that of the typical Christian ascetic. He had no use for it personally and regarded its influence as positively harmful. It must be said that there was little such learning in his day, for the old Latin and Greek culture had now reached a very low stage. Gregory took the ground that the churches should have learned bishops, but their learning was to consist exclusively in a knowledge of the Scriptures, the writings of the Church fathers, and the stories of the martyrs. As a matter of fact not only were the people generally quite unable to understand the Latin services of the Church, but great numbers of the clergy themselves stumbled blindly through the ritual without knowing what they were saying; and this condition of things prevailed for centuries after Gregory's day. [See Charlemagne's letter *De Litteris Colendis*, p. 146.]

[3] That is, more simple and less self-satisfied in their own knowledge.

ness they should pass, as from a nearer neighborhood, to true wisdom.

But in the midst of these things we are brought back by the earnest desire of charity to what we have already said above; that every preacher should give forth a sound more by his deeds than by his words, and rather by good living imprint footsteps for men to follow than by speaking show them the way to walk in. For that cock, too, whom the Lord in his manner of speech takes to represent a good preacher, when he is now preparing to crow, first shakes his wings, and by smiting himself makes himself more awake; since it is surely necessary that those who give utterance to words of holy preaching should first be well awake **Emphasis on the importance of setting a right example** in earnestness of good living, lest they arouse others with their voice while themselves torpid in performance; that they should first shake themselves up by lofty deeds, and then make others solicitous for good living; that they should first smite themselves with the wings of their thoughts; that whatsoever in themselves is unprofitably torpid they should discover by anxious investigation, and correct by strict self-discipline, and then at length set in order the life of others by speaking; that they should take heed to punish their own faults by bewailings, and then denounce what calls for punishment in others; and that, before they give voice to words of exhortation, they should proclaim in their deeds all that they are about to speak.

CHAPTER VII.

THE RISE OF MOHAMMEDANISM

13. Selections from the Koran

The Koran comprises all of the recorded speeches and sayings of the prophet Mohammed and it has for nearly fifteen centuries been the absolute law and gospel of the Mohammedan religion. The teachings and revelations which are contained in it are believed by Mohammedans to have proceeded directly from God. They were delivered orally by Mohammed from time to time in the presence of his followers and until after the prophet's death in 632 no attempt was made to put them in organized written form. Many of the disciples, however, remembered the words their master had uttered, at least until they could inscribe them on palm leaves, bits of wood, bleached bones, or other such articles as happened to be at hand. In the reign of Abu-Bekr (632–634), Mohammed's successor, it became apparent that unless some measure was adopted to bring these scattered sayings together they were in a fair way to be lost for all time to come. Hence the caliph intrusted to a certain young man by the name of Zaid the task of collecting and putting in some sort of system all the teachings that had survived, whether in written form or merely in the minds of men. Zaid had served Mohammed in a capacity which we should designate perhaps as that of secretary, and so should have been well qualified for the work. In later years (about 660) the Koran, or "the reading," as the collection began to be called, was again thoroughly revised. Thereafter all older copies were destroyed and no farther changes in any respect were ever made.

The Koran is made up of one hundred and fourteen chapters, called *surahs*, arranged loosely in the order of their length, beginning with the longest. This arrangement does not correspond either to the dates at which the various passages were uttered by the prophet or to any sequence of thought and meaning, so that when one takes up the book to read it as it is ordinarily printed it seems about as confused as anything can well be. Scholars, however, have recently discovered the chronological order of the various parts and this knowledge has already come to be of no little assistance in the work of interpretation. Like all sacred books, the Koran abounds in repetitions; yet, taken all in all, it contains not more than two-thirds as many verses as the New Testament, and, as one writer has rather curiously observed, it is not more than one-third as lengthy as the ordinary Sunday edition of the New York *Herald*. The teachings which are most emphasized are (1) the unity and greatness of God, (2) the sin of worshipping idols, (3) the certainty of the resurrection of the body and the last judgment, (4) the necessity of a belief in the Scriptures as revelations from God communicated through angels to the line of prophets, (5) the luxuries of heaven and the torments of hell, (6) the doctrine of predestination, (7) the authoritativeness of Mohammed's teachings, and (8) the four cardinal obligations of worship (including purification and prayer), fasting, pilgrimages, and alms-giving. Intermingled with these are numerous popular legends and sayings of the Arabs before Mohammed's day, stories from the Old and New Testaments derived from Jewish and Christian settlers in Arabia, and certain definite and practical rules of everyday conduct. The book is not only thus haphazard in subject-matter but it is also very irregular in interest and elegance. Portions of it abound in splendid imagery and lofty conceptions, and represent the literary quality of the Arabian language at its best, though of course this quality is very largely lost in translation. The later surahs—those which appear first in the printed copy—are largely argumentative and legislative in character and naturally fall into a more prosaic and monotonous strain. From an almost inexhaustible maze of precepts, exhortations, and revelations, the following widely separated passages have been selected in the hope that they will serve to show something of the character of the Koran itself, as well as the nature of some of the more important Mohammedan beliefs and ideals. It will be found profitable to make a comparison of Christian beliefs on the same points as drawn from the New Testament.

Source—Text in Edward William Lane, *Selections from the Kur-án*, edited by
        Stanley Lane-Poole (London, 1879), *passim.*

In the name of God, the Compassionate, the Merciful.

Praise be to God, the Lord of the Worlds,

The opening   The Compassionate, the Merciful,
prayer [1]   The King of the day of judgment.

Thee do we worship, and of Thee seek we help.

Guide us in the right way,

The way of those to whom Thou hast been gracious,

Not of those with whom Thou art wroth, nor of the erring.[2]

> Say, He is God, One [God];
>
> God, the Eternal.
>
> He begetteth not nor is begotten,
>
> And there is none equal unto Him.[3]

God! There is no God but He, the *Ever*-Living, the Ever-Subsisting. Slumber seizeth Him not, nor sleep. To Him be-
The "throne   longeth whatsoever is in the Heavens and whatso-
verse"   ever is in the Earth. Who is he that shall intercede
with Him, unless by His permission? He knoweth what [hath
been] before them and what [shall be] after them, and they shall
not compass aught of His knowledge save what He willeth. His
Throne comprehendeth the Heavens and the Earth, and the care
of them burdeneth Him not. And He is the High, The Great.[4]

[1] This prayer of the Mohammedans corresponds in a way to the Lord's
Prayer of Christian peoples. It is recited several times in each of the five
daily prayers, and on numerous other occasions.

[2] The petition is for guidance in the "right way" of the Mohammedan,
marked out in the Koran. By those with whom God is "wroth," and by the
"erring," is meant primarily the Jews. Mohammed regarded the Jews and
Chistians as having corrupted the true religion.

[3] "This chapter is held in particular veneration by the Mohammedans and
is declared, by a tradition of their prophet, to be equal in value to a third
part of the whole Koran."—Sale, quoted in Lane, *Selections from the Kur-án*,
p. 5.

[4] This passage, known as the "throne verse," is regarded by Mohammedans as one of the most precious in the Koran and is often recited at the end
of the five daily prayers. It is sometimes engraved on a precious stone or an
ornament of gold and worn as an amulet.

When the earth is shaken with her shaking,

And the earth hath cast forth her dead,

The day of resurrection And man shall say, 'What aileth her?'

On that day shall she tell out her tidings,

Because thy Lord hath inspired her,

On that day shall men come one by one to behold their works,

And whosoever shall have wrought an ant's weight of good shall behold it,

And whosoever shall have wrought an ant's weight of ill shall behold it.

When the heaven shall be cloven asunder,

And when the stars shall be scattered,

And when the seas shall be let loose,

And when the graves shall be turned upside-down,[1]

Every soul shall know what it hath done and left undone.

O man! what hath seduced thee from thy generous Lord,

Who created thee and fashioned thee and disposed thee aright?

In the form which pleased Him hath He fashioned thee.

Nay, but ye treat the Judgment as a lie.

Verily there are watchers over you,

The coming judgment Worthy recorders,

Knowing what ye do.

Verily in delight shall the righteous dwell;

And verily the wicked in Hell [-Fire];

They shall be burnt at it on the day of doom,

And they shall not be hidden from it.

And what shall teach thee what the Day of Judgment is?

Again: What shall teach thee what is the Day of Judgment?

It is a day when one soul shall be powerless for another soul; and all on that day shall be in the hands of God.

When one blast shall be blown on the trumpet,

---

[1] These are all to be signs of the day of judgment.

And the earth shall be raised and the mountains, and be broken
    to dust with one breaking,
On that day the Calamity shall come to pass:
And the heavens shall cleave asunder, being frail on that day,
And the angels on the sides thereof; and over them on that day
    eight *of the angels* shall bear the throne of thy Lord.

The reward of the righteous   On that day ye shall be presented *for the reckoning;*
none of your secrets shall be hidden.

And as to him who shall have his book [1] given to him in his right
    hand, he shall say, 'Take ye, read my book;'
Verily I was sure I should come to my reckoning.
And his [shall be] a pleasant life
In a lofty garden,
Whose clusters [shall be] near at hand.
'Eat ye and drink with benefit on account of that which ye paid
    beforehand in the past days.'

But as to him who shall have his book given to him in his left
    hand, he shall say, 'O would that I had not had my book
    given to me,
Nor known what [was] my reckoning!
O would that *my death* had been the ending *of me!*

The fate of the wicked   My wealth hath not profited me!
My power is passed from me!'

'Take him and chain him,
Then cast him into hell to be burnt,
Then in a chain of seventy cubits bind him:
For he believed not in God, the Great,
Nor urged to feed the poor;
Therefore he shall not have here this day a friend,
Nor any food save filth
Which none but the sinners shall eat.'

---

[1] The record of his deeds during life on earth.

When the Calamity shall come to pass

There shall not be *a soul* that will deny its happening,

[It will be] an abaser *of some,* an exalter *of others;*

When the earth shall be shaken with a *violent* shaking,

And the mountains shall be crumbled with a violent crumbling,

And shall become fine dust scattered abroad;

And ye shall be three classes.[1]

And the people of the right hand, what shall be the people of the right hand!

And the people of the left hand, what the people of the left hand!

And the Preceders, the Preceders![2]

"The preceders"   These [shall be] the brought-nigh [unto God]
In the gardens of delight,—

A crowd of the former generations,

And a few of the latter generations,

Upon inwrought couches,

Reclining thereon, face to face.

Youths ever-young shall go unto them round about

With goblets and ewers and a cup of flowing wine,

Their [heads] shall ache not with it, neither shall they be drunken;

And with fruits of the [sorts] which they shall choose,

And the flesh of birds of the [kinds] which they shall desire.

And damsels with eyes like pearls laid up

We will give them as a reward for that which they have done.

Therein shall they hear no vain discourse nor accusation of sin,

But [only] the saying, 'Peace! Peace!'

[1] The three classes are: (1) the "preceders," (2) the people of the right hand, i. e., the good, and (3) the people of the left hand, i. e., the evil. The future state of each of the three is described in the lines that follow.

[2] "Either the first converts to Mohammedanism, or the prophets, who were the respective leaders of their people, or any persons who have been eminent examples of piety and virtue, may be here intended. The original words literally rendered are, *The Leaders, The Leaders:* which repetition, as some suppose, was designed to express the dignity of these persons and the certainty of their future glory and happiness."—Sale, quoted in Wherry, *Comprehensive Commentary on the Qur-án*, Vol. IV., pp. 109–110.

And the people of the right hand—what [shall be] the people of
    the right hand!

[They shall dwell] among lote-trees without thorns

And bananas loaded with fruit,

The pleasures   And a shade *ever-spread*,
of paradise   And water *ever*-flowing,

And fruits abundant

Unstayed and unforbidden,[1]

And couches raised.[2]

Verily we have created them [3] by a [peculiar] creation,

And have made them virgins,

Beloved of their husbands, of equal age [with them],

For the people of the right hand,

A crowd of the former generations

And a crowd of the latter generations.

And the people of the left hand—what [shall be] the people of
    the left hand!

[They shall dwell] amidst burning wind and scalding water,

And a shade of blackest smoke,

Not cool and not grateful.

For before this they were blest with wordly goods,

And they persisted in heinous sin,

And said, 'When we shall have died and become dust and bones,
    shall we indeed be raised to life,

The torments   And our fathers the former generations?'
of hell   Say, verily the former and the latter generations

Shall be gathered together for the appointed time of a known day.

---

[1] The luxuries of paradise—the flowing rivers, the fragrant flowers, the delicious fruits—are sharply contrasted with the conditions of desert life most familiar to Mohammed's early converts. Such a description of the land of the blessed must have appealed strongly to the imaginative Arabs. It should be said that in the modern Mohammedan idea of heaven the spiritual element has a rather more prominent place.

[2] Lofty beds.

[3] The "damsels of paradise."

Then ye, O ye erring, belying [people],
Shall surely eat of the tree of Ez-Zakkoom,[1]
And fill therewith [your] stomachs,
And drink thereon boiling water,
And ye shall drink as thirsty camels drink.—
This [shall be] their entertainment on the day of retribution.

[1] A scrubby bush bearing fruit like almonds, and extremely bitter. It was familiar to Arabs and hence was made to stand as a type of the tree whose fruit the wicked must eat in the lower world.

CHAPTER VIII.

THE BEGINNINGS OF THE CAROLINGIAN DYNASTY OF FRANK-ISH KINGS

14. Pepin the Short Takes the Title of King (751)

During the seventh and eighth centuries the Merovingian line of Frankish kings degenerated to a condition of weakness both pitiable and ridiculous. As the royal family became less worthy, the powers of government gradually slipped from its hands into those of a series of ministers commonly known by the title of Mayor of the Palace (*Maior Domus*). The most illustrious of these uncrowned sovereigns was Charles Martel, the victor over the Saracens near Poitiers, in whose time the Frankish throne for four years had no occupant at all. Martel contrived to make his peculiar office hereditary, and at his death in 741 left it to be filled jointly by his two elder sons, Karlmann and Pepin the Short. They decided that it would be to their interest to keep up the show of Merovingian royalty a little longer and in 743 allowed Childeric III. to mount the throne—a weakling destined to be the last of his family to wear the Frankish crown. Four years later Karlmann renounced his office and withdrew to the monastery of Monte Cassino, southeast of Rome, leaving Pepin sole "mayor" and the only real ruler of the Franks. Before many more years had passed, the utter uselessness of keeping up a royal line whose members were notoriously unfit to govern had impressed itself upon the nation to such an extent that when Pepin proceeded to put young Childeric in a monastery and take the title of king for himself, nobody offered the slightest objection. The sanction of the Pope was obtained for the act because Pepin thought that his course would thus be made to appear less like an outright usurpation. The Pope's reward came four years later when Pepin bestowed upon him the lands in northern and central Italy which eventually constituted, in the main, the so-called States of the Church. In later times, after the reign of Pepin's famous son Charlemagne, the new dynasty established by Pepin's elevation to the throne came to be known as the Carolingian (from *Karolus*, or Charles).

The following account of the change from the Merovingian to the Carolingian line is taken from the so-called *Lesser Annals of Lorsch*. At the monastery of Lorsch, as at nearly every other such place in the Middle Ages, records or "annals" of one sort or another were pretty regularly kept. They were often very inaccurate and their writers had a curious way of filling up space with matters of little importance, but sometimes, as in the present instance, we can get from them some very interesting information. The monastery of Lorsch was about twelve miles distant from Heidelberg, in southern Germany.

Source—*Annales Laurissenses Minores* ["Lesser Annals of Lorsch"]. Text in *Monumenta Germaniæ Historica, Scriptores* (Pertz ed.), Vol. I., p. 116.

In the year 750 [1] of the Lord's incarnation Pepin sent ambassadors to Rome to Pope Zacharias,[2] to inquire concerning the kings of the Franks who, though they were of the royal line and were called kings, had no power in the kingdom, except that charters and privileges were drawn up in their names. They had absolutely no kingly authority, but did whatever the Major Domus of the Franks desired.[3] But on the first day of March in the Campus

[1] The date is almost certainly wrong. Pepin was first acknowledged king by the Frankish nobles assembled at Soissons in November, 751. It was probably in 751 (possibly 752) that Pope Zacharias was consulted. In 754 Pepin was crowned king by Pope Stephen III., successor of Zacharias, who journeyed to France especially for the purpose.

[2] Zacharias was pope from 741 to 752.

[3] Einhard, the secretary of Charlemagne [see p. 108], in writing a biography of his master, described the condition of Merovingian kingship as follows: "All the resources and power of the kingdom had passed into the control of the prefects of the palace, who were called the 'mayors of the palace,' and who exercised the supreme authority. Nothing was left to the king. He had to content himself with his royal title, his flowing locks, and long beard. Seated in a chair of state, he was wont to display an appearance of power by receiving foreign ambassadors on their arrival, and, on their departure, giving them, as if on his own authority, those answers which he had been taught or commanded to give. Thus, except for his empty title, and an uncertain allowance for his sustenance, which the prefect of the palace used to furnish at his pleasure, there was nothing that the king could call his own, unless it were the income from a single farm, and that a very small one, where he made his home, and where such servants as were

Martius,[1] according to ancient custom, gifts were offered to these kings by the people, and the king himself sat in the royal seat with the army standing round him and the Major Domus in his presence, and he commanded on that day whatever was decreed by the Franks; but on all other days thenceforward he remained quietly at home.   Pope Zacharias, therefore, in the exercise of his apostolic authority, replied to their inquiry that it seemed to him better and more expedient that the man who held power in the kingdom should be called king and be king, rather than he who falsely bore that name.   Therefore the aforesaid pope commanded the king and people of the Franks that Pepin, who was exercising royal power, should be called king, and should be established on the throne.   This was therefore done by the anointing of the holy archbishop Boniface in the city of Soissons.   Pepin was proclaimed king, and Childeric, who was falsely called king, was shaved and sent into a monastery.

needful to wait on him constituted his scanty household. When he went anywhere he traveled in a wagon drawn by a yoke of oxen, with a rustic oxherd for charioteer. In this manner he proceeded to the palace, and to the public assemblies of the people held every year for the dispatch of the business of the kingdom, and he returned home again in the same sort of state. The administration of the kingdom, and every matter which had to be undertaken and carried through, both at home and abroad, was managed by the mayor of the palace."—Einhard, *Vita Caroli Magni,* Chap. 1.

[1] See p. 52, note 1.

CHAPTER IX.

THE AGE OF CHARLEMAGNE

15. Charlemagne the Man

BIOGRAPHICAL writings make up a not inconsiderable part of mediæval literature, but unfortunately the greater portion of them are to be trusted in only a limited degree by the student of history. Many biographies, especially the lives of the saints and other noted Christian leaders, were prepared expressly for the purpose of giving the world concrete examples of how men ought to live. Their authors, therefore, were apt to relate only the good deeds of the persons about whom they wrote, and these were often much exaggerated for the sake of effect. The people of the time generally were superstitious and easily appealed to by strange stories and the recital of marvelous events. They were not critical, and even such of them as were able to read at all could be made to believe almost anything that the writers of books cared to say. And since these writers themselves shared in the superstition and credulousness of the age, naturally such biographies as were written abounded in tales which anybody to-day would know at a glance could not be true. To all this Einhard's *Life of Charles the Great* stands as a notable exception. It has its inaccuracies, but it still deserves to be ranked almost in a class of its own as a trustworthy biographical contribution to our knowledge of the earlier Middle Ages.

Einhard (or Eginhard) was a Frank, born about 770 near the Odenwald in Franconia. After being educated at the monastery of Fulda he was presented at the Frankish court, some time between 791 and 796, where he remained twenty years as secretary and companion of the king, and later emperor, Charlemagne. He was made what practically corresponds to a modern minister of public works and in that capacity is thought to have supervised the building of the palace and basilica of the temple at Aachen, the palace of Ingelheim, the bridge over the

Rhine at Mainz, and many other notable constructions of the king, though regarding the precise work of this sort which he did there is a general lack of definite proof. Despite the fact that he was a layman, he was given charge of a number of abbeys. His last years were spent at the Benedictine monastery of Seligenstadt, where he died about 840. There is a legend that Einhard's wife, Emma, was a daughter of Charlemagne, but this is to be regarded as merely a twelfth-century invention.

The *Vita Caroli Magni* was written as an expression of the author's gratitude to his royal friend and patron, though it did not appear until shortly after the latter's death in 814. "It contains the history of a very great and distinguished man," says Einhard in his preface, "but there is nothing in it to wonder at, besides his deeds, except the fact that I, who am a barbarian, and very little versed in the Roman language, seem to suppose myself capable of writing gracefully and respectably in Latin." It is considered ordinarily that Einhard endeavored to imitate the style of the Roman Suetonius, the biographer of the first twelve Cæsars, though in reality his writing is perhaps superior to that of Suetonius and there are scholars who hold that if he really followed a classical model at all that model was Julius Cæsar. Aside from the matter of literary style, there can be no reasonable doubt that the idea of writing a biography of his master was suggested to Einhard by the biographies of Suetonius, particularly that of the Emperor Augustus. Despite his limitations, says Mr. Hodgkin, the fact remains that "almost all our real, vivifying knowledge of Charles the Great is derived from Einhard, and that the *Vita Caroli* is one of the most precious literary bequests of the early Middle Ages." [1] Certainly few mediæval writers had so good an opportunity as did Einhard to know the truth about the persons and events they undertook to describe.

Source—Einhard, *Vita Caroli Magni* ["Life of Charles the Great"], Chaps. 22–27. Text in *Monumenta Germaniæ Historica, Scriptores* (Pertz ed.), Vol. II., pp. 455–457. Adapted from translation by Samuel Epes Turner in "Harper's School Classics" (New York, 1880), pp. 56–65.

22. Charles was large and strong, and of lofty stature, though not excessively tall. The upper part of his head was round, his

[1] Thomas Hodgkin, *Charles the Great* (London, 1903), p. 222.

eyes very large and animated, nose a little long, hair auburn, and face laughing and merry. His appearance was always stately and dignified, whether he was standing or sitting, although his neck was thick and somewhat short and his abdomen rather prominent. The symmetry of the rest of his body concealed these defects. His gait was firm, his whole carriage manly, and **Personal** his voice clear, but not so strong as his size led **appearance** one to expect. His health was excellent, except during the four years preceding his death, when he was subject to frequent fevers; toward the end of his life he limped a little with one foot. Even in his later years he lived rather according to his own inclinations than the advice of physicians; the latter indeed he very much disliked, because they wanted him to give up roasts, to which he was accustomed, and to eat boiled meat instead. In accordance with the national custom, he took frequent exercise on horseback and in the chase, in which sports scarcely any people in the world can equal the Franks. He enjoyed the vapors from natural warm springs, and often indulged in swimming, in which he was so skilful that none could surpass him; and hence it was that he built his palace at Aix-la-Chapelle, and lived there constantly during his later years.[1] . . .

23. His custom was to wear the national, that is to say, the Frankish, dress—next his skin a linen shirt and linen breeches, and above these a tunic fringed with silk; while hose fastened by

[1] The German name for Aix-la-Chapelle was Aachen. From Roman times the place was noted throughout Europe for its warm sulphur springs and for centuries before Charlemagne's day it had been a favorite resort for health-seekers. It was about the middle of his reign that Charlemagne determined to have the small palace already existing rebuilt, together with its accompanying chapel. Marbles and mosaics were obtained at Rome and Ravenna, and architects and artisans were brought together for the work from all Christendom. The chapel was completed in 805 and was dedicated by Pope Leo III. Both palace and chapel were destroyed a short time before the Emperor's death, probably as the result of an earthquake. The present town-house of Aix-la-Chapelle has been constructed on the ruins of this palace. The chapel, rebuilt on the ancient octagonal plan in 983, contains the tomb of Charlemagne, marked by a stone bearing the inscription "Carolo Magno." Besides Aachen, Charlemagne had many other residences, as Compiègne, Worms, Attigny, Mainz, Paderborn, Ratisbon, Heristal, and Thionville.

bands covered his lower limbs, and shoes his feet. In winter he protected his shoulders and chest by a close-fitting coat of otter or marten skins. Over all he flung a blue cloak, and he always had a sword girt about him, usually one with a gold or silver hilt and belt. He sometimes carried a jeweled sword, but only on

Manner of dress great feast-days or at the reception of ambassa-dors from foreign nations. He despised foreign costumes, however handsome, and never allowed himself to be robed in them, except twice in Rome, when he donned the Roman tunic, chlamys,[1] and shoes; the first time at the request of Pope Hadrian,[2] the second to gratify Leo, Hadrian's successor.[3] On great feast-days he made use of embroidered clothes, and shoes adorned with precious stones; his cloak was fastened with a golden buckle, and he appeared crowned with a diadem of gold and gems; but on other days his dress differed little from that of ordinary people.

24. Charles was temperate in eating, and especially so in drinking, for he abhorred drunkenness in anybody, much more in himself and those of his household; but he could not easily abstain from food, and often complained that fasts injured his health. He gave entertainments but rarely, only on great feast-days, and then to large numbers of people. His meals consisted ordinarily of four courses, not counting the roast, which his hunts-men were accustomed to bring in on the spit; he was more fond of this than of any other dish. While at table, he listened to reading or music. The subjects of the readings were the stories and deeds of olden time. He was fond, too, of St. Augustine's books, and especially of the one entitled *The City of God*.[4]

---

[1] A loose, flowing outer garment, or cloak. It was a feature of ancient Greek dress.

[2] Hadrian I., 772–775. Charlemagne's first visit to Rome was in 774.

[3] Leo III., 795–816. The Roman dress was donned by Charlemagne during his visit in 800 [see p. 130].

[4] St. Augustine, the greatest of the Church fathers, was born in Numidia in 354. He spent a considerable part of his early life studying in Rome and other Italian cities. The *De Civitate Dei* ("City of God"), generally re-garded as his most important work, was completed in 426, its purpose being

He was so moderate in the use of wine and all sorts of drink that he rarely allowed himself more than three cups in the course of a

Every-day life meal. In summer, after the midday meal, he would eat some fruit, drain a single cup, put off his clothes and shoes, just as he did for the night, and rest for two or three hours. While he was dressing and putting on his shoes, he not only gave audience to his friends, but if the Count of the Palace [1] told him of any suit in which his judgment was necessary, he had the parties brought before him forthwith, heard the case, and gave his decision, just as if he were sitting in the judgment-seat. This was not the only business that he transacted at this time, but he performed any duty of the day whatever, whether he had to attend to the matter himself, or to give commands concerning it to his officers.

25. Charles had the gift of ready and fluent speech, and could express whatever he had to say with the utmost clearness. He was not satisfied with ability to use his native language merely, but gave attention to the study of foreign ones, and in particular was such a master of Latin that he could speak it as well as his native tongue; but he could understand Greek better than he could speak it. He was so eloquent, indeed, that he might have been taken for a teacher of oratory. He most zealously cherished the liberal arts, held those who taught them in great esteem, and conferred great honors upon them. He took lessons in grammar of the deacon Peter of Pisa, at that time an aged man. [2] Another

to convince the Romans that even though the supposedly eternal city of Rome had recently been sacked by the barbarian Visigoths, the true "city of God" was in the hearts of men beyond the reach of desecrating invaders. When he wrote the book Augustine was bishop of Hippo, an important city of northern Africa. His death occurred in 430, during the siege of Hippo by Gaiseric and his horde of Vandals.

[1] The Count of the Palace was one of the coterie of officials by whose aid Charlemagne managed the affairs of the state. He was primarily an officer of justice, corresponding in a way to the old Mayor of the Palace, but with very much less power.

[2] When Charlemagne captured Pavia, the Lombard capital, in 774, he found Peter the Pisan teaching in that city. With characteristic zeal for the advancement of education among his own people he proceeded to transfer the learned deacon to the Frankish Palace School [see p. 144].

deacon, Albin of Britain, surnamed Alcuin, a man of Saxon birth, who was the greatest scholar of the day, was his teacher in other

Education and accomplishments
branches of learning.[1] The king spent much time and labor with him studying rhetoric, dialectic, and especially astronomy. He learned to make calculations, and used to investigate with much curiosity and intelligence the motions of the heavenly bodies. He also tried to write, and used to keep tablets and blanks in bed under his pillow, that at leisure hours he might accustom his hand to form the letters; however, as he began his efforts late in life, and not at the proper time, they met with little success.

26. He cherished with the greatest fervor and devotion the principles of the Christian religion, which had been instilled into him from infancy. Hence it was that he built the beautiful basilica at Aix-la-Chapelle, which he adorned with gold and silver and lamps, and with rails and doors of solid brass. He had the columns and marbles for this structure brought from Rome and Ravenna, for he could not find such as were suitable elsewhere.[2] He was a constant worshipper at this church as long as his health permitted, going morning and evening, even after nightfall,

Interest in religion and the Church
besides attending mass. He took care that all the services there conducted should be held in the best possible manner, very often warning the sextons not to let any improper or unclean thing be brought into the building, or remain in it. He provided it with a number of sacred vessels of gold and silver, and with such a quantity of clerical robes that not even the door-keepers, who filled the humblest office in the church, were obliged to wear their everyday clothes when in the performance of their duties. He took

---

[1] Alcuin was born at York in 735. He took up his residence at Charlemagne's court about 782, and died in the office of abbot of St. Martin of Tours in 804.

[2] During the Napoleonic period many of these columns were taken possession of by the French and transported to Paris. Only recently have they been replaced in the Aix-la-Chapelle cathedral. Most of them came originally from the palace of the Exarch of Ravenna.

great pains to improve the church reading and singing, for he was well skilled in both, although he neither read in public nor sang, except in a low tone and with others.

27. He was very active in aiding the poor, and in that open generosity which the Greeks call alms; so much so, indeed, that he not only made a point of giving in his own country and his own kingdom, but when he discovered that there were Christians living in poverty in Syria, Egypt, and Africa, at Jerusalem, Alexandria, and Carthage, he had compassion on their wants, and used to send money over the seas to them. The reason that he earnestly strove to make friends with the kings beyond seas was that he might get help and relief to the Christians living **Generosity** under their rule. He cared for the Church of St. **and charities** Peter the Apostle at Rome above all other holy and sacred places, and heaped high its treasury with a vast wealth of gold, silver, and precious stones. He sent great and countless gifts to the popes;[1] and throughout his whole reign the wish that he had nearest his heart was to re-establish the ancient authority of the city of Rome under his care and by his influence, and to defend and protect the Church of St. Peter, and to beautify and enrich it out of his own store above all other churches. Nevertheless, although he held it in such veneration, only four times[2] did he repair to Rome to pay his vows and make his supplications during the whole forty-seven years that he reigned.[3]

16. The War with the Saxons (772–803)

WHEN Charlemagne became sole ruler of the Franks, in 771, he found his kingdom pretty well hemmed in by a belt of kindred,

[1] These statements of Einhard respecting the lavishness of Charlemagne's gifts must be taken with some allowance. They were doubtless considerable for the day, but Charlemagne's revenues were not such as to enable him to display wealth which in modern times would be regarded as befitting a monarch of so exalted rank.

[2] In 774, 781, 787, and 800.

[3] Charlemagne became joint ruler of the Franks with his brother Karlmann in 768; hence when he died, in 814, he had reigned only forty-six years instead of forty-seven.

though more or less hostile, Germanic peoples. The most important of these were the Visigoths in northern Spain, the Lombards in the Po Valley, the Bavarians in the region of the upper Danube, and the Saxons between the Rhine and the Elbe. The policy of the new king, perhaps only dimly outlined at the beginning of the reign but growing ever more definite as time went on, was to bring all of these neighboring peoples under the Frankish dominion, and so to build up a great state which should include the whole Germanic race of western and northern continental Europe. Most of the king's time during the first thirty years, or two-thirds, of the reign was devoted to this stupendous task. The first great step was taken in the conquest of the Lombards in 774, after which Charlemagne assumed the title of King of the Lombards. In 787 Bavaria was annexed to the Frankish kingdom, the settlement in this case being in the nature of a complete absorption rather than a mere personal union such as followed the Lombard conquest. The next year an expedition across the Pyrenees resulted in the annexation of the Spanish March—a region in which the Visigoths had managed to maintain some degree of independence against the Saracens. In all these directions little fighting was necessary and for one reason or another the sovereignty of the Frankish king was recognized without much delay or resistance.

The problem of reducing the Saxons was, however, a very different one. The Saxons of Charlemagne's day were a people of purest Germanic stock dwelling in the land along the Rhine, Ems, Weser, and Elbe, and inland as far as the low mountains of Hesse and Thuringia—the regions which now bear the names of Hanover, Brunswick, Oldenburg, and Westphalia. The Saxons, influenced as yet scarcely at all by contact with the Romans, retained substantially the manner of life described seven centuries earlier by Tacitus in the *Germania*. They lived in small villages, had only the loosest sort of government, and clung tenaciously to the warlike mythology of their ancestors. Before Charlemagne's time they had engaged in frequent border wars with the Franks and had shown capacity for making very obstinate resistance. And when Charlemagne himself undertook to subdue them he entered upon a task which kept him busy much of the time for over thirty years, that is, from 772 to 803. In all not fewer than eighteen distinct campaigns were made into the enemy's territory. The ordinary course

of events was that Charlemagne would lead his army across the Rhine
in the spring, the Saxons would make some little resistance and then
disperse or withdraw toward the Baltic, and the Franks would leave
a garrison and return home for the winter. As soon as the enemy's
back was turned the Saxons would rally, expel or massacre the garrison,
and assert their complete independence of Frankish authority. The
next year the whole thing would have to be done over again. There
were not more than two great battles in the entire contest; the war
consisted rather of a monotonous series of "military parades," apparent
submissions, revolts, and re-submissions. As Professor Emerton puts
it, "From the year 772 to 803, a period of over thirty years, this war
was always on the programme of the Frankish policy, now resting for
a few years, and now breaking out with increased fury, until finally
the Saxon people, worn out with the long struggle against a superior
foe, gave it up and became a part of the Frankish Empire." [1]

It is to be regretted that we have no Saxon account of the great
contest except the well-meant, but very inadequate, history by Widukind, a monk of Corbie, written about the middle of the tenth century.
However, the following passage from Einhard, the secretary and
biographer of Charlemagne, doubtless describes with fair accuracy the
conditions and character of the struggle. A few of the writer's strongest
statements regarding Saxon perfidy should be accepted only with some
allowance for Frankish prejudice.

Source—Einhard, *Vita Caroli Magni*, Chap. 7. Text in *Monumenta Ger-
          maniæ Historica, Scriptores* (Pertz ed.), Vol. II., pp. 446–447.
          Adapted from translation by Samuel Epes Turner in " Harper's
          School Classics " (New York, 1880), pp. 26–28.

No war ever undertaken by the Frankish nation was carried
on with such persistence and bitterness, or cost so much labor,
because the Saxons, like almost all the tribes of Germany, were
a fierce people, given to the worship of devils and hostile to our
religion, and did not consider it dishonorable to transgress and
violate all law, human and divine. Then there were peculiar

circumstances that tended to cause a breach of peace every day. Except in a few places, where large forests or mountain-ridges

Lack of a natural frontier intervened and made the boundaries certain, the line between ourselves and the Saxons passed almost in its whole extent through an open country, so that there was no end to the murders, thefts, and arsons on both sides. In this way the Franks became so embittered that they at last resolved to make reprisals no longer, but to come to open war with the Saxons.

Accordingly, war was begun against them, and was waged for thirty-three successive years [1] with great fury; more, however, to the disadvantage of the Saxons than of the Franks. It could doubtless have been brought to an end sooner, had it not been for the faithlessness of the Saxons. It is hard to say how often they were conquered, and, humbly submitting to the king,

Faithlessness of the Saxons promised to do what was enjoined upon them, gave without hesitation the required hostages, and received the officers sent them from the king. They were sometimes so much weakened and reduced that they promised to renounce the worship of devils and to adopt Christianity; but they were no less ready to violate these terms than prompt to accept them, so that it is impossible to tell which came easier to them to do; scarcely a year passed from the beginning of the war without such changes on their part. But the king did not suffer his high purpose and steadfastness—firm alike in good and evil fortune—to be wearied by any fickleness on their part, or to be turned from the task that he had undertaken; on the contrary,

Charlemagne's settlement of Saxons in Gaul and Germany he never allowed their faithless behavior to go unpunished, but either took the field against them in person, or sent his counts with an army to wreak vengeance and exact righteous satisfaction.[2] At last, after con-

---

[1] The war really lasted only thirty, or at the most thirty-one, years.

[2] The only notable act of vengeance during the war was the beheading of 4,500 Saxons in a single day at Verden, on the Weser. It was occasioned by a great Saxon revolt in 782, led by the chieftain Widukind.

quering and subduing all who had offered resistance, he took
ten thousand of those who lived on the banks of the Elbe, and
settled them, with their wives and children, in many different
bodies here and there in Gaul and Germany. The war that had
lasted so many years was at length ended by their acceding to
The terms of   the terms offered by the king; which were re-
peace   nunciation of their national religious customs and
the worship of devils, acceptance of the sacraments of the Christian
religion,[1] and union with the Franks to form one people.

17. The Capitulary Concerning the Saxon Territory (cir. 780)

JUST as the Saxons were the most formidable of Charlemagne's
foes to meet and defeat in open battle, so were they the most difficult
to maintain in anything like orderly allegiance after they had been
tentatively conquered. This was true in part because of their untamed, freedom-loving character, but also in no small measure because
of the thoroughgoing revolution which the Frankish king sought 'to
work in their conditions of life, and especially in their religion. Before
the Saxon war was far advanced it had very clearly assumed the character of a crusade of the Christian Franks against the "pagans of the

---

[1] The formula of renunciation and confession generally employed in the
Christianizing of the Germans, and therefore in all probability in the conversion of the Saxons, was as follows:

Question. Forsakest thou the devil?
Answer. I forsake the devil.
Ques. And all the devil's service?
Ans. And I forsake all the devil's service.
Ques. And all the devil's works?
Ans. And I forsake all the devil's works and words. Thor and Woden and
        Saxnot and all the evil spirits that are their companions.
Ques. Believest thou in God the Almighty Father?
Ans. I believe in God the Almighty Father.
Ques. Believest thou in Christ the Son of God?
Ans. I believe in Christ the Son of God.
Ques. Believest thou in the Holy Ghost?
Ans. I believe in the Holy Ghost.

"Accepting Christianity was to the German very much like changing of
allegiance from one political sovereign to another. He gave up Thor and
Woden (Odin) and Saxnot, and in their place took the Father, the Son, and
the Holy Ghost."—Emerton, *Introduction to the Study of the Middle Ages*,
pp. 155–156. Text of these "Interrogationes et Responsiones Baptismales"
is in the *Monumenta Germaniæ Historica, Leges* (Boretius ed.), Vol. II.,
No. 107.

north." And when the Saxon had been brought to give sullen promise of submission, it was his dearest possession—his fierce, heroic mythology —that was first to be swept away. By the stern decree of the conqueror Woden and Thor and Freya must go. In their stead was to be set up the Christian religion with its churches, its priests, its fastings, its ceremonial observances. Death was to be the penalty for eating meat during Lent, if done "out of contempt for Christianity," and death also for "causing the body of a dead man to be burned in accordance with pagan rites." Even for merely scorning "to come to baptism," or "wishing to remain a pagan," a man was to forfeit his life. The selections which follow are taken from the capitulary *De Partibus Saxoniæ*, which was issued by Charlemagne probably at the Frankish assembly held at Paderborn in 780. If this date is correct (and it cannot be far wrong) the regulations embodied in the capitulary were established for the Saxon territories when there perhaps seemed to be a good prospect of peace but when, as later events showed, there yet remained twenty-three years of war before the final subjugation. From the beginning of the struggle the Church had been busy setting up new centers of influence—some abbeys and especially the great bishoprics of Bremen, Minden, Paderborn, Verden, Osnabrück, and Halberstadt— among the Saxon pagans, and the primary object of Charlemagne in this capitulary was to give to these ecclesiastical foundations the task of civilizing the country and to protect them, together with his counts or governing agents, while they should be engaged in this work. The severity of the Saxon war was responsible for the unusually stringent character of this body of regulations. In 797, at a great assembly at Aix-la-Chapelle, another capitulary for the Saxons was issued, known as the *Capitulum Saxonicum*, and in this the harsh features of the earlier capitulary were considerably relaxed. By 797 the resistance of the Saxons was pretty well broken, and it had become Charlemagne's policy to give his conquered subjects a government as nearly as possible like that the Franks themselves enjoyed. The chief importance of Charlemagne's conquests toward the east lies in the fact that by them broad stretches of German territory were brought for the first time within the pale of civilization.

These capitularies, like the hundreds of others that were issued by the various kings of the Franks, were edicts or decrees drawn up under the king's direction, discussed and adopted in the assembly of the people, and published in the local districts of the kingdom by the counts and bishops. They were of a less permanent and fixed character than the so-called "leges," or laws established by long usage and custom.

Source—Text in *Monumenta Germaniæ Historica, Leges* (Boretius ed.), Vol. I., No. 26, pp. 68–70. Translated by Dana C. Munro in *University of Pennsylvania Translations and Reprints*, Vol. VI., No. 5, pp. 2–5.

First, concerning the greater chapters it has been enacted:[1]

It is pleasing to all that the churches of Christ, which are now being built in Saxony and consecrated to God, should not have less, but greater and more illustrious honor than the shrines of the idols have had.

2. If any one shall have fled to a church for refuge, let no one presume to expel him from the church by violence, but he shall **The churches as places of refuge** be left in peace until he shall be brought to the judicial assemblage; and on account of the honor due to God and the saints, and the reverence due to the church itself, let his life and all his members be granted to him. Moreover, let him plead his cause as best he can and he shall be judged; and so let him be led to the presence of the lord king, and the latter shall send him where it shall seem fitting to his clemency.

3. If any one shall have entered a church by violence and shall have carried off anything in it by force or theft, or shall have burned the church itself, let him be punished by death.[2]

[1] That is, the more important offenses, involving capital punishment, as contrasted with the later "lesser chapters" dealing with minor misdemeanors.

[2] The Saxons were to be won to the Church through the protection it afforded, but they were likewise to be made to stand in awe of the sanctity of its property.

4. If any one, out of contempt for Christianity, shall have
despised the holy Lenten feast and shall have eaten
Offenses
against the   flesh, let him be punished by death. But, neverthe-
Church   less, let it be taken into consideration by a priest,
lest perchance any one from necessity has been led to eat flesh.[1]

5. If any one shall have killed a bishop or priest or deacon
let him likewise be punished capitally.

6. If any one, deceived by the devil, shall have believed, after
the manner of the pagans, that any man or woman is a witch
and eats men, and on this account shall have burned the person,
or shall have given the person's flesh to others to eat, or shall
have eaten it himself, let him be punished by a capital sentence.

7. If any one, in accordance with pagan rites, shall have
caused the body of a dead man to be burned, and shall have reduced his bones to ashes, let him be punished capitally.

8. If any one of the race of the Saxons hereafter, concealed
among them, shall have wished to hide himself unbaptized,
Refusal to be   and shall have scorned to come to baptism,
baptized   and shall have wished to remain a pagan, let
him be punished by death.

9. If any one shall have sacrificed a man to the devil, and,
after the manner of the pagans, shall have presented him as a
victim to the demons, let him be punished by death.

10. If any one shall have formed a conspiracy with the pagans
against the Christians, or shall have wished to join with them
Conspiracy   in opposition to the Christians, let him be pun-
against Chris-   ished by death; and whosoever shall have con-
tians   sented fraudulently to this same against the
king and the Christian people, let him be punished by death.

11. If any one shall have shown himself unfaithful to the
lord king, let him be punished with a capital sentence.

[1] The apparent harshness of this whole body of regulations was considerably diminished in practice by the large discretion left to the priests, as in
this case. They were exhorted to exercise care and to take circumstances
into account in judging a man's guilt or innocence.

13. If any one shall have killed his lord or lady, let him be punished in a like manner.

14. If, indeed, for these mortal crimes secretly committed any one shall have fled of his own accord to a priest, and after confession shall have wished to do penance, let him be freed by the testimony of the priest from death. . . .[1]

18. On the Lord's day no meetings or public judicial assemblages shall be held, unless perchance in a case of great necessity, or when war compels it, but all shall go to **Observance of the Sabbath and of festival days** church to hear the word of God, and shall be free for prayers or good works. Likewise, also, on the special festivals they shall devote themselves to God and to the services of the Church, and shall refrain from secular assemblies.

19. Likewise, it has been pleasing to insert in these decrees that all infants shall be baptized within a year; and we have **Baptism of infants** decreed this, that if any one shall have refused to bring his infant to baptism within the course of a year, without the advice or permission of the priest, if he is a noble he shall pay 120 *solidi*[2] to the treasury; if a freeman, 60; if a *litus*, 30.[3]

20. If any one shall have contracted a prohibited or illegal marriage, if a noble, 60 *solidi ;* if a freeman, 30; if a *litus*, 15.

21. If any one shall have made a vow at springs or trees or **Keeping up heathen rites** groves,[4] or shall have made an offering after the manner of the heathen and shall have partaken of a repast in honor of the demons, if he shall be a noble, 60

---

[1] From this point the capitulary deals with the "lesser chapters," i. e., non-capital offenses.

[2] For the value of the *solidus*, see p. 61.

[3] Three classes of society are distinguished—nobles, freemen, and serfs. The ordinary freeman pays half as much as the noble, and the serf half as much as the freeman.

[4] A prominent characteristic of the early Teutonic religion was that its ceremonies were invariably conducted out of doors. Tacitus, in the *Germania* (Chap. 9), tells us that the Germans had no temples or other buildings for religious purposes, but worshipped in sacred groves. The "Irmensaule," probably a giant tree-trunk, was the central shrine of the Saxon people, and Charlemagne's destruction of it in 772 was the most serious offense that could have been committed against them.

solidi ; if a freeman, 30; if a *litus,* 15. If, indeed, they have not the means of paying at once, they shall be given into the service of the Church until the *solidi* are paid.

22. We command that the bodies of Saxon Christians shall be carried to the church cemeteries, and not to the mounds of the pagans.

23. We have ordered that diviners and soothsayers shall be handed over to the churches and priests.

24. Concerning robbers and malefactors who shall have fled from one county to another, if any one shall receive them into

Fugitive criminals

his protection and shall keep them with him for seven nights,[1] except for the purpose of bringing them to justice, let him pay our ban.[2] Likewise, if a count [3] shall have concealed them, and shall be unwilling to bring them forward so that justice may be done, and is not able to excuse himself for this, let him lose his office.

26. No one shall presume to impede any man coming to us to seek justice; and if any one shall have attempted to do this, he shall pay our ban.

34. We have forbidden that Saxons shall hold public assemblies in general, unless perchance our *missus* [4] shall have caused

Public assemblies

them to come together in accordance with our command; but each count shall hold judicial assemblies and administer justice in his jurisdiction. And this shall be cared for by the priests, lest it be done otherwise.[5]

[1] The Germans reckoned by nights rather than by days, as explained by Tacitus, *Germania,* Chap. 11 [see p. 27].

[2] A sum assessed by the king, in this case against the illegal harboring of criminals.

[3] The counts, together with the bishops, were the local representatives or agents of the king. They presided over judicial assemblies, collected revenues, and preserved order. There were about three hundred of them in Charlemagne's empire when at its greatest extent.

[4] An officer sent out by the king to investigate the administration of the counts and render judgment in certain cases. As a rule two were sent together, a layman and an ecclesiastic [see p. 134].

[5] Under ordinary circumstances the priests were thus charged with the responsibility of seeing that local government in their various communities was just and legal.

18. The Capitulary Concerning the Royal Domains (cir. 800)

THE revenues which came into Charlemagne's treasury were derived chiefly from his royal domains. There was no system of general taxation, such as modern nations maintain, and the funds realized from gifts, fines, rents, booty, and tribute money, were quite insufficient to meet the needs of the court, modest though they were. Charlemagne's interest in his villas, or private farms, was due therefore not less to his financial dependence upon them than to his personal liking for thrifty agriculture and thoroughgoing administration. The royal domains of the Frankish kingdom, already extensive at Charlemagne's accession, were considerably increased during his reign. It has been well said that Charlemagne was doubtless the greatest landed proprietor of the realm and that he "supervised the administration of these lands as a sovereign who knows that his power rests partly on his riches." [1] He gave the closest personal attention to his estates and was always watchful lest he be defrauded out of even the smallest portion of their products which was due him. The capitulary *De Villis*, from which the following passages have been selected, is a lengthy document in which Charlemagne sought to prescribe clearly and minutely the manifold duties of the stewards in charge of these estates. We may regard it, however, as in the nature of an ideal catalogue of what the king would like to have on his domains rather than as a definite statement of what was always actually to be found there. From it may be gleaned many interesting facts regarding rural life in western Europe during the eighth and ninth centuries. Its date is uncertain, but it was about 800—possibly somewhat earlier.

Source—Text in *Monumenta Germaniæ Historica, Leges* (Boretius ed.), Vol. I., No. 32, pp. 82–91. Translated by Roland P. Falkner in *Univ. of Pa. Translations and Reprints*, Vol. III., No. 2, pp. 2–4.

62.[2] We desire that each steward shall make an annual statement of all our income, with an account of our lands cultivated by the oxen which our plowmen drive, and of our lands which

---

[1] Bémont and Monod, *Mediæval Europe* (New York, 1902), p. 202.

[2] Chapter 62 is here given out of order because it contains a comprehensive survey of the products and activities upon which the royal stewards were expected to report. The other chapters are more specific. It is likely that they have not come down to us in their original order.

the tenants of farms ought to plow;[1] an account of the pigs, of the rents,[2] of the obligations and fines; of the game taken in our forests without our permission; of the various compositions;[3] of the mills, of the forest, of the fields, and of the bridges and ships; of the freemen and the districts under obligations to our treasury; of markets, vineyards, and those who owe wine to us; of

Report to be made to the king by his stewards each Christmas-tide

the hay, fire-wood, torches, planks, and other kinds of lumber; of the waste-lands; of the vegetables, millet, and panic;[4] and of the wool, flax, and hemp; of the fruits of the trees; of the nut trees, larger and smaller; of the grafted trees of all kinds; of the gardens; of the turnips; of the fish-ponds; of the hides, skins, and horns; of the honey and wax; of the fat, tallow and soap; of the mulberry wine, cooked wine, mead, vinegar, beer, wine new and old; of the new grain and the old; of the hens and eggs; of the geese; of the number of fishermen, smiths, sword-makers, and shoe-makers; of the bins and boxes; of the turners and saddlers; of the forges and mines, that is iron and other mines; of the lead mines; of the colts and fillies. They shall make all these known to us, set forth separately and in order, at Christmas, in order that we may know what and how much of each thing we have.

23. On each of our estates our stewards are to have as many

Domestic animals

cow-houses, pig-sties, sheep-folds, stables for goats, as possible, and they ought never to be without these. And let them have in addition cows furnished by our

---

[1] The ordinary estate in this period, whether royal or not, consisted of two parts. One was the demesne, which the owner kept under his immediate control; the other was the remaining lands, which were divided among tenants who paid certain rentals for their use and also performed stated services on the lord's demesne. Charlemagne instructs his stewards to report upon both sorts of land.

[2] Probably payments for the right to keep pigs in the woods. The most common meat in the Middle Ages was pork and the use of the oak forests as hog pasture was a privilege of considerable value.

[3] Fines imposed upon offenders to free them from crime or to repair damages done.

[4] Panic was a kind of grass, the seeds of which were not infrequently used for food.

serfs [1] for performing their service, so that the cow-houses and plows shall be in no way diminished by the service on our demesne. And when they have to provide meat, let them have steers lame, but healthy, and cows and horses which are not mangy, or other beasts which are not diseased and, as we have said, our cow-houses and plows are not to be diminished for this.

34. They must provide with the greatest care that whatever is prepared or made with the hands, that is, lard, smoked meat, **Cleanliness enjoined** salt meat, partially salted meat, wine, vinegar, mulberry wine, cooked wine, *garns*,[2] mustard, cheese, butter, malt, beer, mead, honey, wax, flour, all should be prepared and made with the greatest cleanliness.

40. That each steward on each of our domains shall always have, for the sake of ornament, swans, peacocks, pheasants, ducks, pigeons, partridges, turtle-doves.

42. That in each of our estates, the chambers shall be provided with counterpanes, cushions, pillows, bed-clothes, coverings **Household furniture** for the tables and benches; vessels of brass, lead, iron and wood; andirons, chains, pot-hooks, adzes, axes, augers, cutlasses, and all other kinds of tools, so that it shall never be necessary to go elsewhere for them, or to borrow them. And the weapons, which are carried against the enemy, shall be well-cared for, so as to keep them in good condition; and when they are brought back they shall be placed in the chamber.

43. For our women's work they are to give at the proper time, as has been ordered, the materials, that is the linen, wool, woad,[3] vermilion, madder,[4] wool-combs, teasels,[5] soap, grease, vessels, and the other objects which are necessary.

[1] The serfs were a semi-free class of country people. They did not own the land on which they lived and were not allowed to move off it without the owner's consent. They cultivated the soil and paid rents of one kind or another to their masters—in the present case, to the agents of the king.

[2] A variety of fermented liquor made of salt fish.

[3] A blue coloring matter derived from the leaves of a plant of the same name.

[4] A red coloring matter derived from a plant of the same name.

[5] Burrs of the teasel plant, stiff and prickly, with hooked bracts; used in primitive manufacturing for raising a nap on woolen cloth.

44. Of the food products other than meat, two-thirds shall be sent each year for our own use, that is of the vegetables, fish, **Supplies to be furnished the king** cheese, butter, honey, mustard, vinegar, millet, panic, dried and green herbs, radishes, and in addition of the wax, soap and other small products; and they shall tell us how much is left by a statement, as we have said above; and they shall not neglect this as in the past; because from those two-thirds, we wish to know how much remains.

45. That each steward shall have in his district good workmen, namely, blacksmiths, gold-smith, silver-smith, shoe-makers, **Workmen on the estates** turners, carpenters, sword-makers, fishermen, foilers, soap-makers, men who know how to make beer, cider, berry, and all the other kinds of beverages, bakers to make pastry for our table, net-makers who know how to make nets for hunting, fishing and fowling, and the others who are too numerous to be designated.

19. An Inventory of One of Charlemagne's Estates

IN the following inventory we have a specimen of the annual statements required by Charlemagne from the stewards on his royal domains. The location of Asnapium is unknown, but it is evident that this estate was one of the smaller sort. Like all the rest, it was liable occasionally to become the temporary abiding place of the king. The detailed character of the inventory is worthy of note, as is also the number of industries which must have been engaged in by the inhabitants of the estate and its dependent villas.

Source—Text in *Monumenta Germaniæ Historica, Leges* (Pertz ed.), Vol. I., pp. 178–179.

We found in the imperial estate of Asnapium a royal house **Buildings on the estate of Asnapium** built of stone in the very best manner, having 3 rooms. The entire house was surrounded with balconies and it had 11 apartments for women. Underneath was 1 cellar. There were 2 porticoes. There were 17 other houses built of wood within the court-yard, with a similar number of rooms and other fixtures, all well constructed. There was 1 stable, 1 kitchen, 1 mill, 1 granary, and 3 barns.

The yard was enclosed with a hedge and a stone gateway, and above was a balcony from which distributions can be made. There was also an inner yard, surrounded by a hedge, well arranged, and planted with various kinds of trees.

Of vestments: coverings for 1 bed, 1 table-cloth, and 1 towel.

Of utensils: 2 brass kettles; 2 drinking cups; 2 brass cauldrons; 1 iron cauldron; 1 frying-pan; 1 gramalmin; 1 pair of andirons; 1 lamp; 2 hatchets; 1 chisel; 2 augers; 1 axe; 1 knife; 1 large plane; 1 small plane; 2 scythes; 2 sickles; 2 spades edged with iron; and a sufficient supply of utensils of wood.

Of farm produce: old spelt [1] from last year, 90 baskets which can be made into 450 weight [2] of flour; and 100 measures [3] of **Supplies of** barley. From the present year, 110 baskets of **various sorts** spelt, of which 60 baskets had been planted, but the rest we found; 100 measures of wheat, 60 sown, the rest we found; 98 measures of rye all sown; 1,800 measures of barley, 1,100 sown, the rest we found; 430 measures of oats; 1 measure of beans; 12 measures of peas. At 5 mills were found 800 measures of small size. At 4 breweries, 650 measures of small size, 240 given to the prebendaries, [4] the rest we found. At 2 bridges, 60 measures of salt and 2 shillings. At 4 gardens, 11 shillings. Also honey, 3 measures; about 1 measure of butter; lard, from last year 10 sides; new sides, 200, with fragments and fats; cheese from the present year, 43 weights.

Of cattle: 51 head of larger cattle; 5 three-year olds; 7 two-year olds; 7 yearlings; 10 two-year old colts; 8 yearlings; 3

---

[1] A kind of grain still widely cultivated for food in Germany and Switzerland; sometimes known as German wheat.

[2] The unit of weight was the pound. Charlemagne replaced the old Gallic pound by the Roman, which was a tenth less.

[3] The unit of measure was the *muid*. Charlemagne had a standard measure (*modius publicus*) constructed and in a number of his capitularies enjoined that it be taken as a model by all his subjects. It contained probably a little less than six pecks. A smaller measure was the *setier*, containing about five and two-thirds pints.

[4] Clergymen attached to the church on or near the estate.

stallions; 16 cows; 2 asses; 50 cows with calves; 20 young bulls; 38 yearling calves; 3 bulls; 260 hogs; 100 pigs; 5 boars; 150 **Kinds and num-** sheep with lambs; 200 yearling lambs; 120 rams; **ber of animals** 30 goats with kids; 30 yearling kids; 3 male goats; 30 geese; 80 chickens; 22 peacocks.

Also concerning the manors [1] which belong to the above mansion. In the villa of Grisio we found domain buildings, where there are 3 barns and a yard enclosed by a hedge. There were, besides, 1 garden with trees, 10 geese, 8 ducks, 30 chickens.

In another villa we found domain buildings and a yard surrounded by a hedge, and within 3 barns; 1 arpent [2] of vines; 1 garden with trees; 15 geese; 20 chickens.

In a third villa, domain buildings, with 2 barns; 1 granary; 1 garden and 1 yard well enclosed by a hedge.

We found all the dry and liquid measures just as in the palace. We did not find any goldsmiths, silversmiths, blacksmiths, huntsmen, or persons engaged in other services.

The garden herbs which we found were lily, putchuck,[3] mint, parsley, rue, celery, libesticum, sage, savory, juniper, leeks, gar- **Vegetables** lic, tansy, wild mint, coriander, scullions, onions, **and trees** cabbage, kohlrabi,[4] betony.[5] Trees: pears, apples, medlars, peaches, filberts, walnuts, mulberries, quinces.[6]

---

[1] "Attached to the royal villa, in the center of which stood the palace or manse, were numerous dependent and humbler dwellings, occupied by mechanics, artisans, and tradesmen, or rather manufacturers and craftsmen, in great numbers. The dairy, the bakery, the butchery, the brewery, the flour-mill were there. . . . The villa was a city in embryo, and in due course it grew into one, for as it supplied in many respects the wants of the surrounding country, so it attracted population and became a center of commerce."—Jacob I. Mombert, *Charles the Great* (New York, 1888), pp. 401–402.

[2] An ancient Gallic land measure, equivalent to about half a Roman *jugerum* (the *jugerum* was about two-thirds of an acre). The arpent in modern France has varied greatly in different localities. In Paris it is 4,088 square yards.

[3] The same as "pachak." The fragrant roots of this plant are still exported from India to be used for burning as incense.

[4] A kind of cabbage. The edible part is a large turnip-like swelling of the stem above the surface of the ground.

[5] A plant used both as a medicine and as a dye.

[6] "All the cereals grown in the country were cultivated. The flower gar-

20. Charlemagne Crowned Emperor (800)

THE occasion of Charlemagne's presence in Rome in 800 was a con-flict between Pope Leo III. and a faction of the populace led by two nephews of the preceding pope, Hadrian I. It seems that in 799 Leo had been practically driven out of the papal capital and imprisoned in a neighboring monastery, but that through the planning of a sub-ordinate official he had soon contrived to escape. At any rate he got out of Italy as speedily as he could and made his way across the Alps to seek aid at the court of Charlemagne. The Frankish king was still busy with the Saxon war and did not allow the prospect of a papal visit to interfere with his intended campaign; but at Paderborn, in the very heart of the Saxon country, where he could personally direct the operations of his troops, he established his headquarters and awaited the coming of the refugee pope. The meeting of the two dignitaries resulted in a pledge of the king once more to take up the burden of defending the Roman Church and the Vicar of Christ, this time not against outside foes but against internal disturbers. After about a year Charlemagne repaired to Rome and called upon the Pope and his adversaries to appear before him for judgment. When the leaders of the hostile faction refused to comply, they were summarily con-demned to death, though it is said that through the generous advice of Leo they were afterwards released on a sentence of exile. During the ceremonies which followed in celebration of Christmas occurred the famous coronation which is described in the two passages given below.

Although the coronation has been regarded as so important as to have been called "the central event of the Middle Ages," [1] it is by no means an easy task to determine precisely what significance it was thought to have at the time. We can look back upon it now and see

dens were furnished with the choicest specimens for beauty and fragrance, the orchards and kitchen gardens produced the richest and best varieties of fruit and vegetables. Charles specified by name not less than seventy-four varieties of herbs which he commanded to be cultivated; all the vege-tables still raised in Central Europe, together with many herbs now found in botanical gardens only, bloomed on his villas; his orchards yielded a rich harvest in cherries, apples, pears, prunes, peaches, figs, chestnuts, and mulberries. The hill-sides were vineyards laden with the finest varieties of grapes."—Mombert, *Charles the Great*, p. 400.

[1] James Bryce, *The Holy Roman Empire* (new ed., New York, 1904), p. 50.

that it marked the beginning of the so-called "Holy Roman Empire"— a creation that endured in *fact* only a very short time but whose name and theory survived all the way down to Napoleon's reorganization of the German states in 1806. One view of the matter is that Charlemagne's coronation meant that a Frankish king had become the successor of Emperor Constantine VI., just deposed at Constantinople, and that therefore the universal Roman Empire was again to be ruled from a western capital as it had been before the time of the first Constantine. It will be observed that extract (a), taken from the Annals of Lauresheim, and therefore of German origin, at least suggests this explanation. But, whether or not precisely this idea was in the mind of those who took part in the ceremony, in actual fact no such transfer of universal sovereignty from Constantinople to the Frankish capital ever took place. The Eastern Empire lived right on under its own line of rulers and, so far as we know, aside from some rather vague negotiations for a marriage of Charlemagne and the Empress Irene, the new western Emperor seems never to have contemplated the extension of his authority over the East. His great aspiration had been to consolidate all the Germanic peoples of western continental Europe under the leadership of the Franks; that, by 800, he had practically done; he had no desire to go farther. His dominion was always limited strictly to the West, and at the most he can be regarded after 800 as not more than the reviver of the old western half of the Empire, and hence as the successor of Romulus Augustulus. But even this view is perhaps somewhat strained. The chroniclers of the time liked to set up fine theories of the sort, and later it came to be to the interest of papal and imperial rivals to make large use, in one way or another, of such theories. But we to-day may look upon the coronation as nothing more than a formal recognition of a condition of things already existing. By his numerous conquests Charlemagne had drawn under his control such a number of peoples and countries that his position had come to be that which we think of as an emperor's rather than that of simple king of the Franks. The Pope did not give Charlemagne his empire; the energetic king had built it for himself. At the most, what Leo did was simply to bestow a title already earned and to give with it presumably the blessing and favor of the Church, whose devoted servant Charlemagne repeatedly professed to be. That the idea of imperial

unity still survived in the West is certain, and without doubt many
men looked upon the ceremony of 800 as re-establishing such unity;
but as events worked out it was not so much Charlemagne's empire
as the papacy itself that was the real continuation of the power of the
Cæsars.   Conditions had so changed that it was impossible in the
nature of things for Charlemagne to be a Roman emperor in the old
sense.   The coronation gave him a new title and new prestige, but
no new subjects, no larger army, no more princely income.   The basis
of his power continued to be, in every sense, his Frankish kingdom.
The structural element in the revived empire was Frankish; the Roman
was merely ornamental.

Sources—(a) *Annales Laureshamensis* ["Annals of Lauresheim"], Chap. 34.
    Text in *Monumenta Germaniæ Historica, Scriptores* (Pertz ed.),
    Vol. I., p. 38.

    (b) *Vitæ Pontificorum Romanorum* ["Lives of the Roman Pontiffs"].
    Text in Muratori, *Rerum Italicarum Scriptores*, Vol. III., pp. 284–
    285.

(a)

And because the name of emperor had now ceased among the
Greeks, and their empire was possessed by a woman,[1] it seemed
both to Leo the pope himself, and to all the holy fathers who
were present in the self-same council,[2] as well as to the rest of
the Christian people, that they ought to take to be emperor
Charles, king of the Franks, who held Rome herself, where the
Cæsars had always been wont to sit, and all the other regions

[1] Irene, the wife of Emperor Leo IV.   After the death of her husband in
780 she became regent during the minority of her son, Constantine VI., then
only nine years of age.   In 790 Constantine succeeded in taking the government out of her hands; but seven years afterwards she caused him to be
blinded and shut up in a dungeon, where he soon died.   The revolting crimes
by which Irene established her supremacy at Constantinople were considered,
even in her day, a disgrace to Christendom.

[2] This expression has given rise to a view which will be found in some
books that Pope Leo convened a general council of Frankish and Italian
clergy to consider the advisability of giving the imperial title to Charlemagne.   The whole matter is in doubt, but it does not seem likely that there
was any such formal deliberation.   Leo certainly ascertained that the leading
lay and ecclesiastical magnates would approve the contemplated step, but
that a definite election in council took place may be pretty confidently denied.   The writer of the Annals of Lauresheim was interested in making the
case of Charlemagne, and therefore of the later emperors, as strong as possible.

which he ruled through Italy and Gaul and Germany; and inasmuch as God had given all these lands into his hand, it seemed right that with the help of God, and at the prayer of the whole Christian people, he should have the name of emperor also. [The Pope's] petition King Charles willed not to refuse,[1] but submitting himself with all humility to God, and at the prayer of the priests, and of the whole Christian people, on the day of the nativity of our Lord Jesus Christ, he took on himself the name of emperor, being consecrated by the Pope Leo. . . . . For this also was done by the will of God . . . that the heathen might not mock the Christians if the name of emperor should have ceased among them.

(b)

After these things, on the day of the birth of our Lord Jesus Christ, when all the people were assembled in the Church of the blessed St. Peter,[2] the venerable and gracious Pope with his own hands crowned him [Charlemagne] with an exceedingly precious crown. Then all the faithful Romans, beholding the choice of such a friend and defender of the holy Roman Church, and of

---

[1] Einhard, Charlemagne's biographer, says that the king at first had such aversion to the titles of Emperor and Augustus "that he declared he would not have set foot in the church the day that they were conferred, although it was a great feast-day, if he could have foreseen the design of the Pope" (*Vita Caroli Magni*, Chap. 28). Despite this statement, however, we are not to regard the coronation as a genuine surprise to anybody concerned. In all probability there had previously been a more or less definite understanding between the king and the Pope that in due time the imperial title should be conferred. It is easy to believe, though, that Charlemagne had had no idea that the ceremony was to be performed on this particular occasion and it is likely enough that he had plans of his own as to the proper time and place for it, plans which Leo rather rudely interfered with, but which the manifest good-will of everybody constrained the king to allow to be sacrificed. It may well be that Charlemagne had decided simply to assume the imperial crown without a papal coronation at all, in order that the whole question of papal supremacy, which threatened to be a troublesome one, might be kept in the background.

[2] The celebration of the Nativity was by far the greatest festival of the Church. At this season the basilica of St. Peter at Rome was the scene of gorgeous ceremonials, and to its sumptuous shrine thronged the devout of all Christendom. Its magnificence on the famous Christmas of 800 was greater than ever, for only recently Charlemagne had bestowed the most costly of all his gifts upon it—the spoils of the Avar wars.

the pontiff, did by the will of God and of the blessed Peter, the key-bearer of the heavenly kingdom, cry with a loud voice, "To Charles, the most pious Augustus, crowned of God, the great and peace-giving Emperor, be life and victory." While he, before the altar of the church, was calling upon many of the saints, it was proclaimed three times, and by the common voice of all he was chosen to be emperor of the Romans. Then the most holy high priest and pontiff anointed Charles with holy oil, and also his most excellent son to be king,[1] upon the very day of the birth of our Lord Jesus Christ.

21. The General Capitulary for the Missi (802)

THROUGHOUT the larger part of Charlemagne's dominion the chief local unit of administration was the county, presided over by the count. The count was appointed by the Emperor, generally from among the most important landed proprietors of the district. His duties included the levy of troops, the publication of the royal decrees or capitularies, the administration of justice, and the collection of revenues. On the frontiers, where the need of defense was greatest, these local officers exercised military functions of a special character and were commonly known as "counts of the march," or dukes, or sometimes as margraves. In order that these royal officials, in whatever part of the country, might not abuse their authority as against their fellow-subjects, or engage in plots against the unity of the empire, Charlemagne devised a plan of sending out at stated intervals men who were known as *missi dominici* ("the lord's messengers") to visit the various counties, hear complaints of the people, inquire into the administration of the counts, and report conditions to the Emperor. They were to serve as connecting links between the central and local governments and as safeguards against the ever powerful forces of disintegration. Such itinerant royal agents had not been unknown in Merovingian times, and they had probably been made use of pretty frequently by Charles Martel

---

[1] Charles, the eldest son, since 789 king of Maine. In reality, of course, he was but an under-king, since Maine was an integral part of Charlemagne's dominion. He was anointed by Pope Leo in 800 as heir-apparent to the new imperial dignity of his father.

and Pepin the Short. But it was Charlemagne who reduced the employment of *missi* to a system and made it a fixed part of the governmental machinery of the Frankish kingdom. This he did mainly by the *Capitulare Missorum Generale*, promulgated early in 802 at an assembly at the favorite capital Aix-la-Chapelle. The whole empire was divided into districts, or *missaticæ*, and each of these was to be visited annually by two of the *missi*. A churchman and a layman were usually sent out together, probably because they were to have jurisdiction over both the clergy and the laity, and also that they might restrain each other from injustice or other misconduct. They were appointed by the Emperor, at first from his lower order of vassals, but after a time from the leading bishops, abbots, and nobles of the empire. They were given power to depose minor officials for misdemeanors, and to summon higher ones before the Emperor. By 812, at least, they were required to make four rounds of inspection each year.

In the capitulary for the *missi* Charlemagne took occasion to include a considerable number of regulations and instructions regarding the general character of the local governments, the conduct of local officers, the manner of life of the clergy, the management of the monasteries, and other things of vital importance to the strength of the empire and the well-being of the people. The capitulary may be regarded as a broad outline of policy and conduct which its author, lately become emperor, wished to see realized throughout his vast dominion.

Source—Text in *Monumenta Germaniæ Historica, Leges* (Boretius ed.), Vol. I., No. 33, pp. 91–99. Translated by Dana C. Munro in *Univ. of Pa. Translations and Reprints*, Vol. VI., No. 5, pp. 16–27.

1. Concerning the embassy sent out by the lord emperor.

Therefore, the most serene and most Christian lord emperor Charles has chosen from his nobles the wisest and most prudent **The missi** men, both archbishops and some of the other **sent out** bishops also, and venerable abbots and pious laymen, and has sent them throughout his whole kingdom, and through them he would have all the various classes of persons mentioned in the following chapters live in accordance with the correct law. Moreover, where anything which is not right and just has been enacted in the law, he has ordered them to inquire into this most diligently and to inform him of it. He desires, God granting, to reform it. And let no one, through his cleverness or craft, dare to oppose or thwart the written law, as many are wont to do, or the judicial sentence passed upon him, or to do injury to the churches of God, or the poor, or the widows, or the wards, or any Christian. But all shall live entirely in accordance with God's precept, honestly and under a just rule, and each one shall be admonished to live in harmony with his fellows in his business or profession; the canonical clergy [1] ought to observe in every respect a canonical life without heeding base gain; nuns ought to keep diligent watch over their lives; laymen and the secular clergy [2] ought rightly to observe their laws without malicious fraud; and all ought to live in mutual charity and perfect peace.

And let the *missi* themselves make a diligent investigation whenever any man claims that an injustice has been done him by any one, just as they desire to deserve the grace of omnipotent God and to keep their fidelity promised to Him, so that in all cases, in accordance with the will and fear of God, they shall administer the law fully and justly in the case of the holy churches of God and of the poor, of wards and widows, and of the whole people. And if there be anything of such a nature that they,

The duties of the missi together with the provincial counts, are not able of themselves to correct it and to do justice concerning it, they shall, without any reservation, refer it, together with their reports, to the judgment of the emperor; and

---

[1] The term "canonical" was applied more particularly to the clergy attached to a cathedral church, the clergy being known individually as "canons," collectively as a "chapter." In the present connection, however, it probably refers to the monks, who, living as they did by "canons" or rules, were in that sense " canonical clergy."

[2] The secular clergy were the bishops, priests, deacons, and other church officers, who lived with the people in the *sæculum*, or world, as distinguished from the monks, ascetics, cenobites, anchorites, and others, who dwelt in monasteries or other places of seclusion.

the straight path of justice shall not be impeded by any one on account of flattery or gifts, or on account of any relationship, or from fear of the powerful.[1]

2. Concerning the fidelity to be promised to the lord emperor.

He has commanded that every man in his whole kingdom, whether ecclesiastic or layman, and each one according to his **Oath to be taken to Charlemagne as emperor** vow and occupation, should now promise to him as emperor the fidelity which he had previously promised to him as king; and all of those who had not yet made that promise should do likewise, down to those who were twelve years old. And that it shall be announced to all in public, so that each one might know, how great and how many things are comprehended in that oath; not merely, as many have thought hitherto, fidelity to the lord emperor as regards his life, and not introducing any enemy into his kingdom out of enmity, and not consenting to or concealing another's faithlessness to him; but that all may know that this oath contains in itself the following meaning:

3. First, that each one voluntarily shall strive, in accordance with his knowledge and ability, to live completely in the holy **What the new oath was to mean** service of God, in accordance with the precept of God and in accordance with his own promise, because the lord emperor is unable to give to all individually the necessary care and discipline.

4. Secondly, that no man, either through perjury or any other wile or fraud, or on account of the flattery or gift of any one, shall refuse to give back or dare to take possession of or conceal a serf of the lord emperor, or a district, or land, or anything that belongs to him; and that no one shall presume, through perjury or other wile, to conceal or entice away his fugitive fis-

---

[1] This is really as splendid a guarantee of equality before the law as is to be found in Magna Charta or the Constitution of the United States. Unfortunately there was not adequate machinery in the Frankish government to enforce it, though we may suppose that while the *missi* continued efficient (which was not more than a hundred years) considerable progress was made in this direction.

caline serfs [1] who unjustly and fraudulently say that they are free.

5. That no one shall presume to rob or do any injury fraudulently to the churches of God, or widows, or orphans, or pilgrims;[2] for the lord emperor himself, under God and His saints, has constituted himself their protector and defender.

6. That no one shall dare to lay waste a benefice [3] of the lord emperor, or to make it his own property.

7. That no one shall presume to neglect a summons to war from the lord emperor; and that no one of the counts shall be so presumptuous as to dare to excuse any one of those who owe military service, either on account of relationship, or flattery, or gifts from any one.

8. That no one shall presume to impede at all in any way a ban [4] or command of the lord emperor, or to tamper with his work, or to impede, or to lessen, or in any way to act contrary to his will or commands. And that no one shall dare to neglect to pay his dues or tax.

9. That no one, for any reason, shall make a practice in court of defending another unjustly, either from any desire of gain when the cause is weak, or by impeding a just judgment by his skill in reasoning, or by a desire of oppressing when the cause is

Justice to be rendered in the courts
weak. But each one shall answer for his own cause or tax or debt, unless any one is infirm or ignorant of pleading;[5] for these the *missi*, or the chiefs who are in the court, or the judge who knows the case in question, shall plead before the court; or, if it is necessary, such

[1] Serfs who worked on the fiscal lands, or, in other words, on the royal estates.

[2] Compare chapters 14 and 27.

[3] A benefice, as the term is here used, was land granted by the Emperor to a friend or dependent. The holder was to use such land on stated terms for his own and the Emperor's gain, but was in no case to claim ownership of it.

[4] The word has at least three distinct meanings—a royal edict, a judicial fine, and a territorial jurisdiction. It is here used in the first of these senses.

[5] There was little room under Charlemagne's system for professional lawyers or advocates.

a person may be allowed as is acceptable to all and knows the case well; but this shall be done wholly according to the convenience of the chiefs or *missi* who are present. But in every case it shall be done in accordance with justice and the law; and no one shall have the power to impede justice by a gift, reward, or any kind of evil flattery, or from any hindrance of relationship. And no one shall unjustly consent to another in anything, but with all zeal and good-will all shall be prepared to carry out justice.

For all the above mentioned ought to be observed by the imperial oath.[1]

10. [We ordain] that bishops and priests shall live according to the canons [2] and shall teach others to do the same.

11. That bishops, abbots, and abbesses who are in charge of others, with the greatest veneration shall strive to surpass their **Obligations of the clergy** subjects in this diligence and shall not oppress their subjects with a harsh rule or tyranny, but with a sincere love shall carefully guard the flock committed to them with mercy and charity, or by the examples of good works.

14. That bishops, abbots and abbesses, and counts shall be mutually in accord, following the law in order to render a just judgment with all charity and unity of peace, and that they shall live faithfully in accordance with the will of God, so that always everywhere through them and among them a just judgment shall be rendered. The poor, widows, orphans, and pilgrims shall have consolation and defense from them; so that we, through the good-will of these, may deserve the reward of eternal life rather than punishment.

19. That no bishops, abbots, priests, deacons, or other members of the clergy shall presume to have dogs for hunting, or hawks, falcons, and sparrow-hawks, but each shall observe fully

[1] In other words, when the oath of allegiance is taken, as it must be by every man and boy above the age of twelve, all the obligations mentioned from Chap. 3 to Chap. 9 are to be considered as assumed along with that of fidelity to the person and government of the Emperor.

[2] That is, the laws of the Church.

the canons or rule of his order.[1] If any one shall presume to do so, let him know that he shall lose his office. And in addition he shall suffer such punishment for his misconduct that the others will be afraid to possess such things for themselves.

27. And we command that no one in our whole kingdom shall dare to deny hospitality to rich, or poor, or pilgrims; that is, let no one deny shelter and fire and water to pilgrims traversing our country in God's name, or to any one traveling for the love of God, or for the safety of his own soul.

28. Concerning embassies coming from the lord emperor. That the counts and *centenarii* [2] shall provide most carefully, as

The missi to be helped on their way
they desire the good-will of the lord emperor, for the *missi* who are sent out, so that they may go through their territories without any delay; and the emperor commands all everywhere that they see to it that no delay is encountered anywhere, but they shall cause the *missi* to go on their way in all haste and shall provide for them in such a manner as they may direct.

32. Murders, by which a multitude of the Christian people perish, we command in every way to be shunned and to be

The crime of murder
forbidden. . . . Nevertheless, lest sin should also increase, in order that the greatest enmities may not arise among Christians, when by the persuasions of the devil murders happen, the criminal shall immediately hasten to make amends and with all speed shall pay to the relatives of the murdered man the fitting composition for the evil done. And we forbid firmly that the relatives of the murdered man shall dare in any way to continue their enmities on account of the evil done, or shall refuse to grant peace to him who asks it, but, having given their pledges, they shall receive the fitting com-

---

[1] One of the greatest temptations of the mediæval clergy was to spend time in hunting, to the neglect of religious duties. Apparently this evil was pretty common in Charlemagne's day.

[2] The *centenarii* were minor local officials, subordinate to the counts, and confined in authority to their particular district or "hundred."

position and shall make a perpetual peace; moreover, the guilty one shall not delay to pay the composition.[1] . . . But if any one shall have scorned to make the fitting composition, he shall be deprived of his property until we shall render our decision.[2]

39. That in our forests no one shall dare to steal our game, which we have already many times forbidden to be done; and

Theft of game from the royal forests

now we again strictly forbid that any one shall do so in the future; just as each one desires to preserve the fidelity promised to us, so let him take heed to himself. . . .

40. Lastly, therefore, we desire all our decrees to be known in the whole kingdom through our *missi* now sent out, either among the men of the Church, bishops, abbots, priests, deacons, canons, all monks or nuns, so that each one in his ministry or profession may keep our ban or decree, or where it may be fitting to thank the citizens for their good-will, or to furnish aid, or where there may be need still of correcting anything. . . . Where we believe there is anything unpunished, we shall so strive to correct it with all our zeal and will that with God's aid we may bring it to correction, both for our own eternal glory and that of all our faithful.

22. A Letter of Charlemagne to Abbot Fulrad

IN Charlemagne's governmental and military system the clergy, both regular and secular, had a place of large importance. From early Frankish times the bishoprics and monasteries had been acquiring

---

[1] In the Frankish kingdom, as commonly among Germanic peoples of the period, murder not only might be, but was expected to be, atoned for by a money payment to the slain man's relatives. The payment, known as the *wergeld*, would vary according to the rank of the man killed. If it were properly made, such "composition" was bound to be accepted as complete reparation for the injury. In this regulation we can discern a distinct advance over the old system of blood-feud under which a murder almost invariably led to family and clan wars. Plainly the Franks were becoming more civilized.

[2] If a murderer refused to pay the required composition his property was to be taken possession of by the Emperor's officers and the case must be laid before the Emperor himself. If the latter chose, he might order the restoration of the property, but this he was not likely to do.

large landed estates on which they enjoyed peculiar political and judicial privileges. These lands came to the church authorities partly by purchase, largely by gift, and not infrequently through concessions by small land-holders who wished to get the Church's favor and protection without actually moving off the little farms they had been accustomed to cultivate. However acquired, the lands were administered by the clergy with larger independence than was apt to be allowed the average lay owner. Still, they were as much a part of the empire as before and the powerful bishops and abbots were expected to see that certain services were forthcoming when the Emperor found himself in need of them. Among these was the duty of leading, or sending, a quota of troops under arms to the yearly assembly. In the selection below we have a letter written by Charlemagne some time between 804 and 811 to Fulrad, abbot of St. Quentin (about sixty miles northeast of Paris), respecting the fulfilment of this important obligation. The closing sentence indicates very clearly the price exacted by the Emperor in return for concessions of temporal authority to ecclesiastical magnates.

Source—Text in *Monumenta Germaniæ Historica, Leges* (Boretius ed.), Vol. I., No. 75, p. 168.

In the name of the Father, Son and Holy Ghost. Charles, most serene, august, crowned of God, great pacific Emperor, who, by God's mercy, is King of the Franks and Lombards, to Abbot Fulrad.

Let it be known to you that we have determined to hold our general assembly [1] this year in the eastern part of Saxony, on the River Bode, at the place which is known as Strassfurt.[2] There-

[1] Beginning with the reign of Charlemagne there were really two assemblies each year—one in the spring, the other in the autumn; but the one in the spring, the so-called "May-field," was much the more important. All the nobles and higher clergy attended, and if a campaign was in prospect all who owed military service would be called upon to bring with them their portion of the war-host, with specified supplies. Charlemagne proposed all measures, the higher magnates discussed them with him, and the lower ones gave a perfunctory sanction to acts already determined upon. The meeting place was changed from year to year, being rotated irregularly among the royal residences, as Aix-la-Chapelle, Paderborn, Ingelheim, and Thionville; occasionally they were held, as in this instance, in places otherwise almost unknown.

[2] Strassfurt was some distance south of Magdeburg.

fore, we enjoin that you come to this meeting-place, with all your men well armed and equipped, on the fifteenth day before the Kalends of July, that is, seven days before the festival of St. John the Baptist.[1] Come, therefore, so prepared with your men to the aforesaid place that you may be able to go thence well equipped in any direction in which our command shall direct; that is, with arms and accoutrements also, and other provisions

The troops to be brought: their equipment for war in the way of food and clothing. Each horseman will be expected to have a shield, a lance, a sword, a dagger, a bow, and quivers with arrows; and in your carts shall be implements of various kinds, that is, axes, planes, augers, boards, spades, iron shovels, and other utensils which are necessary in an army. In the wagons also should be supplies of food for three months, dating from the time of the assembly, together with arms and clothing for six months. And furthermore we command that you see to it that you proceed peacefully to the aforesaid place, through whatever part of our realm your journey shall be made; that is, that you presume to take nothing except fodder, wood, and water. And let the followers of each one of your vassals march along with the carts and horsemen, and let the leader always be with them until they reach the aforesaid place, so that the absence of a lord may not give to his men an opportunity to do evil.

Send your gifts,[2] which you ought to present to us at our assembly in the middle of the month of May, to the place where

Gifts for the Emperor we then shall be. If it happens that your journey shall be such that on your march you are able in person to present these gifts of yours to us, we shall be greatly

---

[1] The date of the festival of St. John the Baptist was June 22.

[2] From earliest Germanic times we catch glimpses of this practice of requiring gifts from a king's subjects. By Charlemagne's day it had crystallized into an established custom and was a very important source of revenue, though other sources had been opened up which were quite unknown to the German sovereigns of three or four hundred years before. Ordinarily these gifts, in money, jewels, or provisions, were presented to the sovereign each year at the May assembly.

pleased. Be careful to show no negligence in the future if you care to have our favor.

23. The Carolingian Revival of Learning

ONE of Charlemagne's chief claims to distinction is that his reign, largely through his own influence, comprised the most important period of the so-called Carolingian renaissance, or revival of learning. From the times of the Frankish conquest of Gaul until about the middle of the eighth century, education in western Europe, except in Ireland and Britain, was at a very low ebb and literary production quite insignificant. The old Roman intellectual activity had nearly ceased, and two or three centuries of settled life had been required to bring the Franks to the point of appreciating and encouraging art and letters. Even by Charlemagne's time people generally were far from being awake to the importance of education, though a few of the more far-sighted leaders, and especially Charlemagne himself, had come to lament the gross ignorance which everywhere prevailed and were ready to adopt strong measures to overcome it. Charlemagne was certainly no scholar, judged even by the standards of his own time; but had he been the most learned man in the world his interest in education could not have been greater. Before studying the selection given below, it would be well to read what Einhard said about his master's zeal for learning and the amount of progress he made personally in getting an education [see pp. 112–113].

The most conspicuous of Charlemagne's educational measures was his enlarging and strengthening of the Scola Palatina, or Palace School. This was an institution which had existed in the reign of his father Pepin, and probably even earlier. It consisted of a group of scholars gathered at the Frankish court for the purpose of studying and writing literature, educating the royal household, and stimulating learning throughout the country. It formed what we to-day might call an academy of sciences. Under Charlemagne's care it came to include such men of distinction as Paul the Deacon, historian of the Lombards, Paulinus of Aquileia, a theologian, Peter of Pisa, a grammarian, and above all Alcuin, a skilled teacher and writer from the school of York in England. Its history falls into three main periods: (1) from the middle of the eighth century to the year 782—the period during which it was dominated by Paul the Deacon and his Italian colleagues; (2) from 782 to about 800, when its leading spirit was Alcuin; and (3) from 800 to the years of its decadence in the later ninth century, when Frankish rather than foreign names appear most prominently in its annals.

It was Charlemagne's ideal that throughout his entire dominion opportunity should be open to all to obtain at least an elementary education and to carry their studies as much farther as they liked. To this end a regular system of schools was planned, beginning with the village school, in charge of the parish priest for the most elementary studies, and leading up through monastic and cathedral schools to the School of the Palace. In the intermediate stages, corresponding to our high schools and academies to-day, the subjects studied were essentially the same as those which received attention in the Scola Palatina. They were divided into two groups: (1) the *trivium*, including grammar, rhetoric, and dialectic (or philosophy), and (2) the *quadrivium*, including geometry, arithmetic, astronomy, and music. The system thus planned was never fully put in operation throughout Frankland, for after Charlemagne's death the work which he had so well begun was seriously interfered with by the falling off in intellectual aggressiveness of the sovereigns, by civil war, and by the ravages of the Hungarian and Norse invaders [see p. 163]. A capitulary of Louis the Pious in 817, for example, forbade the continuance of secular education in monastic schools. Still, much of what had been done remained, and never thereafter did learning among the Frankish people fall to quite so low a stage as it had passed through in the sixth and seventh centuries.

Charlemagne's interest in education may be studied best of all in his capitularies. In the extract below we have the so-called letter *De Litteris Colendis*, written some time between 780 and 800, which, though addressed personally to Abbot Baugulf, of the monastery of Fulda, was in reality a capitulary establishing certain regulations regarding education in connection with the work of the monks. To the Church was intrusted the task of raising the level of intelligence among the masses, and the clergy were admonished to bring together the children of both freemen and serfs in schools in which they might be trained, even as the sons of the nobles were trained at the royal court.

Source—Text in *Monumenta Germaniæ Historica, Leges* (Boretius ed.), Vol. I., No. 29, pp. 78–79. Adapted from translation by Dana C. Munro in *Univ. of Pa. Translations and Reprints*, Vol. VI., No. 5, pp. 12–14.

Charles, by the grace of God, king of the Franks and Lombards and Patrician of the Romans.[1] To Abbot Baugulf, and to all the congregation—also to the faithful placed under your care—we have sent loving greetings by our ambassadors in the name of all-powerful God.

Be it known, therefore, to you, devoted and acceptable to God, that we, together with our faithful, have deemed it expe-

Men of the Church charged with the work of education dient that the bishoprics and monasteries intrusted by the favor of Christ to our control, in addition to the order of monastic life and the relationships of holy religion, should be zealous also in the cherishing of letters, and in teaching those who by the gift of God are able to learn, according as each has capacity. So that, just as the observance of the rule [2] adds order and grace to the integrity of morals, so also zeal in teaching and learning may do the same for sentences, to the end that those who wish to please God by living rightly should not fail to please Him also by speaking correctly. For it is written, "Either from thy words thou shall be justified or from thy words thou shalt be condemned" [Matt., xii. 37]. Although right conduct may be better than knowledge, nevertheless knowledge goes before conduct. Therefore each one ought to study what he desires to accomplish, in order that so much the more fully the mind may know what ought to be done,

[1] The title "Patricius of Rome" was conferred on Charlemagne by Pope Hadrian I., in 774. Its bestowal was a token of papal appreciation of the king's renewal of Pepin's grant of lands to the papacy. In practice the title had little or no meaning. It was dropped in 800 when Charlemagne was crowned emperor [see p. 130].

[2] That is, the law of the Church; in case of the monasteries, more especially the regulations laid down for their order, e.g., the Benedictine Rule.

as the tongue speeds in the praises of all-powerful God without the hindrances of mistakes. For while errors should be shunned **Even the clergy** by all men, so much the more ought they to be **often unable** avoided, as far as possible, by those who are **to speak and write correctly** chosen for this very purpose alone.[1] They ought to be the specially devoted servants of truth. For often in recent years when letters have been written to us from monasteries, in which it was stated that the brethren who dwelt there offered up in our behalf sacred and pious prayers, we have recognized, in most cases, both correct thoughts and uncouth expressions; because what pious devotion dictated faithfully to the mind, the tongue, uneducated on account of the neglect of study, was not able to express in the letter without error. Whence it happened that we began to fear lest perchance, as the skill in writing was less, so also the wisdom for understanding the Holy Scriptures might be much less than it rightly ought to be. And we all know well that, although errors of speech are dangerous, far more dangerous are errors of the understanding.

Therefore, we exhort you not only not to neglect the study of letters, but also with most humble mind, pleasing to God, to **Education es-** study earnestly in order that you may be able **sential to an** more easily and more correctly to penetrate the **understanding of the Scrip-** mysteries of the divine Scriptures. Since, more-**tures** over, images [similes], tropes[2] and like figures are found in the sacred pages, nobody doubts that each one in reading these will understand the spiritual sense more quickly if previously he shall have been fully instructed in the mastery of letters. Such men truly are to be chosen for this work as have both the will and the ability to learn and a desire to instruct

[1] In the Middle Ages it was assumed that churchmen were educated; few other men had any claim to learning. Charlemagne here says that it is bad indeed when men who have been put in ecclesiastical positions because of their supposed education fall into errors which ought to be expected only from ordinary people.

[2] In rhetoric a trope is ordinarily defined as the use of a word or expression in a different sense from that which properly belongs to it. The most common varieties are metaphor, metonomy, synechdoche, and irony.

others. And may this be done with a zeal as great as the earnestness with which we command it. For we desire you to be, as the soldiers of the Church ought to be, devout in mind, learned in discourse, chaste in conduct, and eloquent in speech, so that when any one shall seek to see you, whether out of reverence for God or on account of your reputation for holy conduct, just as he is edified by your appearance, he may also be instructed by the wisdom which he has learned from your reading or singing, and may go away gladly, giving thanks to Almighty God.

CHAPTER X.

THE ERA OF THE LATER CAROLINGIANS

24. The Oaths of Strassburg (842)

The broad empire of Germanic peoples built up by Charlemagne was
extremely difficult to hold together. Even before the death of its
masterful creator, in 814, it was already showing signs of breaking up,
and after that event the process of dissolution set in rapidly. It will
not do to look upon this falling to pieces as caused entirely by the
weakness of Charlemagne's successors. The trouble lay deeper, in the
natural love of independence common to all the Germans, in the wide
differences that had come to exist among Saxons, Lombards, Bavarians,
Franks, and other peoples in the empire, and finally in the prevailing
ill-advised principle of royal succession by which the territories making
up the empire, like those composing the old Frankish kingdom, were
regarded as personal property to be divided among the sovereign's
sons, just as was the practice respecting private possessions. As a
consequence of these things the generation following the death of
Charlemagne was a period of much confusion in western Europe. The
trouble first reached an acute stage in 817 when Emperor Louis the
Pious, Charlemagne's son and successor, was constrained to make a
division of the empire among his three sons, Lothair, Pepin, and Louis.
The Emperor expressly stipulated that despite this arrangement there
was to be still "one sole empire, and not three"; but it is obvious that
the imperial unity was at least pretty seriously threatened, and when,
in 823, Louis's second wife, Judith of Bavaria, gave birth to a son and
immediately set up in his behalf an urgent demand for a share of the
empire, civil war among the rival claimants could not be averted.   In the
struggle that followed the distracted Emperor completely lost his throne
for a time (833). Thereafter he was ready to accept almost any arrangement that would enable him to live out his remaining days in

peace. When he died, in 840, two of the sons, Louis the German and Judith's child, who came to be known as Charles the Bald, combined against their brother Lothair (Pepin had died in 838) with the purpose of wresting from him the imperial crown, which the father, shortly before his death, had bestowed upon him. At least they were determined that this mark of favor from the father should not give the older brother any superiority over them. In the summer of 841 the issue was put to the test in a great battle at Fontenay, a little distance east of Orleans, with the result that Lothair was badly defeated. In February of the following year Louis and Charles, knowing that Lothair was still far from regarding himself as conquered, bound themselves by oath at Strassburg, in the valley of the Rhine, to keep up their joint opposition until they should be entirely successful.

The pledges exchanged on this occasion are as interesting to the student of language as to the historian. The army which accompanied Louis was composed of men of almost pure Germanic blood and speech, while that with Charles was made up of men from what is now southern and western France, where the people represented a mixture of Frankish and old Roman and Gallic stocks. As a consequence Louis took the oath in the *lingua romana* for the benefit of Charles's soldiers, and Charles reciprocated by taking it in the *lingua teudisca*, in order that the Germans might understand it. Then the followers of the two kings took oath, each in his own language, that if their own king should violate his agreement they would not support him in acts of hostility against the other brother, provided the latter had been true to his word. The *lingua romana* employed marks a stage in the development of the so-called Romance languages of to-day—French, Spanish, and Italian— just as the *lingua teudisca* approaches the character of modern Teutonic languages—German, Dutch, and English. The oaths and the accompanying address of the kings are the earliest examples we have of the languages used by the common people of the early Middle Ages. Latin was of course the language of literature, records, and correspondence, matters with which ordinary people had little or nothing to do. The necessity under which the two kings found themselves of using two quite different modes of speech in order to be understood by all the soldiers is evidence that already by the middle of the ninth century the Romance and Germanic languages were becoming essentially distinct. It was prophetic, too, of the fast approaching cleavage of the northern and southern peoples politically.

Nithardus, whose account of the exchange of oaths at Strassburg is translated below, was an active participant in the events of the first half of the ninth century. He was born about 790, his mother being Charlemagne's daughter Bertha and his father the noted courtier and poet Angilbert. In the later years of Charlemagne's reign, and probably under Louis the Pious and Charles the Bald, he was in charge of the defense of the northwest coasts against the Northmen. He fought for Charles the Bald at Fontenay and was frequently employed in those troublous years between 840 and 843 in the fruitless negotiations among the rival sons of Louis. Neither the date nor the manner of his death is known. There are traditions that he was killed in 858 or 859 while fighting the Northmen; but other stories just as well founded tell us that he became disgusted with the turmoil of the world, retired to a monastery, and there died about 853. His history of the wars of the sons of Louis the Pious (covering the period 840–843) was undertaken at the request of Charles the Bald. The first three books were written in 842, the fourth in 843. Aside from a rather too favorable attitude toward Charles, the work is very trustworthy, and the claim is even made by some that among all of the historians of the Carolingian period, not even Einhard excepted, no one surpassed Nithardus in spirit, method, and insight. It may further be noted that Nithardus was the first historical writer of any importance in the Middle Ages who was not some sort of official in the Church.

Source—Nithardus, *Historiarum Libri IV*. ["Four Books of Histories"], Bk. III., Chaps. 4–5. Text in *Monumenta Germaniæ Historica, Scriptores* (Pertz ed.), Vol. II., pp. 665–666.

Lothair was given to understand that Louis and Charles were supporting each other with considerable armies.[1] Seeing that his plans were crushed in every direction, he made a long but profitless expedition and abandoned the country about Tours.

[1] After the battle of Fontenay, June 25, 841, Charles and Louis had separated and Lothair had formed the design of attacking and conquering first one and then the other. He made an expedition against Charles, but was unable to accomplish anything before his two enemies again drew together at Strassburg.

At length he returned into France,[1] worn out with fatigue, as was also his army. Pepin,[2] bitterly repenting that he had been

Movements of the hostile parties in 841–842 on Lothair's side, withdrew into Aquitaine. Charles, learning that Otger, bishop of Mainz, objected to the proposed passage of Louis by way of Mainz to join his brother, set out by way of the city of Toul[3] and entered Alsace at Saverne. When Otger heard of this, he and his supporters abandoned the river and sought places where they might hide themselves as speedily as possible. On the fifteenth of February Louis and Charles came together in the city formerly called Argentoratum, now known as Strassburg, and there they took the mutual oaths which are given herewith, Louis in the *lingua romana* and Charles in the *lingua teudisca*. Before the exchange of oaths they addressed the assembled people, each in his own language, and Louis, being the elder, thus began:

"How often, since the death of our father, Lothair has pursued my brother and myself and tried to destroy us, is known to you all. So, then, when neither brotherly love, nor Christian feeling, nor any reason whatever could bring about a peace between us upon fair conditions, we were at last compelled to bring the matter before God, determined to abide by whatever issue He might decree. And we, as you know, came off victorious;[4] our brother was beaten, and with his followers got away, each as best he

The speech of Louis the German could. Then we, moved by brotherly love and having compassion on our Christian people, were not willing to pursue and destroy them; but, still, as before, we begged that justice might be done to each.

---

[1] The name "Francia" was as yet confined to the country lying between the Loire and the Scheldt.

[2] This Pepin was a son of Pepin, the brother of Charles, Louis, and Lothair. Upon the death of the elder Pepin in 838 his part of the empire—the great region between the Loire and the Pyrenees, known as Aquitaine—had been taken possession of by Charles, without regard for the two surviving sons. It was natural, therefore, that in the struggle which ensued between Charles and Louis on the one side and Lothair on the other, young Pepin should have given such aid as he could to the latter.

[3] On the upper Moselle.

[4] This refers to the battle of Fontenay.

He, however, after all this, not content with the judgment of God, has not ceased to pursue me and my brother with hostile purpose, and to harass our peoples with fire, plunder, and murder. Wherefore we have been compelled to hold this meeting, and, since we feared that you might doubt whether our faith was fixed and our alliance secure, we have determined to make our oaths thereto in your presence. And we do this, not from any unfair greed, but in order that, if God, with your help, shall grant us peace, we may the better provide for the common welfare. But if, which God forbid, I shall dare to violate the oath which I shall swear to my brother, then I absolve each one of you from your allegiance and from the oath which you have sworn to me."

After Charles had made the same speech in the *lingua romana*, Louis, as the elder of the two, swore first to be faithful to his alliance:

Pro Deo amur et pro christian poblo et nostro commun salvament, dist di in avant, in quant Deus savir et podir me dunat, si **The oath** *salvaraeio cist meon fradre Karlo et in adiudha* **of Louis** *et in cadhuna cosa, si cum om per dreit son fradra salvar dist, in o quid il mi altresi fazet ; et ab Ludher nul plaid numquam prindrai, qui meon vol cist meon fradre Karle in damno sit.*[1]

When Louis had taken this oath, Charles swore the same thing in the *lingua teudisca*:

In Godes minna ind in thes christianes folches ind unser bedhero gealtnissi, fon thesemo dage frammordes, so fram so mir **The oath** *Got gewizci indi madh furgibit, so haldih tesan* **of Charles** *minan bruodher, soso man mit rehtu sinan bruodher scal, in thiu, thaz er mig sosoma duo ; indi mit Ludheren*

---

[1] The translation of this oath is as follows: "For the love of God, and for the sake as well of our peoples as of ourselves, I promise that from this day forth, as God shall grant me wisdom and strength, I will treat this my brother as one's brother ought to be treated, provided that he shall do the same by me. And with Lothair I will not willingly enter into any dealings which may injure this my brother."

in nohheiniu thing ne gegango, the minan willon imo ce scadhen werhen.

The oath which the subjects of the two kings then took, each [people] in its own language, reads thus in the *lingua romana:*

The oath taken by the subjects of the two kings

Si Lodhwigs sagrament qua son fradre Karlo jurat, conservat, et Karlus meos sendra, de suo part, non lo stanit, si io returnar non lint pois, ne io ne neuls cui eo returnar int pois, in nulla aiudha contra Lodhuwig nun li iver.[1]

And in the *lingua teudisca:*

Oba Karl then eid then, er sineno bruodher Ludhuwige gesuor, geleistit, indi Ludhuwig min herro then er imo gesuor, forbrihchit, obih ina es irwenden ne mag, noh ih no thero nohhein then ih es irwended mag, widhar Karle imo ce follusti ne wirdhic.

25. The Treaty of Verdun (843)

AFTER the meeting at Strassburg, Charles and Louis advanced against Lothair, who now abandoned Aachen and retreated southward past Châlons-sur-Marne toward Lyons. When the brothers had come into the vicinity of Châlons-sur-Saône, they were met by ambassadors from Lothair who declared that he was weary of the struggle and was ready to make peace if only his imperial dignity should be properly recognized and the share of the kingdom awarded to him should be somewhat the largest of the three. Charles and Louis accepted their brother's overtures and June 15, 842, the three met on an island in the Saône and signed preliminary articles of peace. It was agreed that a board of a hundred and twenty prominent men should assemble October 1 at Metz, on the Moselle, and make a definite division of the kingdom. This body, with the three royal brothers, met at the appointed time, but adjourned to Worms, and subsequently to Verdun, on the upper

---

[1] This oath, taken by the followers of the two kings, may be thus translated: "If Louis [or Charles] shall observe the oath which he has sworn to his brother Charles [or Louis], and Charles [or Louis], our lord, on his side, should be untrue to his oath, and we should be unable to hold him to it, neither we nor any whom we can deter, shall give him any support." The oath taken by the two armies was the same, with only the names of the kings interchanged.

Meuse, in order to have the use of maps at the latter place. The treaty which resulted during the following year was one of the most important in all mediæval times. Unfortunately the text of it has not survived, but all its more important provisions are well known from the writings of the chroniclers of the period. Two such accounts of the treaty, brief but valuable, are given below.

Louis had been the real sovereign of Bavaria for sixteen years and to his kingdom were now added all the German districts on the right bank of the Rhine (except Friesland), together with Mainz, Worms, and Speyer on the left bank, under the general name of *Francia Orientalis*. Charles retained the western countries—Aquitaine, Gascony, Septimania, the Spanish March, Burgundy west of the Saône, Neustria, Brittany, and Flanders—designated collectively as *Francia Occidentalis*.[1] The intervening belt of lands, including the two capitals Rome and Aachen, and extending from Terracina in Italy to the North Sea, went to Lothair.[2] With it went the more or less nominal imperial dignity. In general, Louis's portion represented the coming Germany and Charles's the future France. But that of Lothair was utterly lacking in either geographical or racial unity and was destined not long to be held together. Parts of it, particularly modern Alsace and Lorraine, have remained to this day a bone of contention between the states on the east and west. "The partition of 843," says Professor Emerton, "involved, so far as we know, nothing new in the relations of the three brothers to each other. The theory of the empire was preserved, but the meaning of it disappeared. There is no mention of any actual superiority of the Emperor (Lothair) over his brothers, and there is nothing to show that the imperial name was anything but an empty title, a memory of something great which men could not quite let die, but which for a hundred years to come was to be powerless for good or evil."[3] The empire itself was never afterwards united under the rule of one man, except for two years (885–887) in the time of Charles the Fat.

---

[1] This name in the course of time became simply "Francia," then "France." In the eastern kingdom, "Francia" gradually became restricted to the region about the Main, or "Franconia."

[2] It was commonly known as "Lotharii regnum," later as "Lotharingia," and eventually (a fragment of the kingdom only) as "Lorraine."

[3] Emerton, *Mediæval Europe* (Boston, 1903), p. 30.

Sources—(a) *Annales Bertiniani* ["Annals of Saint Bertin"]. Translated from text in *Monumenta Germaniæ Historica, Scriptores* (Pertz ed.), Vol. I., p. 440.

(b) *Rudolfi Fuldensis Annales* ["Annals of Rudolph of Fulda"]. Text in *Monumenta Germaniæ Historica, Scriptores* (Pertz ed.), Vol. I., p. 362.

(a)

Charles set out to find his brothers, and they met at Verdun. By the division there made Louis received for his share all the

A statement from the annals of Saint Bertin

country beyond the Rhine,[1] and on this side Speyer, Worms, Mainz, and the territories belonging to these cities. Lothair received that which is between the Scheldt and the Rhine toward the sea, and that lying beyond Cambrésis, Hainault, and the counties adjoining on this side of the Meuse, down to the confluence of the Saône and Rhone, and thence along the Rhone to the sea, together with the adjacent counties. Charles received all the remainder, extending to Spain. And when the oath was exchanged they went their several ways.

(b)

The realm had from early times been divided in three portions, and in the month of August the three kings, coming together at

Another from those of Rudolph of Fulda

Verdun in Gaul, redivided it among themselves. Louis received the eastern part, Charles the western. Lothair, who was older than his brothers, received the middle portion. After peace was firmly established and oaths exchanged, each brother returned to his dominion to control and protect it. Charles, presuming to regard Aquitaine as belonging properly to his share, was given much trouble by his nephew Pepin,[2] who annoyed him by frequent incursions and caused great loss.

[1] This statement is only approximately true. In reality Friesland (Frisia) and a strip up the east bank of the Rhine almost to the mouth of the Moselle went to Lothair.

[2] See p. 152, note 2.

26. A Chronicle of the Frankish Kingdom in the Ninth Century

THE following passages from the Annals of Xanten are here given for two purposes—to show something of the character of the period of the Carolingian decline, and to illustrate the peculiar features of the mediæval chronicle. Numerous names, places, and events neither very clearly understood now, nor important if they were understood, occur in the text, and some of these it is not deemed worth while to attempt to explain in the foot-notes. The selection is valuable for the general impressions it gives rather than for the detailed facts which it contains, though some of the latter are interesting enough.

Annals as a type of historical writing first assumed considerable importance in western Europe in the time of Charles Martel and Charlemagne. Their origin, like that of most forms of mediæval literary production, can be traced directly to the influence of the Church. The annals began as mere occasional notes jotted down by the monks upon the "Easter tables," which were circulated among the monasteries so that the sacred festival might not fail to be observed at the proper date. The Easter tables were really a sort of calendar, and as they were placed on parchment having a broad margin it was very natural that the monks should begin to write in the margin opposite the various years some of the things that had happened in those years. An Easter table might pass through a considerable number of hands and so have events recorded upon it by a good many different men. All sorts of things were thus made note of—some important, some unimportant— and of course it is not necessary to suppose that everything written down was actually true. Many mistakes were possible, especially as the writer often had only his memory, or perhaps mere hearsay, to rely upon. And when, as frequently happened, these scattered Easter tables were brought together in some monastery and there revised, fitted together, and written out in one continuous chronicle, there were chances at every turn for serious errors to creep in. The compilers were sometimes guilty of wilful misrepresentation, but more often their fault was only their ignorance, credulity, and lack of critical discernment. In these annals there was no attempt to write history as we now understand it; that is, the chroniclers did not undertake to work out the causes and results and relations of things. They merely

recorded year by year such happenings as caught their attention—
the succession of a new pope, the death of a bishop, the coronation of
a king, a battle, a hail-storm, an eclipse, the birth of a two-headed
calf—all sorts of unimportant, and from our standpoint ridiculous,
items being thrown in along with matters of world-wide moment.
Heterogeneous as they are, however, the large collections of annals
that have come down to us have been used by modern historians with
the greatest profit, and but for them we should know far less than we
do about the Middle Ages, and especially about the people and events
of the ninth, tenth, and eleventh centuries.

The Annals of Xanten here quoted are the work originally of a number of ninth century monks. The fragments from which they were
ultimately compiled are thought to have been brought together at
Cologne, or at least in that vicinity. They cover especially the years
831–873.

Source—*Annales Xantenses* ["Annals of Xanten"]. Text in *Monumenta Ger-
    maniæ Historica, Scriptores* (Pertz ed.), Vol. II., p. 227. Adapted
    from translation in James H. Robinson, *Readings in European
    History* (New York, 1904), Vol. I., pp. 158–162.

844. Pope Gregory departed this world and Pope Sergius
followed in his place.[1] Count Bernhard was killed by Charles.
Pepin, king of Aquitaine, together with his son and the son of
Bernhard, routed the army of Charles,[2] and there fell the abbot
Hugo. At the same time King Louis advanced with his army
against the Wends,[3] one of whose kings, Gestimus by name,
was killed; the rest came to Louis and pledged him their fidelity,
which, however, they broke as soon as he was gone. Thereafter
Lothair, Louis, and Charles came together for council in Dieden-
hofen, and after a conference they went their several ways in
peace.

[1] Gregory IV. (827–844) was succeeded in the papal office by Sergius II.
(844–847).
[2] By the treaty of Verdun in 843 Charles the Bald had been given Aquitaine, along with the other distinctively Frankish regions of western Europe.
His nephew Pepin, however, who had never been reconciled to Charles's
taking possession of Aquitaine in 838, called himself king of that country
and made stubborn resistance to his uncle's claims of sovereignty [see p.
156].
[3] The Wends were a Slavonic people living in the lower valley of the Oder.

845. Twice in the canton of Worms there was an earthquake; the first in the night following Palm Sunday, the second in the holy night of Christ's Resurrection. In the same year the heathen[1] broke in upon the Christians at many points, but more than twelve thousand of them were killed by the Frisians. Another party of invaders devastated Gaul; of these more than six hundred men perished. Yet, owing to his indolence, Charles agreed to give them many thousand pounds of gold and silver if they would leave Gaul, and this they did. Nevertheless the cloisters of most of the saints were destroyed and many of the Christians were led away captive.

The Northmen in Frisia and Gaul

After this had taken place King Louis once more led a force against the Wends. When the heathen had learned this they sent ambassadors, as well as gifts and hostages, to Saxony, and asked for peace. Louis then granted peace and returned home from Saxony. Thereafter the robbers were afflicted by a terrible pestilence, during which the chief sinner among them, by the name of Reginheri, who had plundered the Christians and the holy places, was struck down by the hand of God. They then took counsel and threw lots to determine from which of their gods they should seek safety; but the lots did not fall out happily, and on the advice of one of their Christian prisoners that they should cast their lot before the God of the Christians, they did so, and the lot fell happily. Then their king, by the name of Rorik, together with all the heathen people, refrained from meat and drink for fourteen days, when the plague ceased, and they sent back all their Christian prisoners to their country.

846. According to their custom, the Northmen plundered eastern and western Frisia and burned the town of Dordrecht, with two other villages, before the eyes of Lothair, who was then in the castle of Nimwegen,

The Northmen again in Frisia

---

[1] By "the heathen" are meant the Norse pirates from Denmark and the Scandinavian peninsula. On their invasions see p. 163.

but could not punish the crime. The Northmen, with their boats filled with immense booty, including both men and goods, returned to their own country.

In the same year Louis sent an expedition from Saxony against the Wends across the Elbe. He personally, however, went with his army against the Bohemians, whom we call Beuwinitha, but with great risk. . . . Charles advanced against the Britons, but accomplished nothing.

At this same time, as no one can mention or hear without great sadness, the mother of all churches, the basilica of the apostle **Rome attacked by the Saracens** Peter, was taken and plundered by the Moors, or Saracens, who had already occupied the region of Beneventum.[1] The Saracens, moreover, slaughtered all the Christians whom they found outside the walls of Rome, either within or without this church. They also carried men and women away prisoners. They tore down, among many others, the altar of the blessed Peter, and their crimes from day to day bring sorrow to Christians. Pope Sergius departed life this year.

847. After the death of Sergius no mention of the apostolic see has come in any way to our ears. Rabanus [Maurus], master and abbot of Fulda,[2] was solemnly chosen archbishop as the successor of Bishop Otger, who had died. Moreover, the Northmen here and there plundered the Christians and engaged in a battle with the counts Sigir and Liuthar. They continued up the Rhine as far as Dordrecht, and nine miles farther to Meginhard, when they turned back, having taken their booty.

---

[1] This Saracen attack upon Rome was made by some Arab pirates who in the Mediterranean were playing much the same rôle of destruction as were the Northmen on the Atlantic coasts. A league of Naples, Gaeta, and Amalfi defeated the pirates in 849, and delivered Rome from her oppressors long enough for new fortifications to be constructed. Walls were built at this time to include the quarter of St. Peter's—a district known to this day as the "Leonine City" in memory of Leo IV., who in 847 succeeded Sergius as pope [see above text under date 850].

[2] Fulda was an important monastery on one of the upper branches of the Weser, northeast of Mainz.

848. On the fourth of February, towards evening, it lightened and there was thunder heard. The heathen, as was their custom,

An outbreak of heresy repressed

inflicted injury on the Christians. In the same year King Louis held an assembly of the people near Mainz. At this synod a heresy was brought forward by a few monks in regard to predestination. These were convicted and beaten, to their shame, before all the people. They were sent back to Gaul whence they had come, and, thanks be to God, the condition of the Church remained uninjured.

849. While King Louis was ill, his army of Bavaria took its way against the Bohemians. Many of these were killed and the remainder withdrew, much humiliated, into their own country. The heathen from the North wrought havoc in Christendom as usual and grew greater in strength; but it is painful to say more of this matter.

850. On January 1st of that season, in the octave of the Lord,[1] towards evening, a great deal of thunder was heard and a mighty flash of lightning seen; and an overflow of water afflicted the human race during this winter. In the following summer an all too great heat of the sun burned the earth. Leo, pope of the

Further ravages by the Northmen and the Saracens

apostolic see, an extraordinary man, built a fortification around the church of St. Peter the apostle. The Moors, however, devastated here and there the coast towns in Italy. The Norman Rorik, brother of the above-mentioned younger Heriold, who earlier had fled dishonored from Lothair, again took Dordrecht and did much evil treacherously to the Christians. In the same year so great a peace existed between the two brothers—Emperor Lothair and King Louis—that they spent many days together in Osning [Westphalia] and there hunted, so that many were astonished thereat; and they went each his way in peace.

851. The bodies of certain saints were sent from Rome to

[1] An octave, in the sense here meant, is the week (strictly eight days) following a church festival; in this case, the eight days following the anniversary of Christ's birth, or Christmas.

Saxony—that of Alexander, one of seven brethren, and those of Romanus and Emerentiana. In the same year the very noble Empress, Irmingard by name, wife of the Emperor Lothair,

The Northmen again in Frisia and Saxony departed this world. The Normans inflicted much harm in Frisia and about the Rhine. A mighty army of them collected by the River Elbe against the Saxons, and some of the Saxon towns were besieged, others burned, and most terribly did they oppress the Christians. A meeting of our kings took place on the Maas [Meuse].

852. The steel of the heathen glistened; excessive heat; a famine followed. There was not fodder enough for the animals. The pasturage for the swine was more than sufficient.

853. A great famine in Saxony, so that many were forced to live on horse meat.

854. The Normans, in addition to the very many evils which

The Northmen burn the church of St. Martin at Tours they were everywhere inflicting upon the Christians, burned the church of St. Martin, bishop of Tours, where his body rests.

855. In the spring Louis, the eastern king, sent his son of the same name to Aquitaine to obtain possession of the heritage of his uncle Pepin.

856. The Normans again chose a king of the same name as the preceding one, and related to him, and the Danes made a fresh incursion by sea, with renewed forces, against the Christians.

857. A great sickness prevailed among the people. This produced a terrible foulness, so that the limbs were separated from the body even before death came.

858. Louis, the eastern king, held an assembly of the people of his territory in Worms.

859. On the first of January, as the early Mass was being said, a single earthquake occurred in Worms and a triple one in Mainz before daybreak.

860. On the fifth of February thunder was heard. The king

returned from Gaul after the whole empire had gone to destruction, and was in no way bettered.

861. The holy bishop Luitbert piously furnished the cloister which is called the Freckenhorst with many relics of the saints,

Sacred relics brought together at the Freckenhorst

namely, of the martyrs Boniface and Maximus, and of the confessors Eonius and Antonius, and added a portion of the manger of the Lord and of His grave, and likewise of the dust of the Lord's feet as He ascended to heaven. In this year the winter was long and the above-mentioned kings again had a secret consultation on the island near Coblenz, and they laid waste everything round about.

27. The Northmen in the Country of the Franks.

UNDER the general name of Northmen in the ninth and tenth centuries were included all those peoples of pure Teutonic stock who inhabited the two neighboring peninsulas of Denmark and Scandinavia. In this period, and after, they played a very conspicuous part in the history of western Europe—at first as piratical invaders along the Atlantic coast, and subsequently as settlers in new lands and as conquerors and state-builders. *Northmen* was the name by which the people of the continent generally knew them, but to the Irish they were known as *Ostmen* or *Eastmen*, and to the English as *Danes*, while the name which they applied to themselves was *Vikings* ["Creekmen"]. Their prolonged invasions and plunderings, which fill so large a place in the ninth and tenth century chronicles of England and France, were the result of several causes and conditions: (1) their natural love of adventure, common to all early Germanic peoples; (2) the fact that the population of their home countries had become larger than the limited resources of these northern regions would support; (3) the proximity of the sea on every side, with its fiords and inlets inviting the adventurer to embark for new shores; and (4) the discontent of the nobles, or jarls, with the growing rigor of kingly government. In consequence of these and other influences large numbers of the people became pirates, with no other occupation than the plundering of the more civilized and wealthier countries to the east, west, and south.

Those from Sweden visited most commonly the coasts of Russia, those from Norway went generally to Scotland and Ireland, and those from Denmark to England and France. In fast-sailing vessels carrying sixty or seventy men, and under the leadership of "kings of the sea" who never "sought refuge under a roof, nor emptied their drinking-horns at a fireside," they darted along the shores, ascended rivers, converted islands into temporary fortresses, and from thence sallied forth in every direction to burn and pillage and carry off all the booty upon which they could lay hands. So swift and irresistible were their operations that they frequently met with not the slightest show of opposition from the terrified inhabitants.

It was natural that Frankland, with its numerous large rivers flowing into the ocean and leading through fertile valleys dotted with towns and rich abbeys, should early have attracted the marauders; and in fact they made their appearance there as early as the year 800. Before the end of Charlemagne's reign they had pillaged Frisia, and a monk-ish writer of the time tells us that upon one occasion the great Emperor burst into tears and declared that he was overwhelmed with sorrow as he looked forward and saw what evils they would bring upon his offspring and people. Whether or not this story is true, certain it is that before the ninth century was far advanced incursions of the barbarians—"the heathen," as the chroniclers generally call them—had come to be almost annual events. In 841 Rouen was plundered and burned; in 843 Nantes was besieged, the bishop killed, and many captives carried off; in 845 the invaders appeared at Paris and were prevented from attacking the place only by being bribed; and so the story goes, until by 846 we find the annalists beginning their melan-choly record of the year's events with the matter-of-course statement that, "according to their custom," the Northmen plundered such and such a region [see p. 159]. Below are a few passages taken from the Annals of Saint-Bertin, the poem of Abbo on the siege of Paris, and the Chronicle of Saint-Denys, which show something of the character of the Northmen's part in early French history, first as mere invaders and afterwards as permanent settlers.

The Annals of Saint-Bertin are so called because they have been copied from an old manuscript found in the monastery of that name. The period which they cover is 741–882. Several writers evidently had a hand in their compilation. The portion between the dates 836 and 861 is attributed to Prudence, bishop of Troyes, and that between 861 and 882 to Hincmar, archbishop of Rheims.

Abbo, the author of the second selection given below, was a monk of St. Germain des Prés, at Paris. He wrote a poem in which he undertook to give an account of the siege of Paris by the Northmen in 885 and 886, and of the struggles of the Frankish people with the invaders to the year 896. As literature the poem has small value, but for the historian it possesses some importance.

The account of Rollo's conversion comes from a history of the Normans written in the twelfth century by William of Jumièges. The work covers the period 851–1137, its earlier portions (to 996) being based on an older history written by Dudo, dean of St. Quentin, in the eleventh century. The Chronicle of St.-Denys was composed at a later time and served to preserve most of the history recorded by Dudo and William of Jumièges.

Sources—(a) *Annales Bertiniani* [" Annals of St. Bertin "]. Text in *Monumenta Germaniæ Historica Scriptores* (Pertz ed.), Vol. I., pp. 439–454.

  (b) Abbonis Monachi S. Germani Parisiensis, *De Bellis Parisiacæ Urbis, et Odonis Comitis, post Regis, adversus Northmannos urbem ipsam obsidentes, sub Carolo Crasso Imp. ac Rege Francorum* [Abbo's "Wars of Count Odo with the Northmen in the Reign of Charles the Fat"]. Text in Bouquet, *Recueil des Historiens des Gaules et de la France*, Vol. VIII., pp. 4–26.

  (c) *Chronique de Saint-Denys d'après Dudo et Guillaume de Jumièges* ["Chronicle of St. Denys based on Dudo and William of Jumièges"], Vol. III., p. 105.

(a) THE EARLIER RAVAGES OF THE NORTHMEN

843. Pirates of the Northmen's race came to Nantes, killed the bishop and many of the clergy and laymen, both men and women, and pillaged the city. Thence they set out to plunder the lands of lower Aquitaine. At length they arrived at a certain island [1] and carried materials thither from the mainland to build themselves houses; and they settled there for the winter, as if that were to be their permanent dwelling-place.

[1] The isle of Rhé, near Rochelle, north of the mouth of the Garonne.

844. The Northmen ascended the Garonne as far as Toulouse and pillaged the lands along both banks with impunity. Some, after leaving this region went into Galicia [1] and perished, part of them by the attacks of the cross-bowmen who had come to resist them, part by being overwhelmed by a storm at sea. But others of them went farther into Spain and engaged in long and desperate combats with the Saracens; defeated in the end, they withdrew.

845. The Northmen with a hundred ships entered the Seine on the twentieth of March and, after ravaging first one bank and then the other, came without meeting any re-

The Northmen bought off at Paris

sistance to Paris. Charles [2] resolved to hold out against them; but seeing the impossibility of gaining a victory, he made with them a certain agreement and by a gift of 7,000 livres he bought them off from advancing farther and persuaded them to return.

Euric, king of the Northmen, advanced, with six hundred vessels, along the course of the River Elbe to attack Louis of Germany.[3] The Saxons prepared to meet him, gave battle, and with the aid of our Lord Jesus Christ won the victory.

The Northmen returned [from Paris] down the Seine and coming to the ocean pillaged, destroyed, and burned all the regions along the coast.

846. The Danish pirates landed in Frisia.[4] They were able to force from the people whatever contributions they wished and, being victors in battle, they remained masters of almost the entire province.

847. The Northmen made their appearance in the part of Gaul inhabited by the Britons [5] and won three victories. Noménoé,[6]

---

[1] Galicia was a province in the extreme northwest of the Spanish peninsula.

[2] Charles the Bald, who by the treaty of Verdun in 843, had obtained the western part of the empire built up by Charlemagne [see p. 154].

[3] Louis, a half-brother of Charles the Bald, who had received the eastern portion of Charlemagne's empire by the settlement of 843.

[4] Frisia, or Friesland, was the northernmost part of the kingdom of Lothair.

[5] That is, in Brittany.

[6] Noménoé was a native chief of the Britons. Charles the Bald made

although defeated, at length succeeded in buying them off with presents and getting them out of his country.

853–854. The Danish pirates, making their way into the country eastward from the city of Nantes, arrived without **The burning** opposition, November eighth, before Tours. This **of Tours** they burned, together with the church of St. Martin and the neighboring places. But that incursion had been foreseen with certainty and the body of St. Martin had been removed to Cormery, a monastery of that church, and from there to the city of Orleans. The pirates went on to the château of Blois [1] and burned it, proposing then to proceed to Orleans and destroy that city in the same fashion. But Agius, bishop of Orleans, and Burchard, bishop of Chartres,[2] had gathered soldiers and ships to meet them; so they abandoned their design and returned to the lower Loire, though the following year [855] they ascended it anew to the city of Angers.[3]

855. They left their ships behind and undertook to go overland to the city of Poitiers;[4] but the Aquitanians came to meet them and defeated them, so that not more than 300 escaped.

856. On the eighteenth of April, the Danish pirates came to the city of Orleans, pillaged it, and went away without meeting **Orleans** opposition. Other Danish pirates came into the **pillaged** Seine about the middle of August and, after plundering and ruining the towns on the two banks of the river, and even the monasteries and villages farther back, came to a well located place near the Seine called Jeufosse, and, there quietly passed the winter.

859. The Danish pirates having made a long sea-voyage (for

many efforts to reduce him to obedience, but with little success. In 848 or 849 he took the title of king. During his brief reign (which ended in 851) he invaded Charles's dominions and wrought almost as much destruction as did the Northmen themselves.

[1] Tours, Blois, and Orleans were all situated within a range of a hundred miles along the lower Loire.

[2] Chartres was some eighty miles northwest of Orleans.

[3] About midway between Nantes and Tours.

[4] Poitiers was about seventy miles southwest of Tours.

they had sailed between Spain and Africa) entered the Rhone, where they pillaged many cities and monasteries and established themselves on the island called Camargue. . . . They devastated everything before them as far as the city of Valence.[1] Then after ravaging all these regions they returned to the island where they had fixed their habitation. Thence they went on toward Italy, capturing and plundering Pisa and other cities.

(b) The Siege of Paris

885. The Northmen came to Paris with 700 sailing ships, not counting those of smaller size which are commonly called barques. At one stretch the Seine was lined with the vessels for more than two leagues, so that one might ask in astonishment in what cavern the river had been swallowed up, since it was not to be seen. The second day after the fleet of the Northmen arrived

The Northmen arrive at the city under the walls of the city, Siegfred, who was then king only in name [2] but who was in command of the expedition, came to the dwelling of the illustrious bishop. He bowed his head and said: "Gauzelin, have compassion on yourself and on your flock. We beseech you to listen to us, in order that you may escape death. Allow us only the freedom of the city. We will do no harm and we will see to it that whatever belongs either to you or to Odo shall be strictly respected." Count Odo, who later became king, was then the defender of the city.[3] The bishop replied to Siegfred, "Paris has been entrusted to us by the Emperor Charles, who, after God, king and lord of the powerful, rules over almost all the world.

[1] Valence was on the Rhone, nearly a hundred and fifty miles back from the Mediterranean coast.

[2] The Northmen who ravaged France really had no kings, but only military chieftains.

[3] Odo, or Eudes, was chosen king by the Frankish nobles and clergy in 888, to succeed the deposed Charles the Fat. He was not of the Carolingian family but a Robertian (son of Robert the Strong), and hence a forerunner of the Capetian line of kings regularly established on the French throne in 987 [see p. 177]. His election to the kingship was due in a large measure to his heroic conduct during the siege of Paris by the Northmen.

He has put it in our care, not at all that the kingdom may be
ruined by our misconduct, but that he may keep it and be assured
of its peace. If, like us, you had been given the duty of defending
these walls, and if you should have done that which you ask us to
do, what treatment do you think you would deserve?" Siegfred
replied: "I should deserve that my head be cut off and thrown
to the dogs. Nevertheless, if you do not listen to my demand,
on the morrow our war machines will destroy you with poisoned
arrows. You will be the prey of famine and of pestilence and
these evils will renew themselves perpetually every year." So
saying, he departed and gathered together his comrades.

In the morning the Northmen, boarding their ships, approached
the tower and attacked it.[1] They shook it with their engines
The attack   and stormed it with arrows. The city resounded
upon the tower with clamor, the people were aroused, the bridges
trembled. All came together to defend the tower. There Odo,
his brother Robert,[2] and the Count Ragenar distinguished themselves for bravery; likewise the courageous Abbot Ebolus,[3] the
nephew of the bishop. A keen arrow wounded the prelate, while
at his side the young warrior Frederick was struck by a sword.
Frederick died, but the old man, thanks to God, survived. There
perished many Franks; after receiving wounds they were lavish
of life. At last the enemy withdrew, carrying off their dead.
The evening came. The tower had been sorely tried, but its
foundations were still solid, as were also the narrow *baies* which
surmounted them. The people spent the night repairing it with
boards. By the next day, on the old citadel had been erected a
new tower of wood, a half higher than the former one. At sunrise
the Danes caught their first glimpse of it. Once more the latter
engaged with the Christians in violent combat. On every side
arrows sped and blood flowed. With the arrows mingled the

[1] The tower blocked access to the city by the so-called "Great Bridge,"
which connected the right bank of the Seine with the island on which the
city was built. The tower stood on the present site of the Châtelet.
[2] In time Robert also became king. He reigned only from 922 to 923.
[3] Abbot Ebolus was head of the monastery of St. Germain des Prés.

stones hurled by slings and war-machines; the air was filled with
them. The tower which had been built during the night groaned

Fierce fighting under the strokes of the darts, the city shook with the struggle, the people ran hither and thither, the
bells jangled. The warriors rushed together to defend the totter-
ing tower and to repel the fierce assault. Among these warriors
two, a count and an abbot [Ebolus], surpassed all the rest in
courage. The former was the redoubtable Odo who never ex-

The bravery of Count Odo perienced defeat and who continually revived the spirits of the worn-out defenders. He ran along
the ramparts and hurled back the enemy. On those who were
secreting themselves so as to undermine the tower he poured oil,
wax, and pitch, which, being mixed and heated, burned the Danes
and tore off their scalps. Some of them died; others threw
themselves into the river to escape the awful substance. . . .[1]

Meanwhile Paris was suffering not only from the sword outside
but also from a pestilence within which brought death to many
noble men. Within the walls there was not ground in which to
bury the dead. . . . Odo, the future king, was sent to Charles,
emperor of the Franks,[2] to implore help for the stricken city.

One day Odo suddenly appeared in splendor in the midst of
three bands of warriors. The sun made his armor glisten and

Odo's mission to Emperor Charles the Fat greeted him before it illuminated the country around. The Parisians saw their beloved chief at a distance, but the enemy, hoping to prevent
his gaining entrance to the tower, crossed the Seine and took up
their position on the bank. Nevertheless Odo, his horse at a
gallop, got past the Northmen and reached the tower, whose
gates Ebolus opened to him. The enemy pursued fiercely the

---

[1] The Northmen were finally compelled to abandon their efforts against
the tower. They then retired to the bank of the Seine near the abbey of
Saint-Denys and from that place as a center ravaged all the country lying
about Paris. In a short time they renewed the attack upon the city itself.

[2] Charles the Fat, under whom during the years 885–887 the old empire
of Charlemagne was for the last time united under a single sovereign. When
Odo went to find him in 886 he was at Metz in Germany. German and
Italian affairs interested him more than did those of the Franks.

comrades of the count who were trying to keep up with him and get refuge in the tower. [The Danes were defeated in the attack.]

Now came the Emperor Charles, surrounded by soldiers of all nations, even as the sky is adorned with resplendent stars. A **Terms of peace arranged by Charles** great throng, speaking many languages, accompanied him. He established his camp at the foot of the heights of Montmartre, near the tower. He allowed the Northmen to have the country of Sens to plunder;[1] and in the spring he gave them 700 pounds of silver on condition that by the month of March they leave France for their own kingdom.[2] Then Charles returned, destined to an early death.[3]

(c) THE BAPTISM OF ROLLO AND THE ESTABLISHMENT OF THE NORMANS IN FRANCE [4]

The king had at first wished to give to Rollo the province of Flanders, but the Norman rejected it as being too marshy. Rollo

[1] Sens was about a hundred miles southeast of Paris. Charles abandoned the region about Sens to the Northmen to plunder during the winter of 886–887. His very lame excuse for doing this was that the people of the district did not properly recognize his authority and were deserving of such punishment.

[2] The twelve month siege of Paris thus brought to an end had many noteworthy results. Chief among these was the increased prestige of Odo as a national leader and of Paris as a national stronghold. Prior to this time Paris had not been a place of importance, even though Clovis had made it his capital. In the period of Charlemagne it was distinctly a minor city and it gained little in prominence under Louis the Pious and Charles the Bald. The great Carolingian capitals were Laon and Compiègne. The siege of 885–886, however, made it apparent that Paris occupied a strategic position, commanding the valley of the Seine, and that the inland city was one of the true bulwarks of the kingdom. Thereafter the place grew rapidly in population and prestige, and when Odo became king (in 888) it was made his capital. As time went on it grew to be the heart of the French kingdom and came to guide the destinies of France as no other city of modern times has guided a nation.

[3] He was deposed in 887, largely because of his utter failure to take any active measures to defend the Franks against their Danish enemies. From Paris he went to Germany where he died, January 13, 888, at a small town on the Danube.

[4] After the famous siege of Paris in 885–886 the Northmen, or Normans as they may now be called, continued to ravage France just as they had

refused to kiss the foot of Charles when he received from him the duchy of Normandy. "He who receives such a gift," said the bishops to him, "ought to kiss the foot of the king." "Never," replied he, "will I bend the knee to any one, or kiss anybody's foot." Nevertheless, impelled by the entreaties of the Franks, he ordered one of his warriors to perform the act in his stead. This man seized the foot of the king and lifted it to his lips, kissing it without bending and so causing the king to tumble over backwards. At that there was a loud burst of laughter and a great commotion in the crowd of onlookers. King Charles,

Rollo receives Normandy from Charles the Simple Robert, Duke of the Franks,[1] the counts and magnates, and the bishops and abbots, bound themselves by the oath of the Catholic faith to Rollo, swearing by their lives and their bodies and by the honor of all the kingdom, that he might hold the land and transmit it to his heirs from generation to generation throughout all time to come. When these things had been satisfactorily performed, the king returned in good spirits into his dominion, and Rollo with Duke Robert set out for Rouen.

In the year of our Lord 912 Rollo was baptized in holy water in the name of the sacred Trinity by Franco, archbishop of

Rollo becomes a Christian Rouen. Duke Robert, who was his godfather, gave to him his name. Rollo devotedly honored God and the Holy Church with his gifts. . . . The pagans,

done before that event. In 910 one of their greatest chieftains, Rollo, appeared before Paris and prepared to take the city. In this project he was unsuccessful, but his warriors caused so much devastation in the surrounding country that Charles the Simple, who was now king, decided to try negotiations. A meeting was held at Saint-Clair-sur-Epte where, in the presence of the Norman warriors and the Frankish magnates, Charles and Rollo entered into the first treaty looking toward a permanent settlement of Northmen on Frankish territory. Rollo promised to desist from his attacks upon Frankland and to become a Christian. Charles agreed to give over to the Normans a region which they in fact already held, with Rouen as its center, and extending from the Epte River on the east to the sea on the west. The arrangement was dictated by good sense and proved a fortunate one for all parties concerned.

[1] Robert was Odo's brother. "Duke of the Franks" was a title, at first purely military, but fast developing to the point where it was to culminate in its bearer becoming the first Capetian king [see p. 177].

seeing that their chieftain had become a Christian, abandoned their idols, received the name of Christ, and with one accord desired to be baptized. Meanwhile the Norman duke made ready for a splendid wedding and married the daughter of the king [Gisela] according to Christian rites.

Rollo gave assurance of security to all those who wished to dwell in his country. The land he divided among his followers, and, as it had been a long time unused, he improved it by the construction of new buildings. It was peopled by the Norman warriors and by immigrants from outside regions. The duke **His work in Normandy** established for his subjects certain inviolable rights and laws, confirmed and published by the will of the leading men, and he compelled all his people to live peaceably together. He rebuilt the churches, which had been entirely ruined; he restored the temples, which had been destroyed by the ravages of the pagans; he repaired and added to the walls and fortifications of the cities; he subdued the Britons who rebelled against him; and with the provisions obtained from them he supplied all the country that had been granted to him.

28. Later Carolingian Efforts to Preserve Order

THE ninth century is chiefly significant in Frankish history as an era of decline of monarchy and increase of the powers and independence of local officials and magnates. Already by Charlemagne's death, in 814, the disruptive forces were at work, and under the relatively weak successors of the great Emperor the course of decentralization went on until by the death of Charles the Bald, in 877, the royal authority had been reduced to a condition of insignificance. This century was the formative period *par excellence* of the feudal system—a type of social and economic organization which the conditions of the time rendered inevitable and under which great monarchies tended to be dissolved into a multitude of petty local states. Large landholders began to regard themselves as practically independent; royal officials, particularly the counts, refused to be parted from their positions and used them primarily to enhance their own personal authority; the churches and monasteries stretched their royal grants of immunity so far as almost to refuse to acknowledge any obligations to the central government. In these and other ways the Carolingian monarchy was shorn of its powers, and as it was quite lacking in money, lands, and soldiers who could be depended on, there was little left for it to do but to legislate and ordain without much prospect of being able to enforce its laws and ordinances. The rapidity with which the kings of the period were losing their grip on the situation comes out very clearly from a study of the capitularies which they issued from time to time. In general these capitularies, especially after about 840, testify to the disorder everywhere prevailing, the usurpations of the royal officials, and the popular contempt of the royal authority, and reiterate commands for the preservation of order until they become fairly wearisome to the reader. Royalty was at a bad pass and its weakness is reflected unmistakably in its attempts to govern by mere edict without any backing of enforcing power. In 843, 853, 856, 857, and many other years of Charles the Bald's reign, elaborate decrees were issued prohibiting brigandage and lawlessness, but with the tell-tale provision that violators were to be "admonished with Christian love to repent," or that they were to be punished "as far as the local officials could remember them," or that the royal agents were themselves to take oath not to become highway robbers! Sometimes the king openly confessed his weakness and proceeded to implore, rather than to command, his subjects to obey him.

The capitulary quoted below belongs to the last year of the short reign of Carloman (882–884), son of Louis the Stammerer and grandson of Charles the Bald. It makes a considerable show of power, ordaining the punishment of criminals as confidently as if there had really been means to assure its enforcement. But in truth all the provisions in it had been embodied in capitularies of Carloman's predecessors with scarcely perceptible effect, and there was certainly no reason to expect better results now. With the nobles practicing, if not asserting, independence, the churches and monasteries heeding the royal authority hardly at all, the country being ravaged by Northmen and the people turning to the great magnates for the protection they could no longer get from the king, and the counts and *missi dominici* making their lands and offices the basis for hereditary local authority, the king had come to be almost powerless in the great realm where less than a hundred years before Charlemagne's word, for all practical purposes, was law. Even Charlemagne himself, however, could have done little to avert the state of anarchy which conditions too strong for any sovereign to cope with had brought about.

Source—Text in *Monumenta Germaniæ Historica, Leges* (Boretius ed.), Vol. II., pp. 371–375.

1. According to the custom of our predecessors, we desire that in our palace shall prevail the worship of God, the honor of **The keeping of the peace enjoined** the king, piety, concord, and a condition of peace; and that that peace established in our palace by the sanction of our predecessors shall extend to, and be observed throughout, our entire kingdom.

2. We desire that all those who live at our court, and all who come there, shall live peaceably. If any one, in breach of the peace, is guilty of violence, let him be brought to a hearing at our palace, by the authority of the king and by the order of our *missus*, as it was ordained by the capitularies of our predecessors, that he may be punished according to a legal judgment and may pay a triple composition with the royal ban.[1]

3. If the offender has no lord, or if he flees from our court, our *missus* shall go to find him and shall order him, in our name, to appear at the palace.[2] If he should be so rash as to disdain to come, let him be brought by force. If he spurns both us and our *missus*, and while refusing to obey summons is killed in resisting, and any of his relatives or friends undertake to exercise against our agents who have killed him the right of vengeance,[3] we will oppose them there and will give our agents all the aid of our royal authority.

5. The bishop of the diocese in which the crime shall have

[1] See p. 138, note 4.
[2] If the offender had a lord, this lord would be expected to produce his accused vassal at court.
[3] That is, the old blood-feud of the Germans.

been committed ought, through the priest of the place, to give
three successive invitations to the offender to repent and to
The bishop's make reparation for his fault in order to set
part in re- himself right with God and the church that he
pressing crime has injured.   If he scorns and rejects this summons and invitation, let the bishop wield upon him the pastoral
rod, that is to say, the sentence of excommunication; and let
him separate him from the communion of the Holy Church until
he shall have given the satisfaction that is required.

9. In order that violence be entirely brought to an end and
order restored, it is necessary that the bishop's authority should
Obligations of be supplemented by that of the public officials.
lay officials Therefore we and our faithful have judged it
to restrain
violence expedient that the *missi dominici* should discharge
faithfully the duties of their office.[1]   The count shall enjoin to
the viscount,[2] to his *vicarii* and *centenarii*,[3] and to all the public
officials, as well as to all Franks who have a knowledge of the
law, that all should give as much aid as they can to the Church,
both on their own account and in accord with the requests of
the clergy, every time they shall be called upon by the bishop, the
officers of the bishop, or even by the needy.   They should do this
for the love of God, the peace of the Holy Church, and the fidelity
that they owe to us.

[1] The office of *missus* had by this time fallen pretty much into decay.
Many of the *missi* were at the same time counts—a combination of authority
directly opposed to the earlier theory of the administrative system.   The
missus had been supposed to supervise the counts and restrain them from
disloyalty to the king and from indulgence in arbitrary or oppressive measures of local government.

[2] The viscount (*vicecomes*) was the count's deputy.   By Carloman's time
there were sometimes several of these in a county.   They were at first
appointed by the count, but toward the end of the ninth century they became hereditary.

[3] The *vicarii* and *centenarii* were local assistants of the count in administrative and judicial affairs.   In Merovingian times their precise duties are
not clear, but under the Carolingians the two terms tended to become
synonyms.   The *centenarius*, or hundredman, was charged mainly with
the administration of justice in the smallest local division, i. e., the hundred.
In theory he was elected by the people of the hundred, but in practice he
was usually appointed by the count.

29. The Election of Hugh Capet (987)

THE election of Hugh Capet as king of France in 987 marked the establishment of the so-called Capetian line of monarchs, which occupied the French throne in all not far from eight centuries—a record not equaled by any other royal house in European history. The circumstances of the election were interesting and significant. For more than a hundred years there had been keen rivalry between the Carolingian kings and one of the great ducal houses of the Franks, known as the Robertians. In the disorder which so generally prevailed in France in the ninth and tenth centuries, powerful families possessing extensive lands and having large numbers of vassals and serfs were able to make themselves practically independent of the royal power. The greatest of these families was the Robertians, the descendants of Robert the Strong, father of the Odo who distinguished himself at the siege of Paris in 885–886 [see p. 170]. Between 888 and 987 circumstances brought it about three different times that members of the Robertian house were elevated to the Frankish throne (Odo, 888–898; Robert I., 922–923; and Rudolph—related to the Robertians by marriage only,—923–936). The rest of the time the throne was occupied by Carolingians (Charles the Simple, 898–922; Louis IV., 936–954; Lothair, 954–986; and Louis V., 986–987). With the death of the young king Louis V., in 987, the last direct descendant of Charlemagne passed away and the question of the succession was left for solution by the nobles and higher clergy of the realm. As soon as the king was dead, such of these magnates as were assembled at the court to attend the funeral bound themselves by oath to take no action until a general meeting could be held at Senlis (a few miles north of Paris) late in May, 987. The proceedings of this general meeting are related in the passage below. Apparently it had already been pretty generally agreed that the man to be elected was Hugh Capet, great-grandson of Robert the Strong and the present head of the famous Robertian house, and the speech of Adalbero, archbishop of Rheims, of which Richer gives a resumé, was enough to ensure this result. There was but one other claimant of importance. That was the late king's uncle, Charles of Lower Lorraine. He was not a man of force and Adalbero easily disposed of his candidacy, though the rejected prince was subsequently able to make his successful rival a good deal of trouble. Hugh owed his election to his large material resources, the military prestige of his ancestors, the active support of the Church, and the lack of direct heirs of the Carolingian dynasty.

Richer, the chronicler whose account of the election is given below, was a monk living at Rheims at the time when the events occurred which he describes. His "Four Books of Histories," discovered only in .1833, is almost our only considerable source of information on Frankish affairs in the later tenth century. In his writing he endeavored to round out his work into a real history and to give more than the bare outline of events characteristic of the mediæval annalists. In this he was only partially successful, being at fault mainly in indulging in too much rhetoric and in allowing partisan motives sometimes to guide him in what he said. His partisanship was on the side of the fallen Carolingians. The period covered by the "Histories" is 888–995; they are therefore roughly continuous chronologically with the Annals of Saint Bertin [see p. 164].

Source—Richer, *Historiarum Libri IV*. ["Four Books of Histories"], Bk. IV., Chaps. 11–12. Text in *Monumenta Germaniæ Historica, Scriptores* (Pertz ed.), Vol. III., pp. 633–634.

Meanwhile, at the appointed time the magnates of Gaul who had taken the oath came together at Senlis. When they had all taken their places in the assembly and the duke [1] had given the sign, the archbishop [2] spoke to them as follows: [3]

"King Louis, of divine memory, having been removed from the world, and having left no heirs, it devolves upon us to take

Adalbero's speech at Senlis

serious counsel as to the choice of a successor, so that the state may not suffer any injury through neglect and the lack of a leader. On a former occasion [4] we thought it advisable to postpone that deliberation in order that each of you might be able to come here and, in the presence of the assembly, voice the sentiment which God should have inspired in you, and that from all these different expressions of opinion we might be able to find out what is the general will.

[1] Hugh Capet, whose title prior to 987 was "Duke of the Franks."
[2] Adalbero, archbishop of Rheims.
[3] We are not to suppose that Richer here gives a literal reproduction of Adalbero's speech, but so far as we can tell the main points are carefully stated.
[4] At the funeral of Louis.

"Here we are assembled. Let us see to it, by our prudence and honor, that hatred shall not destroy reason, that love shall not interfere with truth. We are aware that Charles[1] has his partisans, who claim that the throne belongs to him by right of birth. But if we look into the matter, the throne is not acquired by hereditary right, and no one ought to be placed at the head of the kingdom unless he is distinguished, not only by nobility of body, but also by strength of mind—only such a one as honor and generosity recommend.[2] We read in the annals of rulers of illustrious descent who were deposed on account of their unworthiness and replaced by others of the same, or even lesser, rank.[3]

Election, not heredity, the true basis of Frankish kingship

"What dignity shall we gain by making Charles king? He is not guided by honor, nor is he possessed of strength. Then, too, he has compromised himself so far as to have become the dependent of a foreign king[4] and to have married a girl taken from among his own vassals. How could the great duke endure that a woman of the low rank of vassal should become queen and rule over him? How could he tender services to this woman, when his equals, and even his superiors, in birth bend the knee before him and place their hands under his feet? Think of this seriously and you will see that Charles must be rejected for his own faults

Objections to Charles of Lorraine

[1] Charles of Lower Lorraine, uncle of Louis V.

[2] The elective principle here asserted had prevailed in the choice of French and German kings for nearly a century. The kings chosen, however, usually came from one family, as the Carolingians in France.

[3] Almost exactly a century earlier there had been such a case among the Franks, when Charles the Fat was deposed and Odo, the defender of Paris, elevated to the throne (888).

[4] Charles had been made duke of Lower Lorraine by the German emperor. This passage in Adalbero's speech looks like something of an appeal to Frankish pride, or as we would say in these days, to national sentiment. Still it must be remembered that while a sense of common interest was undoubtedly beginning to develop among the peoples represented in the assembly at Senlis, these peoples were still far too diverse to be spoken of accurately as making up a unified nationality. Adalbero was indulging in a political harangue and piling up arguments for effect, without much regard for their real weight.

rather than on account of any wrong done by others. Make a decision, therefore, for the welfare rather than for the injury of the state. If you wish ill to your country, choose Charles to be king; if you have regard for its prosperity, choose Hugh, the illustrious duke. . . . Elect, then, the duke, a man who is

Election of Hugh Capet urged recommended by his conduct, by his nobility, and by his military following. In him you will find a defender, not only of the state, but also of your private interests. His large-heartedness will make him a father to you all. Who has ever fled to him for protection without receiving it? Who that has been deserted by his friends has he ever failed to restore to his rights?"

This speech was applauded and concurred in by all, and by unanimous consent the duke was raised to the throne. He was

The beginning of his reign crowned at Noyon[1] on the first of June[2] by the archbishop and the other bishops as king of the Gauls, the Bretons, the Normans, the Aquitanians, the Goths, the Spaniards and the Gascons.[3] Surrounded by the nobles of the king, he issued decrees and made laws according to royal custom, judging and disposing of all matters with success.

[1] Noyon was a church center about fifty miles north of Paris. That the coronation really occurred at this place has been questioned by some, but there seems to be small reason for doubting Richer's statement in the matter.

[2] M. Pfister in Lavisse, *Histoire de France*, Vol. II., p. 412, asserts that the coronation occurred July 3, 987.

[3] This method of describing the extent of the new king's dominion shows how far from consolidated the so-called Frankish kingdom really was. The royal domain proper, that is, the land over which the king had immediate control, was limited to a long fertile strip extending from the Somme to a point south of Orléans, including the important towns of Paris, Orléans, Étampes, Senlis, and Compiègne. Even this was not continuous, but was cut into here and there by the estates of practically independent feudal lords. By far the greater portion of modern France (the name in 987 was only beginning to be applied to the whole country) consisted of great counties and duchies, owing comparatively little allegiance to the king and usually rendering even less than they owed. Of these the most important was the county (later duchy) of Normandy, the county of Bretagne (Brittany), the county of Flanders, the county of Anjou, the county of Blois, the duchy of Burgundy, the duchy of Aquitaine, the county of Toulouse, the county of Gascony, and the county of Barcelona (south of the Pyrenees). The "Goths" referred to by Richer were the inhabitants of the "march," or border county, of Gothia along the Mediterranean coast between the lower Rhone and the Pyrenees (old Septimania).

CHAPTER XI.

ALFRED THE GREAT IN WAR AND IN PEACE

30. The Danes in England

THE earliest recorded visit of the Danes, or Northmen, to England somewhat antedates the appearance of these peoples on the Frankish coast in the year 800. In 787 three Danish vessels came to shore at Warham in Dorset and their sailors slew the unfortunate reeve who mistook them for ordinary foreign merchants and tried to collect port dues from them. Thereafter the British coasts were never free for many years at a time from the depredations of the marauders. In 793 the famous church at Lindisfarne, in Northumberland, was plundered; in 795 the Irish coasts began to suffer; in 833 a fleet of twenty-five vessels appeared at the mouth of the Thames; in 834 twelve hundred pillagers landed in Dorset; in 842 London and Rochester were sacked and their population scattered; in 850 a fleet of 350 ships carrying perhaps ten or twelve thousand men, wintered at the mouth of the Thames and in the spring caused London again to suffer; and from then on until the accession of King Alfred, in 871, destructive raids followed one another with distressing frequency.

The account of the Danish invasions given below is taken from a biography of King Alfred commonly attributed to Asser, a monk of Welsh origin connected with the monastery of St. David (later bishop of Sherborne) and a close friend and adviser of the great king. It gives us some idea of the way in which Alfred led his people through the darkest days in their history, and of the settlement known as the "Peace of Alfred and Guthrum" by which the Danish leader became a Christian and the way was prepared for the later division of the English country between the two contending peoples.

Source—Johannes Menevensis Asserius, *De rebus gestis Ælfredi Magni* [Asser, "The Deeds of Alfred the Great"], Chaps. 42–55 *passim*. Adapted from translation by J. A. Giles in *Six Old English Chronicles* (London, 1866), pp. 56–63.

In the year 871 Alfred, who up to that time had been of only secondary rank, while his brothers were alive, by God's permission, undertook the government of the whole kingdom, welcomed by all the people.   Indeed, if he had cared to, he might have done so earlier, even while his brother was still alive; [1] for in wisdom

Alfred becomes king (871) and other qualities he excelled all of his brothers, and, moreover, he was courageous and victorious in all his wars.   He became king almost against his will, for he did not think that he could alone withstand the numbers and the fierceness of the pagans, though even during the lifetime of his brothers he had carried burdens enough for many men.   And when he had ruled one month, with a small band of followers and on very unequal terms, he fought a battle with the entire army of the pagans.   This was at a hill called Wilton, on the south bank of the River Wily, from which river the whole of that district is named.[2]   And after a long and fierce engagement the pagans, seeing the danger they were in, and no longer able to meet the attacks of their enemies, turned their backs and fled.   But, oh, shame to say, they deceived the English, who pursued them too boldly, and, turning swiftly about, gained the victory.   Let no one be surprised to learn that the Christians had only a small number of men, for the Saxons had been worn out by eight battles with the pagans in one year.   In these they had slain one king, nine dukes, and innumerable troops of soldiers.   There had also been numberless skirmishes,

The struggle with the Danes both by day and by night, in which Alfred, with his ministers and chieftains and their men, were engaged without rest or relief against the pagans.   How many thousands of pagans fell in these skirmishes God only knows,

[1] That is, Ethelred I., whom Alfred succeeded.
[2] Wiltshire, on the southern coast, west of the Isle of Wight.

over and above the numbers slain in the eight battles before mentioned. In the same year the Saxons made peace with the invaders, on condition that they should take their departure, and
they did so.

In the year 877 the pagans, on the approach of autumn,
partly settled in Exeter[1] and partly marched for plunder into
Mercia.[2] The number of that disorderly horde increased every
day, so that, if thirty thousand of them were slain in one battle,
others took their places to double the number. Then King Alfred
commanded boats and galleys, i. e., long ships, to be built
throughout the kingdom, in order to offer battle by sea to
the enemy as they were coming.[3] On board these he placed
Alfred's plan sailors, whom he commanded to keep watch on
to meet the
pagans on the the seas. Meanwhile he went himself to Exe-
sea ter, where the pagans were wintering and, having
shut them up within the walls, laid siege to the town. He also
gave orders to his sailors to prevent the enemy from obtaining
any supplies by sea. In a short time the sailors were encountered
by a fleet of a hundred and twenty ships full of armed soldiers,
who were on their way to the relief of their countrymen. As soon
as the king's men knew that the ships were manned by pagan
soldiers they leaped to their arms and bravely attacked those
barbaric tribes. The pagans, who had now for almost a month
been tossed and almost wrecked among the waves of the sea,
fought vainly against them. Their bands were thrown into
confusion in a very short time, and all were sunk and drowned
in the sea, at a place called Swanwich.[4]

[1] The same as the modern city of the name.
[2] Mercia was one of the seven old Anglo-Saxon kingdoms. It lay east of
Wales.
[3] This marked a radical departure in methods of fighting the invaders.
On the continent, and hitherto in England, there had been no effort to prevent the enemy from getting into the country they proposed to plunder.
Alfred's creation of a navy was one of his wisest acts. Although the English had by this time grown comparatively unaccustomed to seafaring life
they contrived to win their first naval encounter with the enemy.
[4] In Dorsetshire.

In 878, which was the thirtieth year of King Alfred's life, the pagan army left Exeter and went to Chippenham. This latter place was a royal residence situated in the west of Wiltshire, on the eastern bank of the river which the Britons called the Avon. They spent the winter there and drove many of the inhabitants of the surrounding country beyond the sea by the force of their arms, and by the want of the necessities of life. They reduced almost entirely to subjection all the people of that country.

The same year, after Easter, King Alfred, with a few followers, made for himself a stronghold in a place called Athelney,[1] and

Alfred in refuge at Athelney

from thence sallied, with his companions and the nobles of Somersetshire, to make frequent assaults upon the pagans. Also, in the seventh week after Easter, he rode to Egbert's stone, which is in the eastern part of the wood that is called Selwood.[2] Here he was met by all the folk of Somersetshire and Wiltshire and Hampshire, who had not fled beyond the sea for fear of the pagans; and when they saw the king alive after such great tribulation they received him, as he deserved, with shouts of joy, and encamped there for one night. At dawn on the following day the king broke camp and went to Okely, where he encamped for one night. The next morning he moved to Ethandune[3] and there fought bravely and persistently against the whole army of the pagans.

The battle of Ethandune and the establishment of peace (878)

By the help of God he defeated them with great slaughter and pursued them flying to their fortification. He at once slew all the men and carried off all the booty that he could find outside the fortress, which he immediately laid siege to with his entire army. And when he had been there fourteen days the pagans, driven

[1] Athelney was in Somersetshire, northeast of Exeter, in the marshes at the junction of the Tone and the Parret.

[2] The modern Brixton Deverill, in Wiltshire, near Warminster.

[3] In Wiltshire, a little east of Westbury. In January the Danes had removed from Exeter to Chippenham. Edington (or Ethandune) was eight miles from the camp at the latter place. The Danes were first defeated in an open battle at Edington, and then forced to surrender after a fourteen days' siege at Chippenham.

by famine, cold, fear, and finally by despair, asked for peace on the condition that they should give the king as many hostages as he should ask, but should receive none from him in return. Never before had they made a treaty with any one on such terms. The king, hearing this, took pity upon them and received such hostages as he chose. Then the pagans swore that they would immediately leave the kingdom, and their king, Guthrum, promised to embrace Christianity and receive baptism at Alfred's hands. All of these pledges he and his men fulfilled as they had promised.[1]

31. Alfred's Interest in Education

As an epoch of literary and educational advancement the reign of Alfred in England (871–901) was in many respects like that of Charlemagne among the Franks (768–814). Like Charlemagne, Alfred grew up with very slight education, at least of a literary sort; but both sovereigns were strongly dissatisfied with their ignorance, and both made earnest efforts to overcome their own defects and at the same time to raise the standard of intelligence among their people at large. When one considers how crowded were the reigns of both with wars and the pressing business of administration, such devotion to the interests of learning appears the more deserving of praise.

In the first passage below, taken from Asser's life of Alfred, the anxiety of the king for the promotion of his own education and that of his children is clearly and strongly stated. We find him following Charlemagne's plan of bringing scholars from foreign countries. He brought them, too, from parts of Britain not under his direct control, and used them at the court, or in bishoprics, to perform the work of instruction. Curiously enough, whereas Charlemagne had found the chief of his Palace School, Alcuin, in England, Alfred was glad to secure the services of two men (Grimbald and John) who had made

[1] This so-called "Peace of Alfred and Guthrum" in 878 provided only for the acceptance of Christianity by the Danish leader. It is sometimes known as the treaty of Chippenham and is not to be confused with the treaty of Wedmore, of a few weeks later, by which Alfred and Guthrum divided the English country between them. The text of this second treaty will be found in Lee's *Source-Book of English History* (pp. 98–99), though the introductory statement there given is somewhat misleading. This assignment of the Danelaw to Guthrum's people may well be compared with the yielding of Normandy to Rollo by Charles the Simple in 911 [see p. 172].

their reputations in monasteries situated within the bounds of the old Frankish empire.

Aside from some native songs and epic poems, all the literature known to the Saxon people was in Latin, and but few persons in the kingdom knew Latin well enough to read it. The king himself did not, until about 887. It was supposed, of course, that the clergy were able to use the Latin Bible and the Latin ritual of the Church, but when Alfred came to investigate he found that even these men were often pretty nearly as ignorant as the people they were charged to instruct. What the king did, then, was to urge more study on the part of the clergy, under the direction of such men as Plegmund, Asser, Grimbald, John, and Werfrith. The people in general could not be expected to master a foreign language; hence, in order that they might not be shut off entirely from the first-hand use of books, Alfred undertook the translation of certain standard works from the Latin into the Saxon. Those thus translated were Boethius's *Consolations of Philosophy*, Orosius's *Universal History of the World*, Bede's *Ecclesiastical History of England*, and Pope Gregory the Great's *Pastoral Rule*. The second passage given below is Alfred's preface to his Saxon edition of the last-named book, taking the form of a letter to the scholarly Bishop Werfrith of Worcester. The *Pastoral Rule* [see p. 90] was written by Pope Gregory the Great (590–604) as a body of instructions in doctrine and conduct for the clergy. Alfred's preface, as a picture of the ruin wrought by the long series of Danish wars, is of the utmost importance in the study of ninth and tenth century England, as well as a most interesting revelation of the character of the great king.

Sources—(a) Asser, *De rebus gestis Ælfredi Magni.* Chaps. 75–78. Adapted from translation by J. A. Giles in *Six Old English Chronicles* (London, 1866), pp. 68–70.

      (b) King Alfred's West-Saxon Version of Pope Gregory's *Pastoral Rule*. Edited by Henry Sweet in the Publications of the Early English Text Society (London, 1871), p. 2.

(a)

Ethelwerd, the youngest [of Alfred's children],[1] by the divine counsels and the admirable prudence of the king, was consigned

[1] Ethelwerd was Alfred's fifth living child.

to the schools of learning, where, with the children of almost all the nobility of the country, and many also who were not noble, he prospered under the diligent care of his teachers. Books in both languages, namely, Latin and Saxon, were read in the school.[1]

The education of Alfred's children They also learned to write, so that before they were of an age to practice manly arts, namely, hunting and such pursuits as befit noblemen, they became studious and clever in the liberal arts. Edward[2] and Ælfthryth[3] were reared in the king's court and received great attention from their attendants and nurses; nay, they continue to this day with the love of all about them, and showing friendliness, and even gentleness, towards all, both natives and foreigners, and in complete subjection to their father. Nor, among their other studies which pertain to this life and are fit for noble youths, are they suffered to pass their time idly and unprofitably without learning the liberal arts; for they have carefully learned the Psalms and Saxon books, especially the Saxon poems, and are continually in the habit of making use of books.

In the meantime the king, during the frequent wars and other hindrances of this present life, the invasions of the pagans, and **The varied activities of the king** his own infirmities of body, continued to carry on the government, and to practice hunting in all its branches; to teach his workers in gold and artificers of all kinds, his falconers, hawkers and dog-keepers; to build houses, majestic and splendid, beyond all the precedents of his ancestors, by his new mechanical inventions; to recite the Saxon books, and especially to learn by heart the Saxon poems,

[1] This was, of course, not a school in the modern sense of the word. All that is meant is simply that young Ethelwerd, along with sons of nobles and non-nobles, received instruction from the learned men at the court. It had been customary before Alfred's day for the young princes and sons of nobles to receive training at the court, but not in letters.

[2] This was Edward the Elder who succeeded Alfred as king and reigned from 901 to 925. He was Alfred's eldest son.

[3] Ælfthryth was Alfred's fourth child. She became the wife of Baldwin II. of Flanders.

and to make others learn them.[1] And he alone never desisted from studying most diligently to the best of his ability. He attended the Mass and other daily services of religion. He was **His devout character** diligent in psalm-singing and prayer, at the hours both of the day and of the night. He also went to the churches, as we have already said, in the night-time to pray, secretly and unknown to his courtiers. He bestowed alms and gifts on both natives and foreigners of all countries. He was affable and pleasant to all, and curiously eager to investigate things unknown. Many Franks, Frisians, Gauls, pagans, Britons, Scots, and Armoricans,[2] noble and low-born, came voluntarily to his domain; and all of them, according to their nation and deserving, were ruled, loved, honored and enriched with money and power.[3] Moreover, the king was in the habit of hearing the divine Scriptures read by his own countrymen, or, if by any chance it so happened, in company with foreigners, and he attended to it with care and solicitude. His bishops, too, and all ecclesiastics, his earls and nobles, ministers[4] and friends, were loved by him with wonderful affection, and their sons, who were reared in the royal household, were no less dear to him than his own. He had them instructed in all kinds of good morals, and, among other things, never ceased to teach them letters night and day.

But, as if he had no consolation in all these things, and though

[1] Among other labors in behalf of learning, Alfred made a collection of the ancient epics and lyrics of the Saxon people. Unfortunately, except in the case of the epic Beowulf, only fragments of these have survived. Beowulf was, so far as we know, the earliest of the Saxon poems, having originated before the migration to Britain, though it was probably put in its present form by a Christian monk of the eighth century.

[2] Armorica was the name applied in Alfred's time to the region southward from the mouth of the Seine to Brittany.

[3] There is a good deal of independent evidence that Alfred was peculiarly hospitable to foreigners. He delighted in learning from them about their peoples and experiences.

[4] The word in the original is *ministeriales*. It is not Saxon but Franco-Latin and is an instance of the Frankish element in Asser's vocabulary. Here, as among the Franks, the *ministeriales* were the officials of second-rate importance surrounding the king, the highest being known as the *ministri*.

he suffered no other annoyance, either from within or without,
he was harassed by daily and nightly affliction, so that he

Regret at his lack of education complained to God and to all who were admitted
to his intimate fondness, that Almighty God had
made him ignorant of divine wisdom, and of
the liberal arts—in this emulating the pious, the wise, and
wealthy Solomon, king of the Hebrews, who at first, despising all
present glory and riches, asked wisdom of God and found both,
namely, wisdom and worldly glory; as it is written: "Seek first
the kingdom of God and his righteousness, and all these things
shall be added unto you." But God, who is always the observer
of the thoughts of the mind within and the author of all good
intentions, and a most plentiful helper that good desires may be
formed (for He would not prompt a man to good intentions, unless
He also amply supplied that which the man justly and properly
wishes to have) stimulated the king's mind within: as it is written,
"I will hearken what the Lord God will say concerning me."
He would avail himself of every opportunity to procure co-workers
in his good designs, to aid him in his strivings after wisdom that
he might attain to what he aimed at. And, like a prudent bee,
which, going forth in summer with the early morning from its cell,
steers its rapid flight through the uncertain tracks of ether and
descends on the manifold and varied flowers of grasses, herbs,
and shrubs, discovering that which pleases most, that it may
bear it home, so did he direct his eyes afar and seek without
that which he had not within, that is, in his own kingdom.[1]

But God at that time, as some relief to the king's anxiety,

Learned men from Mercia brought to the English court yielding to his complaint, sent certain lights to
illuminate him, namely, Werfrith, bishop of the
church of Worcester, a man well versed in divine
Scripture, who, by the king's command, first turned the books

---

[1] This comparison of the gathering of learning to the operations of a
bee in collecting honey is very common among classical writers and also
among those of the Carolingian renaissance. It occurs in Lucretius, Seneca,
Macrobius, Alcuin, and the poet Candidus.

of the Dialogues of Pope Gregory and Peter, his disciple, from
Latin into Saxon, and sometimes putting sense for sense, inter-
preted them with clearness and elegance. After him was Plegmund,[1] a Mercian by birth, archbishop of the church of Canterbury, a venerable man, and endowed with wisdom; Ethelstan
also,[2] and Werwulf,[3] his priests and chaplains,[4] Mercians by birth
and learned. These four had been invited from Mercia by King
Alfred, who exalted them with many honors and powers in the
kingdom of the West Saxons, besides the privileges which Archbishop Plegmund and Bishop Werfrith enjoyed in Mercia. By
their teaching and wisdom the king's desires increased unceas-
ingly, and were gratified. Night and day, whenever he had
leisure, he commanded such men as these to read books to him,
for he never suffered himself to be without one of them; wherefore
he possessed a knowledge of every book, though of himself he
could not yet understand anything of books, for he had not yet
learned to read anything.[5]

But the king's commendable desire could not be gratified even

Grimbald and John brought from the continent in this; wherefore he sent messengers beyond the sea to Gaul, to procure teachers, and he invited from thence Grimbald,[6] priest and monk, a venerable man and good singer, adorned with every kind of

[1] Plegmund became archbishop of Canterbury in 890, but it is probable
that he was with Alfred some time before his election to the primacy.

[2] This Ethelstan was probably the person of that name who was consecrated bishop of Ramsbury in 909.

[3] From another document it appears that Werwulf was a friend of Bishop
Werfrith in Mercia before either took up residence at Alfred's court.

[4] In Chap. 104 of Asser's biography the *capellani* are described as supplying
the king with candles, by whose burning he measured time. The word
capellanus is of pure Frankish origin and was originally applied to the clerks
(*clerici capellani*) who were charged with the custody of the cope (*cappa*)
of St. Martin, which was kept in the *capella*. From this the term *capella*
came to mean a room especially devoted to religious uses, that is, a chapel.
It was used in this sense as early as 829 in Frankland. Whether by *capellanus*
Asser meant mere clerks, or veritable "chaplains" in the later sense, cannot
be known, though his usage was probably the latter.

[5] Chapter 87 of Asser informs us that Alfred mastered the art of reading
in the year 887.

[6] Grimbald came from the Flemish monastery of St. Bertin at St. Omer.
He was recommended to Alfred by Fulco, archbishop of Rheims, who had

ecclesiastical training and good morals, and most learned in holy Scripture. He also obtained from thence John,[1] also priest and monk, a man of most energetic talents, and learned in all kinds of literary science, and skilled in many other arts. By the teaching of these men the king's mind was much enlarged, and he enriched and honored them with much influence.

(b)

King Alfred greets Bishop Werfrith with loving words and with friendship.

I let it be known to thee that it has very often come into my mind what wise men there formerly were throughout England,

Alfred writes to Bishop Werfrith on the state of learning in England both within the Church and without it; also what happy times there were then and how the kings who had power over the nation in those days obeyed God and His ministers; how they cherished peace, morality, and order at home, and at the same time enlarged their territory abroad; and how they prospered both in war and in wisdom. Often have I thought, also, of the sacred orders, how zealous they were both in teaching and learning, and in all the services they owed to God; and how foreigners came to this land in search of wisdom and instruction, which things we should now have to get from abroad if we were to have them at all.

So general became the decay of learning in England that there were very few on this side of the Humber [2] who could understand the rituals [3] in English, or translate a letter from Latin into

once been abbot of St. Bertin. We do not know in what year Grimbald went to England, though there is some evidence that it was not far from 887.

[1] John the Old Saxon is mentioned by Alfred as his mass-priest. It is probable that he came from the abbey of Corbei on the upper Weser. Not much is known about the man, but if he was as learned as Asser says he was, he must have been a welcome addition to Alfred's group of scholars particularly as the language which he used was very similar to that of the West Saxons in England.

[2] That is, south of the Humber.

[3] The service of the Church.

English; and I believe that there were not many beyond the Humber who could do these things. There were so few, in fact, that I cannot remember a single person south of the Thames when I came to the throne. Thanks be to Almighty God that we now have some teachers among us. And therefore I enjoin thee to free thyself, as I believe thou art ready to do, from worldly matters, that thou mayst apply the wisdom which God has given thee wherever thou canst. Consider what punishments would come upon us if we neither loved wisdom ourselves nor allowed other men to obtain it. We should then care for the name only of Christian, and have regard for very few of the Christian virtues.

When I thought of all this I remembered also how I saw the country before it had been all ravaged and burned; how the churches throughout the whole of England stood filled with treasures and books. There was also a great multitude of God's servants, but they had very little knowledge of books, for they could not understand anything in them because they were not written in their own language.[1] When I remembered all this I

Learning in the days before the Danish invasions wondered extremely that the good and wise men who were formerly all over England and had learned perfectly all the books, did not wish to translate them into their own language. But again I soon answered myself and said: "Their own desire for learning was so great that they did not suppose that men would ever become so indifferent and that learning would ever so decay; and they wished, moreover, that wisdom in this land might increase with our knowledge of languages." Then I remembered how the law was first known in Hebrew and when the Greeks had learned it how they translated the whole of it into their own tongue,[2] and

---

[1] They were written, of course, in Latin.

[2] By the middle of the third century A. D. as many as three different translations of the Old Testament into Greek had been made—those of Aquila, Theodotion, and Symmochus. These eventually took fixed shape in the so-called Septuagint version of the Old Testament.

all other books besides. And again the Romans, when they had learned it, translated the whole of it into their own language.[1] And also all other Christian nations translated a part of it into their languages.

Therefore it seems better to me, if you agree, for us also to translate some of the books which are most needful for all men

Plan to translate Latin books into English

to know into the language which we can all understand. It shall be your duty to see to it, as can easily be done if we have tranquility enough,[2] that all the free-born youth now in England, who are rich enough to be able to devote themselves to it, be set to learn as long as they are not fit for any other occupation, until they are well able to read English writing. And let those afterwards be taught more in the Latin language who are to continue learning and be promoted to a higher rank.

When I remembered how the knowledge of Latin had decayed through England, and yet that many could read English writing, I began, among other various and manifold troubles of this kingdom, to translate into English the book which is called in

The translation of Pope Gregory's Pastoral Care

Latin *Pastoralis*, and in English *The Shepherd's Book*, sometimes word for word, and sometimes according to the sense, as I had learned it from Plegmund, my archbishop, and Asser, my bishop, and Grimbald, my mass-priest, and John, my mass-priest. And when I had learned it, as I could best understand it and most clearly interpret it, I translated it into English.

I will send a copy of this book to every bishopric in my kingdom, and on each copy there shall be a clasp worth fifty mancuses.[3] And I command in God's name that no man take the

[1] About the year 385 St. Jerome revised the older Latin translation of the New Testament and translated the Old Testament directly from the Hebrew. This complete version gradually superseded all others for the whole Latin-reading Church, being known as the "Vulgate," that is, the version commonly accepted. It was in the form of the Vulgate that the Scriptures were known to the Saxons and all other peoples of western Europe.

[2] In other words, sufficient relief from the Danish incursions.

[3] The *mancus* was a Saxon money value equivalent to a mark.

Med. His.—13

clasp from the book, or the book from the minster.[1]   It is uncertain how long there may be such learned bishops as, thanks be to God, there now are almost everywhere; therefore, I wish these copies always to remain in their places, unless the bishop desires to take them with him, or they be loaned out anywhere, or any one wishes to make a copy of them.

32. Alfred's Laws

· HERE are a few characteristic laws included by Alfred in the code which he drew up on the basis of old customs and the laws of some of the earlier Saxon kings.   On the nature of the law of the early Germanic peoples, see p. 59.

Source—Text in Benjamin Thorpe, *The Ancient Laws and Institutes of England* (London, 1840), pp. 20-44 *passim.*

If any one smite his neighbor with a stone, or with his fist, and he nevertheless can go out with a staff, let him get him a physician and do his work as long as he himself cannot.

If an ox gore a man or a woman, so that they die, let it be stoned, and let not its flesh be eaten. The owner shall not be liable if the ox were wont to push with its horns for two or three days before, and he knew it not; but if he knew it, and would not shut it in, and it then shall have slain a man or a woman, let it be stoned; and let the master be slain, or the person killed be paid for, as the "witan"[2] shall decree to be right.

Injure ye not the widows and the stepchildren, nor hurt them anywhere; for if ye do otherwise they will cry unto me and I will hear them, and I will slay you with my sword; and I will cause that your own wives shall be widows, and your children shall be stepchildren.

If a man strike out another's eye, let him pay sixty shillings,

[1] A minster was a church attached to a monastery.
[2] The witan was the gathering of "wisemen"—members of the royal family, high officials in the Church, and leading nobles—about the Anglo-Saxon king to assist in making ordinances and supervising the affairs of state.

and six shillings, and six pennies, and a third part of a penny, as 'bot.'[1] If it remain in the head, and he cannot see anything with it, let one-third of the 'bot' be remitted.

If a man strike out another's tooth in the front of his head,

Penalties for various crimes of violence let him make 'bot' for it with eight shillings; if it be the canine tooth, let four shillings be paid as 'bot.' A man's grinder is worth fifteen shillings.

If the shooting finger be struck off, the 'bot' is fifteen shillings; for its nail it is four shillings.

If a man maim another's hand outwardly, let twenty shillings be paid him as 'bot,' if he can be healed; if it half fly off, then shall forty shillings be paid as 'bot.'

[1] Compensation rendered to an injured person.

CHAPTER XII.

THE ORDEAL

33. Tests by Hot Water, Cold Water, and Fire

AMONG the early Germans the settling of disputes and the testing of the guilt or innocence of an accused person were generally accomplished through the employment of one or both of two very interesting judicial practices—compurgation and the ordeal. According to the German conception of justice, when one person was accused of wrong-doing by another and chose to defend himself, he was not under obligation to prove directly that he did not commit the alleged misdeed; rather it was his business to produce, if he could, a sufficient number of persons who would take oath that they believed the accused to be a trustworthy man and that he was telling the truth when he denied that he was guilty. The persons brought forward to take this oath were known as compurgators, or "co-swearers," and the legal act thus performed was called compurgation. The number of compurgators required to free a man was usually from seven to twelve, though it varied greatly among different tribes and according to the rank of the parties involved. Naturally they were likely to be relatives or friends of the accused man, though it was not essential that they be such. It was in no wise expected that they be able to give facts or evidence regarding the case; in other words, they were not to serve at all as witnesses, such as are called in our courts to-day.

If the accused succeeded in producing the required number of compurgators, and they took the oath in a satisfactory manner, the defendant was usually declared to be innocent and the case was dropped. If, however, the compurgators were not forthcoming, or there appeared some irregularity in their part of the procedure, resort would ordinarily be had to the ordeal. The ordeal was essentially an appeal to the gods for decision between two contending parties. It was based on the belief that the gods would not permit an innocent person to suffer by reason of an unjust accusation and that when the opportunity was offered under certain prescribed conditions the divine power would indicate who was in the right and who in the wrong. ʿThe ordeal, having its origin far back in the times when the Germans were pagans and before their settlements in the Roman Empire, was retained in common usage after the Christianizing and civilizing of the barbarian tribes. The administering of it simply passed from the old pagan priests to the Christian clergy, and the appeals were directed to the Christian's God instead of to Woden and Thor. Under Christian influence, the wager of battle (or personal combat to settle judicial questions), which had been exceedingly common, was discouraged as much as possible, and certain new modes of appeal to divine authority were introduced. Throughout the earlier Middle Ages the chief forms of the ordeal were: (1) the ordeal by walking through fire; (2) the ordeal by hot iron, in which the accused either carried a piece of hot iron a certain distance in his hands or walked barefoot over pieces of the same material; (3) the ordeal by hot water, in which the accused was required to plunge his bared arm into boiling water and bring forth a stone or other object from the bottom; (4) the ordeal by cold water, in which the accused was thrown, bound hand and foot, into a pond or stream, to sink if he were innocent, to float if he were guilty; (5) the ordeal of the cross, in which the accuser and accused stood with arms outstretched in the form of a cross until one of them could endure the strain of the unnatural attitude no longer; (6) the ordeal of the sacrament, in which the accused partook of the sacrament, the idea being that divine vengeance would certainly fall upon him in so doing if he were guilty; (7) the ordeal of the bread and cheese, in which the accused, made to swallow morsels of bread and cheese, was expected to choke if he were guilty; and (8) the judicial combat, which was generally reserved for freemen, and which, despite the opposition of the Church, did not die out until the end of the mediæval period.

The three passages quoted below illustrate, respectively, the ordeal by hot water, by cold water, and by fire. The first (a) is a story told by the Frankish historian Gregory of Tours [see p. 46]. The second (b) is an explanation of the cold water ordeal written by Hincmar, an archbishop of Rheims in the ninth century. The third (c) is an account, by Raymond of Agiles, of how Peter Bartholomew was put to the test by the ordeal of fire. This incident occurred at Antioch during the first crusade. Peter Bartholomew had just discovered a lance which he claimed was the one thrust into the side of Christ at the crucifixion and, some of the crusaders being skeptical as to the genuineness of the relic, the discoverer was submitted to the ordeal by fire to test the matter.

Sources—(a) Gregorius Episcopus Turonensis, *Libri Miraculorum* [Gregory of Tours, "Books of Miracles"], Chap. 80. Text in *Monumenta Germaniæ Historica, Scriptores Merovingicarum*, Vol. I., p. 542. Translated by Arthur C. Howland in *Univ. of Pa. Translations and Reprints*, Vol. IV., No. 4, pp. 10–11.

(b) Hincmari Archiepiscopi Rhemensis, *De divortio Lotharii regis et Tetbergæ reginæ* [Hincmar, Archbishop of Rheims, "The Divorce of King Lothair and Queen Teutberga"], Chap. 6. Text in Migne, *Patrologiæ Cursus Completus*, Second Series, Vol. CXXV., cols. 668–669. Translated by Arthur C. Howland, *ibid.*

(c) Raimundus de Agiles, *Historia Francorum qui ceperunt Jerusalem* [Raimond of Agiles, "History of the Franks who captured Jerusalem"], Chap. 18. Text in Migne, *Patrologiæ Cursus Completus*, Second Series, Vol. CLV., cols. 619–621.

An Arian presbyter, disputing with a deacon of our religion, made venomous assertions against the Son of God and the Holy Ghost, as is the habit of that sect.[1] But when the deacon had discoursed a long time concerning the reasonableness of our faith, and the heretic, blinded by the fog of unbelief, continued to reject the truth (according as it is written, "Wisdom shall not enter

[1] The principal difference between Arian and orthodox Christians arose out of the much discussed problem as to whether Jesus was of the same substance as God and co-eternal with Him. The Arians maintained that while Jesus was truly the Son of God, He must necessarily have been inferior to the Father, else there would be two gods. Arianism was formally condemned by the Council of Nicaea in 325, but it continued to be the prevalent belief in many parts of the Roman Empire; and when the Germans became Christians, it was Christianity of the Arian type (except in the case of the Franks) that they adopted—because it happened to be this creed that the missionaries carried to them. The Franks became orthodox Christians, which in part explains their close relations with the papacy in the earlier Middle Ages [see p. 50]. Of course Gregory of Tours, who relates the story of the Arian presbyter, as a Frank, was a hater of Arianism, and therefore we need not be surprised at the expressions of contempt which he employs in referring to "the heretic."

the mind of the wicked") the former said: "Why weary ourselves with long discussions? Let acts demonstrate the truth.

A challenge to the ordeal by hot water Let a kettle be heated over the fire and some one's ring be thrown into the boiling water. Let him who shall take it from the heated liquid be approved as a follower of the truth, and afterwards let the other
party be converted to the knowledge of this truth. And do thou
understand, O heretic, that this our party will fulfill the conditions with the aid of the Holy Ghost; thou shalt confess that there
is no inequality, no dissimilarity, in the Holy Trinity." The
heretic consented to the proposition and they separated, after
appointing the next morning for the trial. But the fervor of
faith in which the deacon had first made this suggestion began
to cool through the instigation of the enemy [i. e., Satan]. Rising
with the dawn, he bathed his arm in oil and smeared it with
ointment. But nevertheless he made the round of the sacred
places and called in prayer on the Lord. What more shall I say?
About the third hour they met in the market place. The people
came together to see the show. A fire was lighted, the kettle was

Preparations for the ordeal placed upon it, and when it grew very hot the ring was thrown into the boiling water. The
deacon invited the heretic to take it out of the water first. But
he promptly refused, saying, "Thou who didst propose this trial
art the one to take it out." The deacon, all of a tremble, bared
his arm. And when the heretic presbyter saw it besmeared with
ointment he cried out: "With magic arts thou hast thought to
protect thyself, that thou hast made use of these salves, but what
thou hast done will not avail." While they were thus quarreling,
there came up a deacon from Ravenna named Iacinthus, who
inquired what the trouble was about. When he learned the truth,
he drew his arm out from under his robe at once and plunged his
right hand into the kettle. Now the ring that had been thrown
in was a little thing and very light, so that it was tossed about
by the water as chaff would be blown about by the wind; and,

searching for it a long time, he found it after about an hour.
Meanwhile the flame beneath the kettle blazed up mightily, so
that the greater heat might make it difficult for the ring to be
followed by the hand; but the deacon extracted it at length and
Result of the   suffered no harm, protesting rather that at the
ordeal   bottom the kettle was cold while at the top it was
just pleasantly warm.   When the heretic beheld this, he was
greatly confused and audaciously thrust his hand into the kettle
saying, "My faith will aid me." As soon as his hand had been
thrust in, all the flesh was boiled off the bones clear up to the
elbow. And so the dispute ended.

(b)

Now the one about to be examined is bound by a rope and cast
into the water because, as it is written, "each one shall be holden
with the cords of his iniquity." And it is manifest that he is bound
for two reasons, namely, that he may not be able to practice any
fraud in connection with the judgment, and that he may be drawn
out at the right time if the water should receive him as innocent,
so that he perish not. For as we read that Lazarus, who had been
dead four days (by whom is signified each one buried under a
load of crimes), was buried wrapped in bandages and, bound by
the same bands, came forth from the sepulchre at the word of
How the or-   the Lord and was loosed by the disciples at His
deal of cold   command; so he who is to be examined by this
water is to be
conducted   judgment is cast into the water bound, and is
drawn forth again bound, and is either immediately set free by
the decree of the judges, being purged, or remains bound until the time of his purgation and is then examined by the court.
. . . And in this ordeal of cold water whoever, after the in-
vocation of God, who is the Truth, seeks to hide the truth by a
lie, cannot be submerged in the waters above which the voice of
the Lord God has thundered; for the pure nature of the water
recognizes as impure, and therefore rejects as inconsistent with

itself, such human nature as has once been regenerated by the waters of baptism and is again infected by falsehood.

(c)

All these things were pleasing to us and, having enjoined on him a fast, we declared that a fire should be prepared upon the day on which the Lord was beaten with stripes and put upon the cross for our salvation. And the fourth day thereafter was the day before the Sabbath. So when the appointed day came round, a fire was prepared after the noon hour. The leaders and the people to the number of 60,000 came together. The priests **Preparations for the ordeal by fire** were there also with bare feet, clothed in ecclesiastical garments. The fire was made of dry olive branches, covering a space thirteen feet long; and there were two piles, with a space about a foot wide between them. The height of these piles was four feet. Now when the fire had been kindled so that it burned fiercely, I, Raimond, in the presence of the whole multitude, said: "If Omnipotent God has spoken to this man face to face, and the blessed Andrew has shown him our Lord's lance while he was keeping his vigil,[1] let him go through the fire unharmed. But if it is false, let him be burned, together with the lance, which he is to carry in his hand." And all responded on bended knees, "Amen."

The fire was growing so hot that the flames shot up thirty cubits high into the air and scarcely any one dared approach **Peter Bartholomew passes through the flames** it. Then Peter Bartholomew, clothed only in his tunic and kneeling before the bishop of Albar,[2] called God to witness that "he had seen Him face to face on the cross, and that he had heard from Him those things above written." . . . Then, when the bishop had placed the lance in his hand, he knelt and made the sign of

---

[1] The story as told by Raimond of Agiles was that Peter Bartholomew had been visited by Andrew the Apostle, who had revealed to him the spot where the lance lay buried beneath the Church of St. Peter in Antioch.

[2] Albar, or Albara, was a town southeast of Antioch, beyond the Orontes.

the cross and entered the fire with the lance, firm and unter-
rified. For an instant's time he paused in the midst of the flames,
and then by the grace of God passed through. . . . But
when Peter emerged from the fire so that neither his tunic was
burned nor even the thin cloth with which the lance was wrapped
up had shown any sign of damage, the whole people received him,
after he had made over them the sign of the cross with the lance
in his hand and had cried, "God help us!" All the people, I
say, threw themselves upon him and dragged him to the ground
and trampled on him, each one wishing to touch him, or to get a
piece of his garment, and each thinking him near some one else.
And so he received three or four wounds in the legs where the
flesh was torn away, his back was injured, and his sides bruised.
Peter had died on the spot, as we believe, had not Raimond Pelet,
a brave and noble soldier, broken through the wild crowd with a
band of friends and rescued him at the peril of their lives. . . .
After this, Peter died in peace at the hour appointed to him by
God, and journeyed to the Lord; and he was buried in the place
where he had carried the lance of the Lord through the fire.[1]

[1] Owing to Peter's early death after undergoing the ordeal, a serious controversy arose as to whether he had really passed through it without injury
from the fire. His friends ascribed his death to the wounds he had received
from the enthusiastic crowd, but his enemies declared that he died from
burns.

CHAPTER XIII.

THE FEUDAL SYSTEM

34. Older Institutions Involving Elements of Feudalism

THE history of the feudal system in Europe makes up a very large part of the history of the Middle Ages, particularly of the period between the ninth and the fourteenth centuries. This is true because feudalism, in one way or another, touched almost every phase of the life of western Europe during this long era. More than anything else, it molded the conditions of government, the character and course of war, the administration of justice, the tenure of land, the manner of everyday life, and even the relations of the Church with sovereigns and people. "Coming into existence," says a French historian, "in the obscure period that followed the dissolution of the Carolingian empire, the feudal régime developed slowly, without the intervention of a government, without the aid of a written law, without any general understanding among individuals; rather only by a gradual transformation of customs, which took place sooner or later, but in about the same way, in France, Italy, Christian Spain, and Germany. Then, toward the end of the eleventh century, it was transplanted into England and into southern Italy, in the twelfth and thirteenth into the Latin states of the East, and beginning with the fourteenth into the Scandinavian countries. This régime, established thus not according to a general plan but by a sort of natural growth, never had forms and usages that were everywhere the same. It is impossible to gather it up into a perfectly exact picture, which would not be in contradiction to several cases." [1]

The country in which feudalism reached its fullest perfection was France and most of the passages here given to illustrate the subject

[1] Charles Seignobos, *The Feudal Régime* (translated in "Historical Miscellany" series), New York, 1904, p. 1.

have to do with French life and institutions. In France, speaking generally, feudalism took shape during the ninth and tenth centuries, developed steadily until the thirteenth, and then slowly declined, leaving influences on society which have not yet all disappeared. When the system was complete—say by the tenth century—we can see in it three essential elements which may be described as the personal, the territorial, and the governmental. The personal element, in brief, was the relation between lord and vassal under which the former gave protection in return for the latter's fidelity. The territorial element was the benefice, or fief, granted to the vassal by the lord to be used on certain conditions by the former while the title to it remained with the latter. The governmental element was the rights of jurisdiction over his fief usually given by a lord to his vassal, especially if the fief were an important one. At one time it was customary to trace back all these features of the feudal system to the institutions of Rome. Later it became almost as customary to trace them to the institutions of the early Germans. But recent scholarship shows that it is quite unnecessary, in fact very misleading, to attempt to ascribe them wholly to either Roman or German sources, or even to both together. All that we can say is that in the centuries preceding the ninth these elements all existed in the society of western Europe and that, while something very like them ran far back into old Roman and German times, they existed in sixth and seventh century Europe primarily because conditions were then such as to *demand* their existence. Short extracts to illustrate the most important of these old feudal elements are given below. It should constantly be borne in mind that no one of these things—whether vassalage, the benefice, or the immunity—was in itself feudalism. Most of them could, and did, exist separately, and it was only when they were united, as commonly became the case in the ninth and tenth centuries, that the word feudalism can properly be brought into use, and then only as applied to the complete product.

(1) VASSALAGE

FOR the personal element in feudalism it is possible to find two prototypes, one Roman and the other German. The first was the institution of the later Empire known as the *patrocinium*—the relation established between a powerful man (patron) and a weak one (client) when the latter pledged himself to perform certain services for the former in return for protection. The second was the German *comitatus*—a band of young warriors who lived with a prince or noble and went on campaigns under his leadership. The *patrocinium* doubtless survived in Roman Gaul long after the time of the Frankish invasion, but it is not likely that the *comitatus* ever played much part in that country. It seems that, with the exception of the king, the Frankish men of influence did not have bands of personal followers after the settlement on Roman soil. But, wholly aside from earlier practices, the conditions which the conquest, and the later struggles of the rival kings, brought about made it still necessary for many men who could not protect themselves or their property to seek the favor of some one who was strong enough to give them aid. The name which came to be applied to the act of establishing this personal relation was *commendation*. The man who promised the protection was the lord, and the man who pledged himself to serve the lord and be faithful to him was the *homo*, after the eighth century known as the vassal (*vassus*). In the eighth century, when the power of the Merovingian kings was ebbing away and the people were left to look out for themselves, large numbers entered into the vassal relation; and in the ninth century, when Carolingian power was likewise running low and the Northmen, Hungarians, and Saracens were ravaging the country, scarcely a free man was left who did not secure for himself the protection of a lord. The relation of vassalage was first recognized as legal in the capitularies of Charlemagne. Here is a Frankish formula of commendation dating from the seventh century—practically a blank application in which the names of the prospective lord and vassal could be inserted as required.

Source—Eugène de Rozière, *Recueil Général des Formules usitées dans l'Empire des Francs du Ve au Xe siècle* ["General Collection of Formulae employed in the Frankish Empire from the Fifth to the Tenth Century"], Vol. I., p. 69. Translated by Edward P. Cheyney in *Univ. of Pa. Translations and Reprints*, Vol. IV., No. 3, pp. 3-4.

To that magnificent lord ————, I, ————. Since it is well known to all how little I have wherewith to feed and clothe myself, I have therefore petitioned your piety, and your good-will has decreed to me, that I should hand myself over, or commend myself, to your guardianship, which I have thereupon done; that is to say, in this way, that you should aid and succor me, as well with food as with clothing, according as I shall be able to serve you and deserve it.

And so long as I shall live I ought to provide service and honor to you, compatible with my free condition;[1] and I shall not, during the time of my life, have the right to withdraw from your control or guardianship; but must remain during the days of my life under your power or defense. Wherefore it is proper that if either of us shall wish to withdraw himself from these agreements, he shall pay ———— shillings to the other party, and this agreement shall remain unbroken.[2]

(Wherefore it is fitting that they should make or confirm between themselves two letters drawn up in the same form on this matter; which they have thus done.)

(2) The Benefice

The benefice, or grant of land to a vassal by a lord, by the Church, or by the king, had its origin among the Franks in what were known as the *precaria* of the Church. At the time of the Frankish settlement in Gaul, it was quite customary for the Church to grant land to men in answer to *preces* ("prayers," or requests), on condition that it might be recalled at any time and that the temporary holder should be unable to enforce any claims as against the owner. For the use of such land a small rent in money, in produce, or in service was usually paid. This form of tenure among the Franks was at first restricted to church lands, but by the eighth century lay owners, even the king himself, had come to employ it. The term *precarium* dropped out of use and all such grants, by whomsoever made, came to be known as benefices ("bene-

---

[1] A man was not supposed in any way to sacrifice his freedom by becoming a vassal and the lord's right to his service would be forfeited if this principle were violated.

[2] The relation of lord and vassal was, at this early time, limited to the lifetime of the two parties. When one died, the other was liberated from his contract. But in the ninth and tenth centuries vassalage became generally hereditary.

fits," or "favors"). The ordinary vassal might or might not once have had land in his own name, but if he had such he was expected to give over the ownership of it to his lord and receive it back as a benefice to be used on certain prescribed conditions. In time it became common, too, for lords to grant benefices out of their own lands to landless vassals. A man could be a vassal without having a benefice, but rarely, at least after the eighth century, could he have a benefice without entering into the obligations of vassalage. Benefices were at first granted by the Church with the understanding that they might be recalled at any time; later they were granted by Church, kings, and seigniors for life, or for a certain term of years; and finally, in the ninth and tenth centuries, they came generally to be regarded as hereditary. By the time the hereditary principle had been established, the name "fief" (*feodum*, *feudum*—whence our word feudal) had supplanted the older term "benefice." The tendency of the personal element of vassalage and the territorial element of the benefice, or fief, to merge was very strong, and by the tenth century nearly every vassal was also a fief-holder. The following formulæ belong to the seventh century. The first (a) is for the grant of lands to a church or monastery; the second (b) for their return to the grantor as a *precarium*—or what was known a century later as a benefice.

Source—Eugène de Rozière, *Recueil Général des Formules*, Vol. I., p. 473. Translated by E. P. Cheyney in *Univ. of Pa. Translations and Reprints*, Vol. IV., No. 3, pp. 6–8.

(a)

I, ———, in the name of God. I have settled in my mind that I ought, for the good of my soul, to make a gift of something from my possessions, which I have therefore done. And this is what I hand over, in the district named ———, in the place of which the name is ————, all those possessions of mine which there my father left me at his death, and which, as against my brothers, or as against my co-heirs, the lot legitimately brought me in the division,[1] or those which I was able afterward

---

[1] Casting lots for the property of a deceased father was not uncommon among the Franks. All sons shared in the inheritance, but particular parts of the property were often assigned by lot.

to add to them in any way, in their whole completeness, that is to say, the courtyard with its buildings, with slaves, houses, **Description of** lands (cultivated and uncultivated), meadows, **property yield-** woods, waters, mills, etc. These, as I have said **ed to a church** **or monastery** before, with all the things adjacent or belonging to them, I hand over to the church, which was built in honor of Saint ————, to the monastery which is called ————, where the Abbot ———— is acknowledged to rule regularly over God's flock. On these conditions: that so long as life remains in my body, I shall receive from you as a benefice for **Terms of** usufruct the possessions above described, and the **the contract** due payment I will make to you and your successors each year, that is ———— [amount named]. And my son shall have the same possessions for the days of his life, and shall make the above-named payment; and if my children should survive me, they shall have the same possessions during the days of their lives and shall make the same payment; and if God shall give me a son from a legitimate wife, he shall have the same possessions for the days of his life only, after the death of whom the same possessions, with all their improvements, shall return to your hands to be held forever; and if it should be my chance to beget sons from a legitimate marriage, these shall hold the same possessions after my death, making the above-named payment, during the time of their lives. If not, however, after my death, without subterfuge of any kind, by right of your authority, the same possessions shall revert to you, to be retained forever. If any one, however (which I do not believe will ever occur)—if I myself, or any other person—shall wish to violate the firmness and validity of this grant, the order of truth opposing him, may his falsity in no degree succeed; and **Penalty for** for his bold attempt may he pay to the afore- **faithlessness** said monastery double the amount which his ill-ordered cupidity has been prevented from abstracting; and moreover let him be indebted to the royal authority for ————

solidi of gold; and, nevertheless, let the present charter remain inviolate with all that it contains, with the witnesses placed below.

Done in ————, publicly, those who are noted below being present, or the remaining innumerable multitude of people.

(b)

In the name of God, I, Abbot ————, with our commissioned brethren. Since it is not unknown how you, ————, by the suggestion of divine exhortation, did grant to ———— [monastery named], to the church which is known to be constructed in honor of Saint ————, where we by God's authority exercise our pastoral care, all your possessions which you seemed to have in the district named, in the vill [village] named, which your father on his death bequeathed to you there, or which by your own labor you were able to gain there, or which, as against your brother or against ————, a co-heir,

The property again described a just division gave you, with courtyard and buildings, gardens and orchards, with various slaves, ———— by name, houses, lands, meadows, woods (cultivated and uncultivated), or with all the dependencies and appurtenances belonging to it, which it would be extremely long to enumerate, in all their completeness; but

Returned to the original owner to be used by him afterwards, at your request, it has seemed proper to us to cede to you the same possessions to be held for usufruct; and you will not neglect to pay at annual periods the due *census* [i. e., the rental] hence, that is ———— [amount named]. And if God should give you a son by your legal wife, he shall have the same possessions for the days of his life only, and shall not presume to neglect the above payment, and similarly your sons which you are seen to have at present, shall do for the days of their lives; after the death of whom, all the possessions above-named shall revert to us and our successors perpetually. Moreover, if no sons shall have been begotten by you, immediately after your death, without any harmful contention, the possessions shall revert to the rulers or guardians of the above-named church, forever. Nor may any one, either ourselves or our successors, be successful in a rash attempt inordinately to destroy these agreements, but just as the time has demanded in the present *precaria*, may that be sure to endure unchanged which we, with the consent of our brothers, have decided to confirm.

Done in ————, in the presence of ———— and of others whom it is not worth while to enumerate. [Seal of the same abbot who has ordered this *precaria* to be made.]

(3) The Immunity

The most important element in the governmental phase of feudalism was what was known as the immunity. In Roman law immunity meant exemption from taxes and public services and belonged especially to the lands owned personally by the emperors. Such exemptions were, however, sometimes allowed to the lands of imperial officers and of men in certain professions, and in later times to the lands held by the Church. How closely this Roman immunity was connected with the feudal immunity of the Middle Ages is not clear. Doubtless the institution survived in Gaul, especially on church lands, long after the Frankish conquest. It is best, however, to look upon the typical Frankish immunity as of essentially independent origin. From the time of Clovis, the kings were accustomed to make grants of the sort to land-holding abbots and bishops, and by the time of Charlemagne nearly all such prelates had been thus favored. But such grants were not confined to ecclesiastics. Even in the seventh and eighth centuries lay holders of royal benefices often received the privileges of the immunity also. Speaking generally, the immunity exempted the lands to which it applied from the jurisdiction of the local royal officials, especially of the counts. The lands were supposed to be none the less ultimately subject to the royal authority, but by the grant of immunity the sovereign took their financial and judicial administration from the counts, who would ordinarily have charge, and gave it to the holders of the lands.   The counts were forbidden to enter the specified territories to collect taxes or fines, hold courts, and sometimes even to arrange for military service.   The layman, or the bishop, or the abbot, who held the lands performed these services and was responsible only to the crown for them.   The king's chief object in granting the immunity was to reward or win the support of the grantees and to curtail the authority of his local representatives, who in many cases threatened to become too powerful for the good of the state; but by every such grant the sovereign really lost some of his own power, and this practice came to be in no small measure responsible for the weakness of monarchy in feudal times.

The first of the extracts below (a) is a seventh-century formula for the grant of an immunity by the king to a bishop.   The second (b) is a grant made by Charlemagne, in 779, confirming an old immunity enjoyed by the monastery at Châlons-sur-Saône.

Sources—(a) Text in *Monumenta Germaniæ Historica, Legum Sectio V., Formulæ*, Part I., pp. 43–44.

(b) Text in *Monumenta Germaniæ Historica, Leges* (Pertz ed.), Vol. II., p. 287.   Adapted from translation in Ephraim Emerton, *Introduction to the Study of the Middle Ages* (new ed., Boston, 1903), p. 246.

(a)

We believe that we give our royal authority its full splendor if, with benevolent intentions, we bestow upon churches—or upon any persons—the favors which they merit, and if, with the aid of God, we give a written assurance of the continuance of these favors.   We wish, then, to make known that at the request of a prelate, lord of ————— [the estate named] and bishop of ————— [the church named], we have accorded to him, for the sake of our eternal salvation, the following benefits: that in the domains of the bishop's church, both those which it possesses

A formula for a grant of immunity to-day and those which by God's grace it may later acquire, no public official shall be permitted to enter, either to hold courts or to exact fines, on any account; but let these prerogatives be vested in full in the bishop and his successors.   We ordain therefore that neither you nor your subordinates,[1] nor those who come after you, nor any person endowed with a public office, shall ever enter the domains of that church, in whatever part of our kingdom they may be situated, either to hold trials or to collect fines. All the taxes and other revenues which the royal treasury has a right to demand from the people on the lands of the said church, whether they be freemen or slaves, Romans or barbarians, we now bestow on the said church for our future salvation, to be used by the officials of the church forever for the best interests of the church.

(b)

Charles, by the grace of God King of the Franks and Lombards and Patrician of the Romans, to all having charge of our affairs, both present and to come:

By the help of the Lord, who has raised us to the throne of this kingdom, it is the chief duty of our clemency to lend a gracious ear to the need of all, and especially ought we devoutly to regard that which we are persuaded has been granted by preceding kings to church foundations for the saving of souls, and not to deny fitting benefits, in order that we may deserve to be partakers of the reward, but to confirm them in still greater security.

Now the illustrious Hubert, bishop and ruler of the church of St. Marcellus, which lies below the citadel of Châlons,[2] where the

The old immunity enjoyed by the monastery at Châlons

precious martyr of the Lord himself rests in the body, has brought it to the attention of our Highness that the kings who preceded us, or our lord and father of blessed memory, Pepin, the preceding king, had by their charters granted complete immunities to that monastery, so that in the towns or on the lands

---

[1] The grant of immunity was thus brought to the attention of the count in whose jurisdiction the exempted lands lay.

[2] Châlons-sur-Saône was about eighty miles north of the junction of the Saône with the Rhone. It should not be confused with Châlons-sur-Marne where the battle was fought with Attila's Huns in 451.

belonging to it no public judge, nor any one with power of hearing cases or exacting fines, or raising sureties, or obtaining lodging or entertainment, or making requisitions of any kind, should enter.

Moreover, the aforesaid bishop, Hubert, has presented the original charters of former kings, together with the confirmations of them, to be read by us, and declares the same favors to be preserved to the present day; but desiring the confirmation of our clemency, he prays that our authority may confirm this grant anew to the monastery.

Wherefore, having inspected the said charters of former kings, we command that neither you, nor your subordinates, nor your successors, nor any person having judicial powers, shall presume to enter into the villages which may at the present time be in possession of that monastery, or which hereafter may have been bestowed by God-fearing men [or may be about to be so bestowed].[1] Let no public officer enter for the hearing of cases, **The immunity** or for exacting fines, or procuring sureties, or **confirmed** obtaining lodging or entertainment, or making any requisitions; but in full immunity, even as the favor of former kings has been continued down to the present day, so in the future also shall it, through our authority, remain undiminished. And if in times past, through any negligence of abbots, or lukewarmness of rulers, or the presumption of public officers, anything has been changed or taken away, removed or withdrawn, from these immunities, let it, by our authority and favor, be restored. And, further, let neither you nor your subordinates presume to infringe upon or violate what we have granted.

But if there be any one, *dominus*,[2] *comes* [count], *domesticus*,[3] *vicarius*,[4] or one vested with any judicial power whatsoever, by

---

[1] There is some doubt at this point as to the correct translation. That given seems best warranted.
[2] *Dominus* was a common name for a lord.
[3] A member of the king's official household.
[4] A subordinate officer under the count [see p. 176, note 3].

the indulgence of the good or by the favor of pious Christians or kings, who shall have presumed to infringe upon or violate these **Penalties for its violation** immunities, let him be punished with a fine of six hundred *solidi*,[1] two parts to go to the library of this monastery, and the third part to be paid into our treasury, so that impious men may not rejoice in violating that which our ancestors, or good Christians, may have conceded or granted. And whatever our treasury may have had a right to expect from this source shall go to the profit of the men of this church of St. Marcellus the martyr, to the better establishment of our kingdom and the good of those who shall succeed us.

And that this decree may firmly endure we have ordered it to be confirmed with our own hand under our seal.

35. The Granting of Fiefs

THE most obvious feature of feudalism was a peculiar divided tenure of land under which the title was vested in one person and the use in another. The territorial unit was the fief, which in extent might be but a few acres, a whole county, or even a vast region like Normandy or Burgundy. Fiefs were granted to vassals by contracts which bound both grantor and grantee to certain specific obligations. The two extracts below are examples of the records of such feudal grants, bearing the dates 1167 and 1200 respectively. It should be remembered, however, that fiefs need not necessarily be land. Offices, payments of money, rights to collect tolls, and many other valuable things might be given by one man to another as fiefs in just the same way that land was given. Du Cange, in his *Glossarium Mediæ et Infimæ Latinitatis*, mentions eighty-eight different kinds of fiefs, and it has been said that this does not represent more than one-fourth of the total number. Nevertheless, the typical fief consisted of land. The term might therefore be defined in general as the land for which the vassal, or hereditary possessor, rendered to the lord, or hereditary proprietor, services of a special character which were considered honorable, such as military aid and attendance at courts.

[1] See p. 61, note 2.

Sources—(a) Nicolas Brussel, *Nouvel Examen de l'Usage général des Fiefs en France pendant le XI, le XII, le XIII, et le XIVe Siècle* ["New Examination of the Customs of Fiefs in the 11th, the 12th, the 13th, and the 14th Century"], Paris, 1727, Vol. I., p. 3, note. Translated by Edward P. Cheyney in *Univ. of Pa. Translations and Reprints*, Vol. IV., No. 3, pp. 15–16.

(b) Maximilien Quantin, *Recueil de Pièces du XIIIe Siècle* ["Collection of Documents of the Thirteenth Century"], Auxerre, 1873, No. 2, pp. 1–2. Translated by Cheyney, *ibid.*

(a)

In the name of the Holy and Undivided Trinity, Amen. I, Louis,[1] by the grace of God king of the French, make known to all present as well as to come, that at Mante in our presence, Count Henry of Champagne[2] conceded the fief of Savigny to

The count of Champagne grants a fief to the bishop of Beauvais

Bartholomew, bishop of Beauvais,[3] and his successors. And for that fief the said bishop has made promise and engagement for one knight and justice and service to Count Henry;[4] and he also agreed that the bishops who shall come after him will do likewise. In order that this may be understood and known to posterity we have caused the present charter to be attested by our seal. Done at Mante, in the year of the Incarnate Word, 1167; present in our palace those whose names and seals are appended: seal of Thiebault, our steward; seal of Guy, the butler; seal of Matthew, the chamberlain; seal of Ralph, the constable. Given by the hand of Hugh, the chancellor.

(b)

I, Thiebault, count palatine of Troyes,[5] make known to those present and to come that I have given in fee[6] to Jocelyn d'Avalon

[1] Louis VII., king of France, 1137–1180.
[2] The county of Champagne lay to the east of Paris. It was established by Charlemagne and, while at first insignificant, grew until by the twelfth and thirteenth centuries it was one of the most important in France.
[3] Beauvais was about sixty miles northwest of Paris.
[4] That is, the bishop of Beauvais was bound to furnish his lord, the count of Champagne, the service of one knight for his army, besides ordinary feudal obligations.
[5] The county of Troyes centered about the city of that name on the upper Seine. It was eventually absorbed by Champagne.
[6] As a fief.

and his heirs the manor which is called Gillencourt,[1] which is of
the castellanerie [2] of La Ferté-sur-Aube; and whatever the same
Jocelyn shall be able to acquire in the same manor I have granted
to him and his heirs in enlargement of that fief. I have granted,
moreover, to him that in no free manor of mine will I retain men
who are of this gift.[3] The same Jocelyn, moreover, on account
of this has become my liege man, saving, however, his allegiance
to Gerad d'Arcy, and to the lord duke of Bur-
gundy, and to Peter, count of Auxerre.[4] Done
at Chouaude, by my own witness, in the year of
the Incarnation of our Lord 1200, in the month of January.
Given by the hand of Walter, my chancellor.

A grant by
Count Thie-
bault

36. The Ceremonies of Homage and Fealty

THE personal relation between lord and vassal was established by
the double ceremony of homage and fealty. Homage was the act by
which the vassal made himself the man (*homo*) of the lord, while fealty
was the oath of fidelity to the obligations which must ordinarily be
assumed by such a man. The two were really distinct, though because
they almost invariably went together they finally became confounded in
the popular mind. The details of the ceremonies varied much in different times and places, but, in general, when homage was to be performed,
the prospective vassal presented himself before his future seigneur

[1] A manor, in the general sense, was a feudal estate.
[2] A castellanerie was a feudal holding centering about a castle.
[3] That is, Count Thiebault promises Jocelyn not to deprive him of the
services of men who rightfully belong on the manor which is being granted.
[4] Here is an illustration of the complexity of the feudal system. Count
Thiebault is Jocelyn's *fourth* lord, and loyalty and service are owed to all
of the four at the same time. Accordingly, Thiebault must be content with
only such allegiance of his new vassal as will not involve a breach of the
contracts which Jocelyn has already entered into with his other lords.
For example, Thiebault could not expect Jocelyn to aid him in war against
the duke of Burgundy, for Jocelyn is pledged to fidelity to that duke. In
general, when a man had only one lord he owed him full and unconditional
allegiance (*liege homage*), but when he became vassal to other lords he could
promise them allegiance only so far as would not conflict with contracts
already entered into. It was by no means unusual for a man to have
several lords, and it often happened that A was B's vassal for a certain
piece of land while at the same time B was A's vassal for another piece.
Not infrequently the king himself was thus a vassal of one or more of his
own vassals.

bareheaded and without arms; knelt, placed his hands in those of the seigneur, and declared himself his man; then he was kissed by the seigneur and lifted to his feet. In the act of fealty, the vassal placed his hand upon sacred relics, or upon the Bible, and swore eternal faithfulness to his seigneur. The so-called "act of investiture" generally followed, the seigneur handing over to the vassal a bit of turf, a stick, or some other object symbolizing the transfer of the usufruct of the property in question. The whole process was merely a mode of establishing a binding contract between the two parties. Below we have: (a) a mediæval definition of homage, taken from the customary law of Normandy; (b) an explanation of fealty, given in an old English law-book; (c) a French chronicler's account of the rendering of homage and fealty to the count of Flanders in the year 1127; and (d) a set of laws governing homage and fealty, written down in a compilation of the ordinances of Saint Louis (king of France, 1226–1270), but doubtless showing substantially the practice in France for a long time before King Louis's day.

Sources—(a) *L'Ancienne Coutume de Normandie* ["The Old Custom of Normandy"], Chap. 29.

    (b) Sir Thomas Lyttleton, *Treatise of Tenures in French and English* (London, 1841), Bk. II., Chap. 2, p. 123.

    (c) Galbert de Bruges, *De Multro, Traditione, et Occisione gloriosi Karoli comitis Flandriarum* ["Concerning the Murder, Betrayal, and Death of the glorious Charles, Count of Flanders"]. Text in Henri Pirenne, *Histoire du Meurtre de Charles le Bon, comte de Flandre, par Galbert de Bruges* (Paris, 1891). Translated by Edward P. Cheyney in *Univ. of Pa. Translations and Reprints*, Vol. IV., No. 3, p. 18.

    (d) *Les Établissements de Saint Louis* ["The Ordinances of St. Louis"], Bk. II., Chap. 19. Text in Paul Viollet's edition (Paris, 1881), Vol. II., pp. 395–398

(a)

Homage is a pledge to keep faith in respect to matters that are right and necessary, and to give counsel and aid. He who

A Norman definition of homage

would do homage ought to place his hands between those of the man who is to be his lord, and speak these words: "I become your man, to keep faith with you against all others, saving my allegiance to the duke of Normandy."

(b)

And when a free tenant shall swear fealty to his lord, let him place his right hand on the book [1] and speak thus: "Hear thou this, my lord, that I will be faithful and loyal to you and will keep my pledges to you for the lands which I claim to hold of

The oath of fealty   you, and that I will loyally perform for you the services specified, so help me God and the saints."

Then he shall kiss the book; but he shall not kneel when he swears fealty, nor take so humble a posture as is required in homage.

(c)

Through the whole remaining part of the day those who had been previously enfeoffed by the most pious count Charles, did homage to the count,[2] taking up now again their fiefs and offices and whatever they had before rightfully and legitimately obtained. On Thursday, the seventh of April, homages were again made to the count, being completed in the following order of faith and security:

First they did their homage thus. The count asked if he was willing to become completely his man, and the other replied,

The rendering of homage and fealty to the count of Flanders   "I am willing"; and with clasped hands, surrounded by the hands of the count, they were bound together by a kiss. Secondly, he who had done homage gave his fealty to the representative

of the count in these words, "I promise on my faith that I will in future be faithful to Count William, and will observe my homage to him completely, against all persons, in good faith and without deceit." Thirdly, he took his oath to this upon the relics of the saints. Afterwards, with a little rod which the count held in his hand, he gave investitures to all who by this agree-

---

[1] The Bible. Sometimes only the Gospels were used.
[2] Charles, count of Flanders, had just died and had been succeeded by his son William. All persons who had received fiefs from the deceased count were now brought together to renew their homage and fealty to the new count.

ment had given their security and homage and accompanying oath.

(d)

If any one would hold from a lord in fee, he ought to seek his lord within forty days. And if he does not do it within forty days, the lord may and ought to seize his fief for default of homage, and the things which are found there he should seize without compensation; and yet the vassal should be obliged to pay to his lord the redemption.[1] When any one wishes to enter into the fealty of a lord, he ought to seek him, as we have said above, and should speak as follows: "Sir, I request you, as my lord, to **An ordinance** put me in your fealty and in your homage for **of St. Louis on** such and such a thing situated in your fief, which **homage and fealty** I have bought." And he ought to say from what man, and this one ought to be present and in the fealty of the lord;[2] and whether it is by purchase or by escheat[3] or by inheritance he ought to explain; and with his hands joined, to speak as follows: "Sir, I become your man and promise to you fealty for the future as my lord, towards all men who may live or die, rendering to you such service as the fief requires, making to you your relief as you are the lord." And he ought to say whether for guardianship,[4] or as an escheat, or as an inheritance, or as a purchase.

The lord should immediately reply to him: "And I receive you and take you as my man, and give you this kiss as a sign of faith, saving my right and that of others," according to the usage of the various districts.

---

[1] Such a case as this would be most apt to arise when a lord died and a vassal failed to renew his homage to the successor; or when a vassal died and his heir failed to do homage as was required.

[2] This law would apply also to a case where a man who is already a vassal of a lord should acquire from another vassal of the same lord some additional land and so become indebted to the lord for a new measure of fealty.

[3] Reversion to the original proprietor because of failure of heirs.

[4] Such land might be acquired for temporary use only, i. e., for guardianship, during the absence or disability of its proprietor.

37. The Mutual Obligations of Lords and Vassals

THE feudal relation was essentially one of contract involving recipro-
cal relations between lord and vassal. In the following letter, written
in the year 1020 by Bishop Fulbert of Chartres [1] to the duke of Aquitaine, we find laid down the general principles which ought to govern
the discharge of these mutual obligations. It is affirmed that there
were six things that no loyal vassal could do, and these are enumerated
and explained. Then comes the significant statement that these
negative duties must be supplemented with positive acts for the service
and support of the lord. What some of these acts were will appear in
the extracts in § 38. Bishop Fulbert points out also that the lord is
himself bound by feudal law not to do things detrimental to the safety,
honor, or prosperity of his vassal. The letter is an admirable statement of the spirit of the feudal system at its best. Already by 1020 a
considerable body of feudal customs having the force of law had come
into existence and it appears that Fulbert had made these customs the
subject of some special study before answering the questions addressed
to him by Duke William.

Source—Text in Martin Bouquet, *Recueil des Historiens des Gaules et de la
        France* [" Collection of the Historians of Gaul and of France "],
        Vol. X., p. 463.

To William, most illustrious duke of the Aquitanians, Bishop
Fulbert, the favor of his prayers:

Requested to write something regarding the character of
fealty, I have set down briefly for you, on the authority of the
books, the following things. He who takes the oath of fealty to

**What the vas-
sal owes the
lord**
his lord ought always to keep in mind these six
things: what is harmless, safe, honorable, useful,
easy, and practicable.[2] *Harmless*, which means
that he ought not to injure his lord in his body; *safe*, that he
should not injure him by betraying his confidence or the defenses upon which he depends for security; *honorable*, that he

---

[1] Chartres was somewhat less than twenty miles southwest of Paris.
[2] The terms used in the original are *incolume, tutum, honestum, utile, facile,
et possibile.*

should not injure him in his justice, or in other matters that relate to his honor; *useful*, that he should not injure him in his property; *easy*, that he should not make difficult that which his lord can do easily; and *practicable*, that he should not make impossible for the lord that which is possible.

However, while it is proper that the faithful vassal avoid these injuries, it is not for doing this alone that he deserves his holding: for it is not enough to refrain from wrongdoing, unless that which is good is done also. It remains, therefore, that in the same six things referred to above he should faithfully advise and aid his lord, if he wishes to be regarded as worthy of his benefice and to be safe concerning the fealty which he has sworn.

The lord also ought to act toward his faithful vassal in the same manner in all these things. And if he fails to do this, he **The obligations of the lord** will be rightfully regarded as guilty of bad faith, just as the former, if he should be found shirking, or willing to shirk, his obligations would be perfidious and perjured.[1]

I should have written to you at greater length had I not been busy with many other matters, including the rebuilding of our city and church, which were recently completely destroyed by a terrible fire. Though for a time we could not think of anything but this disaster, yet now, by the hope of God's comfort, and of yours also, we breathe more freely again.

38. Some of the More Important Rights of the Lord

THE obligations of vassals to lords outlined in the preceding selection were mainly of a moral character—such as naturally grew out of the general idea of loyalty and fidelity to a benefactor. They were largely

---

[1] In the English customary law of the twelfth century we read that, "it is allowable to any one, without punishment, to support his lord if any one assails him, and to obey him in all legitimate ways, except in theft, murder, and in all such things as are not conceded to any one to do and are reckoned infamous by the laws;" also that, "the lord ought to do likewise equally with counsel and aid, and he may come to his man's assistance in his vicissitudes in all ways."—Thorpe, *Ancient Laws and Institutes*, Vol. I., p. 590.

negative and were rather vague and indefinite. So far as they went, they were binding upon lords and vassals alike. There were, however, several very definite and practical rights which the lords possessed with respect to the property and persons of their dependents. Some of these were of a financial character, some were judicial, and others were military. Five of the most important are illustrated by the passages given below.

(a) AIDS

UNDER the feudal system the idea prevailed that the vassal's purse as well as his body was to be at the lord's service. Originally the right to draw upon his vassals for money was exercised by the lord whenever he desired, but by custom this ill-defined power gradually became limited to three sorts of occasions when the need of money was likely to be especially urgent, i. e., when the eldest son was knighted, when the eldest daughter was married, and when the lord was to be ransomed from captivity. In the era of the crusades, the starting of the lord on an expedition to the Holy Land was generally regarded as another emergency in which an aid might rightfully be demanded. The following extract from the old customary law of Normandy represents the practice in nearly all feudal Europe.

Source—*L'Ancienne Coutume de Normandie*, Chap. 35.

In Normandy there are three chief aids. The first is to help make the lord's eldest son a knight; the second is to marry his eldest daughter; the third is to ransom the body of the lord from prison when he shall be taken captive during a war for the

The three aids   duke.[1] By this it appears that the *aide de chevalerie* [knighthood-aid] is due when the eldest son of the lord is made a knight. The eldest son is he who has the dignity of primogeniture.[2] The *aide de mariage* [marriage-aid] is

[1] The duke of Normandy. Outside of Normandy, of course, other feudal princes would be substituted.

[2] It was the feudal system that first gave the eldest son in France a real superiority over his brothers. This may be seen most clearly in the change wrought by feudalism whereby the old Frankish custom of allowing all the sons to inherit their father's property equally was replaced by the mediæval rule of primogeniture (established by the eleventh century) under which the younger sons were entirely, or almost entirely, excluded from the inheritance.

due when the eldest daughter is married. The *aide de rançon* [ransom-aid] is due when it is necessary to deliver the lord from the prisons of the enemies of the duke. These aids are paid in some fiefs at the rate of half a relief, and in some at the rate of a third.[1]

(b) MILITARY SERVICE

FROM whatever point of view feudalism is regarded—whether as a system of land tenure, as a form of social organization, or as a type of government—the military element in it appears everywhere important. The feudal period was the greatest era of war the civilized world has ever known. Few people between the tenth and fourteenth centuries, except in the peasant classes, were able to live out their lives entirely in peace. Of greatest value to kings and feudal magnates, greater even than money itself, was a goodly following of soldiers; hence the almost universal requirement of military service by lords from their vassals. Fiefs were not infrequently granted out for no other purpose than to get the military service which their holders would owe. The amount of such service varied greatly in different times and places, but the following arrangement represents the most common practice.

Source—*Les Établissements de Saint Louis*, Bk. I., Chap. 65. Text in Paul Viollet's edition (Paris, 1881), Vol. II., pp. 95–96.

The baron and the vassals of the king ought to appear in his army when they shall be summoned, and ought to serve at their own expense for forty days and forty nights, with whatever number of knights they owe.[2] And he possesses the right to exact **The conditions of military service** from them these services when he wishes and when he has need of them. If, however, the king shall wish to keep them more than forty days and forty nights at their own expense, they need not remain unless

[1] Relief is the term used to designate the payment made to the lord by the son of the deceased vassal before taking up the inheritance [see p. 225]. The "custom" says that sometimes the amount paid as an aid to the lord was equal to half that paid as relief and sometimes it was only a third.

[2] The number of men brought by a vassal to the royal army depended on the value of his fief and the character of his feudal contract. Greater vassals often appeared with hundreds of followers.

they desire.[1] But if he shall wish to retain them at his cost for the defense of the kingdom, they ought lawfully to remain. But if he shall propose to lead them outside of the kingdom, they need not go unless they are willing, for they have already served their forty days and forty nights.

(c) WARDSHIP AND MARRIAGE

VERY important among the special prerogatives of the feudal lord was his right to manage, and enjoy the profits of, fiefs inherited by minors. When a vassal died, leaving an heir who was under age, the lord was charged with the care of the fief until the heir reached his or her majority. On becoming of age, a young man was expected to take control of his fief at once. But a young woman remained under wardship until her marriage, though if she married under age she could get possession of her fief immediately, just as she would had she waited until older. The control of the marriage of heiresses was largely in the hands of their lords, for obviously it was to the lord's interest that no enemy of his, nor any shiftless person, should become the husband of his ward. The lord could compel a female ward to marry and could oblige her to accept as a husband one of the candidates whom he offered her; but it was usually possible for the woman to purchase exemption from this phase of his jurisdiction. After the thirteenth century the right of wardship gradually declined in France, though it long continued in England. The following extract from the customs of Normandy sets forth the typical feudal law on the subject.

Source—*L'Ancienne Coutume de Normandie*, Chap. 33.

Heirs should be placed in guardianship until they reach the age of twenty years; and those who hold them as wards should

---

[1] This provision rendered the ordinary feudal army much more inefficient than an army made up of paid soldiers. Under ordinary circumstances, when their forty days of service had expired, the feudal troops were free to go home, even though their doing so might force the king to abandon a siege or give up a costly campaign only partially completed. By the thirteenth century it had become customary for the king to accept extra money payments instead of military service from his vassals. With the revenues thus obtained, soldiers could be hired who made war their profession and who were willing to serve indefinitely.

give over to them all the fiefs which came under their control by reason of wardship, provided they have not lost anything by judicial process. . . . When the heirs pass out of the condition of wardship, their lords shall not impose upon them any reliefs for their fiefs, for the profits of wardship shall be reckoned in place of the relief.

When a female ward reaches the proper age to marry, she should be married by the advice and consent of her lord, and by

The marriage of a female ward the advice and consent of her relatives and friends, according as the nobility of her ancestry and the value of her fief may require; and upon her marriage the fief which has been held in guardianship should be given over to her. A woman cannot be freed from wardship except by marriage; and let it not be said that she is of age until she is twenty years old. But if she be married at the age at which it is allowable for a woman to marry, the fact of her marriage makes her of age and delivers her fief from wardship.

The fiefs of those who are under wardship should be cared for attentively by their lords, who are entitled to receive the

The lord's obligation to care for the fief of his ward produce and profits.[1] And in this connection let it be known that the lord ought to preserve in their former condition the buildings, the manorhouses, the forests and meadows, the gardens, the ponds, the mills, the fisheries, and the other things of which he has the profits. And he should not sell, destroy, or remove the woods, the houses, or the trees.

(d) RELIEFS

A relief was a payment made to the lord by an heir before entering upon possession of his fief. The history of reliefs goes back to the time when benefices were not hereditary and when, if a son succeeded his father in the usufruct of a piece of property, it was regarded as an un-

---

[1] Every fief-holder was supposed to render some measure of military service. As neither a minor nor a woman could do this personally, it was natural that the lord should make up for the deficiency by appropriating the produce of the estate during the period of wardship.

usual thing—a special favor on the part of the owner to be paid for by the new tenant. Later, when fiefs had become almost everywhere hereditary, the custom of requiring reliefs still survived. The amount was at first arbitrary, being arranged by individual bargains; but in every community, especially in France, the tendency was toward a fixed custom regarding it. Below are given some brief extracts from English Treasury records which show how men in England between the years 1140 and 1230 paid the king for the privilege of retaining the fiefs held by their fathers.

Source—Thomas Madox, *History and Antiquities of the Exchequer of the Kings of England* (London, 1769), Vol. I., pp. 312–322 *passim*.

Walter Hait renders an account of 5 marks of silver for the relief of the land of his father.

Walter Brito renders an account of £66, 13s. and 4d. for the relief of his land.

Richard of Estre renders an account of £15 for the relief for 3 knights' fees which he holds from the honor of Mortain.

Walter Fitz Thomas, of Newington, owes 28s. 4d. for having a fourth part of one knight's fee which had been seized into the hand of the king for default of relief.

John of Venetia renders an account of 300 marks for the fine of his land and for the relief of the land which was his father's which he held from the king *in capite*.[1]

John de Balliol owes £150 for the relief of 30 knights' fees which Hugh de Balliol, his father, held from the king *in capite*, that is 100s. for each fee.

Peter de Bruce renders an account of £100 for his relief for the barony which was of Peter his father.

(e) FORFEITURE

THE lord's most effective means of compelling his vassals to discharge their obligations was his right to take back their fiefs for breach of feudal contract. Such a breach, or felony, as it was technically

[1] Tenants *in capite* in England were those who held their land by direct royal grant.

called, might consist in refusal to render military service or the required aids, ignoring the sovereign authority of the lord, levying war against the lord, dishonoring members of the lord's family, or, as in the case below, refusing to obey the lord's summons to appear in court. In practice the lords generally found it difficult to enforce the penalty of forfeiture and after the thirteenth century the tendency was to substitute money fines for dispossession, except in the most aggravated cases. The following is an account of the condemnation of Arnold Atton, a nobleman of south France, by the feudal court of Raymond, count of Toulouse, in the year 1249. The penalty imposed was the loss of the valuable château of Auvillars.

Source—Teulet, *Layettes du Trésor des Cartes* ["Bureau of Treasury Accounts"], No. 3778, Vol. III., p. 70. Translated by Edward P. Cheyney in *Univ. of Pa. Translations and Reprints*, Vol. IV., No. 3. pp. 33–34.

Raymond, by the grace of God count of Toulouse, marquis of Provence, to the nobleman Arnold Atton, viscount of Lomagne, greeting:

Let it be known to your nobility by the tenor of these presents what has been done in the matter of the complaints which we have made about you before the court of Agen; that you have not taken the trouble to keep or fulfill the agreements sworn by you to us, as is more fully contained in the instrument drawn up there, sealed with our seal by the public notary; and that you have refused contemptuously to appear before the said court for the purpose of doing justice, and have otherwise committed multiplied and great delinquencies against us. As your faults

The court's sentence upon Arnold Atton have required, the aforesaid court of Agen has unanimously and concordantly pronounced sentence against you, and for these matters have condemned you to hand over and restore to us the château of Auvillars and all that land which you hold from us in fee, to be had and held by us by right of the obligation by which you have bound it to us for fulfilling and keeping the said agreements.

Likewise it has declared that we are to be put into possession of the said land and that it is to be handed over to us, on account of your contumacy, because you have not been willing to appear before the same court on the days which were assigned to you. Moreover, it has declared that you shall be held and required to restore the said land in whatsoever way we wish to receive it, with few or many, in peace or in anger, in our own person, by right of lordship. Likewise it has declared that you shall restore to us all the expenses which we have incurred, or the court itself has incurred, on those days which were assigned to you, or because of those days, and has condemned you to repay these to us.[1]

Moreover, it has declared that the nobleman Gerald d'Armagnac, whom you hold captive, you shall liberate, and deliver him free to us. We demand, moreover, by right of our lordship that you liberate him.

We call, therefore, upon your discretion in this matter, strictly enjoining you and commanding that you obey the aforesaid sentences in all things and fulfill them in all respects and in no way delay the execution of them.

39. The Peace and the Truce of God

WAR rather than peace was the normal condition of feudal society. Peasants were expected to settle their disputes in the courts of law, but lords and seigneurs possessed a legal right to make war upon their enemies and were usually not loath to exercise it. Private warfare was indeed so common that it all the time threatened seriously the lives and property of the masses of the people and added heavily to the afflictions which flood, drought, famine, and pestilence brought repeatedly upon them. The first determined efforts to limit, if not to abolish, the ravages of private war were made by the Church, partly because

[1] Apparently the king's court had been assembled several times to consider the charges against Viscount Atton, but had been prevented from taking action because of the latter's failure to appear. At last the court decided that it was useless to delay longer and proceeded to condemn the guilty noble and send him a statement of what had been done. He was not only to lose his château of Auvillars but also to reimburse the king for the expenses which the court had incurred on his account.

the Church itself often suffered by reason of them, partly because its ideal was that of peace and security, and partly because it recognized its duty as the protector of the poor and oppressed. Late in the tenth century, under the influence of the Cluniacs [see p. 245], the clergy of France, both secular and regular, began in their councils to promulgate decrees which were intended to establish what was known as the Peace of God. These decrees, which were enacted by so many councils between 989 and 1050 that they came to cover pretty nearly all France, proclaimed generally that any one who should use violence toward women, peasants, merchants, or members of the clergy should be excommunicated. The principle was to exempt certain classes of people from the operations of war and violence, even though the rest of the population should continue to fight among themselves. It must be said that these decrees, though enacted again and again, had often little apparent effect.

Effort was then made in another direction. From about 1027 the councils began to proclaim what was known as the Truce of God, sometimes alone and sometimes in connection with the Peace. The purport of the Truce of God was that all men should abstain from warfare and violence during a certain portion of each week, and during specified church festivals and holy seasons. At first only Sunday was thus designated; then other days, until the time from Wednesday night to Monday morning was all included; then extended periods, as Lent, were added, until finally not more than eighty days remained of the entire year on which private warfare was allowable. As one writer has stated it, "the Peace of God was intended to protect certain classes at all times and the Truce to protect all classes at certain times." It was equally difficult to secure the acquiescence of the lawless nobles in both, and though the efforts of the Church were by no means without result, we are to think of private warfare as continuing quite common until brought gradually to an end by the rise of strong monarchies, by the turning of men to commerce and trade, and by the drawing off of military energies into foreign and international wars.

The decree given below, which combines features of both the Peace and the Truce, was issued by the Council of Toulouges (near Perpignan) in 1041, or, as some scholars think, in 1065. Its substance was many times reënacted, notably by the Council of Clermont, in 1095, upon the occasion of the proclamation of the first Crusade. It should have procured about 240 days of peace in every year and reduced war to about 120 days, but, like the others, it was only indifferently observed.

Source—Text in Martin Bouquet, *Recueil des Historiens des Gaules et de la France* ["Collection of the Historians of Gaul and of France"], Paris, 1876, Vol. XI., pp. 510–511.

1. This Peace has been confirmed by the bishops, by the abbots, by the counts and viscounts and the other God-fearing nobles in this bishopric, to the effect that in the future, beginning with this day, no man may commit an act of violence in a church, **Acts of violence forbidden in or near churches** or in the space which surrounds it and which is covered by its privileges, or in the burying-ground, or in the dwelling-houses which are, or may be, within thirty paces of it.

2. We do not include in this measure the churches which have been, or which shall be, fortified as châteaux, or those in which plunderers and thieves are accustomed to store their ill-gotten booty, or which give them a place of refuge. Nevertheless we desire that such churches be under this protection until complaint of them shall be made to the bishop, or to the chapter. If the bishop or chapter [1] act upon such information and lay hold of the malefactors, and if the latter refuse to give themselves up to the justice of the bishop or chapter, the malefactors and all their possessions shall not be immune, even within the church. A man who breaks into a church, or into the space within thirty paces around it, must pay a fine for sacrilege, and double this amount to the person wronged.

3. Furthermore, it is forbidden that any one attack the clergy, who do not bear arms, or the monks and religious persons, or do **Attacks upon the clergy prohibited** them any wrong; likewise it is forbidden to despoil or pillage the communities of canons, monks, and religious persons, the ecclesiastical lands which are under the protection of the Church, or the clergy, who do not

[1] The chapter was the body of clergy attached to a cathedral church. Its members were known as canons.

bear arms; and if any one shall do such a thing, let him pay a double composition.[1]

5. Let no one burn or destroy the dwellings of the peasants and the clergy, the dove-cotes and the granaries. Let no man dare to kill, to beat, or to wound a peasant or serf, or the wife of either, or to seize them and carry them off, except for misdemeanors which they may have committed; but it is not forbidden

Protection extended to the peasantry to lay hold of them in order to bring them to justice, and it is allowable to do this even before they shall have been summoned to appear. Let not the raiment of the peasants be stolen; let not their ploughs, or their hoes, or their olive-fields be burned.

6. . . . Let any one who has broken the peace, and has not paid his fines within a fortnight, make amends to him whom he has injured by paying a double amount, which shall go to the bishop and to the count who shall have had charge of the case.

7. The bishops of whom we have spoken have solemnly confirmed the Truce of God, which has been enjoined upon all

The Truce of God confirmed Christians, from the setting of the sun of the fourth day of the week, that is to say, Wednesday, until the rising of the sun on Monday, the second day. . . . If any one during the Truce shall violate it, let him pay a double composition and subsequently undergo the ordeal of cold water.[2] When any one during the Truce shall kill

Penalties for violations of the Truce a man, it has been ordained, with the approval of all Christians, that if the crime was committed intentionally the murderer shall be condemned to perpetual exile, but if it occurred by accident the slayer shall be banished for a period of time to be fixed by the bishops and

---

[1] That is, the penalty for using violence against peaceful churchmen, or despoiling their property was to be twice that demanded by the law in case of similar offenses committed against laymen.

[2] The ordeal of cold water was designed to test a man's guilt or innocence. The accused person was thrown into a pond and if he sank he was considered innocent; if he floated, guilty, on the supposition that the pure water would refuse to receive a person tainted with crime [see p. 200].

the canons. If any one during the Truce shall attempt to seize
a man or to carry him off from his château, and does not succeed in his purpose, let him pay a fine to the bishop and to the
chapter, just as if he had succeeded. It is likewise forbidden
during the Truce, in Advent and Lent, to build any château
or fortification, unless it was begun a fortnight before the
time of the Truce. It has been ordained also that at all times
disputes and suits on the subject of the Peace and Truce of God
shall be settled before the bishop and his chapter, and likewise
for the peace of the churches which have before been enumerated. When the bishop and the chapter shall have pronounced
sentences to recall men to the observance of the Peace and the
Truce of God, the sureties and hostages who show themselves
hostile to the bishop and the chapter shall be excommunicated
by the chapter and the bishop, with their protectors and partisans, as guilty of violating the Peace and the Truce of the
Lord; they and their possessions shall be excluded from the
Peace and the Truce of the Lord.

CHAPTER XIV.

THE NORMAN CONQUEST

40. The Battle of Hastings: the English and the Normans

THE Northmen, under the leadership of the renowned Rollo, got their first permanent foothold in that important part of France since known as Normandy in the year 911 [see p. 171]. Almost from the beginning the new county (later duchy) increased rapidly both in territorial extent and in political influence. The Northmen, or Normans, were a vigorous, ambitious, and on the whole very capable people, and they needed only the polishing which peaceful contact with the French could give to make them one of the most virile elements in the population of western Europe. They gave up their old gods and accepted Christianity, ceased to speak their own language and began the use of French, and to a considerable extent became ordinary soldiers and traders instead of the wild pirates their forefathers had been. The spirit of unrest, however, and the love of adventure so deeply ingrained in their natures did not die out, and we need not be surprised to learn that they continued still to enjoy nothing quite so much as war, especially if it involved hazardous expeditions across seas. Some went to help the Christians of Spain against the Saracens; some went to aid the Eastern emperors against the Turks; others went to Sicily and southern Italy, where they conquered weak rulers and set up principalities of their own; and finally, under the leadership of Duke William the Bastard, in 1066, they entered upon the greatest undertaking of all, i. e., the conquest of England and the establishment of a Norman chieftain upon the throne of the Anglo-Saxon kingdom.

Duke William was one of the greatest and most ambitious feudal lords of France—more powerful really than the French king himself. He had overcome practically all opposition among his unruly vassals in Normandy, and by 1066, when the death of King Edward the Confessor occurred in England, he was ready to engage in great enterprises which gave promise of enhanced power and renown. He had long cherished a claim to the English throne, and when he learned that in utter disregard of this claim the English witan had chosen Harold, son of the West Saxon Earl Godwin, to be Edward's successor, he prepared to invade the island kingdom and force an acknowledgment of what he pretended at least to believe were his rights. Briefly stated, William claimed the English throne on the ground (1) that through his wife Matilda, a descendant of Emma, Edward the Confessor's mother, he was a nearer heir than was Harold, who was only the late king's brother-in-law; (2) that on the occasion of a visit to England in 1051 Edward had promised him the inheritance; and (3) that Harold himself, when some years before he had been shipwrecked on the coast of Normandy, had sworn on sacred relics to help him gain the crown. There is some doubt as to the actual facts in connection with both of these last two points, but the truth is that all of William's claims taken together were not worth much, since the recognized principle of the English government was that the king should be chosen by the wisemen, or witan. Harold had been so chosen and hence was in every way the legitimate sovereign.

William, however, was determined to press his claims and, after obtaining the blessing of the Pope (Alexander II.), he gathered an army of perhaps 65,000 Normans and adventurers from all parts of France and prepared a fleet of some 1,500 transports at the mouth of the Dive to carry his troops across the Channel. September 28, 1066, the start was made and the following day the host landed at Pevensey in Sussex. Friday, the 29th, Hastings was selected and fortified to serve as headquarters. The English were taken at great disadvantage. Only two days before the Normans crossed the Channel Harold with all the troops he could muster had been engaged in a great battle at Stamford Bridge, in Northumberland, with Harold Hardrada, king of Norway, who was making an independent invasion. The English had won the fight, but they were not in a position to meet the Normans as they might otherwise have been. With admirable energy, however, Harold marched his weary army southward to Senlac, a hill near the town of Hastings, and there took up his position to await an attack by the duke's army. The battle came on Saturday, October 14, and after a very stubborn contest, in which Harold was slain, it resulted in a decisive victory for the Normans. Thereafter the conquest of the entire kingdom, while by no means easy, was inevitable.

William of Malmesbury, from whose *Chronicle of the Kings of England* our account of the battle and of the two contending peoples is taken, was a Benedictine monk, born of a Norman father and an English mother. He lived about 1095–1150 and hence wrote somewhat over half a century after the Conquest. While thus not strictly a contemporary, he was a man of learning and discretion and there is every reason to believe that he made his history as accurate as he was able, with the materials at his command. His parentage must have enabled him to understand both combatants in an unusual degree and, though his sympathies were with the conquerors, we may take his characterizations of Saxon and Norman alike to be at least fairly reliable. His *Chronicle* covers the period 449–1135, and for the years after 1066 it is the fullest, most carefully written, and most readable account of English affairs that we have.

Source—Guilielmus Monachi Malmesburiensis, *De gestis regum Anglorum* [William of Malmesbury, "Chronicle of the Kings of England"], Bk. III. Adapted from translation by John Sharpe (London, 1815), pp. 317–323.

The courageous leaders mutually prepared for battle, each according to his national custom. The English passed the night [1] without sleep, in drinking and singing, and in the morning proceeded without delay against the enemy. All on foot, armed with battle-axes, and covering themselves in front by joining

How the English prepared for battle their shields, they formed an impenetrable body which would assuredly have secured their safety that day had not the Normans, by a pretended flight, induced them to open their ranks, which until that time, according to their custom, had been closely knit together. King Harold himself, on foot, stood with his brothers near the standard in order that, so long as all shared equal danger, none could think of retreating. This same standard William sent, after his victory, to the Pope. It was richly embroidered with

[1] Friday night, October 13.

gold and precious stones, and represented the figure of a man fighting.

On the other hand, the Normans passed the whole night in confessing their sins, and received the communion of the Lord's body in the morning. Their infantry, with bows and arrows, formed the vanguard, while their cavalry, divided into wings, **How the Nor-** was placed in the rear. The duke, with serene **mans prepared** countenance, declaring aloud that God would favor his as being the righteous side, called for his arms; and when, through the haste of his attendants, he had put on his hauberk[1] the rear part before, he corrected the mistake with a laugh, saying, "The power of my dukedom shall be turned into a kingdom." Then starting the song of Roland,[2] in order that the warlike example of that hero might stimulate the soldiers, and calling on God for assistance, the battle commenced on both sides, and was fought with great ardor, neither side yielding ground during the greater part of the day.

Observing this, William gave a signal to his troops, that, pretending flight, they should withdraw from the field.[3] By means of this device the solid phalanx of the English opened for the purpose of cutting down the fleeing enemy and thus brought upon itself swift destruction; for the Normans, facing about, **William's** attacked them, thus disordered, and compelled **stratagem** them to fly. In this manner, deceived by stratagem, they met an honorable death in avenging their country;

[1] A long coat of mail made of interwoven metal rings.

[2] Roland, count of Brittany, was slain at the pass of Roncesvalles in the famous attack of the Gascons upon Charlemagne's retreating army in 778. One of the chronicles says simply, "In this battle Roland, count of Brittany, was slain," and we have absolutely no other historical knowledge of the man. His career was taken up by the singers of the Middle Ages, however, and employed to typify all that was brave and daring and romantic. It was some one of the many "songs of Roland" that William used at Hastings to stimulate his men.

[3] In a battle so closely contested this was a dangerous stratagem and its employment seems to indicate that William despaired of defeating the English by direct attack. His main object, in which he was altogether successful, was to entice the English into abandoning their advantageous position on the hilltop.

nor indeed were they at all without their own revenge, for, by frequently making a stand, they slaughtered their pursuers in heaps. Getting possession of a higher bit of ground, they drove back the Normans, who in the heat of pursuit were struggling up the slope, into the valley beneath, where, by hurling their javelins and rolling down stones on them as they stood below, the English easily destroyed them to a man. Besides, by a short passage with which they were acquainted, they avoided a deep ditch and trod underfoot such a multitude of their enemies in that place that the heaps of bodies made the hollow level with the plain. This alternating victory, first of one side and then of the other, continued as long as Harold lived to check the retreat; but when he fell, his brain pierced by an arrow, the flight of the English ceased not until night.[1]

In the battle both leaders distinguished themselves by their bravery. Harold, not content with the duties of a general and with exhorting others, eagerly assumed himself the work of a common soldier. He was constantly striking down the enemy **The valor of Harold** at close quarters, so that no one could approach him with impunity, for straightway both horse and rider would be felled by a single blow. So it was at long range, as I have said, that the enemy's deadly arrow brought him to his death. One of the Norman soldiers gashed his thigh with a sword, as he lay prostrate; for which shameful and cowardly action he was branded with ignominy by William and expelled from the army.

William, too, was equally ready to encourage his soldiers by his voice and by his presence, and to be the first to rush forward to attack the thickest of the foe. He was everywhere fierce and furious. He lost three choice horses, which were that day killed

[1] After the Norman victory was practically assured, William sought to bring the battle to an end by having his archers shoot into the air, that their arrows might fall upon the group of soldiers, including the king, who were holding out in defense of the English standard. It was in this way that Harold was mortally wounded; he died immediately from the blows inflicted by Norman knights at close hand.

under him. The dauntless spirit and vigor of the intrepid general, however, still held out. Though often called back by the **William's bravery and ardor** thoughtful remonstrance of his bodyguard, he still persisted until approaching night crowned him with complete victory. And no doubt the hand of God so protected him that the enemy could draw no blood from his person, though they aimed so many javelins at him.

This was a fatal day to England, and melancholy havoc was wrought in our dear country during the change of its lords.[1] For it had long before adopted the manners of the Angles, which had indeed altered with the times; for in the first years of their arrival they were barbarians in their look and manner, warlike in their usages, heathen in their rites.

After embracing the faith of Christ, by degrees and, in process of time, in consequence of the peace which they enjoyed, they consigned warfare to a secondary place and gave their whole attention to religion. I am not speaking of the poor, the meanness of whose fortune often restrains them from overstepping the bounds of justice; I omit, too, men of ecclesiastical rank, whom sometimes respect for their profession and sometimes the fear of shame suffers not to deviate from the true path; I speak of princes, who from the greatness of their power might have full liberty to indulge in pleasure. Some of these in their own country, and others at Rome, changing their habit, obtained a heavenly kingdom and a saintly fellowship. Many others during their whole lives devoted themselves in outward appearance to worldly affairs, but in order that they might expend their treasures on the poor or divide them amongst monasteries.

Religious zeal of the Saxons before the Conquest

[1] The victory at Hastings did not at once make William king, but it revealed to both himself and the English people that the crown was easily within his grasp. After the battle he advanced past London into the interior of the country. Opposition melted before him and on Christmas day, 1066, the Norman duke, having already been regularly elected by the witan, was crowned at London by the archbishop of York. In the early years of his reign he succeeded in making his power recognized in the more turbulent north.

What shall I say of the multitudes of bishops, hermits, and abbots? Does not the whole island blaze with such numerous relics of its own people that you can scarcely pass a village of any consequence without hearing the name of some new saint? And of how many more has all remembrance perished through the want of records?

Nevertheless, the attention to literature and religion had gradually decreased for several years before the arrival of the Normans. The clergy, contented with a little confused learning, could scarcely stammer out the words of the sacraments; and a person who understood grammar was an object of wonder and astonishment.[1] The monks mocked the rule of their order **Recent decline of learning and religion** by fine vestments and the use of every kind of food. The nobility, given up to luxury and wantonness, went not to church in the morning after the manner of Christians, but merely, in a careless manner, heard matins and masses from a hurrying priest in their chambers, amid the blandishments of their wives. The community, left unprotected, became a prey to the most powerful, who amassed fortunes, either by seizing on their property or by selling their persons into foreign countries; although it is characteristic of this people to be more inclined to reveling than to the accumulation of wealth.

Drinking in parties was an universal practice, in which occupation they passed entire nights as well as days. They consumed their whole substance in mean and despicable houses, unlike the Normans and French, who live frugally in noble and splendid mansions. The vices attendant on drunkenness, which enervate the human mind, followed; hence it came about that when they resisted William, with more rashness and precipitate fury than military skill, they doomed themselves and their country to slavery by a single, and that an easy, victory.[2] For

[1] The work of Alfred had not been consistently followed up during the century and a half since his death [see p. 185].

[2] The conquest of England by the Normans was really far from an en-

nothing is less effective than rashness; and what begins with violence quickly ceases or is repelled. The English at that time

The English people described wore short garments, reaching to the mid-knee; they had their hair cropped, their beards shaven, their arms laden with golden bracelets, their skin adorned with tattooed designs. They were accustomed to eat until they became surfeited, and to drink until they were sick. These latter qualities they imparted to their conquerors; as for the rest, they adopted their manners. I would not, however, have these bad characteristics ascribed to the English universally; I know that many of the clergy at that day trod the path of sanctity by a blameless life. I know that many of the laity, of all ranks and conditions, in this nation were well-pleasing to God. Be injustice far from this account; the accusation does not involve the whole, indiscriminately. But as in peace the mercy of God often cherishes the bad and the good together, so, equally, does His severity sometimes include them both in captivity.

The Normans—that I may speak of them also—were at that time, and are even now, exceedingly particular in their dress and delicate in their food, but not so to excess. They are a race accustomed to war, and can hardly live without it; fierce in rushing against the enemy, and, where force fails to succeed, ready

A description of the Normans to use stratagem or to corrupt by bribery. As I have said, they live in spacious houses with economy, envy their superiors, wish to excel their equals, and plunder their subjects, though they defend them from others; they are faithful to their lords, though a slight offense alienates them. They weigh treachery by its chance of success, and change their sentiments for money. The most hospitable, however, of all nations, they esteem strangers worthy of equal honor with themselves; they also intermarry with their vassals. They revived, by their arrival, the rule of religion

slavement. Norman rule was strict, but hardly more so than conditions warranted.

which had everywhere grown lifeless in England.[1] You might
see churches rise in every village, and monasteries in the towns
and cities, built after a style unknown before; you might behold
the country flourishing with renewed rites; so that each wealthy
man accounted that day lost to him which he had neglected to
signalize by some beneficent act.

41. William the Conqueror as Man and as King

IN the following passage, taken from the Saxon Chronicle, we have
an interesting summary of the character of the Conqueror and of his
conduct as king of England. Both the good and bad sides of the
picture are clearly brought out and perhaps it is not quite easy to say
which is given the greater prominence. On the one hand there is
William's devotion to the Church, his establishment of peace and order,
his mildness in dealing with all but those who had antagonized him,
and the virtue of his personal life; on the other is his severity, rapacity, and pride, his heavy taxes and his harsh forest laws. As one writer
says, "the Conquest was bad as well as good for England; but the
harm was only temporary, the good permanent." It is greatly to the
credit of the English chronicler that he was able to deal so fairly with
the character of one whom he had not a few patriotic reasons for ma-
ligning.

Source—*The Saxon Chronicle*. Translated by J. A. Giles (London, 1847),
    pp. 461–462.

If any one would know what manner of man King William
was, the glory that he obtained, and of how many lands he was
lord, then will we describe him as we have known him, we who
have looked upon him and who once lived at his court. This
King William, of whom we are speaking, was a very wise and a
great man, and more honored and more powerful than any of

[1] It seems to be true, as William of Malmesbury says, that the century
preceding the Norman Conquest had been an era of religious as well as
literary decline among the English. After 1066 the native clergy, ignorant
and often grossly immoral, were gradually replaced by Normans, who on
the whole were better men. By 1088 there remained only one bishop of
English birth in the entire kingdom. One should be careful, however, not
to exaggerate the moral differences between the two peoples.

his predecessors. He was mild to those good men who loved
God, but severe beyond measure towards those who withstood
William's his will. He founded a noble monastery on the
religious zeal spot where God permitted him to conquer England, and he established monks in it, and he made it very rich.[1]
In his days the great monastery at Canterbury was built,[2] and
many others also throughout England; moreover, this land was
filled with monks who lived after the rule of St. Benedict; and
such was the state of religion in his days that all who would
might observe that which was prescribed by their respective
orders.

King William was also held in much reverence. He wore his
crown three times every year when he was in England: at Easter
he wore it at Winchester,[3] at Pentecost at Westminster,[4] and at
Christmas at Gloucester.[5] And at these times all the men of
His strong England were with him, archbishops, bishops,
government abbots and earls, thanes [6] and knights.[7] So also
was he a very stern and a wrathful man, so that none durst
do anything against his will, and he kept in prison those earls

[1] The story goes that just before entering the battle of Hastings in 1066
William made a vow that if successful he would establish a monastery on
the site where Harold's standard stood. The vow was fulfilled by the
founding of the Abbey of St. Martin, or Battle Abbey, in the years 1070–
1076. The monastery was not ready for consecration until 1094.

[2] Christchurch. This cathedral monastery had been organized before the
Conqueror's day, but it was much increased in size and in importance by
Lanfranc, William's archbishop of Canterbury; and the great building
which it occupied in the later Middle Ages was constructed at this time.

[3] In Hampshire, in the southern part of the kingdom.

[4] In Middlesex, near London.

[5] On the Severn, in the modern county of Gloucester.

[6] A thane (or thegn) was originally a young warrior; then one who became
a noble by serving the king in arms; then the possessor of five hides of land.
A hide was a measure of arable ground varying in extent at the time of
William the Conqueror, but by Henry II.'s reign (1154–1189) fixed at about
100 acres. The thane before the Conquest occupied nearly the same position
socially as the knight after it.

[7] This assembly of dignitaries, summoned by the king three times a year,
was the so-called Great Council, which in Norman times superseded the
old Saxon witan. Its duties were mainly judicial. It acted also as an advisory body, but the king was not obliged to consult it or to carry out its
recommendations [see p. 307, note 2].

who acted against his pleasure. He removed bishops from their
sees [1] and abbots from their offices, and he imprisoned thanes,
and at length he spared not his own brother Odo. This Odo was
a very powerful bishop in Normandy. His see was that of
Bayeux,[2] and he was foremost to serve the king. He had an
earldom in England, and when William was in Normandy he
[Odo] was the first man in this country [England], and him did
William cast into prison.[3]

Amongst other things, the good order that William established
is not to be forgotten. It was such that any man, who was himself aught, might travel over the kingdom with a bosom full of
gold unmolested; and no man durst kill another, however great
the injury he might have received from him. He reigned over
England, and being sharp-sighted to his own interest, he sur-
veyed the kingdom so thoroughly that there was not a single
The extent of   hide of land throughout the whole of which he
his power   knew not the possessor, and how much it was
worth, and this he afterwards entered in his register.[4] The land
of the Britons [Wales] was under his sway, and he built castles
therein; moreover he had full dominion over the Isle of Man; [5]
Scotland also was subject to him, from his great strength; the
land of Normandy was his by inheritance, and he possessed the
earldom of Maine;[6] and had he lived two years longer, he would
have subdued Ireland by his prowess, and that without a battle.[7]

Truly there was much trouble in these times, and very great

---

[1] The *see* of a bishop is his ecclesiastical office; the area over which his
authority extends is more properly known as his diocese.

[2] On the Orne River, near the English Channel.

[3] Odo, though a churchman, was a man of brutal instincts and evil character. Through his high-handed course, both as a leading ecclesiastical
dignitary in Normandy and as earl of Kent and vicegerent in England, he
gave William no small amount of trouble. The king finally grew tired of
his brother's conduct and had him imprisoned in the town of Rouen where
he was left for four years, or until the end of the reign (1087).

[4] This was the famous Domesday Survey, begun in 1085.

[5] In the Irish Sea.

[6] Maine lay directly to the south of Normandy.

[7] This statement is doubtful, though it is true that Lanfranc made a beginning by consecrating a number of bishops in Ireland.

distress. He caused castles to be built and oppressed the poor.
The king was also of great sternness, and he took from his subjects many marks of gold, and many hundred pounds of silver,
and this, either with or without right, and with little need. He
was given to avarice, and greedily loved gain.[1] He made large
forests for the deer, and enacted laws therewith, so that whoever
killed a hart or a hind should be blinded. As he forbade killing
His faults   the deer, so also the boars; and he loved the tall
as a ruler   stags as if he were their father. He also commanded concerning the hares, that they should go free.[2] The
rich complained and the poor murmured, but he was so sturdy
that he recked nought of them; they must will all that the king
willed, if they would live, or would keep their lands, or would hold
their possessions, or would be maintained in their rights. Alas
that any man should so exalt himself, and carry himself in his
pride over all! May Almighty God show mercy to his soul, and
grant him the forgiveness of his sins! We have written concerning him these things, both good and bad, that virtuous men
may follow after the good, and wholly avoid the evil, and
may go in the way that leadeth to the kingdom of heaven.

[1] All of the early Norman kings were greedy for money and apt to bear
heavily upon the people in their efforts to get it. Englishmen were not
accustomed to general taxation and felt the new régime to be a serious
burden. There was consequently much complaint, but, as our historian
says, William was strong enough to be able to ignore it.

[2] Most of William's harsh measures can be justified on the ground that
they were designed to promote the ultimate welfare of his people. This
is not true, however, of his elaborate forest laws, which undertook to deprive Englishmen of their accustomed freedom of hunting when and where
they pleased. William's love of the chase amounted to a passion and he
was not satisfied with merely enacting such stringent measures as that the
slayer of a hart or a hind in his forests should be blinded, but also set apart
a great stretch of additional country, the so-called New Forest, as his own
exclusive hunting grounds.

CHAPTER XV.

THE MONASTIC REFORMATION OF THE TENTH, ELEVENTH, AND TWELFTH CENTURIES

42. The Foundation Charter of the Monastery of Cluny (910)

THROUGHOUT the earlier Middle Ages the Benedictine Rule [see p. 83] was the code under which were governed practically all the monastic establishments of western Europe. There was a natural tendency, however, for the severe and exacting features of the Rule to be softened considerably in actual practice. As one writer puts it, "the excessive abstinence and many other of the mechanical observances of the rule were soon found to have little real utility when simply enforced by a rule, and not practiced willingly for the sake of self-discipline." The obligation of manual labor, for example, was frequently dispensed with in order that the monks might occupy themselves with the studies for which the Benedictines have always been famous. Too often such relaxation was but a pretext for the indulgence of idleness or vice. The disrepute into which such tendencies brought the monastics in the tenth and eleventh centuries gave rise to numerous attempts to revive the primitive discipline, the most notable of which was the so-called "Cluniac movement."

The monastery of Cluny, on the borders of Aquitaine and Burgundy, was established under the terms of a charter issued by William the Pious, duke of Aquitaine and count of Auvergne, September 11, 910. The conditions of its foundation, set forth in the text of the charter given below, were in many ways typical. The history of the monastery was, however, quite exceptional. During the invasions and civil wars of the latter half of the ninth century, many of the monasteries of western Europe had fallen under the control of unscrupulous laymen who used them mainly to satisfy their greed or ambition, and in consequence by the time that Cluny was founded the standard of monastic life and service had been seriously impaired. The monks had grown worldly, education was neglected, and religious services had become empty formalities. Powerful nobles used their positions of advantage to influence, and often to dictate, the election of bishops and abbots, and the men thus elected were likely enough to be unworthy of their offices in both character and ability. The charter of the Cluny monastery, however, expressly provided that the abbot should be chosen by canonical election, i. e., by the monks, and without any sort of outside interference. The life of the monastery was to be regulated by the Benedictine Rule, though with rather less stress on manual labor and rather more on religious services and literary employment. Cluny, indeed, soon came to be one of the principal centers of learning in western Europe, as well as perhaps the greatest administrator of charity.

Another notable achievement of Cluny was the building up of the so-called "Cluny Congregation." Hitherto it had been customary for monasteries to be entirely independent of one another, even when founded by monks sent out from a parent establishment. Cluny, however, kept under the control of her own abbot all monasteries founded by her agents and made the priors of these monasteries directly responsible to him. Many outside abbeys were drawn into the new system, so that by the middle of the twelfth century the Cluny congregation was comprised of more than two thousand monasteries, all working harmoniously under a single abbot-general. The majority of these were in France, but there were many also in Spain, Italy, Poland, Germany, and England. It was the Cluny monks who gave the Pope his chief support in the struggle to free the Church from lay investiture and simony and to enforce the ideal of a celibate clergy. This movement for reform may properly be said, indeed, to have originated with the Cluniacs and to have been taken up only later by the popes, chiefly by Gregory VII. By the end of the eleventh century Cluniac discipline had begun to grow lax and conditions were gradually shaped for another wave of monastic reform, which came with the establishment of the Carthusians (in 1084) and of the Cistercians (in 1098).

Source—Text in Martin Bouquet, *Recueil des Historiens des Gaules et de la France* ["Collection of the Historians of Gaul and of France"] (Paris, 1874), Vol. IX., pp. 709–711.

To all who think wisely it is evident that the providence of God has made it possible for rich men, by using well their temporal possessions, to be able to merit eternal rewards. . . . I, William, count and duke, after diligent reflection, and desiring to provide for my own safety while there is still time, have decided that it is advisable, indeed absolutely necessary, that

Motives for Duke William's benefaction from the possessions which God has given me I should give some portion for the good of my soul. I do this, indeed, in order that I who have thus increased in wealth may not at the last be accused of having spent all in caring for my body, but rather may rejoice, when fate at length shall snatch all things away, in having preserved something for myself. I cannot do better than follow the precepts of Christ and make His poor my friends. That my gift may be durable and not transitory I will support at my own expense a congregation of monks. And I hope that I shall receive the reward of the righteous because I have received those whom I believe to be righteous and who despise the world, although I myself am not able to despise all things.[1]

Therefore be it known to all who live in the unity of the faith and who await the mercy of Christ, and to those who shall succeed them and who shall continue to exist until the end of the world, that, for the love of God and of our Saviour Jesus Christ, I hand over from my own rule to the holy apostles, namely,

The land and other property ceded Peter and Paul, the possessions over which I hold sway—the town of Cluny, with the court and demesne manor, and the church in honor of St. Mary, the mother of God, and of St. Peter, the prince of the apostles, together with all the things pertaining to it, the villas,

[1] In other words, it is Duke William's hope that, though not himself willing to be restricted to the life of a monk, he may secure substantially an equivalent reward by patronizing men who *are* thus willing.

the chapels, the serfs of both sexes, the vines, the fields, the meadows, the woods, the waters and their outlets, the mills, the incomes and revenues, what is cultivated and what is not, all without reserve. These things are situated in or about the county of Mâcon,[1] each one marked off by definite bounds. I give, moreover, all these things to the aforesaid apostles—I, William, and my wife Ingelberga—first for the love of God; then for the soul of my lord King Odo, of my father and my mother; for myself and my wife,—for the salvation, namely, of our souls and bodies; and not least, for that of Ava, who left me these things in her will; for the souls also of our brothers and sisters and nephews, and of all our relatives of both sexes; for our faithful ones who adhere to our service; for the advancement, also, and integrity of the Catholic religion. Finally, since all of us Christians are held together by one bond of love and faith, let this donation be for all—for the orthodox, namely, of past, present, or future times.

I give these things, moreover, with this understanding, that in Cluny a monastery shall be constructed in honor of the holy apostles Peter and Paul, and that there the monks shall congregate and live according to the rule of St. Benedict, and that **A monastery to be established.** they shall possess and make use of these same things for all time. In such wise, however, that the venerable house of prayer which is there shall be faithfully frequented with vows and supplications, and that heavenly conversations shall be sought after with all desire and with the deepest ardor; and also that there shall be diligently directed to God prayers and exhortations, as well for me as for all, according to the order in which mention has been made of them above. And let the monks themselves, together with all aforesaid possessions, be under the power and dominion of the abbot Berno, who, as long as he shall live, shall preside over

---

[1] Mâcon, the seat of the diocese in which Cluny was situated, was on the Saône, a short distance to the southeast.

them regularly according to his knowledge and ability.[1] But
after his death, those same monks shall have power and per-

**Election of
abbots to be
" canonical "**

mission to elect any one of their order whom
they please as abbot and rector, following the will
of God and the rule promulgated by St. Bene-
dict—in such wise that neither by the intervention of our own or
of any other power may they be impeded from making a purely canonical election.   Every five years, moreover, the aforesaid monks
shall pay to the church of the apostles at Rome ten shillings to
supply them with lights; and they shall have the protection of
those same apostles and the defense of the Roman pontiff; and
those monks may, with their whole heart and soul, according to
their ability and knowledge, build up the aforesaid place.

We will, further, that in our times and in those of our successors, according as the opportunities and possibilities of that

**Works of char-
ity enjoined**

place shall allow, there shall daily, with the greatest zeal, be performed works of mercy towards
the poor, the needy, strangers, and pilgrims.[2]   It has pleased us
also to insert in this document that, from this day, those same
monks there congregated shall be subject neither to our yoke,
nor to that of our relatives, nor to the sway of the royal might,
nor to that of any earthly power.   And, through God and all His
saints, and by the awful day of judgment, I warn and admonish
that no one of the secular princes, no count, no bishop, not even
the pontiff of the aforesaid Roman see, shall invade the property
of these servants of God, or alienate it, or diminish it, or exchange it, or give it as a benefice to any one, or set up any prelate
over them against their will.[3]

[1] Berno served as abbot of Cluny from 910 until 927.

[2] That the charitable side of the monastery's work was well attended
to is indicated by the fact that in a single year, late in the eleventh century,
seventeen thousand poor were given assistance by the monks.

[3] The remainder of the charter consists of a series of imprecations of
disaster and punishment upon all who at any time and in any way should
undertake to interfere with the vested rights just granted.   These imprecations were strictly typical of the mediæval spirit—so much so that
many of them came to be mere formulæ, employed to give documents due

43. The Early Career of St. Bernard and the Founding of Clairvaux

THE most important individual who had part in the twelfth century movement for monastic reform was unquestionably St. Bernard, of whom indeed it has been said with reason that for a quarter of a century there was no more influential man in Europe. Born in 1091, he came upon the scene when times were ripe for great deeds and great careers, whether with the crusading hosts in the East or in the vexed swirl of secular and ecclesiastical affairs in the West. Particularly were the times ripe for a great preacher and reformer—one who could avail himself of the fresh zeal of the crusading period and turn a portion of it to the regeneration of the corrupt and sluggish spiritual life which in far too great a measure had crept in to replace the earlier purity and devotion of the clergy. The need of reform was perhaps most conspicuous in the monasteries, for many monastic establishments had not been greatly affected by the Cluniac movement of the previous century, and in many of those which had been touched temporarily the purifying influences had about ceased to produce results. It was as a monastic reformer that St. Bernard rendered greatest service to the Church of his day, though he was far more than a mere zealot. He was, says Professor Emerton, more than any other man, representative of the spirit of the Middle Ages. "The monastery meant to him, not a place of easy and luxurious retirement, where a man might keep himself pure from earthly contact, nor even a home of learning, from which a man might influence his world. It meant rather a place of pitiless discipline, whereby the natural man should be reduced to the lowest terms and thus the spiritual life be given its largest liberty. The aim of Bernard was nothing less than the regeneration of society through the presence in it of devoted men, bound together by a compact organization, and holding up to the world the highest types of an ideal which had already fixed itself in the imagination of the age." [1]

The founding of Clairvaux by St. Bernard, in 1115, was not the beginning of a new monastic order; the Cistercians, to whom the establishment properly belonged, had originated at Cîteaux seventeen years before. But in later times St. Bernard was very properly regarded as a

solemnity, but without any especially direful designs on the part of the writer who used them.

[1] Emerton, *Mediæval Europe*, p. 458.

second founder of the Cistercians, and the story of his going forth from the parent house to establish the new one affords an excellent illustration of the spirit which dominated the leaders in monastic reform in the eleventh and twelfth centuries and of the methods they employed to keep alive the lofty ideals of the old Benedictine system; and, although individual monasteries were founded under the most diverse circumstances, the story is of interest as showing us the precise way in which one monastic house took its origin. By the time of St. Bernard's death (1153) not fewer than a hundred and fifty religious houses had been regenerated under his inspiration.

We are fortunate in possessing a composite biography of the great reformer which is practically contemporary. It is in five books, the first of which was written by William, abbot of St. Thierry of Rheims; the second by Arnold, abbot of Bonneval, near Chartres; and the third, fourth, and fifth by Geoffrey, a monk of Clairvaux and a former secretary of St. Bernard. William of St. Thierry (from whose portion of the biography selection "a" below is taken) wrote about 1140, Arnold and Geoffrey soon after Bernard's death in 1153.

Sources—(a) Guillaume de Saint-Thierry, *Bernardus Clarævallensis* [William of Saint Thierry, "Life of St. Bernard"], Bk. I., Chaps. 1–4.

(b) The *Acta Sanctorum*. Translated in Edward L. Cutts, *Scenes and Characters of the Middle Ages* (London, 1872), pp. 11–12.

(a)

Saint Bernard was born at Fontaines in Burgundy [near Dijon], at the castle of his father. His parents were famed among the famous of that age, most of all because of their piety. His father, Tescelin, was a member of an ancient and knightly family, fearing God and scrupulously just. Even when engaged in holy war he plundered and destroyed no one; he contented himself with his worldly possessions, of which he had an abundance, and used them in all manner of good works. With both **Bernard's parents** his counsel and his arms he served temporal lords, but so as never to neglect to render to the sovereign Lord that which was due Him. Bernard's mother, Alith, of the castle Montbar, mindful of holy law, was submissive to

her husband and, with him, governed the household in the fear
of God, devoting herself to deeds of mercy and rearing her children in strict discipline. She bore seven children, six boys and
one girl, not so much for the glory of her husband as for that
of God; for all the sons became monks and the daughter a
nun.[1] . . .

As soon as Bernard was of sufficient age his mother intrusted
his education to the teachers in the church at Châtillon [2] and
did everything in her power to enable him to make rapid progress. The young boy, abounding in pleasing qualities and endowed with natural genius, fulfilled his mother's every expectation; for he advanced in his study of letters at a speed beyond
his age and that of other children of the same age. But in secular
matters he began already, and very naturally, to humble him-
His early   self in the interest of his future perfection, for
characteristics he exhibited the greatest simplicity, loved to be
in solitude, fled from people, was extraordinarily thoughtful,
submitted himself implicitly to his parents, had little desire to
converse, was devoted to God, and applied himself to his studies
as the means by which he should be able to learn of God through
the Scriptures. . . .

Determined that it would be best for him to abandon the
world, he began to inquire where his soul, under the yoke of
Christ, would be able to find the most complete and sure repose.
The recent establishment of the order of Cîteaux [3] suggested
itself to his thought. The harvest was abundant, but the
He decides to laborers were few, for hardly any one had sought
become a monk happiness by taking up residence there, because of
at Cîteaux   the excessive austerity of life and the poverty
which there prevailed, but which had no terrors for the soul truly
seeking God. Without hesitation or misgivings, he turned his

---

[1] Bernard was the third son.
[2] About sixty miles southeast of Troyes.
[3] Cîteaux (established by Odo, duke of Burgundy, in 1098) was near
Dijon in Burgundy.

steps to that place, thinking that there he would be able to find seclusion and, in the secret of the presence of God, escape the importunities of men; wishing particularly there to gain a refuge from the vain glory of the noble's life, and to win purity of soul, and perhaps the name of saint.

When his brothers, who loved him according to the flesh, discovered that he intended to become a monk, they employed every means to turn him to the pursuit of letters and to attach him to the secular life by the love of worldly knowledge. Without doubt, as he has himself declared, he was not a little moved by their arguments. But the memory of his devout mother urged him importunately to take the step. It often seemed to him that she appeared before him, reproaching him and reminding him that she had not reared him for frivolous things of that sort, and that she had brought him up in quite another hope. Finally, one day when he was returning from the siege of a château called Grancey, and was coming to his brothers, who were with the duke of Burgundy, he began to be violently tormented by these thoughts. Finding by the roadside a church, he went in and there prayed, with flooded eyes, lifting his hands toward Heaven and pouring out his heart like water before the Lord. That day fixed his resolution irrevocably. From that **His struggle** hour, even as the fire consumes the forests and **and his victory** the flame ravages the mountains, seizing everything, devouring first that which is nearest but advancing to objects farther removed, so did the fire which God had kindled in the heart of his servant, desiring that it should consume it, lay hold first of his brothers (of whom only the youngest, incapable yet of becoming a monk, was left to console his old father), then his parents, his companions, and his friends, from whom no one had ever expected such a step. . . .

The number of those who decided to take upon themselves monastic vows increased and, as one reads of the earliest sons of the Church, "all the multitude of those who believed were of one mind and one heart" [Acts v. 32]. They lived together and no one else dared mingle with them. They had at Châtillon a house which they possessed in common and in which they held meetings, dwelt together, and held converse with one another.

Bernard and his companions at Châtillon No one was so bold as to enter it, unless he were a member of the congregation. If any one entered there, seeing and hearing what was done and said (as the Apostle declared of the Christians of Corinth), he was convinced by their prophecies and, adoring the Lord and perceiving that God was truly among them, he either joined himself to the brotherhood or, going away, wept at his own plight and their happy state. . . .

At that time, the young and feeble establishment at Cîteaux, under the venerable abbot Stephen,[1] began to be seriously weakened by its paucity of numbers and to lose all hope of having successors to perpetuate the heritage of holy poverty, for everybody revered the life of these monks for its sancity but held aloof from it because of its austerity. But the monastery was sud-

They enter Cîteaux denly visited and made glad by the Lord in a happy and unhoped-for manner. In 1113, fifteen years after the foundation of the monastery, the servant of God, Bernard, then about twenty-three years of age, entered the establishment under the abbot Stephen, with his companions to the number of more than thirty, and submitted himself to the blessed yoke of Christ. From that day God prospered the house, and that vine of the Lord bore fruit, putting forth its branches from sea to sea.

Such were the holy beginnings of the monastic life of that man of God. It is impossible to any one who has not been imbued as he with the spirit of God to recount the illustrious deeds of his career, and his angelic conduct, during his life on earth. He entered the monastery poor in spirit, still obscure and of no

[1] Stephen Harding, an Englishman, succeeded Alberic as abbot of Cîteaux in 1113.

fame, with the intention of there perishing in the heart and memory of men, and hoping to be forgotten and ignored like a lost vessel. But God ordered it otherwise, and prepared him as a chosen vessel, not only to strengthen and extend the monastic order, but also to bear His name before kings and peoples to the ends of the earth. . . .

At the time of harvest the brothers were occupied, with the fervor and joy of the Holy Spirit, in reaping the grain. Since he [Bernard] was not able to have part in the labor, they bade him sit by them and take his ease. Greatly troubled, he had

Bernard prays for and obtains the ability to reap recourse to prayer and, with much weeping, implored the Lord to grant him the strength to become a reaper. The simplicity of his faith did not deceive him, for that which he asked he obtained. Indeed from that day he prided himself in being more skilful than the others at that task; and he was the more given over to devotion during that labor because he realized that the ability to perform it was a direct gift from God. Refreshed by his employments of this kind, he prayed, read, or meditated continuously. If an opportunity for prayer in solitude offered itself, he seized it; but in any case, whether by himself or with companions, he preserved a solitude in his heart, and thus was everywhere alone. He read gladly, and always with faith and thoughtfulness, the Holy Scriptures, saying that they never seemed to him so clear as when read in the text alone, and he declared his ability to discern their truth and divine virtue much more readily in the

His devotion and knowledge of the Scriptures source itself than in the commentaries which were derived from it. Nevertheless, he read humbly the saints and orthodox commentators and made no pretense of rivaling their knowledge; but, submitting his to theirs, and tracing it faithfully to its sources, he drank often at the fountain whence they had drawn. It is thus that, full of the spirit which has divinely inspired all Holy Scripture, he has served God to this day, as the Apostle says, with so great confidence, and such ability to instruct, convert, and sway. And when he preaches the word of God, he renders so clear and agreeable that which he takes from Scripture to insert in his discourse, and he has such power to move men, that everybody, both those clever in worldly matters and those who possess spiritual knowledge, marvel at the eloquent words which fall from his lips.

(b)

Twelve monks and their abbot, representing our Lord and His apostles, were assembled in the church. Stephen placed a cross in Bernard's hands, who solemnly, at the head of his small band, walked forth from Cîteaux. . . . Bernard struck away to the northward. For a distance of nearly ninety miles he kept this course, passing up by the source of the Seine, by Châtillon, of school-day memories, until he arrived at La Ferté, about equally distant between Troyes and Chaumont, in the diocese of Langres, and situated on the river Aube.[1] About four miles beyond La Ferté was a deep valley opening to the east. Thick umbrageous forests gave it a character of gloom and wildness; but a gushing stream of limpid water which ran through it was sufficient to redeem every disadvantage.

Site selected for the new monastery

In June, 1115, Bernard took up his abode in the "Valley of Wormwood," as it was called, and began to look for means of shelter and sustenance against the approaching winter. The rude fabric which he and his monks raised with their own hands was long preserved by the pious veneration of the Cistercians. It consisted of a building covered by a single roof, under which chapel, dormitory, and refectory were all included. Neither stone nor

The first building constructed

[1] Châtillon was about twelve miles south of La Ferté. The latter was fifty miles southeast of Troyes and only half as far from Chaumont, despite the author's statement that it lay midway between the two places. The Aube is an important tributary of the upper Seine.

wood hid the bare earth, which served for a floor. Windows
scarcely wider than a man's head admitted a feeble light. In
this room the monks took their frugal meals of herbs and water.
Immediately above the refectory was the sleeping apartment.
It was reached by a ladder, and was, in truth, a sort of loft.
Here were the monks' beds, which were peculiar. They were
made in the form of boxes, or bins, of wooden planks, long and
wide enough for a man to lie down in. A small space, hewn out
with an axe, allowed room for the sleeper to get in or out. The
inside was strewn with chaff, or dried leaves, which, with the
woodwork, seem to have been the only covering permitted. . .

The monks had thus got a house over their heads; but they
had very little else. They had left Cîteaux in June. Their
journey had probably occupied them a fortnight; their clearing,
preparations, and building, perhaps two months; and thus they
were near September when this portion of their labor was accomplished. Autumn and winter were approaching, and they
had no store laid by. Their food during the summer had been
a compound of leaves intermixed with coarse grain. Beech-
nuts and roots were to be their main support during the winter.

Hardships   And now to the privations of insufficient food
encountered   was added the wearing out of their shoes and
clothes. Their necessities grew with the severity of the season,
until at last even salt failed them; and presently Bernard heard
murmurs. He argued and exhorted; he spoke to them of the
fear and love of God, and strove to rouse their drooping spirits
by dwelling on the hopes of eternal life and Divine recompense.
Their sufferings made them deaf and indifferent to their abbot's
words. They would not remain in this valley of bitterness; they
would return to Cîteaux. Bernard, seeing they had lost their
trust in God, reproved them no more; but himself sought in
earnest prayer for release from their difficulties. Presently a
voice from heaven said, "Arise, Bernard, thy prayer is granted
thee." Upon which the monks said, "What didst thou ask of

the Lord?"   "Wait, and ye shall see, ye of little faith," was the
reply; and presently came a stranger who gave the abbot ten
livres.

44. A Description of Clairvaux

THE following is an interesting description of the abbey of Clairvaux,
written by William of St. Thierry, the friend and biographer of Bernard.
After giving an account of the external appearance and surroundings
of the monastery, the writer goes on to portray the daily life and devotion of the monks who resided in it.   In reading the description it
should be borne in mind that Clairvaux was a new establishment,
founded expressly to further the work of monastic reform, and that
therefore at the time when William of St. Thierry knew it, it exhibited
a state of piety and industry considerably above that to be found in
the average abbey of the day.

Source—Guillaume de Saint-Thierry, *Bernardus Clarævallensis* [William
    of Saint Thierry, " Life of St. Bernard "], Bk. I., Chap. 7. Trans-
    lated in Edward L. Cutts, *Scenes and Characters of the Middle
    Ages* (London, 1872), pp. 12–14.

At the first glance as you entered Clairvaux by descending the
hill you could see that it was a temple of God; and the still,
silent valley bespoke, in the modest simplicity of its buildings,
the unfeigned humility of Christ's poor.   Moreover, in this valley
full of men, where no one was permitted to be idle, where one
and all were occupied with their allotted tasks, a silence deep
The solitude   as that of night prevailed.   The sounds of labor, or
of Clairvaux   the chants of the brethren in the choral service,
were the only exceptions.   The orderliness of this silence, and
the report that went forth concerning it, struck such a reverence
even into secular persons that they dreaded breaking it,—I will
not say by idle or wicked conversation, but even by proper
remarks.   The solitude, also, of the place—between dense forests
in a narrow gorge of neighboring hills—in a certain sense recalled

---

[1] The famous founder of the monastery of Monte Cassino and the com-
piler of the Benedictine Rule [see p. 83].

the cave of our father St. Benedict,[1] so that while they strove
to imitate his life, they also had some similarity to him in their
habitation and loneliness. . . .

Although the monastery is situated in a valley, it has its
foundations on the holy hills, whose gates the Lord loveth more
than all the dwellings of Jacob. Glorious things are spoken of
it, because the glorious and wonderful God therein worketh great
marvels. There the insane recover their reason, and although
their outward man is worn away, inwardly they are born again.

Marvelous works accomplished there
There the proud are humbled, the rich are made
poor, and the poor have the Gospel preached to
them, and the darkness of sinners is changed
into light. A large multitude of blessed poor from the ends of
the earth have there assembled, yet have they one heart and
one mind; justly, therefore, do all who dwell there rejoice with
no empty joy. They have the certain hope of perennial joy, of
their ascension heavenward already commenced. In Clairvaux,
they have found Jacob's ladder, with angels upon it; some
descending, who so provide for their bodies that they faint not
on the way; others ascending, who so rule their souls that their
bodies hereafter may be glorified with them.

For my part, the more attentively I watch them day by day,
the more do I believe that they are perfect followers of Christ
in all things. When they pray and speak to God in spirit and
in truth, by their friendly and quiet speech to Him, as well
The piety of the monks
as by their humbleness of demeanor, they are
plainly seen to be God's companions and friends.
When, on the other hand, they openly praise God with psalms,
how pure and fervent are their minds, is shown by their posture
of body in holy fear and reverence, while by their careful pro-
nunciation and modulation of the psalms, is shown how sweet to
their lips are the words of God—sweeter than honey to their
mouths. As I watch them, therefore, singing without fatigue
from before midnight to the dawn of day, with only a brief in-

terval, they appear a little less than the angels, but much more than men. . . .

As regards their manual labor, so patiently and placidly, with such quiet countenances, in such sweet and holy order, do they perform all things, that although they exercise themselves at many works, they never seem moved or burdened in anything, whatever the labor may be. Whence it is manifest that that Holy Spirit worketh in them who disposeth of all things with sweetness, in whom they are refreshed, so that they rest even **Their manual** in their toil. Many of them, I hear, are bishops **labor** and earls, and many illustrious through their birth or knowledge; but now, by God's grace, all distinction of persons being dead among them, the greater any one thought himself in the world, the more in this flock does he regard himself as less than the least. I see them in the garden with hoes, in the meadows with forks or rakes, in the fields with scythes, in the forest with axes. To judge from their outward appearance, their tools, their bad and disordered clothes, they appear a race of fools, without speech or sense. But a true thought in my mind tells me that their life in Christ is hidden in the heavens. Among them I see Godfrey of Peronne, Raynald of Picardy, William of St. Omer, Walter of Lisle, all of whom I knew formerly in the old man, whereof I now see no trace, by God's favor. I knew them proud and puffed up; I see them walking humbly under the merciful hand of God.

CHAPTER XVI.

THE CONFLICT OVER INVESTITURE

45. Gregory VII.'s Conception of the Papal Authority

HILDEBRAND, who as pope was known as Gregory VII., was born about the year 1025 in the vicinity of the little Tuscan town of Soana. His education was received in the rich monastery of Saint Mary on the Aventine, of which one of his uncles was abbot. At the age of twenty-five he became chaplain to Pope Gregory VI., after whose fall from power he sought seclusion in the monastery at Cluny. In 1049, however, he again appeared in Italy, this time in the rôle of companion to the new pontiff, Leo IX. In a few years he became sub-deacon and cardinal and was intrusted with the municipal affairs and financial interests of the Holy See. He served as papal legate in France and in 1057 was sent to Germany to obtain the consent of Empress Agnes to the hurried election of Stephen IX. While in these countries he became convinced that the evil conditions—simony, lay investiture, and non-celibacy of the clergy—which the Cluniacs were seeking to reform would never be materially improved by the temporal powers, and consequently that the only hope of betterment lay in the establishing of an absolute papal supremacy before which kings, and even emperors, should be compelled to bow in submission. In April, 1073, Hildebrand himself was made pope, nominally by the vote of the College of Cardinals, but really by the enthusiastic choice of the Roman populace. His whole training and experience had fitted him admirably for the place and had equipped him with the capacity to make of his office something more than had any of his predecessors. When he became pope it was with a very lofty ideal of what the papacy should be, and the surprising measure in which he was able to realize this ideal entitles him without question to be regarded as the greatest of all mediæval popes.

In the document given below, the so-called *Dictatus Papæ*, Pope Gregory's conception of the nature of the papal power and its proper place in the world is stated in the form of a clear and forcible summary. Until recently the *Dictatus* was supposed to have been written by Gregory himself, but it has been fairly well demonstrated that it was composed not earlier than 1087 and was therefore the work of some one else (Gregory died in 1085). It conforms very closely to a collection of the laws of the Church published in 1087 by a certain cardinal by the name of Deusdedit. The document loses little or none of its value by reason of this uncertainty as to its authorship, for it represents Pope Gregory's views as accurately as if he were known to have written it. In judging Gregory's theories it should be borne in mind (1) that it was not personal ambition, but sincere conviction, that lay beneath them; (2) that the temporal states which existed in western Europe in Gregory's day were rife with feudal anarchy and oppression and often too weak to be capable of rendering justice; and (3) that Gregory claimed, not that the Church should actually assume the management of the civil government throughout Europe, but only that in cases of notorious failure of temporal sovereigns to live right and govern well, the supreme authority of the papacy should be brought to bear upon them, either to depose them or to compel them to mend their ways. It is worthy of note, however, that Gregory was careful to lay the foundations of a formidable political power in Italy, chiefly by availing himself of the practices of feudalism, as seen, for example, in the grant of southern Italy to the Norman Robert Guiscard to be held as a fief of the Roman see.

Source—Text in Michael Doeberl, *Monumenta Germaniæ Historica Selecta* (München, 1889), Vol. III., p. 17.

1. That the Roman Church was founded by God alone.
2. That the Roman bishop alone is properly called universal.[1]

---

[1] The incumbent of the papal office was at the same time bishop of Rome, temporal sovereign of the papal lands, and head of the church universal. In earlier times there was always danger that the third of these functions be lost and that the papacy revert to a purely local institution, but by Gregory VII.'s day the universal headship was clearly recognized throughout the West as inherent in the office. It was only when there arose the question as to how far this headship justified the Pope in attempting to control the affairs of the world that serious disagreement manifested itself.

3. That he alone has the power to depose bishops and reinstate them.

4. That his legate, though of inferior rank, takes precedence of all bishops in council, and may give sentence of deposition against them.

5. That the Pope has the power to depose [bishops] in their absence.[1]

6. That we should not even stay in the same house with those who are excommunicated by him.

8. That he alone may use the imperial insignia.[2]

9. That the Pope is the only person whose feet are kissed by all princes.

11. That the name which he bears belongs to him alone.[3]

12. That he has the power to depose emperors.[4]

13. That he may, if necessity require, transfer bishops from one see to another.

16. That no general synod may be called without his consent.

17. That no action of a synod, and no book, may be considered canonical without his authority.[5]

18. That his decree can be annulled by no one, and that he alone may annul the decrees of any one.

19. That he can be judged by no man.

20. That no one shall dare to condemn a person who appeals to the apostolic see.

22. That the Roman Church has never erred, nor ever, by the testimony of Scripture, shall err, to all eternity.[6]

[1] That is, without giving them a hearing at a later date.
[2] On the basis of the forged Donation of Constantine the Pope claimed the right here mentioned. There was no proper warrant for it.
[3] "This is the first distinct assertion of the exclusive right of the bishop of Rome to the title of pope, once applied to all bishops." Robinson, *Readings in European History*, Vol. I., p. 274. The word pope is derived from *papa* (father). It is still used as the common title of all priests in the Greek Church.
[4] This, with the letter given on page 265, sets forth succinctly the papacy's absolute claim of authority as against the highest temporal power in Europe.
[5] That is, pronounced by the canons of the Church to be divinely inspired.
[6] This is, of course, not a claim of *papal* infallibility. The assertion is

26. That no one can be considered Catholic who does not agree with the Roman Church.

27. That he [the Pope] has the power to absolve the subjects of unjust rulers from their oath of fidelity.

46. Letter of Gregory VII. to Henry IV. (December, 1075)

THE high ideal of papal supremacy over temporal sovereigns which Gregory cherished when he became pope in 1073, and which is set forth so forcibly in the *Dictatus*, was one whose validity no king or emperor could be brought to recognize. It involved an attitude of inferiority and submissiveness which monarchs felt to be quite inconsistent with the complete independence which they claimed in the management of the affairs of their respective states. Perhaps one may say that the theory in itself, as a mere expression of religious sentiment, was not especially obnoxious; many an earlier pope had proclaimed it in substance without doing the kings and emperors of Europe material injury. It was the firm determination and the aggressive effort of Gregory to reduce the theory to an actual working system that precipitated a conflict.

The supreme test of Gregory's ability to make the papal power felt in the measure that he thought it should be came early in the pontificate in the famous breach with Henry IV. of Germany. Henry at the time was not emperor in name, but only "king of the Romans," the imperial coronation not yet having taken place.[1] For all practical purposes, however, he may be regarded as occupying the emperor's position, since all that was lacking was the performance of a more or less perfunctory ceremony. Henry's specific grievances against the Pope were that the latter had declared it a sin for an ecclesiastic to be invested with his office by a layman, though this was almost the universal practice in Germany, and that he had condemned five of the king's councilors for simony,[2] suspended the archbishop of Bremen, the bishops of Speyer

merely that in the domain of faith and morals the Roman church, judged by Scriptural principles, has never pursued a course either improper or unwarranted.

[1] It did not occur until 1084. Henry had inherited the office at the death of his father, Henry III., in 1056.

[2] The sin of simony comprised the employment of any corrupt means to obtain appointment or election to an ecclesiastical office. For the origin

and Strassburg, and two Lombard bishops, and deposed the bishop of Florence. Half of the land and wealth of Germany was in the hands of bishops and abbots who, if the Pope were to have his way, would be released from all practical dependence upon the king and so would be free to encourage and take part in the feudal revolts which Henry was exerting himself so vigorously to crush. June 8, 1075, on the banks of the Unstrutt, the king won a signal victory over the rebellious feudal lords, after which he felt strong enough to defy the authority of Gregory with impunity. He therefore continued to associate with the five condemned councilors and, in contempt of recent papal declarations against lay investiture, took it upon himself to appoint and invest a number of bishops and abbots, though always with extreme care that the right kind of men be selected. Pope Gregory was, of course, not the man to overlook such conduct and at once made vigorous protest. The letter given below was written in December, 1075, and is one of a considerable series which passed back and forth across the Alps prior to the breaking of the storm in 1076–1077. At this stage matters had not yet got beyond the possibility of compromise and reconciliation; in fact Gregory writes as much as anything else to get the king's own statement regarding the reports of his conduct which had come to Rome. The tone of the letter is firm, it is true, but conciliatory. The thunder of subsequent epistles to the recreant Henry had not yet been brought into play.

Source—Text in Michael Doeberl, *Monumenta Germaniæ Historica Selecta* (München, 1889), Vol. III., pp. 18–22. Adapted from translation in Oliver J. Thatcher and Edgar H. McNeal, *Source Book for Mediæval History* (New York, 1905), pp. 147–150.

Gregory, bishop, servant of the servants of God, to Henry, the king, greeting and apostolic benediction,—that is, if he be obedient to the apostolic see as is becoming in a Christian king:

It is with some hesitation that we have sent you our apostolic benediction, knowing that for all our acts as pope we must render an account to God, the severe judge. It is reported that you have willingly associated with men who have been excom-

of the term see the incident recorded in Acts, viii. 18–24. The five councilors had been condemned by a synod at Rome in February, 1075.

municated by decree of the Pope and sentence of a synod.[1] If this be true, you are very well aware that you can receive the blessing neither of God nor of the Pope until you have driven

Henry exhorted to confess his sins

them from you and have compelled them to do penance, and have also yourself sought absolution and forgiveness for your transgressions with due repentance and good works. Therefore we advise you that, if you realize your guilt in this matter, you immediately confess to some pious bishop, who shall absolve you with our permission, prescribing for you penance in proportion to the fault, and who shall faithfully report to us by letter, with your permission, the nature of the penance required.

We wonder, moreover, that you should continue to assure us by letter and messengers of your devotion and humility; that you should call yourself our son and the son of the holy mother Church, obedient in the faith, sincere in love, diligent in devotion; and that you should commend yourself to us with all zeal of love and reverence—whereas in fact you are constantly disobeying the canonical and apostolic decrees in important matters of the faith. . . . Since you confess yourself a son of the Church, you should treat with more honor the head of the Church, that is, St. Peter, the prince of the apostles. If you are one of the sheep of the Lord, you have been entrusted to

The Pope's claim to authority over temporal princes

him by divine authority, for Christ said to him: "Peter, feed my sheep" [John, xxi. 16]; and again: "And I will give unto thee the keys of the kingdom of Heaven; and whatsoever thou shalt bind on earth shall be bound in heaven; and whatsoever thou shalt loose on earth shall be loosed in heaven" [Matt., xvi. 19]. And since we, although an unworthy sinner, exercise his authority by divine will, the words which you address to us are in reality addressed directly to him. And although we read or hear only the words, he sees the heart from which the words proceed. There-

---

[1] The five condemned councilors.

fore your highness should be very careful that no insincerity be found in your words and messages to us; and that you show due reverence, not to us, indeed, but to omnipotent God, in those things which especially make for the advance of the Christian faith and the well-being of the Church. For our Lord said to the apostles and to their successors: "He that heareth you heareth me, and he that despiseth you despiseth me" [Luke, x. 16]. For no one will disregard our admonitions if he believes that the decrees of the Pope have the same authority as the words of the apostle himself.[1] . . .

Now in the synod held at the apostolic seat to which the divine will has called us (at which some of your subjects also were present) we, seeing that the Christian religion had been weakened by many attacks and that the chief and proper motive, that of saving souls, had for a long time been neglected and slighted, were alarmed at the evident danger of the destruction of the flock of the Lord, and had recourse to the decrees and the

Abuses in the Church to be corrected doctrine of the holy fathers. We decreed nothing new, nothing of our invention; but we decided that the error should be abandoned and the single primitive rule of ecclesiastical discipline and the familiar way of the saints should be again sought out and followed.[2] For we know that no other door to salvation and eternal life lies open to the sheep of Christ than that which was pointed out by Him who said: "I am the door: by me if any man enter in he shall be saved, and find pasture" [John, x. 9]; and this, we learn from the gospels and from the sacred writings, was preached by the apostles and observed by the holy fathers. And we have decided that this decree—which some, placing human above divine honor, have called an unendurable weight and an immense

[1] This portion of the letter comprises a clear assertion of the "Petrine Supremacy," i. e., the theory that Peter, as the first bishop of Rome, transmitted his superiority over all other bishops to his successors in the Roman see, who in due time came to constitute the line of popes [see p. 78].

[2] This refers to a decree of a Roman synod in 1074 against simony and the marriage of the clergy.

burden, but which we call by its proper name, that is, the truth and light necessary to salvation—is to be received and observed not only by you and your subjects, but also by all princes and peoples of the earth who confess and worship Christ; for it is greatly desired by us, and would be most fitting to you, that as you are greater than others in glory, in honor, and in virtue, so you should be more distinguished in devotion to Christ.

Nevertheless, that this decree may not seem to you beyond measure grievous and unjust, we have commanded you by your faithful ambassadors to send to us the wisest and most pious men whom you can find in your kingdom, so that if they can show or instruct us in any way how we can temper the sentence promulgated by the holy fathers without offense **Gregory disposed to treat Henry fairly** to the eternal King or danger to our souls, we may consider their advice. But, even if we had not warned you in so friendly a manner, it would have been only right on your part, before you violated the apostolic decrees, to ask justice of us in a reasonable manner in any matter in which we had injured or affected your honor. But from what you have since done and decreed it is evident how little you care for our warnings, or for the observance of justice.

But since we hope that, while the long-suffering patience of God still invites you to repent, you may become wiser and your heart may be turned to obey the commands of God, we warn you with fatherly love that, knowing the rule of Christ to be over you, you should consider how dangerous it is to place your honor above His, and that you should not interfere with the liberty of the Church which He has deigned to join to Himself by heavenly union, but rather with faithful devotion you should offer your assistance to the increasing of this liberty to omnipotent God and St. Peter, through whom also your glory may be enhanced. You ought to recognize what you undoubtedly owe to them for giving you victory over your enemies,[1] that as they

[1] In the battle on the Unstrutt, June 8, 1075.

have gladdened you with great prosperity, so they should see
that you are thereby rendered more devout.   And in order that
Henry's obli- the fear of God, in whose hands is all power and
gation to serve all rule, may affect your heart more than these
and obey the
papacy   our warnings, you should recall what happened
to Saul, when, after winning the victory which he gained by
the will of the prophet, he glorified himself in his triumph and
did not obey the warnings of the prophet, and how God reproved
him; and, on the other hand, what grace King David acquired
by reason of his humility, as well as his other virtues.

47. Henry IV.'s Reply to Gregory's Letter (January, 1076)

IN 1059, when Nicholas II. was pope and Hildebrand was yet only a
cardinal, a council assembled at the Lateran decreed that henceforth
the right of electing the sovereign pontiff should be vested exclusively
in the college of cardinals, or in other words, in seven cardinal bishops
in the vicinity of Rome and a certain number of cardinal priests and
deacons attached to the parishes of the city.   The people and clergy
generally were deprived of participation in the election, except so far
as merely to give their consent.   Hildebrand seems to have been the
real author of the decree.   Nevertheless, in 1073, when he was elevated
to the papal chair, the decree of 1059 was in a measure ignored, for he
was elected by popular vote and his choice was only passively sanc-
tioned by the cardinals.   When, therefore, the quarrel between him and
Henry IV. came on, the latter was not slow to make use of the weapon
which Hildebrand's (or Gregory's) uncanonical election placed in his
hands.   In replying, January 24, 1076, to the papal letter of December, 1075, he bluntly addresses himself to "Hildebrand, not pope, but
false monk," and writes a stinging epistle in the tone thus assumed
in his salutation.   In his arraignment of Gregory the king doubtless
went far beyond the truth; but the fact remains that Gregory's dominat-
ing purposes in the interest of the papal authority threatened to cut
deeply into the independence of all temporal sovereigns, and therefore
rendered such resistance as Henry offered quite inevitable.   In the in-
terim between receiving the Pope's letter and dispatching his reply

Henry had convened at Worms a council of the German clergy, and this body had decreed that Gregory, having wrongfully ascended the papal throne, should be compelled forthwith to abdicate it.

Source—Text in Michael Doeberl, *Monumenta Germaniæ Historica Selecta* (München, 1889), Vol. III., pp. 24–25. Translated in Oliver J. Thatcher and Edgar H. McNeal, *Source Book for Mediæval History* (New York, 1905), pp. 151–152.

Henry, king not by usurpation, but by the holy ordination of God, to Hildebrand, not pope, but false monk.

This is the salutation which you deserve, for you have never held any office in the Church without making it a source of confusion and a curse to Christian men, instead of an honor and a blessing. To mention only the most obvious cases out of many, you have not only dared to lay hands on the Lord's anointed, the archbishops, bishops, and priests, but you have scorned **Gregory declared to be only a demagogue** them and abused them, as if they were ignorant servants not fit to know what their master was doing. This you have done to gain favor with the vulgar crowd. You have declared that the bishops know nothing and that you know everything; but if you have such great wisdom you have used it not to build but to destroy. Therefore we believe that St. Gregory, whose name you have presumed to take, had you in mind when he said: "The heart of the prelate is puffed up by the abundance of subjects, and he thinks himself more powerful than all others." All this we have endured because of our respect for the papal office, but you have mistaken our humility for fear, and have dared to make an attack upon the royal and imperial authority which we received **The papal claim to temporal supremacy rejected** from God. You have even threatened to take it away, as if we had received it from you, and as if the Empire and kingdom were in your disposal and not in the disposal of God. Our Lord Jesus Christ has called us to the government of the Empire, but He never called you to the rule of the Church.   This is the way you have gained advancement in the Church: through craft you have obtained wealth; through wealth you have obtained favor; through favor, the power of the sword; and through the power of the sword, the papal seat, which is the seat of peace; and then from the seat of peace you have expelled peace. For you have incited subjects to rebel against their prelates by teaching them to despise the bishops, their rightful rulers. You have given to laymen the authority over priests, whereby they condemn and depose those whom the bishops have put over them to teach them. You have attacked me, who, unworthy as I am, have yet been anointed to rule among the anointed of God, and who, according to the teaching of the fathers, can be judged by no one save God alone, and can be deposed for no crime except infidelity. For the holy fathers in the time of the apostate Julian [1] did not presume to pronounce sentence of deposition against him, but left him to be judged and condemned by God.

Henry also cites Scripture St. Peter himself said, "Fear God, honor the king" [1 Pet., ii. 17]. But you, who fear not God, have dishonored me, whom He hath established. St. Paul, who said that even an angel from heaven should be accursed who taught any other than the true doctrine, did not make an exception in your favor, to permit you to teach false doctrines. For he says, "But though we, or an angel from heaven, preach any other gospel unto you than that which we have preached unto you, let him be accursed" [Gal., i. 8]. Come down, then, from that apostolic seat which you have obtained by violence; for you have been declared accursed by St. Paul for your false doctrines, and have been condemned by us and our bishops for your evil rule. Let another ascend the throne of St. Peter, one who will not use religion as a cloak of violence, but will teach the life-giving doctrine of that prince of the

[1] Julian succeeded Constantine's son Constantius as head of the Roman Empire in 361. He was known as "the Apostate" because of his efforts to displace the Christian religion and to restore the old pagan worship. He died in battle with the Persians in 363.

apostles. I, Henry, king by the grace of God, with all my bishops, say unto you: "Come down, come down, and be accursed through all the ages."

48. Henry IV. Deposed by Pope Gregory (1076)

THE foregoing letter of Henry IV. was received at Rome with a storm of disapproval and the envoys who bore it barely escaped with their lives. A council of French and Italian bishops was convened in the Lateran (Feb. 24, 1076), and the king's haughty epistle, together with the decree of the council at Worms deposing Gregory, were read and allowed to have their effect. With the assent of the bishops, the Pope pronounced the sentence of excommunication against Henry and formally released all the latter's Christian subjects from their oath of allegiance. Naturally the action of Gregory aroused intense interest throughout Europe. In Germany it had the intended effect of detaching many influential bishops and abbots from the imperial cause and stirring the political enemies of the king to renewed activity. The papal ban became a pretext for the renewal of the hostility on part of his dissatisfied subjects which Henry had but just succeeded in suppressing.

In the first part of the papal decree Gregory seeks to defend himself against the charges brought by Henry and the German clergy to the effect that he had mounted the papal throne through personal ambition and the employment of unbecoming means. It was indisputable that his election had not been strictly in accord with the decree of 1059, but it seems equally true that, as Gregory declares, he was placed at the helm of the Church contrary to his personal desires.

Source—Text in Michael Doeberl, *Monumenta Germaniæ Historica Selecta* (München, 1889), Vol. III., p. 26. Translated in Oliver J. Thatcher and Edgar H. McNeal, *Source Book for Mediæval History* (New York, 1905), pp. 155–156.

St. Peter, prince of the apostles, incline thine ear unto me, I beseech thee, and hear me, thy servant, whom thou hast nourished from mine infancy and hast delivered from mine enemies that hate me for my fidelity to thee. Thou art my witness, as are also my mistress, the mother of God, and St. Paul thy brother, and all the other saints, that the Holy Roman Church **Gregory denies** called me to its government against my own will, **that he ever** and that I did not gain thy throne by violence; **sought the** **papal office** that I would rather have ended my days in exile than have obtained thy place by fraud or for worldly ambition. It is not by my efforts, but by thy grace, that I am set to rule over the Christian world which was especially intrusted to thee by Christ. It is by thy grace, and as thy representative that God has given to me the power to bind and to loose in heaven and in earth. Confident of my integrity and authority, I now declare in the name of the omnipotent God, the Father, Son, and Holy Spirit, that Henry, son of the Emperor Henry,[1] is **Henry** deprived of his kingdom of Germany and Italy. **deposed by** I do this by thy authority and in defense of the **papal decree** honor of thy Church, because he has rebelled against it. He who attempts to destroy the honor of the Church should be deprived of such honor as he may have held. He has refused to obey as a Christian should; he has not returned to God from whom he had wandered; he has had dealings with excommunicated persons; he has done many iniquities; he has despised the warnings which, as thou art witness, I sent to him for his salvation; he has cut himself off from thy Church, and has attempted to rend it asunder; therefore, by thy authority, I place him under the curse. It is in thy name that I curse him, that all people may know that thou art Peter, and upon thy rock the Son of the living God has built his Church, and the gates of Hell shall not prevail against it.

49. The Penance of Henry IV. at Canossa (1077)

In his contest with the Pope, Henry's chances of winning were from the outset diminished by the readiness of his subjects to take advantage of his misfortunes to recover political privileges they had lost under his

---

[1] Henry III., emperor from 1039 to 1056.

vigorous rule. In October, 1076, the leading German nobles, lay and clerical, encouraged by the papal decree of the preceding February, assembled at Tribur, near Mainz, and proceeded to formulate a plan of action. Henry, with the few followers who remained faithful, awaited the result at Oppenheim, just across the Rhine. The magnates at last agreed that unless Henry could secure the removal of the papal ban within a year he should be deposed from the throne. By the Oppenheim Convention he was forced to promise to revoke his sentence of deposition against Gregory and to offer him his allegiance. The promise was executed in a royal edict of the same month. Seeing that there remained no hope in further resistance, and hearing that Gregory was about to present himself in Germany to compel a final adjustment of the affair, Henry fled from Speyer, where he had been instructed by the nobles to remain, and by a most arduous winter journey over the Alps arrived at last at the castle of Canossa, in Tuscany,[1] where the Pope, on his way to Germany, was being entertained by one of his allies, the Countess Matilda. Gregory might indeed already have been on the Rhine but that he had heard of the move Henry was making and feared that he was proposing to stir up revolt in the papal dominions. The king was submissive, apparently conquered; yet Gregory was loath to end the conflict at this point. He had hoped to establish a precedent by entering German territory and there disposing of the crown according to his own will. But it was a cardinal rule of the Church that a penitent sincerely seeking absolution could not be denied, and in his request Henry was certainly importunate enough to give every appearance of sincerity. Accordingly, the result of the meeting of king [Emperor] and Pope at Canossa was that the ban of excommunication was revoked by the latter, while the former took an oath fully acknowledging the papal claims.

Inasmuch as he had saved his crown and frustrated the design of Gregory to cross the mountains into Germany, Henry may be said to have won a temporary advantage; and this was followed within a few years, when the struggle broke out again, by the practical expulsion of Gregory from Rome and his death in broken-hearted exile (1085).

---

[1] The castle of Canossa stood on one of the northern spurs of the Apennines, about ten miles southwest of Reggio. Some remains of it may yet be seen.

Nevertheless the moral effect of the Canossa episode, and of the events which followed, in the long run operated decidedly against the king's position and the whole imperial theory. The document below is a letter of Gregory to the German magnates giving an account of the submission of the king at Canossa, and including the text of the oath which he there took.

Source—Text in Michael Doeberl, *Monumenta Germaniæ Historica Selecta* (München, 1889), Vol. III., pp. 33–34. Adapted from translation in Ernest F. Henderson, *Select Historical Documents of the Middle Ages* (London, 1896), pp. 385–388.

Gregory, bishop, servant of the servants of God, to all the archbishops, bishops, dukes, counts, and other princes of the realm of the Germans who defend the Christian faith, greeting and apostolic benediction.

Inasmuch as for love of justice you assumed common cause and danger with us in the struggle of Christian warfare, we have taken care to inform you, beloved, with sincere affection, how the king, humbled to penance, obtained the pardon of absolution and how the whole affair has progressed from his entrance into Italy to the present time.

As had been agreed with the legates who had been sent to us on your part,[1] we came into Lombardy about twenty days before the date on which one of the commanders was to come over the

Gregory's advance into Tuscany
pass to meet us, awaiting his advent that we might cross over to the other side. But when the period fixed upon had already passed, and we were told that at this time on account of many difficulties— as we can readily believe—an escort could not be sent to meet us, we were involved in no little perplexity as to what would be best for us to do, having no other means of coming to you.

[1] The German princes who were hostile to Henry had kept in close touch with the Pope. In the Council of Tribur a legate of Gregory took the most prominent part, and the members of that body had invited the Pope to come to Augsburg and aid in the settling of Henry's crown upon a successor.

Meanwhile, however, we learned that the king was approaching. He also, before entering Italy, sent to us suppliant legates, offering in all things to render satisfaction to God, to St. Peter, and to us. And he renewed his promise that, besides amending his way of living, he would observe all obedience if only he might deserve to obtain from us the favor of absolution and the apostolic benediction. When, after long postponing a decision and holding frequent consultations, we, through all the envoys who

Henry at Canossa

passed, had severely taken him to task for his excesses, he came at length of his own accord, with a few followers, showing nothing of hostility or boldness, to the town of Canossa where we were tarrying. And there, having laid aside all the belongings of royalty, wretchedly, with bare feet and clad in wool, he continued for three days to stand before the gate of the castle. Nor did he desist from imploring with many tears, the aid and consolation of the apostolic mercy until he had moved all of those who were present there, and whom the report of it reached, to such pity and depth of compassion that, interceding for him with many prayers and tears, all wondered indeed at the unaccustomed hardness of our heart, while some actually cried out that we were exercising, not the dignity of apostolic severity, but the cruelty, as it were, of a tyrannical madness.

Finally, won by the persistency of his suit and by the constant supplications of all who were present, we loosed the chain of the anathema [1] and at length received him into the favor of communion and into the lap of the holy mother Church, those being accepted as sponsors for him whose names are written below.

Having thus accomplished these matters, we desire at the first opportunity to cross over to your country in order that, by God's aid, we may more fully arrange all things for the peace

---

[1] Revoked the ban of excommunication. The anathema was a solemn curse by an ecclesiastical authority.

of the Church and the concord of the kingdom, as has long been our wish. For we desire, beloved, that you should know **Gregory's purpose to visit Germany** beyond a doubt that the whole question at issue is as yet so little cleared up—as you can learn from the sponsors mentioned—that both our coming and the concurrence of your counsels are extremely necessary. Wherefore strive ye all to continue in the faith in which you have begun and in the love of justice; and know that we are not otherwise committed to the king save that, by word alone, as is our custom, we have said that he might have hopes from us in those matters in which, without danger to his soul or to our own, we might be able to help him to his salvation and honor, either through justice or through mercy.

OATH OF KING HENRY

I, King Henry, on account of the murmuring and enmity which the archbishops and bishops, dukes, counts and other princes of the realm of the Germans, and others who follow them in the same matter of dissension, bring to bear against me, will, within the term which our master Pope Gregory has constituted, either do justice according to his judgment or conclude peace according to his counsels—unless an absolute impediment should stand in his way or in mine. And on the removal of this impediment I shall be ready to continue in the same course. Likewise, if that same lord Pope Gregory shall wish to go beyond the mountains [i.e., into Germany], or to any other part of the world, he himself, as well as those who shall be in his escort or following, or who are sent by him, or come to him from any parts of the world whatever, shall be secure while going, remaining, or returning, on my part, and on the part of those whom I can constrain, from every injury to life or limb, or from capture. Nor shall he, by my consent, meet any other hindrance that is contrary to his dignity; and if any such be placed in his way I

will aid him according to my ability.   So help me God and this
holy gospel.

50. The Concordat of Worms (1122)

THE veteran Emperor Henry IV. died at Liège in 1106 and was succeeded by his son, Henry V.   The younger Henry had some months before been prompted by Pope Paschal II. to rebel against his father and,
succeeding in this, had practically established himself on the throne
before his legitimate time.   Pope Paschal expected the son to be more
submissive than the father had been and in 1106 issued a decree re-
newing the prohibition of lay investiture.   Outside of Germany this
evil had been brought almost to an end and, now that the vigorous
Henry IV. was out of the way, the Pope felt that the time had come to
make the reform complete throughout Christendom.   But in this he
was mistaken, for Henry V. proved almost as able and fully as determined a power to contend with as had been his father.   In fact, the new
monarch could command a much stronger army, and he was in no wise
loath to use it.   In 1110 he led a host of thirty thousand men across
the Alps, compelled the submission of the north Italian towns, and
marched on Rome.   The outcome was a secret compact (February 4,
1111) by which the king, on the one hand, was to abandon all claim to the
right of investiture and the Pope, on the other, was to see that the ecclesiastical princes of the Empire (bishops and abbots holding large tracts
of land) should give up all the lands which they had received by royal
grant since the days of Charlemagne.   The abandonment of investiture
looked like a surrender on the part of Henry, but in reality all that he
wanted was direct control over all the lands of the Empire, and if the
ecclesiastical princes were to be dispossessed of these he cared little or
nothing about having a part in the mere religious ceremony.   This
settlement was rendered impossible, however, by the attitude of the
princes themselves, who naturally refused to be thus deprived of their
landed property and chief source of income.   The Pope was then forced
to make a second compact surrendering the full right of investiture to
the imperial authority, and Henry also got the coveted imperial coronation.   But his triumph was short-lived.   Rebellions among the German
nobles robbed him of his strength and after years of wearisome bicker-

ings and petty conflicts he again came to the point where he was wiiling to compromise. Calixtus II., who became pope in 1119, was similarly inclined.

Accordingly, in a diet at Worms, in 1122, the whole problem was taken up for settlement, and happily this time with success. The documents translated below contain the concessions made mutually by the two parties. Calixtus, in brief, grants that the elections of bishops and abbots may take place in the presence of the Emperor, or of his agents, and that the Emperor should have the right to invest them with the scepter, i.e., with their dignity as princes of the Empire. Henry, on his side, agrees to give up investiture with the ring and staff, i.e., with spiritual functions, to allow free elections, and to aid in the restoration of church property which had been confiscated during the long struggle now drawing to a close. The settlement was in the nature of a compromise; but on the whole the papacy came off the better. In its largest aspects the great fifty-year struggle over the question of investiture was ended, though minor features of it remained to trouble all parties concerned for a long time to come.

Sources—(a) Text in *Monumenta Germaniæ Historica*, *Leges* (Pertz ed.), Vol. II., pp. 75–76.

   (b) Text in Michael Doeberl, *Monumenta Germaniæ Historica Selecta*, Vol. III., p. 60.

(a)

I, Bishop Calixtus, servant of the servants of God, do grant to thee, by the grace of God august Emperor of the Romans, the right to hold the elections of the bishops and abbots of the German realm who belong to the kingdom, in thy presence, with-**The provision for elections** out simony, and without any resort to violence; it being agreed that, if any dispute arise among those concerned, thou, by the counsel and judgment of the metropolitan [i.e., the archbishop] and the suffragan bishops, shalt extend favor and support to the party which shall seem to you to have the better case. Moreover, the person elected may receive from thee the *regalia* through the scepter, without any exaction being levied;[1] and he shall discharge his rightful obligations to thee for them.[2]

He who is consecrated in other parts of the Empire[3] shall receive the *regalia* from thee through the scepter, within six months, and without any exaction, and shall discharge his

Investiture with the scepter

rightful obligations to thee for them; those rights being excepted, however, which are known to belong to the Roman Church. In whatever cases thou shalt make complaint to me and ask my aid I will support thee according as my office requires. To thee, and to all those who are on thy side, or have been, in this period of strife, I grant a true peace.

(b)

In the name of the holy and indivisible Trinity, I, Henry, by the grace of God august Emperor of the Romans, for the love of God and of the holy Roman Church and of our lord Pope Calixtus, and for the saving of my soul, do give over to God,

Investiture with ring and staff

and to the holy apostles of God, Peter and Paul, and the holy Catholic Church, all investiture through ring and staff; and do concede that in all the churches that are in my kingdom or empire there shall be canonical election and free consecration.

All the property and *regalia* of St. Peter which, from the beginning of this conflict until the present time, whether in the days of my father or in my own, have been confiscated, and

Restoration of confiscated property

which I now hold, I restore to the holy Roman Church. And as for those things which I do not now hold, I will faithfully aid in their restoration. The property also of all other churches and princes and

---

[1] That is, the Emperor was to be allowed to invest the new bishop or abbot with the fiefs and secular powers by a touch of the scepter, but his old claim to the right of investment with the spiritual emblems of ring and crozier was denied.

[2] This means that the ecclesiastical prince—the bishop or abbot—in the capacity of a landholder was to render the ordinary feudal obligations to the Emperor.

[3] Burgundy and Italy.

of every one, whether lay or ecclesiastical, which has been lost in the struggle, I will restore as far as I hold it, according to the counsel of the princes, or according to considerations of justice. I will also faithfully aid in the restoration of those things which I do not hold.

And I grant a true peace to our lord Pope Calixtus, and to the holy Roman Church, and to all those who are, or have been, on its side. In matters where the holy Roman Church shall seek assistance, I will faithfully render it, and when it shall make complaint to me I will see that justice is done.

CHAPTER XVII.

THE CRUSADES

51. Speech of Pope Urban II. at the Council of Clermont (1095)

Within a short time after the death of Mohammed (632) the whole country of Syria, including Palestine, was overrun by the Arabs, and the Holy City of Jerusalem passed out of Christian hands into the control of the infidels. The Arabs, however, shared the veneration of the Christians for the places associated with the life of Christ and did not greatly interfere with the pilgrims who flocked thither from all parts of the Christian world. In the tenth century the strong emperors of the Macedonian dynasty at Constantinople succeeded in winning back all of Syria except the extreme south, and the prospect seemed fair for the permanent possession by a Christian power of all those portions of the Holy Land which were regarded as having associations peculiarly sacred. This prospect might have been realized but for the invasions and conquests of the Seljuk Turks in the latter part of the eleventh century. These Turks came from central Asia and are to be carefully distinguished from the Ottoman Turks of more modern times. They had recently been converted to Mohammedanism and were now the fiercest and most formidable champions of that faith in its conflict with the Christian East. In 1071 Emperor Romanus Diogenes was defeated at Manzikert, in Armenia, and taken prisoner by the sultan Alp Arslan, and as a result not only Asia Minor, but also Syria, was forever lost to the Empire. The Holy City of Jerusalem was definitely occupied in 1076. The invaders established a stronghold at Nicæa, less than a hundred miles across the Sea of Marmora from Constantinople, and even threatened the capital itself, although they did not finally succeed in taking it until 1453.

No sooner were the Turks in possession of Jerusalem and the approaches thither, than pilgrims returning to western Europe began to tell tales, not infrequently as true as they were terrifying, regarding insults and tortures suffered at the hand of the pitiless conquerors. The Emperor Alexius Comnenus (1081–1118) put forth every effort to expel the intruders from Asia Minor, hoping to be able to regain the territories, including Syria, which they had stripped from the Empire; but his strength proved unequal to the task. Accordingly, in 1095, he sent an appeal to Pope Urban II. to enlist the Christian world in a united effort to save both the Empire and the Eastern Church. It used to be thought that Pope Sylvester II., about the year 1000, had suggested a crusade against the Mohammedans of the East, but it now appears that the first pope to advance such an idea was Gregory VII. (1073–1085), who in response to an appeal of Alexius's predecessor in 1074, had actually assembled an army of 50,000 men for the aid of the Emperor and had been prevented from carrying out the project only by the severity of the investiture controversy with Henry IV. of Germany. At any rate, it was not a difficult task for the ambassadors of Alexius to convince Pope Urban that he ought to execute the plan of Gregory. The plea for aid was made at the Council of Piacenza in March, 1095, and during the next few months Urban thought out the best method of procedure.

At the Council of Clermont, held in November, 1095, the crusade was formally proclaimed through the famous speech which the Pope himself delivered after the regular business of the assembly had been transacted. Urban was a Frenchman and he knew how to appeal to the emotions and sympathies of his hearers. For the purpose of stirring up interest in the enterprise he dropped the Latin in which the work of the Council had been transacted and broke forth in his native tongue, much to the delight of his countrymen. There are four early versions of the speech, differing widely in contents, and none, of course, reproducing the exact words used by the speaker. The version given by Robert the Monk, a resident of Rheims, in the opening chapter of his history of the first crusade seems in most respects superior to the others. It was written nearly a quarter of a century after the Council of Clermont, but the writer in all probability had at least heard the speech which he was trying to reproduce; in any event we may take his version of it as a very satisfactory representation of the aspirations and spirit which impelled the first crusaders to their great enterprise. It has been well said that "many orations have been delivered with as much eloquence, and in

as fiery words as the Pope used, but no other oration has ever been able
to boast of as wonderful results."

Source—Robertus Monachus, *Historia Iherosolimitana* [Robert the Monk,
       "History of the Crusade to Jerusalem"], Bk. I., Chap. 1. Re-
       printed in *Recueildes Historiens des Croisades: Historiens Occiden-
       taux* (Paris, 1866), Vol. III., pp. 727–728. Adapted from transla-
       tion by Dana C. Munro in *Univ. of Pa. Translations and Reprints*,
       Vol. I., No. 2, pp. 5–8.

In the year of our Lord's Incarnation one thousand and
ninety-five, a great council was convened within the bounds of
The Council   Gaul, in Auvergne, in the city which is called
of Clermont   Clermont. Over this Pope Urban II. presided,
with the Roman bishops and cardinals. This council was a
famous one on account of the concourse of both French and
German bishops, and of princes as well. Having arranged the
matters relating to the Church, the lord Pope went forth into a
certain spacious plain, for no building was large enough to hold
all the people. The Pope then, with sweet and persuasive eloquence, addressed those present in words something like the
following, saying:

"Oh, race of Franks, race beyond the mountains [the Alps],
race beloved and chosen by God (as is clear from many of your
works), set apart from all other nations by the situation of your
Pope Urban   country, as well as by your Catholic faith and
appeals to the   the honor you render to the holy Church: to you
French   our discourse is addressed, and for you our
exhortations are intended. We wish you to know what a serious
matter has led us to your country, for it is the imminent peril
threatening you and all the faithful that has brought us hither.

" From the confines of Jerusalem and from the city of Constantinople a grievous report has gone forth and has been brought
repeatedly to our ears; namely, that a race from the kingdom
of the Persians, an accursed race, a race wholly alienated from
God, 'a generation that set not their heart aright, and whose
spirit was not steadfast with God' [Ps., lxxviii. 8], has vio-

lently invaded the lands of those Christians and has depopu-
lated them by pillage and fire. They have led away a part of the
The ravages captives into their own country, and a part they
of the Turks have killed by c.uel tortures. They have either
destroyed the churches of God or appropriated them for the rites
of their own religion. They destroy the altars, after having
defiled them with their uncleanness. . . . The kingdom of
the Greeks [the Eastern Empire] is now dismembered by them
and has been deprived of territory so vast in extent that it could
not be traversed in two months' time.

" On whom, therefore, rests the labor of avenging these wrongs
and of recovering this territory, if not upon you—you, upon
whom, above all other nations, God has conferred remarkable
glory in arms, great courage, bodily activity, and strength to
humble the heads of those who resist you? Let the deeds of
your ancestors encourage you and incite your minds to manly
Urban recalls achievements—the glory and greatness of King
the zeal and Charlemagne, and of his son Louis [the Pious],
valor of the
earlier Franks and of your other monarchs, who have destroyed
the kingdoms of the Turks [1] and have extended the sway of the
holy Church over lands previously pagan. Let the holy sepulcher
of our Lord and Saviour, which is possessed by the unclean
nations, especially arouse you, and the holy places which are
now treated with ignominy and irreverently polluted with the
filth of the unclean. Oh most valiant soldiers and descendants
of invincible ancestors, do not degenerate, but recall the valor of
your ancestors.

" But if you are hindered by love of children, parents, or wife,
remember what the Lord says in the Gospel, ' He that loveth
father or mother more than me is not worthy of me' [Matt.,
x. 37]. 'Every one that hath forsaken houses, or brethren, or

---

[1] The term Turks is here used loosely and inaccurately for Asiatic pagan
invaders in general. The French had never destroyed any "kingdoms of the
Turks" in the proper sense of the word, though from time to time they had
made successful resistance to Saracens, Avars and Hungarians.

sisters, or father, or mother, or wife, or children, or lands, for my name's sake, shall receive an hundred-fold, and shall inherit everlasting life' [Matt., xix. 29]. Let none of your possessions restrain you, nor anxiety for your family affairs. For this land which you inhabit, shut in on all sides by the seas and sur-

The crusade as a desirable remedy for over population
rounded by the mountain peaks, is too narrow for your large population; nor does it abound in wealth; and it furnishes scarcely food enough for its cultivators. Hence it is that you murder and devour one another, that you wage war, and that very many among you perish in civil strife.[1]

" Let hatred, therefore, depart from among you; let your quarrels end; let wars cease; and let all dissensions and controversies slumber. Enter upon the road of the Holy Sepulcher; wrest that land from the wicked race, and subject it to yourselves. That

Syria, a rich country
land which, as the Scripture says, 'floweth with milk and honey' [Num., xiii. 27] was given by God into the power of the children of Israel. Jerusalem is the center of the earth; the land is fruitful above all others, like another paradise of delights. This spot the Redeemer of mankind has made illustrious by His advent, has beautified by His sojourn, has consecrated by His passion, has redeemed by His death, has glorified by His burial.

" This royal city, however, situated at the center of the earth, is now held captive by the enemies of Christ and is subjected, by those who do not know God, to the worship of the heathen. She seeks, therefore, and desires to be liberated, and ceases not to implore you to come to her aid. From you especially she asks succor, because, as we have already said, God has conferred

---

[1] Among the acts of the Council of Clermont had been a solemn confirmation of the Truce of God, with the purpose of restraining feudal warfare [see p. 228]. In the version of Urban's speech given by Fulcher of Chartres, the Pope is reported as saying that in some parts of France "hardly any one can venture to travel upon the highways, by night or day, without danger of attack by thieves or robbers; and no one is sure that his property at home or abroad will not be taken from him by the violence or craft of the wicked."

upon you, above all other nations, great glory in arms. Accordingly, undertake this journey eagerly for the remission of your sins, with the assurance of the reward of imperishable glory in the kingdom of heaven."

When Pope Urban had skilfully said these and very many similar things, he so centered in one purpose the desires of all **Response to** who were present that all cried out, "It is the **the appeal** will of God! It is the will of God!" When the venerable Roman pontiff heard that, with eyes uplifted to heaven, he gave thanks to God and, commanding silence with his hand, said:

"Most beloved brethren, to-day is manifest in you what the Lord says in the Gospel, 'Where two or three are gathered together in my name, there am I in the midst of them' [Matt., xviii. 20]. For unless God had been present in your spirits, all of you would not have uttered the same cry; since, although **"Deus vult,"** the cry issued from numerous mouths, yet the **the war cry** origin of the cry was one. Therefore I say to you that God, who implanted this in your breasts, has drawn it forth from you. Let that, then, be your war cry in battle, because it is given to you by God. When an armed attack is made upon the enemy, let this one cry be raised by all the soldiers of God: 'It is the will of God! It is the will of God!'

"And we neither command nor advise that the old or feeble, or those incapable of bearing arms, undertake this journey. Nor ought women to set out at all without their husbands, or brothers, or legal guardians. For such are more of a hindrance than aid, more of a burden than an advantage. Let the rich aid the needy; and according to their wealth let them take with them experienced soldiers. The priests and other clerks [clergy], **Who should go** whether secular or regular, are not to go without **and who should** the consent of their bishop; for this journey **remain** would profit them nothing if they went without permission. Also, it is not fitting that laymen should enter upon the pilgrimage without the blessing of their priests.

"Whoever, therefore, shall decide upon this holy pilgrimage, and shall make his vow to God to that effect, and shall offer himself to Him for sacrifice, as a living victim, holy and acceptable to God, shall wear the sign of the cross of the Lord on his forehead or on his breast. When he shall return from his journey, having fulfilled his vow, let him place the cross on his back between his shoulders. Thus shall ye, indeed, by this twofold action, fulfill the precept of the Lord, as He commands in the Gospel, 'He that taketh not his cross, and followeth after me, is not worthy of me'" [Luke, xiv. 27].

52. The Starting of the Crusaders (1096)

THE appeals of Pope Urban at Clermont and elsewhere met with ready response, especially among the French, but also to a considerable extent among Italians, Germans, and even English. A great variety of people were attracted by the enterprise, and from an equal variety of motives. Men whose lives had been evil saw in the crusade an opportunity of doing penance; criminals who perhaps cared little for penance but much for their own personal safety saw in it an avenue of escape from justice; merchants discovered in it a chance to open up new and valuable trade; knights hailed it as an invitation to deeds of valor and glory surpassing any Europe had yet known; ordinary malcontents regarded it as a chance to mend their fortunes; and a very large number of people looked upon it as a great spiritual obligation laid upon them and necessary to be performed in order to insure salvation in the world to come. By reason of all these incentives, some of them weighing much more in the mediæval mind than we can understand to-day, the crusade brought together men, women, and children from every part of Christendom. Both of the accounts given below of the assembling and starting of the crusaders are doubtless more or less exaggerated at certain points, yet in substance they represent what must have been pretty nearly the actual facts.

William of Malmesbury was an English monk who lived in the first half of the twelfth century and wrote a very valuable *Chronicle of the Kings of England*, which reached the opening of the reign of Stephen (1135). He thus had abundant opportunity to learn of the first crusade

from people who had actually participated in it. His rather humorous
picture of the effects of Pope Urban's call is thus well worth reading.
Better than it, however, is the account by the priest Fulcher of Chartres
(1058–1124)—better because the writer himself took part in the crusade and so was a personal observer of most of the things he undertook
to describe. Fulcher, in 1096, set out upon the crusade in the company
of his lord, Etienne, count of Blois and Chartres, who was a man of
importance in the army of Robert of Normandy. With the rest of Robert's crusaders he spent the winter in Italy and arrived at Durazzo in
the spring of 1097. He had a part in the siege of Nicæa and in the battle
of Dorylæum, but not in the siege of Antioch. Before reaching Jerusalem, in 1099, he became chaplain to a brother of Godfrey of Bouillon
and was already making progress on his "history of the army of God."

Sources—(a) Guilielmus Monachi Malmesburiensis, *De gestis regum Anglorum*
[William of Malmesbury, "Chronicle of the Kings of Eng-
land"], Bk. IV., Chap. 2. Adapted from translation by John
Sharpe (London, 1815), p. 416.

(b) Fulcherius Carnotensis, *Historia Iherosolimitana: gesta Francorum Iherusalem peregrinantium* [Fulcher of Chartres, "History of the Crusade to Jerusalem: the Deeds of the French
Journeying Thither"], Chap. 6. Text in *Recueil des Historiens
des Croisades: Historiens Occidentaux* (Paris, 1866), Vol. III.,
p. 328.

(a)

Immediately the fame of this great event,[1] being spread
through the universe, penetrated the minds of Christians with
its mild breath, and wherever it blew there was no nation, however distant and obscure, that did not send some of its people.
This zeal animated not only the provinces bordering on the
Mediterranean, but all who had ever even heard of the name
Christian in the most remote isles, and among barbarous nations.
Then the Welshman abandoned his forests and neglected his
hunting; the Scotchman deserted the fleas with which he is so

**Universal in-
terest in the
crusade**

familiar; the Dane ceased to swallow his intoxi-
cating draughts; and the Norwegian turned his
back upon his raw fish. The fields were left by
the cultivators, and the houses by their inhabitants; all the cities

[1] Pope Urban's appeal at the Council of Clermont.

were deserted. People were restrained neither by the ties of blood nor the love of country; they saw nothing but God. All that was in the granaries, or was destined for food, was left under the guardianship of the greedy agriculturist. The journey to Jerusalem was the only thing hoped for or thought of. Joy animated the hearts of all who set out; grief dwelt in the hearts of all who remained. Why do I say "of those who remained"? You might have seen the husband setting forth with his wife, with all his family; you would have laughed to see all the *penates* [1] put in motion and loaded upon wagons. The road was too narrow for the passengers, and more room was wanted for the travelers, so great and numerous was the crowd.[2]

(b)

Such, then, was the immense assemblage which set out from the West. Gradually along the march, and from day to day, the army grew by the addition of other armies, coming from every direction and composed of innumerable people. Thus one saw an infinite multitude, speaking different languages and coming from divers countries. All did not, however, come together into **The multitude** a single army until we had reached the city of **of crusaders** Nicæa.[3] What shall I add? The isles of the sea and the kingdoms of the whole earth were moved by God, so that one might believe fulfilled the prophecy of David, who said in his Psalm: "All nations whom Thou hast made shall come and worship before Thee, O Lord, and shall glorify Thy name;" and so that those who reached the holy places afterwards said justly: "We will worship where His feet have stood." Concern-

[1] The *penates* of the Romans were household gods. William of Malmesbury here uses the term half-humorously to designate the various sorts of household articles which the crusaders thought they could not do without on the expedition, and hence undertook to carry with them.

[2] This was in the summer of 1097. The whole body of crusaders, including monks, women, children, and hangers-on, may then have numbered three or four hundred thousand, but the effective fighting force was not likely over one hundred thousand men.

[3] The crusaders reached Nicæa May 6, 1097. After a long siege the city surrendered, although to the Emperor Alexius rather than to the French.

ing this journey we read very many other predictions in the prophets, which it would be tedious to recall.

Oh, how great was the grief, how deep the sighs, what weeping, what lamentations among the friends, when the husband left the wife so dear to him, his children also, and all his possessions of any kind, father, mother, brethren, or kindred! And

Mingled sorrow and joy of the crusaders
yet in spite of the floods of tears which those who remained shed for their friends about to depart, and in their very presence, the latter did not suffer their courage to fail, and, out of love for the Lord, in no way hesitated to leave all that they held most precious, believing without doubt that they would gain an hundred-fold in receiving the recompense which God has promised to those who love Him.

Then the husband confided to his wife the time of his return and assured her that, if he lived, by God's grace he would return to her. He commended her to the Lord, gave her a kiss, and, weeping, promised to return. But the latter, who feared that she would never see him again, overcome with grief, was unable to stand, fell as if lifeless to the ground, and wept over her dear one whom she was losing in life, as if he were already dead. He, then, as if he had no pity (nevertheless he was filled with pity) and was not moved by the grief of his friends (and yet he was secretly moved), departed with a firm purpose. The sadness was for those who remained, and the joy for those who departed. What more can we say? "This is the Lord's doings, and it is marvelous in our eyes."

53. A Letter from a Crusader to his Wife

ONE of the most important groups of sources on the crusades is the large body of letters which has come down to us, written by men who had an actual part in the various expeditions. These letters, addressed to parents, wives, children, vassals, or friends, are valuable alike for the facts which they contain and for the revelation they give of the spirit and motives of the crusaders. A considerable collection of the letters, in English translation, may be found in Roger de Hoveden's *Annals of English History*, Roger of Wendover's *Flowers of History*, and Matthew Paris's *English History* (all in the Bohn Library); also in Michaud's *History of the Crusades*, Vol. III., Appendix. In many respects the letter given below, written at Antioch by Count Stephen of Blois to his wife Adele, under date of March 29, 1098, is unexcelled in all the records of mediæval letter-writing. Count Stephen (a brother-in-law of Robert of Normandy, who was a son of William the Conqueror) was one of the wealthiest and most popular French noblemen who responded to Pope Urban's summons at Clermont. At least three of his letters to his wife survive, of which the one here given is the third in order of time. It discloses the ordinary human sentiments of the crusader and makes us feel that, unlike the modern man as he was, he yet had very much in common with the people of to-day and of all ages. He was at the same time a bold fighter and a tender husband, a religious enthusiast and a practical man of affairs. When the letter was written, the siege of Antioch had been in progress somewhat more than five months; it continued until the following June, when it ended in the capture of the city by the crusaders. Count Stephen was slain in the battle of Ramleh in 1102.

Source—D'Achery, *Spicilegium* ["Gleanings"], 2d edition, Vol. III., pp. 430–433. Adapted from translation by Dana C. Munro in *Univ. of Pa. Translations and Reprints*, Vol. I., No. 4, pp. 5–8.

Count Stephen to Adele, his sweetest and most amiable wife, to his dear children, and to all his vassals of all ranks,—his greeting and blessing.

Count Stephen reports prosperity

You may be very sure, dearest, that the messenger whom I sent to give you pleasure left me before Antioch safe and unharmed and, through God's grace, in the greatest prosperity. And already at that time, together with all the chosen army of Christ, endowed with great valor by Him, we have been continually advancing for twenty-three weeks toward the home of our Lord Jesus. You may know for certain, my beloved, that of gold, silver, and many other kind of riches I now have twice as much as your love had assigned to me when I left you. For all our princes, with the common consent of the whole army, though against my own wishes, have made me up to the present time the leader, chief, and director of their whole expedition.

Doubtless you have heard that after the capture of the city of Nicæa we fought a great battle with the treacherous Turks and, by God's aid, conquered them.[1] Next we conquered for the Lord all Romania, and afterwards Cappadocia.[2] We had learned that there was a certain Turkish prince, Assam, dwelling in Cappadocia; so we directed our course thither. We conquered **Early achieve-** all his castles by force and compelled him to flee **ments of the** to a certain very strong castle situated on a high **crusaders** rock. We also gave the land of that Assam to one of our chiefs, and in order that he might conquer the prince we left there with him many soldiers of Christ. Thence, continually following the wicked Turks, we drove them through the midst of Armenia,[3] as far as the great river Euphrates. Having left all their baggage and beasts of burden on the bank, they fled across the river into Arabia.

The bolder of the Turkish soldiers, indeed, entering Syria, hastened by forced marches night and day, in order to be able to enter the royal city of Antioch before our approach.[4] Hearing of this, the whole army of God gave due praise and thanks to the all-powerful Lord. Hastening with great joy to this **The arrival at** chief city of Antioch, we besieged it and there **Antioch (1097)** had a great number of conflicts with the Turks; and seven times we fought with the citizens of the city and with

---

[1] This battle—the first pitched contest between the crusader and the Turk—was fought at Dorylæum, southeast of Nicæa.

[2] Romania (or the sultanate of Roum) and Cappadocia were regions in northern Asia Minor.

[3] The country immediately southeast of the Black Sea.

[4] Antioch was one of the largest and most important cities of the East. It had been girdled with enormous walls by Justinian and was a strategic position of the greatest value to any power which would possess Syria and Palestine. The siege of the city by the crusaders began October 21, 1097.

the innumerable troops all the time coming to their aid. The latter we rushed out to meet and fought with the fiercest courage under the leadership of Christ. And in all these seven battles, by the aid of the Lord God, we conquered and most assuredly killed an innumerable host of them. In those battles, indeed, and in very many attacks made upon the city, many of our brethren and followers were killed and their souls were borne to the joys of paradise.

We found the city of Antioch very extensive, fortified with the greatest strength and almost impossible to be taken. In addition, more than 5,000 bold Turkish soldiers had entered the city, not counting the Saracens, Publicans, Arabs, Turcopolitans, Syrians, Armenians, and other different races of whom an infinite multitude had gathered together there. In fighting against **The beginning of the siege** these enemies of God and of us we have, by God's grace, endured many sufferings and innumerable hardships up to the present time. Many also have already exhausted all their means in this most holy enterprise. Very many of our Franks, indeed, would have met a bodily death from starvation, if the mercy of God and our money had not come to their rescue. Lying before the city of Antioch, indeed, throughout the whole winter we suffered for our Lord Christ from excessive cold and enormous torrents of rain. What some say about the impossibility of bearing the heat of the sun in Syria is untrue, for the winter there is very similar to our winter in the West.

I delight to tell you, dearest, what happened to us during Lent. Our princes had caused a fortress to be built before a certain gate which was between our camp and the sea. For the Turks, coming out of this gate daily, killed some of our men on their way to the sea. The city of Antioch is about five leagues distant from the sea. For this purpose they sent the excellent Bohemond and Raymond, count of St. Gilles,[1] to the sea with only

[1] Bohemond of Tarentum was the son of Robert Guiscard and the leader

sixty horsemen, in order that they might bring mariners to aid in this work. When, however, they were returning to us with

The Christians defeated near the seashore these mariners, the Turks collected an army, fell suddenly upon our two leaders, and forced them to a perilous flight. In that unexpected fight we lost more than 500 of our foot-soldiers—to the glory of God. Of our horsemen, however, we lost only two, for certain.

On that same day, in order to receive our brethren with joy, and entirely ignorant of their misfortunes, we went out to meet them. When, however, we approached the above-mentioned gate of the city, a mob of foot-soldiers and horsemen from Antioch, elated by the victory which they had won, rushed upon us in the same manner. Seeing these, our leaders went to the camp of the Christians to order all to be ready to follow us into battle. In the meantime our men gathered together and the scattered leaders, namely, Bohemond and Raymond, with the remainder of their army came up and told of the great misfortune which they had suffered.

Our men, full of fury at these most evil tidings, prepared to die for Christ and, deeply grieved for their brethren, rushed upon the wicked Turks. They, enemies of God and of us, hastily fled before us and attempted to enter the city. But by God's grace the affair turned out very differently; for, when they tried to

A notable victory over the Turks cross a bridge built over the great river Moscholum,[1] we followed them as closely as possible, killed many before they reached the bridge, forced many into the river, all of whom were killed, and we also slew many upon the bridge and very many at the narrow entrance to the gate. I am telling you the truth, my beloved, and you may be assured that in this battle we killed thirty emirs, that is, princes, and three hundred other Turkish nobles, not counting the remaining Turks and pagans. Indeed the num-

of the Norman contingent from Italy. Raymond of St. Gilles, count of Toulouse, was leader of the men from Languedoc in south France.

[1] The modern Orontes.

ber of Turks and Saracens killed is reckoned at 1230, but of ours we did not lose a single man.

On the following day (Easter), while my chaplain Alexander was writing this letter in great haste, a party of our men lying in wait for the Turks fought a successful battle with them and killed sixty horsemen, whose heads they brought to the army.

These which I write to you are only a few things, dearest, of the many which we have done; and because I am not able to tell you, dearest, what is in my mind, I charge you to do right, to watch carefully over your land, and to do your duty as you ought to your children and your vassals. You will certainly see me just as soon as I can possibly return to you. Farewell.

CHAPTER XVIII.

THE GREAT CHARTER

54. The Winning of the Charter

THE reign of King John (1199–1216) was an era of humiliation, though in the end one of triumph, for all classes of the English people. The king himself was perhaps the most unworthy sovereign who has ever occupied the English throne and one after another of his deeds and policies brought deep shame to every patriotic Englishman. His surrender to the papacy (1213) and his loss of the English possessions on the continent (1214) were only two of the most conspicuous results of his weakness and mismanagement. Indeed it was not these that touched the English people most closely, for after all it was rather their pride than their real interests that suffered by the king's homage to Innocent III. and his bitter defeat at Bouvines. Worse than these things were the heavy taxes and the illegal extortions of money, in which John went far beyond even his unscrupulous brother and predecessor, Richard. The king's expenses were very heavy, the more so by reason of his French wars, and to meet them he devised all manner of schemes for wringing money from his unwilling subjects. Land taxes were increased, scutage (payments in lieu of military service) was nearly doubled, levies of a thirteenth, a seventh, and other large fractions of the movable property of the realm were made, excessive fines were imposed, old feudal rights were revived and exercised in an arbitrary fashion, and property was confiscated on the shallowest of pretenses. Even the Church was by no means immune from the king's rapacity. The result of these high-handed measures was that all classes of the people—barons, clergy, and commons—were driven into an attitude of open protest. The leadership against the king fell naturally to the barons and it was directly in consequence of their action that John was brought, in 1215, to grant the Great Charter and to pledge himself to govern thereafter according to the ancient and just laws of the kingdom.

The account of the winning of the Charter given below comes from the hand of Roger of Wendover, a monk of St. Albans, a monastery in Hertfordshire which was famous in the thirteenth century for its group of historians and annalists. It begins with the meeting of the barons at St. Edmunds in Suffolk late in November, 1214, and tells the story to the granting of the Charter at Runnymede, June 15, 1215. On this subject, as well as on the entire period of English history from 1189 to 1235, Roger of Wendover is our principal contemporary authority.

Source—Rogerus de Wendover, *Chronica Majora, sive Liber qui dicitur Flores Historiarum* [Roger of Wendover, "Greater Chronicle, or the Book which is called the Flowers of History"]. Translated by J. A. Giles (London, 1849), Vol. II., pp. 303–324 *passim*.

About this time the earls and barons of England assembled at St. Edmunds, as if for religious duties, although it was for another reason;[1] for after they had discoursed together secretly for a time, there was placed before them the charter of King Henry the First, which they had received, as mentioned before, in the city of London from Stephen, archbishop of Canterbury.[2] This charter contained certain liberties and laws granted to the holy Church as well as to the nobles of the kingdom, besides some liberties which the king added of his own accord. All therefore assembled in the church of St. Edmund, the king and martyr, and, commencing with those of the highest rank, they all swore on the great altar that, if the king refused to

A conference held by the barons against King John

grant these liberties and laws, they themselves would withdraw from their allegiance to him, and make war on him until he should, by a charter under his own seal, confirm to them everything that they required; and finally it was unanimously agreed that, after Christmas, they should all go together to the king and demand

[1] The barons attended the meeting under the pretense of making a religious pilgrimage.
[2] This charter, granted at the coronation of Henry I. in 1100, contained a renunciation of the evil practices which had marked the government of William the Conqueror and William Rufus. It was from this document mainly that the barons in 1215 drew their constitutional programme.

the confirmation of the aforesaid liberties to them, and that they should in the meantime provide themselves with horses and arms, so that if the king should endeavor to depart from his oath they might, by taking his castles, compel him to satisfy their demands; and having arranged this, each man returned home. . . .

In the year of our Lord 1215, which was the seventeenth year of the reign of King John, he held his court at Winchester at Christmas for one day, after which he hurried to London, and **They demand** took up his abode at the New Temple;[1] and at **a confirmation of the old liberties** that place the above-mentioned nobles came to him in gay military array, and demanded the confirmation of the liberties and laws of King Edward, with other liberties granted to them and to the kingdom and church of England, as were contained in the charter, and above-mentioned laws of Henry the First. They also asserted that, at the time of his absolution at Winchester,[2] he had promised to restore those laws and ancient liberties, and was bound by his own oath to observe them. The king, hearing the bold tone of the barons in making this demand, much feared an attack from them, as he saw that they were prepared for battle. He, however, made answer that their demands were a matter of im- **A truce arranged** portance and difficulty, and he therefore asked a truce until the end of Easter, that, after due deliberation, he might be able to satisfy them as well as the dignity of his crown. After much discussion on both sides, the

[1] The Knights Templars, having purchased all that part of the banks of the Thames lying between Whitefriars and Essex Street, erected on it a magnificent structure which was known as the New Temple, in distinction from the Old Temple on the south side of Holborn. Meetings of Parliament and of the king's council were frequently held in the New Temple; here also were kept the crown jewels. Ultimately, after the suppression of the Templars by Edward II., the Temple became one of England's most celebrated schools of law.

[2] This refers to the king's absolution at the hands of Stephen Langton, archbishop of Canterbury, July 20, 1213, after his submission to the papacy. At that time John took an oath on the Bible to the effect that he would restore the good laws of his forefathers and render to all men their rights.

king at length, although unwillingly, procured the archbishop of Canterbury, the bishop of Ely, and William Marshal, as his sureties that on the day agreed upon he would, in all reason, satisfy them all; on which the nobles returned to their homes. The king, however, wishing to take precautions against the future, caused all the nobles throughout England to swear fealty to him alone against all men, and to renew their homage to him; and, the better to take care of himself, on the day of St. Mary's purification, he assumed the cross of our Lord, being induced to this more by fear than devotion.[1] . . .

In Easter week of this same year, the above-mentioned nobles assembled at Stamford,[2] with horses and arms. They had now

The truce at an end induced almost all the nobility of the whole kingdom to join them, and constituted a very large army; for in their army there were computed to be two thousand knights, besides horse-soldiers, attendants, and foot-soldiers, who were variously equipped. . . . The king at this time was awaiting the arrival of his nobles at Oxford.[3] On the Monday next after the octave of Easter,[4] the said barons assembled in the town of Brackley.[5] And when the king learned this, he sent the archbishop of Canterbury and William Marshal, earl of Pembroke, with some other prudent men, to them to inquire what the laws

The preliminary demands of the barons and liberties were which they demanded. The barons then delivered to the messengers a paper, containing in great measure the laws and ancient customs of the kingdom, and declared that, unless the king immediately granted them and confirmed them under his own seal, they,

[1] The exact day upon which John took the crusader's vow is uncertain. It was probably Ash Wednesday (March 4), 1215. The king's object was in part to get the personal protection which the sanctity of the vow carried with it and in part to enlist the sympathies of the Pope and make it appear that the barons were guilty of interfering with a crusade.

[2] On the southern border of Lincolnshire.

[3] On the Thames in Oxfordshire. This statement of the chronicler is incorrect. John was yet in London.

[4] Octave means the period of eight days following a religious festival. This Monday was April 27.

[5] Brackley is about twenty-two miles north of Oxford.

by taking possession of his fortresses, would force him to give them sufficient satisfaction as to their before-named demands. The archbishop, with his fellow messengers, then carried the paper to the king, and read to him the heads of the paper one by one throughout. The king, when he heard the purport of these heads, said derisively, with the greatest indignation, "Why, amongst these unjust demands, did not the barons ask for my kingdom also? Their demands are vain and visionary, and are unsupported by any plea of reason whatever." And at length he angrily declared with an oath that he would never grant them such liberties as would render him their slave. The principal of these laws and liberties which the nobles required to be confirmed to them are partly described above in the charter of King Henry,[1] and partly are extracted from the old laws of King Edward,[2] as the following history will show in due time.

As the archbishop and William Marshal could not by any persuasion induce the king to agree to their demands, they

The castle of Northampton besieged by the barons returned by the king's order to the barons, and duly reported to them all that they had heard from the king. And when the nobles heard what John said, they appointed Robert Fitz-Walter commander of their soldiers, giving him the title of "Marshal of the Army of God and the Holy Church," and then, one and all flying to arms, they directed their forces toward Northampton.[3] On their arrival there they at once laid siege to the castle, but after having stayed there for fifteen days, and having gained little or no advantage, they determined to move their camp. Having come without *petrariæ* [4] and other engines of war, they, without accomplishing their purpose, proceeded in confusion to the castle of Bedford.[5] . . .

When the army of the barons arrived at Bedford, they were

[1] Henry I.'s charter, 1100.
[2] Edward the Confessor, king from 1042 to 1066.
[3] In the county of Northampton, in central England.
[4] Engines for hurling stones.
[5] About twenty miles southeast of Northampton.

received with all respect by William de Beauchamp.[1] Messengers from the city of London also came to them there, secretly telling them, if they wished to get into that city, to come there immediately. The barons, encouraged by the arrival of this agreeable message, immediately moved their camp and arrived **The city of** at Ware. After this they marched the whole **London given** night and arrived early in the morning at the city **over to the** **barons** of London, and, finding the gates open, on the 24th of May (which was the Sunday next before our Lord's ascension) they entered the city without any tumult while the inhabitants were performing divine service; for the rich citizens were favorable to the barons, and the poor ones were afraid to murmur against them. The barons, having thus got into the city, placed their own guards in charge of each of the gates, and then arranged all matters in the city at will.[2] They then took security from the citizens, and sent letters through England to those earls, barons, and knights who appeared to be still faithful to the king (though they only pretended to be so) and advised them with threats, as they had regard for the safety of all their property and possessions, to abandon a king who was perjured and who made war against his barons, and together with them to stand firm and fight against the king for their rights and for peace; and that, if they refused to do this, they, the barons, would make war against them all, as against open enemies, and would destroy their castles, burn their houses and other buildings, and pillage their warrens, parks, and orchards. . . . The greatest part of these, on receiving the message of the barons, set out to London and joined them, abandoning the king entirely. . . .

King John, when he saw that he was deserted by almost all, so that out of his regal superabundance of followers he retained

---

[1] The commander of Bedford Castle.
[2] The loss of London by the king was a turning point in the contest. Thereafter the barons' party gained rapidly and its complete success was only a question of time.

scarcely seven knights, was much alarmed lest the barons should attack his castles and reduce them without difficulty, as they **The conference** would find no obstacle to their so doing. He **between the** deceitfully pretended to make peace for a time **king and the barons** with the aforesaid barons, and sent William Marshal, earl of Pembroke, with other trustworthy messengers, to them, and told them that, for the sake of peace and for the exaltation and honor of the kingdom, he would willingly grant them the laws and liberties they demanded. He sent also a request to the barons by these same messengers that they appoint a suitable day and place to meet and carry all these matters into effect. The king's messengers then came in all haste to London, and without deceit, reported to the barons all that had been deceitfully imposed on them. They in their great joy appointed the fifteenth of June for the king to meet them, at a field lying **The charter** between Staines and Windsor.[1] Accordingly, at **granted at** the time and place agreed upon the king and nobles **Runnymede** came to the appointed conference, and when each party had stationed itself some distance from the other, they began a long discussion about terms of peace and the aforesaid liberties. . . . At length, after various points on both sides had been discussed, King John, seeing that he was inferior in strength to the barons, without raising any difficulty, granted the underwritten laws and liberties, and confirmed them by his charter as follows:—

[Here ensues the Charter.]

55. Extracts from the Charter

No document in the history of any nation is more important than the Great Charter; in the words of Bishop Stubbs, the whole of the constitutional history of England is only one long commentary upon it. Its importance lay not merely in the fact that it was won from an unwilling sovereign by the united action of nobles, clergy, and people, but also in

[1] Runnymede, on the Thames.

the admirable summary which it embodies of the fundamental principles of English government, so far as they had ripened by the early years of the thirteenth century. The charter contained almost nothing that was not old. It was not even an instrument, like the Constitution of the United States, providing for the creation of a new government. It merely sought to gather up within a single reasonably brief document all the important principles which the best of the English sovereigns had recognized, but which such rulers as Richard and John had lately been improving every opportunity to evade. The primary purpose of the barons in forcing the king to grant the charter was not to get a new form of government or code of laws, but simply to obtain a remedy for certain concrete abuses, to resist the encroachments of the crown upon the traditional liberties of Englishmen, and to get a full and definite confirmation of these liberties in black and white. Not a new constitution was wanted, but good government in conformity with the old one. Naturally enough, therefore, the charter of 1215 was based in most of its important provisions upon that granted by Henry I. in 1100, even as this one was based on the righteous laws of the good Edward the Confessor. And after the same manner the charter of King John, in its turn, became the foundation for all future resistance of Englishmen to the evils of misgovernment, so that very soon it came naturally to be called *Magna Charta*—the Great Charter—by which designation it is known to this day.

King John was in no true sense the author of the charter. Many weeks before the meeting at Runnymede the barons had drawn up their demands in written form, and when that meeting occurred they were ready to lay before the sovereign a formal document, in forty-nine chapters, to which they simply requested his assent. This preliminary document was discussed and worked over, the number of chapters being increased to sixty-two, but the charter as finally agreed upon differed from it only in minor details. It is a mistake to think of John as "signing" the charter after the fashion of modern sovereigns. There is no evidence that he could write, and at any rate he acquiesced in the terms of the charter only by having his seal affixed to the paper. The original "Articles of the Barons" is still preserved in the British Museum, but there is no *one* original Magna Charta in existence. Duplicate copies of the document were made for distribution among the barons, and papers which are generally supposed to represent four of these still exist, two being in the British Museum.

The charter makes a lengthy document and many parts of it are too technical to be of service in this book; hence only a few of the most important chapters are here given. Translations of the entire document from the original Latin may be found in many places, among them the University of Pennsylvania *Translations and Reprints*, Vol. I., No. 6; Lee, *Source Book of English History*, 169–180; Adams and Stephens, *Select Documents Illustrative of English Constitutional History*, pp. 42–52; and the *Old South Leaflets*, No. 5.

Source—Text in William Stubbs, *Select Charters Illustrative of English Constitutional History* (8th ed., Oxford, 1895), pp. 296–306. Adapted from translation in Sheldon Amos, *Primer of the English Constitution and Government* (London, 1895), pp. 189–201 *passim.*

John, by the grace of God, king of England, lord of Ireland, duke of Normandy, Aquitane, and count of Anjou, to his archbishops, bishops, abbots, earls, barons, justiciaries, foresters, sheriffs, governors, officers, and to all bailiffs, and his faithful subjects, greeting. Know ye, that we, in the presence of God, and for the salvation of our soul, and the souls of all our ancestors and heirs, and unto the honor of God and the advancement of Holy Church, and amendment of our Realm, . . . have, in the first place, granted to God, and by this our present Charter confirmed, for us and our heirs forever:

1. That the Church of England shall be free, and have her whole rights, and her liberties inviolable; and we will have them

Liberties of the English Church guaranteed so observed that it may appear thence that the freedom of elections, which is reckoned chief and indispensable to the English Church, and which we granted and confirmed by our Charter, and obtained the confirmation of the same from our Lord Pope Innocent III., before the discord between us and our barons, was granted of mere free will; which Charter we shall observe, and we do desire it to be faithfully observed by our heirs forever.[1]

[1] The charter referred to, in which the liberties of the Church were con-

Med. Hist.—20

2. We also have granted to all the freemen of our kingdom, for us and for our heirs forever, all the underwritten liberties, to be had and holden by them and their heirs, of us and our heirs forever. If any of our earls, or barons, or others who hold of us in chief by military service,[1] shall die, and at the time of his death his heir shall be of full age, and owe a relief, he shall have his inheritance by the ancient relief—that is to say, the heir or heirs of an earl, for a whole earldom, by a hundred pounds; the heir or heirs of a knight, for a whole knight's fee, by a hundred shillings at most; and whoever oweth less shall give less, according to the ancient custom of fees.[2]

The rate of reliefs

3. But if the heir of any such shall be under age, and shall be in ward, when he comes of age he shall have his inheritance without relief and without fine.[3]

12. No scutage[4] or aid shall be imposed in our kingdom, unless by the general council of our kingdom;[5] except for ransoming our person, making our eldest son a knight, and once for marrying our eldest daughter; and for

The three aids

firmed, was granted in November, 1214, and renewed in January, 1215. It was in the nature of a bribe offered the clergy by the king in the hope of winning their support in his struggle with the barons. The liberty granted was particularly that of "canonical election," i. e., the privilege of the cathedral chapters to elect bishops without being dominated in their choice by the king. Henry I.'s charter (1100) contained a similar provision, but it had not been observed in practice.

[1] Tenants *in capite*, i. e., men holding land directly from the king on condition of military service.

[2] The object of this chapter is, in general, to prevent the exaction of excessive reliefs. The provision of Henry I.'s charter that reliefs should be just and reasonable had become a dead letter.

[3] During the heir's minority the king received the profits of the estate; in consequence of this the payment of relief by such an heir was to be remitted.

[4] Scutage (from *scutum*, shield) was payment made to the king by persons who owed military service but preferred to give money instead. Scutage levied by John had been excessively heavy.

[5] The General, or Great, Council was a feudal body made up of the king's tenants-in-chief, both greater and lesser lords. This chapter puts a definite, even though not very far-reaching, limitation upon the royal power of taxation, and so looks forward in a way to the later régime of taxation by Parliament.

these there shall be paid no more than a reasonable aid. In like manner it shall be concerning the aids of the City of London.[1]

14. And for holding the general council of the kingdom concerning the assessment of aids, except in the three cases aforesaid, and for the assessing of scutage, we shall cause to be summoned the archbishops, bishops, abbots, earls, and greater barons of the realm, singly by our letters. And furthermore, we shall

The Great Council cause to be summoned generally, by our sheriffs and bailiffs, all others who hold of us in chief, for a certain day, that is to say, forty days before their meeting at least, and to a certain place. And in all letters of such summons we will declare the cause of such summons. And summons being thus made, the business shall proceed on the day appointed, according to the advice of such as shall be present, although all that were summoned come not.[2]

15. We will not in the future grant to any one that he may take aid of his own free tenants, except to ransom his body, and to make his eldest son a knight, and once to marry his eldest daughter; and for this there shall be paid only a reasonable aid.[3]

36. Nothing from henceforth shall be given or taken for a writ of inquisition of life or limb, but it shall be granted freely, and not denied.[4]

[1] London had helped the barons secure the charter and was rewarded by being specifically included in its provisions.

[2] Here we have a definite statement as to the composition of the Great Council. The distinction between greater and lesser barons is mentioned as early as the times of Henry I. (1100–1135). In a general way it may be said that the greater barons (together with the greater clergy) developed into the House of Lords and the lesser ones, along with the ordinary free-holders, became the "knights of the shire," who so long made up the backbone of the Commons. In the thirteenth century comparatively few of the lesser barons attended the meetings of the Council. Attendance was expensive and they were not greatly interested in the body's proceedings. It should be noted that the Great Council was in no sense a legislative assembly.

[3] It is significant that the provisions of the charter which prohibit feudal exactions were made by the barons to apply to themselves as well as to the king.

[4] This is an important legal enactment whose purpose is to prevent prolonged imprisonment, without trial, of persons accused of serious crime.

39. No freeman shall be taken or imprisoned, or disseised,[1] or outlawed,[2] or banished, or in any way destroyed, nor will we pass upon him, nor will we send upon him,[3] unless by the lawful judgment of his peers,[4] or by the law of the land.[5]

40. We will sell to no man, we will not deny to any man, either justice or right.[6]

41. All merchants shall have safe and secure conduct to go out of, and to come into, England, and to stay there and to pass as well by land as by water, for buying and selling by the ancient and allowed customs, without any unjust tolls, except in time

Freedom of commercial intercourse of war, or when they are of any nation at war with us. And if there be found any such in our land, in the beginning of the war, they shall be detained, without damage to their bodies or goods, until it be known to us, or to our chief justiciary, how our merchants be

A person accused of murder, for example, could not be set at liberty under bail, but he could apply for a writ *de odio et âtia* ("concerning hatred and malice") which directed the sheriff to make inquest by jury as to whether the accusation had been brought by reason of hatred and malice. If the jury decided that the accusation had been so brought, the accused person could be admitted to bail until the time for his regular trial. This will occur to one as being very similar to the principle of *habeas corpus*. John had been charging heavy fees for these writs *de odio et âtia*, or "writs of inquisition of life and limb," as they are called in the charter; henceforth they were to be issued freely.

1 To disseise a person is to dispossess him of his freehold rights.

2 Henceforth a person could be outlawed, i. e., declared out of the protection of the law, only by the regular courts.

3 That is, use force upon him, as John had frequently done.

4 The term "peers," as here used, means simply equals in rank. The present clause does not yet imply trial by jury in the modern sense. It comprises simply a narrow, feudal demand of the nobles to be judged by other nobles, rather than by lawyers or clerks. Jury trial was increasingly common in the thirteenth century, but it was not guaranteed in the Great Charter.

5 This chapter is commonly regarded as the most important in the charter. It undertakes to prevent arbitrary imprisonment and to protect private property by laying down a fundamental principle of government which John had been constantly violating and which very clearly marked the line of distinction between a limited and an absolute monarchy.

6 The principle is here asserted that justice in the courts should be open to all, and without the payment of money to get judgment hastened or delayed. Extortions of this character did not cease in 1215, but they became less exorbitant and arbitrary.

treated in the nation at war with us; and if ours be safe there, the others shall be safe in our dominions.[1]

42. It shall be lawful, for the time to come, for any one to go out of our kingdom and return safely and securely by land or by water, saving his allegiance to us (unless in time of war, by some short space, for the common benefit of the realm), except prisoners and outlaws, according to the law of the land, and people in war with us, and merchants who shall be treated as is above mentioned.[2]

51. As soon as peace is restored, we will send out of the kingdom all foreign knights, cross-bowmen, and stipendiaries, who are come with horses and arms to the molestation of our people.[3]

60. All the aforesaid customs and liberties, which we have granted to be holden in our kingdom, as much as it belongs to us, all people of our kingdom, as well clergy as laity, shall observe, as far as they are concerned, towards their dependents.[4]

61. And whereas, for the honor of God and the amendment of our kingdom, and for the better quieting the discord that

How the charter was to be enforced

has arisen between us and our barons, we have granted all these things aforesaid. Willing to render them firm and lasting, we do give and grant our subjects the underwritten security, namely, that the barons

[1] The object of this chapter is to encourage commerce by guaranteeing foreign merchants the same treatment that English merchants received in foreign countries. The tolls imposed on traders by the cities, however, were not affected and they continued a serious obstacle for some centuries.

[2] This chapter provides that, except under the special circumstances of war, any law-abiding Englishman might go abroad freely, provided only he should remain loyal to the English crown. The rule thus established continued in effect until 1382, when it was enacted that such privileges should belong only to lords, merchants, and soldiers.

[3] During the struggle with the barons, John had brought in a number of foreign mercenary soldiers or "stipendiaries." All classes of Englishmen resented this policy and the barons improved the opportunity offered by the charter to get a promise from the king to dispense with his continental mercenaries as quickly as possible.

[4] This chapter provides that the charter's regulation of feudal customs should apply to the barons just as to the king. The barons' tenants were to be protected from oppression precisely as were the barons themselves. These tenants had helped in the winning of the charter and were thus rewarded for their services.

may choose five and twenty barons of the kingdom, whom they think convenient, who shall take care, with all their might, to hold and observe, and cause to be observed, the peace and liberties we have granted them, and by this our present Charter confirmed.[1] . . .

63. . . . It is also sworn, as well on our part as on the part of the barons, that all the things aforesaid shall be observed in good faith, and without evil duplicity. Given under our hand, in the presence of the witnesses above named, and many others, in the meadow called Runnymede, between Windsor and Staines, the 15th day of June, in the 17th year of our reign.

[1] The chapter goes on at considerable length to specify the manner in which, if the king should violate the terms of the charter, the commission of twenty-five barons should proceed to bring him to account. Even the right of making war was given them, in case it should become necessary to resort to such an extreme measure.

CHAPTER XIX.

THE REIGN OF SAINT LOUIS

56. The Character and Deeds of the King as Described by Joinville

Louis IX., or St. Louis, as he is commonly called, was the eldest son of Louis VIII. and a grandson of Philip Augustus. He was born in 1214 and upon the death of his father in 1226 he succeeded to the throne of France while yet but a boy of twelve. The recent reign of Philip Augustus (1180–1223) had been a period marked by a great increase in the royal power and by a corresponding lessening of the independent authority of the feudal magnates. The accession of a boy-king was therefore hailed by the discontented nobles as an opportunity to recover something at least of their lost privileges. It would doubtless have been such but for the vigilance, ability, and masculine aggressiveness of the young king's mother, Blanche of Castile. Aided by the clergy and the loyal party among the nobles, she, in the capacity of regent, successfully defended her son's interests against a succession of plots and uprisings, with the result that when Louis gradually assumed control of affairs in his own name, about 1236, the realm was in good order and the dangers which once had been so threatening had all but disappeared. The king's education and moral training had been well attended to, and he arrived at manhood with an equipment quite unusual among princes of his day. His reign extended to 1270 and became in some respects the most notable in all French history. In fact, whether viewed from the standpoint of his personal character or his practical achievements, St. Louis is generally admitted to have been one of the most remarkable sovereigns of mediæval Europe. He was famous throughout Christendom for his piety, justice, wisdom, and ability, being recognized as at once a devoted monk, a brave knight, and a capable king. In him were blended two qualities—vigorous activity and proneness to austere meditation—rarely combined in such measure in one person. His character may

311

be summed up by saying that he had all the virtues of his age and few of its vices. No less cynical a critic than Voltaire has declared that he went as far in goodness as it is possible for a man to go.

Saint Louis being thus so interesting a character in himself, it is very fortunate that we have an excellent contemporary biography of him, from the hand of a friend and companion who knew him well. Sire de Joinville's *Histoire de Saint Louis* is a classic of French literature and in most respects the best piece of biographical writing that has come down to us from the Middle Ages. Joinville, or more properly John, lord of Joinville, was born in Champagne, in northern France, probably in 1225. His family was one of the most distinguished in Champagne and he himself had all the advantages that could come from being brought up at the refined court of the count of this favored district. In 1248, when St. Louis set out on his first crusading expedition, Joinville, only recently become of age, took the cross and became a follower of the king, joining him in Cyprus and there first definitely entering his service. During the next six years the two were inseparable companions, and even after Joinville, in 1254, retired from the king's service in order to manage his estates in Champagne he long continued to make frequent visits of a social character to the court.

Joinville's memoirs of St. Louis were completed about 1309—probably nine years before the death of the author—and they were first published soon after the death of Philip the Fair in 1314. They constitute by far the most important source of information on the history of France in the middle portion of the thirteenth century. Joinville had the great advantage of intimate acquaintance and long association with King Louis and, what is equally important, he seems to have tried to write in a spirit of perfect fairness and justice. He was an ardent admirer of Louis, but his biography did not fall into the tempting channel of mere fulsome and indiscriminate praise. Moreover, the work is a biography of the only really satisfactory type; it is not taken up with a bare recital of events in the life of the individual under consideration, but it has a broad background drawn from the general historical movements and conditions of the time. Its most obvious defects arise from the fact that it comprises largely the reminiscences of an old man, which are never likely to be entirely accurate or well-balanced. In his dedication of the treatise to Louis, eldest son of Philip IV., the author relates that it had been written at the urgent solicitation of the deceased king's widow.

The biography in print makes a good-sized volume and it is possible, of course, to reproduce here but a few significant passages from it. But these are perhaps sufficient to show what sort of man the saint-king really was, and it is just this insight into the character of the men of the Middle Ages that is most worth getting—and the hardest thing, as a rule, to get. Incidentally, the extract throws some light on the methods of warfare employed by the crusaders and the Turks.

Source—Jean, Sire de Joinville, *Histoire de Saint Louis.* Text edited by M. Joseph Noël (Natalis de Wailly) and published by the Société de l'Histoire de France (Paris, 1868). Translated by James Hutton under title of *Saint Louis, King of France* (London, 1868), *passim.*

As I have heard him say, he [Saint Louis] was born on the day of St. Mark the Evangelist,[1] shortly after Easter. On that day **The king's birth** the cross is carried in procession in many places, and in France they are called black crosses. It was therefore a sort of prophecy of the great numbers of people who perished in those two crusades, i.e., in that to Egypt, and in that other, in the course of which he died at Carthage;[2] for many great sorrows were there on that account in this world, and many great joys are there now in Paradise on the part of those who in those two pilgrimages died true crusaders.

God, in whom he put his trust, preserved him ever from his infancy to the very last; and especially in his infancy did He preserve him when he stood in need of help, as you will presently **His early training** hear. As for his soul, God preserved it through the pious instructions of his mother, who taught him to believe in God and to love Him, and placed about him

[1] April 25, 1215.

[2] Louis started on his first crusade in August, 1248. After a series of disasters in Egypt he managed to reach the Holy Land, where he spent nearly four years fortifying the great seaports. He returned to France in July, 1254. Sixteen years later, in July, 1270, he started on his second crusade. He had but reached Carthage when he was suddenly taken ill and compelled to halt the expedition. He died there August 25, 1270. Louis was as typical a crusader as ever lived, but in his day men of his kind were few; the great era of crusading enterprise was past.

none but ministers of religion. And she made him, while he was yet a child, attend to all his prayers and listen to the sermons on saints' days. He remembered that his mother used sometimes to tell him that she would rather he were dead than that he should commit a deadly sin.

Sore need of God's help had he in his youth, for his mother, who came out of Spain, had neither relatives nor friends in all the realm of France. And because the barons of France saw that the king was an infant, and the queen, his mother, a foreigner, they made the count of Boulogne, the king's uncle, their chief, and looked up to him as their lord.[1] After the king was crowned,

Difficulties at the beginning of his reign some of the barons asked of the queen to bestow upon them large domains; and because she would do nothing of the kind all the barons assembled at Corbei.[2] And the sainted king related to me how neither he nor his mother, who were at Montlhéri,[3] dared to return to Paris, until the citizens of Paris came, with arms in their hands, to escort them. He told me, too, that from Montlhéri to Paris the road was filled with people, some with and some without weapons, and that all cried unto our Lord to give him a long and happy life, and to defend and preserve him from his enemies. . . .

After these things it chanced, as it pleased God, that great illness fell upon the king at Paris, by which he was brought to such extremity that one of the women who watched by his side wanted to draw the sheet over his face, saying that he was dead; but another woman, who was on the other side of the bed, would not suffer it, for the soul, she said, had not yet left the

Louis takes the cross body. While he was listening to the dispute between these two, our Lord wrought upon him and quickly sent him health; for before that he was dumb, and could

---

[1] This was Philip, son of Philip Augustus. The lands of the count of Boulogne lay on the coast of the English Channel north of the Somme.

[2] An important church center about seventy miles north of Paris.

[3] A town a few miles south of Paris.

not speak. He demanded that the cross should be given to him, and it was done. When the queen, his mother, heard that he had recovered his speech, she exhibited as much joy as could be; but when she was told by himself that he had taken the cross, she displayed as much grief as if she had seen him dead.

After the king put on the cross, Robert, count of Artois, Alphonse, count of Poitiers, Charles, count of Anjou, who was afterwards king of Sicily—all three brothers of the king—also took the cross; as likewise did Hugh, duke of Burgundy, William, count of Flanders (brother to Count Guy of Flanders, the last who died), the good Hugh, count of Saint Pol, and Monseigneur **Prominent** Walter, his nephew, who bore himself right man-**Frenchmen** fully beyond seas, and would have been of great **who followed** **his example** worth had he lived. There was also the count of La Marche, and Monseigneur Hugh le Brun, his son; the count of Sarrebourg, and Monseigneur d'Apremont, his brother, in whose company I myself, John, Seigneur de Joinville, crossed the sea in a ship we chartered, because we were cousins; and we crossed over in all twenty knights, nine of whom followed the count of Sarrebourg, and nine were with me. . . .

The king summoned his barons to Paris, and made them swear to keep faith and loyalty towards his children if anything happened to himself on the voyage. He asked the same of me, but I refused to take any oath, because I was not his vassal. . . .

In the month of August we went on board our ships at the Rock of Marseilles. The day we embarked the door of the vessel **Embarking on** was opened, and the horses that we were to take **the Mediter-** with us were led inside. Then they fastened the **ranean** door and closed it up tightly, as when one sinks a cask, because when the ship is at sea the whole of the door is under water. When the horses were in, our sailing-master called out to his mariners who were at the prow: "Are you all ready?" And they replied: "Sir, let the clerks and priests come forward." As soon as they had come nigh, he shouted to them: "Chant, in God's name!" And they with one voice chanted, "*Veni, Creator Spiritus.*" Then the master called out to his men: "Set sail, in God's name!" And they did so. And in a little time the wind struck the sails and carried us out of sight of land, so that we saw nothing but sea and sky; and every day the wind bore us farther away from the land where we were born. And thereby I show you how foolhardy he must be who would venture to put himself in such peril with other people's property in his possession, or while in deadly sin; for when you fall asleep at night you know not but that ere the morning you may be at the bottom of the sea.

When we reached Cyprus, the king was already there, and we found an immense supply of stores for him, i.e., wine-stores and granaries. The king's wine-stores consisted of great piles of casks of wine, which his people had purchased two years before the king's arrival and placed in an open field near the seashore.

Preparations made in Cyprus
They had piled them one upon the other, so that when seen from the front they looked like a farmhouse. The wheat and barley had been heaped up in the middle of the field, and at first sight looked like hills; for the rain, which had long beaten upon the corn, had caused it to sprout, so that nothing was seen but green herbage. But when it was desired to transport it to Egypt, they broke off the outer coating with the green herbage, and the wheat and barley within were found as fresh as if they had only just been threshed out.

The king, as I have heard him say, would gladly have pushed on to Egypt without stopping, had not his barons advised him to wait for his army, which had not all arrived. While the king was sojourning in Cyprus, the great Khan of Tartary[1] sent

[1] In the early years of the thirteenth century, an Asiatic chieftain by the name of Genghis Khan built up a vast empire of Mongol or Tartar peoples, which for a time stretched all the way from China to eastern Germany. The rise and westward expansion of this barbarian power spread alarm

envoys to him, the bearers of very courteous messages. Among other things, he told him that he was ready to aid him in conquering the Holy Land and in delivering Jerusalem out of the hands of the Saracens. The king received the messengers very graciously, and sent some to the Khan, who were two years absent before they could return. And with his messengers the king sent to the Khan a tent fashioned like a chapel, which cost a large sum of money, for it was made of fine rich scarlet cloth. And the king, in the hope of drawing the Khan's people to our faith, caused to be embroidered inside the chapel, pictures representing the Annunciation of Our Lady, and other articles of faith. And he sent these things to them by the hands of two friars, who spoke the Saracen language, to teach and point out to them what they ought to believe. . . .

An embassy from the Khan

As soon as March came round, the king, and, by his command, the barons and other pilgrims, gave orders that the ships should be laden with wine and provisions, to be ready to sail when the king should give the signal. It happened that when everything was ready, the king and queen withdrew on board their ship on the Friday before Whitsunday, and the king desired his barons to follow in his wake straight towards Egypt. On Saturday [1] the king set sail, and all the other vessels at the same time, which was a fine sight to behold, for it seemed as if the whole sea, as far as the eye could

The departure from Cyprus

throughout Christendom, and with good reason, for it was with great difficulty that the Tartar sovereigns were prevented from extending their dominion over Germany and perhaps over all western Europe. After the first feeling of terror had passed, however, it began to be considered that possibly the Asiatic conquerors might yet be made to serve the interests of Christendom. They were not Mohammedans, and Christian leaders saw an opportunity to turn them against the Saracen master of the coveted Holy Land. Louis IX.'s reception of an embassy from Ilchikadai, one of the Tartar khans, or sovereigns, was only one of several incidents which illustrate the efforts made in this direction. After this episode the Tartars advanced rapidly into Syria, taking the important cities of Damascus and Aleppo; but a great defeat, September 3, 1260, by the sultan Kutuz at Ain Talut stemmed the tide of invasion and compelled the Tartars to retire to their northern dominions.

[1] May 21, 1249.

reach, was covered with sails, and the number of ships, great and small, was reckoned at 1,800. . . .[1]

Upon the arrival of the count of Poitiers, the king summoned all the barons of the army to decide in what direction he should march, whether towards Alexandria, or towards Babylon.[2] It resulted that the good Count Peter of Brittany, and most of the barons of the army, were of the opinion that the king should lay siege to Alexandria, because that city is possessed of a good

Decision to proceed against Cairo
port where the vessels could lie that should bring provisions for the army. To this the count of Artois was opposed. He said that he could not advise going anywhere except to Babylon, because that was the chief town in all the realm of Egypt; he added, that whosoever wished to kill a serpent outright should crush its head. The king set aside the advice of his barons, and held to that of his brother.

At the beginning of Advent, the king set out with his army to march against Babylon, as the count of Artois had counseled him. Not far from Damietta we came upon a stream of water which issued from the great river [Nile], and it was resolved that the army should halt for a day to dam up this branch, so that it might be crossed. The thing was done easily enough, for the arm was dammed up close to the great river. At the passage of this stream the sultan sent 500 of his knights, the best mounted in his whole army, to harass the king's troops, and retard our march.

On St. Nicholas's day [3] the king gave the order to march and forbade that any one should be so bold as to sally out upon the Saracens who were before us. So it chanced that when the

---

[1] Joinville here gives an account of the first important undertaking of the crusaders—the capture of Damietta. After this achievement the king resolved to await the arrival of his brother, the count of Poitiers, with additional troops. The delay thus occasioned was nearly half a year in length, i.e., until October.

[2] This was a common designation of Cairo, the Saracen capital of Egypt.

[3] December 6.

army was in motion to resume the march and the Turks saw that no one would sally out against them, and learned from their spies that the king had forbidden it, they became emboldened **A skirmish be-** and attacked the Templars,[1] who formed the **tween the Sar-** advance-guard. And one of the Turks hurled to **acens and the** **Templars** the ground one of the knights of the Temple, right before the feet of the horse of Reginald de Bichiers, who was at that time Marshal of the Temple. When the latter saw this, he shouted to the other brethren: "Have at them, in God's name! I cannot suffer any more of this." He dashed in his spurs, and all the army did likewise. Our people's horses were fresh, while those of the Turks were already worn out. Whence it happened, as I have heard, that not a Turk escaped, but all perished, several of them having plunged into the river, where they were drowned. . . .[2]

One evening when we were on duty near the cat castles, they brought against us an engine called *pierrière*,[3] which they had never done before, and they placed Greek fire[4] in the sling of the engine. When Monseigneur Walter de Cureil, the good

---

[1] The order of the Templars was founded in 1119 to afford protection to pilgrims in Palestine. The name was taken from the temple of Solomon, in Jerusalem, near which the organization's headquarters were at first established. The Templars, in their early history, were a military order and they had a prominent part in most of the crusading movements after their foundation.

[2] At this point Joinville gives an extended description of the Nile and its numerous mouths. King Louis found himself on the bank of one of the streams composing the delta, with the sultan's army drawn up on the other side to prevent the Christians from crossing. Louis determined to construct an embankment across the stream, so that his troops might cross and engage in battle with the enemy. To protect the men engaged in building the embankment, two towers, called cat castles (because they were in front of two *cats*, or covered galleries) were erected. Under cover of these, the work of constructing a passageway went on, though the Saracens did not cease to shower missiles upon the laborers.

[3] An instrument intended primarily for the hurling of stones.

[4] Greek fire was made in various ways, but its main ingredients were sulphur, Persian gum, pitch, petroleum, and oil. It was a highly inflammable substance and when once ignited could be extinguished only by the use of vinegar or sand. It was used quite extensively by the Saracens in their battles with the crusaders, being usually projected in the form of fire-balls from hollow tubes.

knight, who was with me, saw that, he said to us: "Sirs, we are in the greatest peril we have yet been in; for if they set fire to our towers, and we remain here, we are dead men, and if we leave our posts which have been intrusted to us, we are put to shame; and no one can rescue us from this peril save God. It is therefore my opinion and my advice to you that each time they discharge the fire at us we should throw ourselves upon our elbows and knees, and pray our Lord to bring us out of this danger."

As soon as they fired we threw ourselves upon our elbows and knees, as he had counseled us. The first shot they fired came between our two cat castles, and fell in front of us on the open place which the army had made for the purpose of damming the river. Our men whose duty it was to extinguish fires were all ready for it; and because the Saracens could not aim at them on account of the two wings of the sheds which the king had erected there, they fired straight up towards the clouds, so that their darts came down from above upon the men. The nature of the Greek fire was in this wise, that it rushed forward as large around as a cask of verjuice,[1] and the tail of the fire which issued from it was as big as a large-sized spear. It made such a noise in coming that it seemed as if it were a thunderbolt from heaven and looked like a dragon flying through the air. It cast such a brilliant light that in the camp they could see as clearly as if it were daytime, because of the light diffused by such a bulk of fire. Three times that night they discharged the Greek fire at us, and four times they sent it from the fixed cross-bows. Each time that our sainted king heard that they had discharged the Greek fire at us, he dressed himself on his bed and stretched out his hands towards our Lord, and prayed with tears: "Fair Sire God, preserve me my people!" And I verily believe that his prayers stood us in good stead in our hour of need. That evening, every

The Saracens make use of Greek fire

---

[1] An acid liquor made from sour apples or grapes.

time the fire fell, he sent one of his chamberlains to inquire in
what state we were and if the fire had done us any damage.
One time when they threw it, it fell close to the cat castle which
Monseigneur de Courtenay's people were guarding, and struck
on the river-bank.   Then a knight named Aubigoiz called to
me and said: "Sir, if you do not help us we are all burnt, for
the Saracens have discharged so many of their darts dipped in
Greek fire that there is of them, as it were, a great blazing
hedge coming towards our tower."

We ran forward and hastened thither and found that he spoke
the truth.   We extinguished the fire, but before we had done
so the Saracens covered us with the darts they discharged from
the other side of the river.

The king's brothers mounted guard on the roof of the cat
castles to fire bolts from cross-bows against the Saracens, and
which fell into their camp.   The king had commanded that when
the king of Sicily [1] mounted guard in the daytime at the cat
castles, we were to do so at night.   One day when the king of
Sicily was keeping watch, which we should have to do at night, we
were in much trouble of mind because the Saracens had shattered
Progress of our cat castles.   The Saracens brought out the
the conflict *pierrière* in the daytime, which they had hitherto
done only at night, and discharged the Greek fire at our towers.
They had advanced their engines so near to the causeway
which the army had constructed to dam the river that no one
dared to go to the towers, because of the huge stones which
the engines flung upon the road.   The consequence was that
our two towers were burned, and the king of Sicily was so en-
raged about it that he came near flinging himself into the fire to
extinguish it.   But if he were wrathful, I and my knights, for
our part, gave thanks to God; for if we had mounted guard at
night, we should all have been burned.   .   .   .[2]

[1] Charles, count of Anjou—a brother of Saint Louis.
[2] Joinville's story of the remainder of the campaign in Egypt is a long one.
Enough has been given to show something of the character of the conflicts

It came to pass that the sainted king labored so much that the king of England, his wife, and children, came to France to treat with him about peace between him and them. The members of his council were strongly opposed to this peace, and said to him:

"Sire, we greatly marvel that it should be your pleasure to yield to the king of England such a large portion of your land, which **The treaty of Paris, 1259** you and your predecessors have won from him, and obtained through forfeiture. It seems to us that if you believe you have no right to it, you do not make fitting restitution to the king of England unless you restore to him all the conquests which you and your predecessors have made; but if you believe that you have a right to it, it seems to us that you are throwing away all that you yield to him."

To this the sainted king replied after this fashion: "Sirs, I am certain that the king of England's predecessors lost most justly the conquests I hold; and the land which I give up to him I do not give because I am bound either towards himself or his heirs, but to create love between his children and mine, who are first cousins. And it seems to me that I am making a good use of what I give to him, because before he was not my vassal, but now he has to render homage to me." [1] . . .

between Saracen and crusader. In the end Louis was compelled to withdraw his shattered army. He then made his way to the Holy Land in the hope of better success, but the four years he spent there were likewise a period of disappointment.

[1] The treaty here referred to is that of Paris, negotiated by Louis IX. and Henry III. in 1259. By it the English king renounced his claim to Normandy, Maine, Anjou, Touraine, and Poitou, while Louis IX. ceded to Henry the Limousin, Périgord, and part of Saintonge, besides the reversion of Agenais and Quercy. The territories thus abandoned by the French were to be annexed to the duchy of Guienne, for which Henry III. was to render homage to the French king, just as had been rendered by the English sovereigns before the conquests of Philip Augustus. Manifestly Louis IX.'s chief motive in yielding possession of lands he regarded as properly his was to secure peace with England and to get the homage of the English king for Guienne. For upwards of half a century the relations of England and France had been strained by reason of the refusal of Henry III. to recognize the conquests of Philip Augustus and to render the accustomed homage. The treaty of Paris was important because it regulated the relations of France and England to the outbreak of the Hundred Years' War. It undertook to perpetuate the

After the king's return from beyond sea, he lived so devoutly that he never afterwards wore furs of different colors, nor minnever,[1] nor scarlet cloth, nor gilt stirrups or spurs. His dress was of camlet [2] and of a dark blue cloth; the linings of his coverlets and garments were of doeskin or hare-legs.

When rich men's minstrels entered the hall after the repast, bringing with them their viols, he waited to hear grace until the minstrel had finished his chant; then he rose and the priests who said grace stood before him. When we were at his court in a private way,[3] he used to sit at the foot of his bed, and when the Franciscans and Dominicans [4] who were there spoke of a book that would give him pleasure, he would say to them: "You shall not read to me, for, after eating, there is no book so pleasant as *quolibets*,"—that is, that every one should say what he likes. When men of quality dined with him, he made himself agreeable to them. . . .

The king's personal traits

Many a time it happened that in the summer he would go and sit down in the wood at Vincennes,[5] with his back to an oak, and make us take our seats around him. And all those who had complaints to make came to him, without hindrance from ushers or other folk. Then he asked them with his own lips: "Is there any one here who has a cause?" [6] Those who had a cause stood up, when he would say to them: "Silence all, and you shall be dispatched one after the other." Then he would call Monseigneur de Fontaines, or Monseigneur Geoffrey de Villette, and would say to one of

His primitive method of dispensing justice

old division of French soil between the English and French monarchs—an arrangement always fruitful of discord and destined, more than anything else, to bring on the great struggle of the fourteenth and fifteenth centuries between the two nations [see p. 417 ff.].

[1] A fur much esteemed in the Middle Ages. It is not known whether it was the fur of a single animal or of several kinds combined.

[2] A woven fabric made of camel's hair.

[3] After his retirement from the royal service in 1254 Joinville frequently made social visits at Louis's court.

[4] On the Franciscans and Dominicans [see p. 360].

[5] To the east from Paris—now a suburb of that city. The château of Vincennes was one of the favorite royal residences.

[6] That is, a case in law.

them: "Dispose of this case for me." When he saw anything to amend in the words of those who spoke for others, he would correct it with his own lips. Sometimes in summer I have seen him, in order to administer justice to the people, come into the garden of Paris dressed in a camlet coat, a surcoat of woollen stuff, without sleeves, a mantle of black taffety around his neck, his hair well combed and without coif, a hat with white peacock's feathers on his head. Carpets were spread for us to sit down upon around him, and all the people who had business to dispatch stood about in front of him. Then he would have it dispatched in the same manner as I have already described in the wood of Vincennes.

CHAPTER XX.

MUNICIPAL ORGANIZATION AND ACTIVITY

57. Some Twelfth Century Town Charters

In the times of the Carolingians the small and scattered towns and villages of western Europe, particularly of France, were inhabited mainly by serfs and villeins, i.e., by a dependent rather than an independent population. With scarcely an exception, these urban centers belonged to the lords of the neighboring lands, who administered their affairs through mayors, provosts, bailiffs, or other agents, collected from them seigniorial dues as from the rural peasantry, and, in short, took entire charge of matters of justice, finance, military obligations, and industrial arrangements. There was no local self-government, nothing in the way of municipal organization separate from the feudal régime, and no important burgher class as distinguished from the agricultural laborers. By the twelfth century a great transformation is apparent. France has come to be dotted with strong and often largely independent municipalities, and a powerful class of bourgeoisie, essentially anti-feudal in character, has risen to play an increasing part in the nation's political and economic life. In these new municipalities there is a larger measure of freedom of person, security of property, and rights of self-government than Europe had known since the days of Charlemagne, perhaps even since the best period of the Roman Empire.

The reason for this transformation—in other words, the origin of these new municipal centers—has been variously explained. One theory is that the municipal system of the Middle Ages was essentially a survival of that which prevailed in western Europe under the fostering influence of Rome. The best authorities now reject this view, for there is every reason to believe that, speaking generally, the barbarian invasions and feudalism practically crushed out the municipal institutions of the Empire. Another theory ascribes the origin of mediæval municipal govern-

325

ment to the merchant and craft guilds, particularly the former; but there is little evidence to support the view. Undeniably the guild was an important factor in drawing groups of burghers together and forming centers of combination against local lords, but it was at best only one of several forces tending to the growth of municipal life. Other factors of larger importance were the military and the commercial. On the one hand, the need of protection led people to flock to fortified places— castles or monasteries—and settle in the neighborhood; on the other, the growth of commerce and industry, especially after the eleventh century, caused strategic places like the intersection of great highways and rivers to become seats of permanent and growing population. The towns which thus sprang up in response to new conditions and necessities in time took on a political as well as a commercial and industrial character, principally through the obtaining of charters from the neighboring lords, defining the measure of independence to be enjoyed and the respective rights of lord and town. Charters of the sort were usually granted by the lord, not merely because requested by the burghers, but because they were paid for and constituted a valuable source of revenue. Not infrequently, however, a charter was wrested from an unwilling lord through open warfare. It was in the first half of the twelfth century that town charters became common. As a rule they were obtained by the larger towns (it should be borne in mind that a population of 10,000 was large in the twelfth century), but not necessarily so, for many villages of two or three hundred people secured them also.

The two great classes of towns were the *villes libres* (free towns) and the *villes franches*, or *villes de bourgeoisie* (franchise, or chartered, towns). The free towns enjoyed a large measure of independence. In relation to their lords they occupied essentially the position of vassals, with the legislative, financial, and judicial privileges which by the twelfth century all great vassals had come to have. The burghers elected their own officers, constituted their own courts, made their own laws, levied taxes, and even waged war. The leading types of free cities were the communes of northern France (governed by a provost and one or more councils, often essentially oligarchical) and the consulates of southern France and northern Italy (distinguished from the communes by the fact that the executive was made up of "consuls," and by the greater participation of the local nobility in town affairs). A typical free town of the commune type, was Laon, in the region of northern Champagne. In 1109 the bishop of Laon, who was lord of the city, consented to the establishment of a communal government. Three years later he sought to abolish it, with the result that an insurrection was stirred up in which he lost his life. King Louis VI. intervened and the citizens were obliged to submit to the authority of the new bishop, though in 1328 fear of another uprising led this official to renew the old grant. The act was ratified by Louis VI. in the text (a) given below.

The other great class of towns—the franchise towns—differed from the free towns in having a much more limited measure of political and economic independence. They received grants of privileges, or "franchises," from their lord, especially in the way of restrictions of rights of the latter over the persons and property of the inhabitants, but they remained politically subject to the lord and their government was partly or wholly under his control. Their charters set a limit to the lord's arbitrary authority, emancipated such inhabitants as were not already free, gave the citizens the right to move about and to alienate property, substituted money payments for the corvée, and in general made old regulations less burdensome; but as a rule no political rights were conferred. Paris, Tours, Orleans, and other more important cities on the royal domain belonged to this class. The town of Lorris, on the royal domain a short distance east of Orleans, became the common model for the type. Its charter, received from Louis VII. in 1155, is given in the second selection (b) below.

Sources—(a) Text in Vilevault and Bréquigny, *Ordonnances des Rois de France de la Troisième Race* ["Ordinances of the Kings of France of the Third Dynasty"], Paris, 1769, Vol. XI., pp. 185–187.

(b) Text in Maurice Prou, *Les Coutumes de Lorris et leur Propagation aux XIIe et XIIIe Siècles* ["The Customs of Lorris and their Spread in the Twelfth and Thirteenth Centuries"], Paris, 1884, pp. 129–141.

(a)

1. Let no one arrest any freeman or serf for any offense without due process of law.[1]

[1] Such guarantees of personal liberty were not peculiar to the charters of communes; they are often found in those of franchise towns.

2. But if any one do injury to a clerk, soldier, or merchant, native or foreign, provided he who does the injury belongs to the

Provisions of the charter of Laon

same city as the injured person, let him, summoned after the fourth day, come for justice before the mayor and jurats.[1]

7. If a thief is arrested, let him be brought to him on whose land he has been arrested; but if justice is not done by the lord, let it be done by the jurats.[2]

12. We entirely abolish mortmain.[3]

18. The customary tallages we have so reformed that every man owing such tallages, at the time when they are due, must pay four pence, and beyond that no more.[4]

19. Let men of the peace not be compelled to resort to courts outside the city.[5]

(b)

1. Every one who has a house in the parish of Lorris shall pay as *cens* sixpence only for his house, and for each acre of land that he possesses in the parish.[6]

2. No inhabitant of the parish of Lorris shall be required to pay a toll or any other tax on his provisions; and let him not be made to pay any measurage fee on the grain which he has raised by his own labor.[7]

---

[1] The chief magistrate of Laon was a mayor, elected by the citizens. In judicial matters he was assisted by twelve "jurats."

[2] This is intended to preserve the judicial privileges of lords of manors.

[3] The citizens of the town were to have freedom to dispose of their property as they chose.

[4] This provision was intended to put an end to arbitrary taxation by the bishop. In the earlier twelfth century serfs were subject to the arbitrary levy of the taille (tallage) and this indeed constituted one of their most grievous burdens. Arbitrary tallage was almost invariably abolished by the town charters.

[5] By "men of the peace" is meant the citizens of the commune. The term "commune" is scrupulously avoided in the charter because of its odious character in the eyes of the bishop. Suits were to be tried at home in the burgesses' own courts, to save time and expense and insure better justice.

[6] This trifling payment of sixpence a year was made in recognition of the lordship of the king, the grantor of the charter. Aside from it, the burgher had full rights over his land.

[7] The burghers, who were often engaged in agriculture as well as commerce,

3. No burgher shall go on an expedition, on foot or on horse-back, from which he cannot return the same day to his home if he desires.[1]

4. No burgher shall pay toll on the road to Étampes, to Orleans, to Milly (which is in the Gâtinais), or to Melun.[2]

5. No one who has property in the parish of Lorris shall forfeit it **The charter** for any offense whatsoever, unless the offense shall **of Lorris** have been committed against us or any of our *hôtes*.[3]

6. No person while on his way to the fairs and markets of Lorris, or returning, shall be arrested or disturbed, unless he shall have committed an offense on the same day.[4]

9. No one, neither we nor any other, shall exact from the burghers of Lorris any tallage, tax, or subsidy.[5]

12. If a man shall have had a quarrel with another, but without breaking into a fortified house, and if the parties shall have reached an agreement without bringing a suit before the provost, no fine shall be due to us or our provost on account of the affair.[6]

are to be exempt from tolls on commodities bought for their own sustenance and from the ordinary fees due the lord for each measure of grain harvested.

[1] The object of this provision is to restrict the amount of military service due the king. The burghers of small places like Lorris were farmers and traders who made poor soldiers and who were ordinarily exempted from service by their lords. The provision for Lorris practically amounted to an exemption, for such service as was permissible under chapter 3 of the charter was not worth much.

[2] The Gâtinais was the region in which Lorris was situated. Étampes, Milly, and Melun all lay to the north of Lorris, in the direction of Paris. Orleans lay to the west. The king's object in granting the burghers the right to carry goods to the towns specified without payment of tolls was to encourage commercial intercourse.

[3] This protects the landed property of the burghers against the crown and crown officials. With two exceptions, fine or imprisonment, not confiscation of land, is to be the penalty for crime. *Hôtes* denotes persons receiving land from the king and under his direct protection.

[4] This provision is intended to attract merchants to Lorris by placing them under the king's protection and assuring them that they would not be molested on account of old offenses.

[5] This chapter safeguards the personal property of the burghers, as chapter 5 safeguards their land. Arbitrary imposts are forbidden and any of the inhabitants who as serfs had been paying arbitrary tallage are relieved of the burden. The nominal *cens* (Chap. 1) was to be the only regular payment due the king.

[6] An agreement outside of court was allowable in all cases except when there was a serious breach of the public peace. The provost was the chief

15. No inhabitant of Lorris is to render us the obligation of *corvée*, except twice a year, when our wine is to be carried to Orleans, and not elsewhere.[1]

16. No one shall be detained in prison if he can furnish surety that he will present himself for judgment.

17. Any burgher who wishes to sell his property shall have the privilege of doing so; and, having received the price of the sale, he shall have the right to go from the town freely and without molestation, if he so desires, unless he has committed some offense in it.

18. Any one who shall dwell a year and a day in the parish of Lorris, without any claim having pursued him there, and without having refused to lay his case before us or our provost, shall abide there freely and without molestation.[2]

35. We ordain that every time there shall be a change of provosts in the town the new provost shall take an oath faithfully to observe these regulations; and the same thing shall be done by new sergeants [3] every time that they are installed.

58. The Colonization of Eastern Germany

In the time of Charlemagne the Elbe River marked a pretty clear boundary between the Slavic population to the east and the Germanic to the west. There were many Slavs west of the Elbe, but no Germans east of it. There had been a time when Germans occupied large portions

officer of the town. He was appointed by the crown and was charged chiefly with the administration of justice and the collection of revenues. All suits of the burghers were tried in his court. They had no active part in their own government, as was generally true of the franchise towns.

[1] Another part of the charter specifies that only those burghers who owned horses and carts were expected to render the king even this service.

[2] This clause, which is very common in the town charters of the twelfth century (especially in the case of towns on the royal domain) is intended to attract serfs from other regions and so to build up population. As a rule the towns were places of refuge from seigniorial oppression and the present charter undertakes to limit the time within which the lord might recover his serf who had fled to Lorris to a year and a day—except in cases where the serf should refuse to recognize the jurisdiction of the provost's court in the matter of the lord's claim.

[3] The sergeants were deputies of the provost, somewhat on the order of town constables.

of eastern Europe, but for one reason or another they gradually became concentrated toward the west, while Slavic peoples pushed in to fill the vacated territory. Under Charlemagne and his successors we can discern the earlier stages of a movement of reaction which has gone on in later times until the political map of all north central Europe has been remodeled. During the ninth, tenth, and eleventh centuries large portions of the "sphere of influence" (to use a modern phrase) which Charlemagne had created eastward from the Elbe were converted into German principalities and dependencies. German colonists pushed down the Danube, well toward the Black Sea, along the Baltic, past the Oder and toward the Vistula, and up the Oder into the heart of modern Poland. The Slavic population was slowly brought under subjection, Christianized, and to a certain extent Germanized. In the tenth century Henry I. (919–936) began a fresh forward movement against the Slavs, or Wends, as the Germans called them. Magdeburg, on the Elbe, was established as the chief base of operations. The work was kept up by Henry's son, Otto I. (936–973), but under his grandson, Otto II. (973–983), a large part of what had been gained was lost for a time through a Slavic revolt called out by the Emperor's preoccupation with affairs in Italy. Thereafter for a century the Slavs were allowed perforce to enjoy their earlier independence, and upon more than one occasion they were able to assume the aggressive against their would-be conquerors. In 1066 the city of Hamburg, on the lower Elbe, was attacked and almost totally destroyed. The imperial power was fast declining and the Franconian sovereigns had little time left from their domestic conflicts and quarrels with the papacy to carry on a contest on the east.

The renewed advance which the Germans made against the Slavs in the later eleventh and earlier twelfth centuries was due primarily to the energy of the able princes of Saxony and to the pressure for colonization, which increased in spite of small encouragement from any except the local authorities. The document given below is a typical charter of the period, authorizing the establishment of a colony of Germans eastward from Hamburg, on the border of Brandenburg. It was granted in 1106 by the bishop of Hamburg, who as lord of the region in which the proposed settlement was to be made exercised the right not merely of giving consent to the undertaking, but also of prescribing the terms and conditions by which the colonists were to be bound.

As appears from the charter, the colony was expected to be a source of profit to the bishop; and indeed it was financial considerations on the part of lords, lay and spiritual, who had stretches of unoccupied land at their disposal, almost as much as regard for safety in numbers and the absolute dominance of Germanic peoples, that prompted these local magnates of eastern Germany so ardently to promote the work of colonization.

Source—Text in Wilhelm Altmann and Ernst Bernheim, *Ausgewählte Urkunden zur Erlauterung der Verfassungsgeschichte Deutschlands im Mittelalter* ["Select Documents Illustrative of the Constitutional History of Germany in the Middle Ages"], 3rd ed., Berlin, 1904, pp. 159–160. Translated in Thatcher and McNeal, *A Source Book for Mediæval History* (New York, 1905), pp. 572–573.

1. In the name of the holy and undivided Trinity. Frederick, by the grace of God bishop of Hamburg, to all the faithful in Christ, gives a perpetual benediction. We wish to make known to all the agreement which certain people living this side of the Rhine, who are called Hollanders,[1] have made with us.

2. These men came to us and earnestly begged us to grant them certain lands in our bishopric, which are uncultivated,
swampy, and useless to our people. We have consulted our subjects about this and, feeling that this would be profitable to us and to our successors, have granted their request.

The Hollanders ask land for a colony

3. The agreement was made that they should pay us every year one *denarius* for every hide of land. We have thought it necessary to determine the dimensions of the hide, in order that no quarrel may thereafter arise about it. The hide shall be 720 royal rods long and thirty royal rods wide. We also grant them the streams which flow through this land.

4. They agreed to give the tithe according to our decree, that is, every eleventh sheaf of grain, every tenth lamb, every tenth pig, every tenth goat, every tenth goose, and a tenth of the

---

[1] These "Hollanders" inhabited substantially the portion of Europe now designated by their name.

honey and of the flax. For every colt they shall pay a *denarius* on St. Martin's day [Nov. 11], and for every calf an obol [penny].

5. They promised to obey me in all ecclesiastical matters,

Obedience promised to the bishop of Hamburg according to the decrees of the holy fathers, the canonical law, and the practice in the diocese of Utrecht.[1]

6. They agreed to pay every year two marks for every 100 hides for the privilege of holding their own courts for the settlement of all their differences about secular matters. They did this because they feared they would suffer from the injustice of

Judicial immunity foreign judges.[2] If they cannot settle the more important cases, they shall refer them to the bishop. And if they take the bishop with them for the purpose of deciding one of their trials,[3] they shall provide for his support as long as he remains there by granting him one third of all the fees arising from the trial; and they shall keep the other two thirds.

7. We have given them permission to found churches wherever they may wish on these lands. For the support of the priests who shall serve God in these churches we grant a tithe of our tithes from these parish churches. They promised that the congregation of each of these churches should endow their church with a hide for the support of their priest.[4] The names of the men who made this agreement with us are: Henry, the priest, to whom we have granted the aforesaid churches for life; and the others are laymen, Helikin, Arnold, Hiko, Fordalt, and Referic. To them and to their heirs after them we have granted the aforesaid land according to the secular laws and to the terms of this agreement.

---

[1] This was the diocese from which the colonists proposed to remove.
[2] That is, judges representing any outside authority.
[3] In other words, if the bishop should go from his seat at Hamburg to the colony.
[4] In each parish of the colony, therefore, the priest would be supported by the income of the hide of land set apart for his use and by the tenth of the regular church tithes which the bishop conceded for the purpose.

59. The League of Rhenish Cities (1254)

ABOUT the middle of the thirteenth century the central authority of
the Holy Roman Empire was for a time practically dissolved. Frederick
II., the last strong ruler of the Hohenstaufen dynasty, died in 1250, and
even he was so largely Italian in character and interests that he could
bring himself to give little attention to German affairs. During the
stormy period of the Interregnum (1254–1273) there was no universally
recognized emperor at all. Germany had reached an advanced stage of
political disintegration and it is scarcely conceivable that even a Henry
IV. or a Frederick Barbarossa could have made the imperial power much
more than a shadow and a name. But while the Empire was broken up
into scores of principalities, independent cities, and other political fragments, its people were enjoying a vigorous and progressive life. The
period was one of great growth of industry in the towns, and especially
of commerce. The one serious disadvantage was the lack of a central
police authority to preserve order and insure the safety of person and
property. Warfare was all but ceaseless, robber-bands infested the
rivers and highways, and all manner of vexatious conditions were imposed upon trade by the various local authorities. The natural result
was the formation of numerous leagues and confederacies for the suppression of anarchy and the protection of trade and industry. The
greatest of these was the Hanseatic League, which came to comprise
one hundred and seventy-two cities, and the history of whose operations
runs through more than three centuries. An earlier organization, which
may be considered in a way a forerunner of the Hansa, was the Rhine
League, established in 1254. At this earlier date Conrad IV., son of
Frederick II., was fighting his half-brother Manfred for their common
Sicilian heritage; William of Holland, who claimed the imperial title,
was recognized in only a small territory and was quite powerless to affect
conditions of disorder outside; the other princes, great and small, were
generally engaged in private warfare; and the difficulties and dangers of
trade and industry were at their maximum. To establish a power
strong enough, and with the requisite disposition, to suppress the robbers and pirates who were ruining commerce, the leading cities of the
Rhine valley—Mainz, Cologne, Worms, Speyer, Strassburg, Basel,
Trier, Metz, and others—entered into a "league of holy peace," to endure

for a period of ten years, dating from July 13, 1254. The more significant terms of the compact are set forth in the selection below.

Source—Text in Wilhelm Altmann and Ernst Bernheim, *Ausgewählte
Urkunden zur Erlauterung der Verfassungsgeschichte Deutschlands
im Mittelalter* ["Select Documents Illustrative of the Constitutional History of Germany in the Middle Ages"], 3rd ed., Berlin,
1904, pp. 251–254. Translated in Thatcher and McNeal, *A Source
Book for Mediæval History* (New York, 1905), pp. 606–609.

In the name of the Lord, amen. In the year of our Lord 1254,
on the octave of St. Michael's day [a week after Sept. 29] we,
the cities of the upper and lower Rhine, leagued together for the
preservation of peace, met in the city of Worms. We held a
conference there and carefully discussed everything pertaining to

**The league
formed at
Worms**
a general peace. To the honor of God, and of the
holy mother Church, and of the holy Empire,
which is now governed by our lord, William,
king of the Romans,[1] and to the common advantage of all, both
rich and poor alike, we made the following laws. They are for
the benefit of all, both poor and great, the secular clergy, monks,
laymen, and Jews. To secure these things, which are for the
public good, we will spare neither ourselves nor our possessions.
The princes and lords who take the oath are joined with us.

1. We decree that we will make no warlike expeditions, except
those that are absolutely necessary and determined on by the
wise counsel of the cities and communes. We will mutually
aid each other with all our strength in securing redress for our
grievances.

2. We decree that no member of the league, whether city

**No dealings
to be had with
enemies of the
league**
or lord, Christian or Jew, shall furnish food,
arms, or aid of any kind, to any one who op-
poses us or the peace.

3. And no one in our cities shall give credit, or make a loan,
to them.

---

[1] All that this means is that the members of the Rhine League recognized
William of Holland as emperor. Most of the Empire did not so recognize
him. He died in 1256, two years after the league was formed.

4. No citizen of any of the cities in the league shall associate with such, or give them counsel, aid, or support. If any one is convicted of doing so, he shall be expelled from the city and punished so severely in his property that he will be a warning to others not to do such things.

5. If any knight, in trying to aid his lord who is at war with us, attacks or molests us anywhere outside of the walled towns of his lord, he is breaking the peace, and we will in some way **A warning** inflict due punishment on him and his possessions, **to enemies** no matter who he is. If he is caught in any of the cities, he shall be held as a prisoner until he makes proper satisfaction. We wish to be protectors of the peasants, and we will protect them against all violence if they will observe the peace with us. But if they make war on us, we will punish them, and if we catch them in any of the cities, we will punish them as malefactors.

6. We wish the cities to destroy all the ferries except those in their immediate neighborhood, so that there shall be no ferries except those near the cities which are in the league. This is to be done in order that the enemies of the peace may be deprived of all means of crossing the Rhine.

7. We decree that if any lord or knight aids us in promoting the peace, we will do all we can to protect him. Whoever does not swear to keep the peace with us, shall be excluded from the general peace.

10. Above all, we wish to affirm that we desire to live in mutual peace with the lords and all the people of the province, and we desire that each should preserve all his rights.

11. Under threat of punishment we forbid any citizen to revile the lords, although they may be our enemies. For although we wish to punish them for the violence they have done us, yet before making war on them we will first warn them to cease from injuring us.

12. We decree that all correspondence about this matter with

the cities of the lower Rhine shall be conducted from Mainz, and from Worms with the cities of the upper Rhine. From these **Mainz and** two cities all our correspondence shall be carried **Worms to be** on and all who have done us injury shall be **the capitals** **of the league** warned. Those who have suffered injury shall send their messengers at their own expense.

13. We also promise, both lords and cities, to send four official representatives to whatever place a conference is to be **The governing** held, and they shall have full authority from **body of the** their cities to decide on all matters. They shall **league** report to their cities all the decisions of the meeting. All who come with the representatives of the cities, or who come to them while in session, shall have peace, and no judgment shall be enforced against them.

14. No city shall receive non-residents, who are commonly called "pfahlburgers," as citizens.[1]

15. We firmly declare that if any member of the league breaks the peace, we will proceed against him at once as if he were not a member, and compel him to make proper satisfaction.

16. We promise that we will faithfully keep each other informed by letter about our enemies and all others who may be able to do us damage, in order that we may take timely counsel to protect ourselves against them.

17. We decree that no one shall violently enter the house of monks or nuns, of whatever order they may be, or quarter themselves upon them, or demand or extort food or any kind of

---

[1] These "pfahlburgers" were subjects of ecclesiastical or secular princes who, in order to escape the burdens of this relation, contrived to get themselves enrolled as citizens of neighboring cities. While continuing to dwell in regions subject to the jurisdiction of their lords, they claimed to enjoy immunity from that jurisdiction, because of their citizenship in those outside cities. The pfahlburgers were a constant source of friction between the towns and the territorial princes. The Golden Bull of Emperor Charles IV. (1356) decreed that pfahlburgers should not enjoy the rights and privileges of the cities unless they became actual residents of them and discharged their full obligations as citizens.

service from them, contrary to their will. If any one does this, he shall be held as a violator of the peace.

18. We decree that each city shall try to persuade each of its neighboring cities to swear to keep the peace. If they do not **The league to** do so, they shall be entirely cut off from the **be enlarged** peace, so that if any one does them an injury, either in their persons or their property, he shall not thereby break the peace.

19. We wish all members of the league, cities, lords, and all others, to arm themselves properly and prepare for war, so that whenever we call upon them we shall find them ready.

20. We decree that the cities between the Moselle and Basel shall prepare 100 war boats, and the cities below the Moselle **Military** shall prepare 500, well equipped with bowmen, **preparations** and each city shall prepare herself as well as **of the league** she can and supply herself with arms for knights and foot-soldiers.

CHAPTER XXI.

UNIVERSITIES AND STUDENT LIFE

THE modern university is essentially a product of the Middle Ages. The Greeks and Romans had provisions for higher education, but nothing that can properly be termed universities, with faculties, courses of study, examinations, and degrees. The word "universitas" in the earlier mediæval period was applied indiscriminately to any group or body of people, as a guild of artisans or an organization of the clergy, and only very gradually did it come to be restricted to an association of teachers and students—the so-called *universitas societas magistrorum discipulorumque*. The origins of mediæval universities are, in most cases, rather obscure. In the earlier Middle Ages the interests of learning were generally in the keeping of the monks and the work of education was carried on chiefly in monastic schools, where the subjects of study were commonly the seven liberal arts inherited from Roman days.[1] By the twelfth century there was a relative decline of these monastic schools, accompanied by a marked development of cathedral schools in which not only the seven liberal arts but also new subjects like law and theology were taught. The twelfth century renaissance brought a notable revival of Roman law, medicine, astronomy, and philosophy; by 1200 the whole of Aristotle's writings had become known; and the general awakening produced immediate results in the larger numbers of students who flocked to places like Paris and Bologna where exceptional teachers were to be found.

Out of these conditions grew the earliest of the universities. No definite dates for the beginnings of Paris, Bologna, Oxford, etc., can be assigned, but the twelfth and thirteenth centuries are to be considered their great formative period. Bologna was specifically the creation of the revived study of the Roman law and of the fame of the great law teacher Irnerius. The university sprang from a series of organizations

[1] That is, the *trivium* (Latin grammar, rhetoric, and logic) and the *quadrivium* (arithmetic, geometry, astronomy, and music).

effected first by the students and later by the masters, or teachers, and modeled after the guilds of workmen. It became the pattern for most of the later Italian and Spanish universities. Paris arose in a different way. It grew directly out of the great cathedral school of Notre Dame and, unlike Bologna, was an organization at the outset of masters rather than of students. It was presided over by the chancellor, who had had charge of education in the cathedral and who retained the exclusive privilege of granting licenses to teach (the *licentia docendi*), or, in other words, degrees.[1] Rising to prominence in the twelfth century, especially by virtue of the teaching of Abelard (1079–1142), Paris became in time the greatest university of the Middle Ages, exerting profound influence not only on learning, but also on the Church and even at times on political affairs. The universities of the rest of France, as well as the German universities and Oxford and Cambridge in England, were copied pretty closely after Paris.

60. Privileges Granted to Students and Masters

THROUGHOUT the Middle Ages numerous special favors were showered upon the universities and their students by the Church. Patronage and protection from the secular authorities were less to be depended on, though the courts of kings were not infrequently the rendezvous of scholars, and the greater seats of learning after the eleventh century generally owed their prosperity, if not their origin, to the liberality of monarchs such as Frederick Barbarossa or Philip Augustus. The recognition of the universities by the temporal powers came as a rule earlier than that by the Church. The edict of the Emperor Frederick I., which comprises selection (a) below, was issued in 1158 and is not to be considered as limited in its application to the students of any particular university, though many writers have associated it solely with

[1] The earliest degrees granted at Bologna, Paris, etc., were those of master of arts and doctor of philosophy. "Master" and "Doctor" were practically equivalent terms and both signified simply that the bearer, after suitable examinations, had been recognized as sufficiently proficient to be admitted to the guild of teachers. The bachelor's degree grew up more obscurely. It might be taken somewhere on the road to the master's degree, but was merely an incidental stamp of proficiency up to a certain stage of advancement. Throughout mediæval times the master's, or doctor's, degree, which carried the right to become a teacher, was the normal goal and few stopped short of its attainment.

the University of Bologna. That the statute was decreed at the solicitation of the Bologna doctors of law admits of little doubt, but, as Rashdall observes, it was "a general privilege conferred on the student class throughout the Lombard kingdom." [1]   By some writers it is said to have been the earliest formal grant of privileges for university students, but this cannot be true as Salerno (notable chiefly for medical studies) received such grants from Robert Guiscard and his son Roger before the close of the eleventh century.

Until the year 1200 the students of Paris enjoyed no privileges such as those conferred upon the Italian institutions by Frederick. In that year a tavern brawl occurred between some German students and Parisian townspeople, in which five of the students lost their lives. The provost of the city, instead of attempting to repress the disorder, took sides against the students and encouraged the populace. Such laxity stirred the king, Philip Augustus, to action. Fearing that the students would decamp *en masse*, he hastened to comply with their appeal for redress. The provost and his lieutenants were arrested and a decree was issued [given, in part, in selection (b)] exempting the scholars from the operation of the municipal law in criminal cases. Pope Innocent III. at once confirmed the privileges and on his part relaxed somewhat the vigilance of the Church. Such liberal measures, however, did not insure permanent peace. In less than three decades another conflict with the provost occurred which was so serious as to result in a total suspension of the university's activities for more than two years.

Sources—(a) Text in *Monumenta Germaniæ Historica*, *Leges* (Pertz ed.), Vol. II., p. 114. Adapted from translation by Dana C. Munro in *Univ. of Pa. Translations and Reprints*, Vol. II., No. 3, pp. 2–4.

(b) Text in *Chartularium Universitatis Parisiensis* ["Cartulary of the University of Paris"], No. 1., p. 59. Adapted from translation in *Univ. of Pa. Translations and Reprints*, *ibid.*, pp. 4–7.

(a)

After a careful consideration of this subject by the bishops, abbots, dukes, counts, judges, and other nobles of our sacred palace, we, from our piety, have granted this privilege to all

[1] Hastings Rashdall, *The Universities of Europe in the Middle Ages* (Oxford, 1895), Vol. I., p. 146.

scholars who travel for the sake of study, and especially to the professors of divine and sacred laws,[1] namely, that they may

Security of travel and residence for scholars

go in safety to the places in which the studies are carried on, both they themselves and their messengers, and may dwell there in security. For we think it fitting that, during good behavior, those should enjoy our praise and protection, by whose learning the world is enlightened to the obedience of God and of us, his ministers, and the life of the subject is molded; and by a special consideration we defend them from all injuries.

For who does not pity those who exile themselves through love for learning, who wear themselves out in poverty in place of riches, who expose their lives to all perils and often suffer bodily injury from the vilest men? This must be endured with vexation. Therefore, we declare by this general and perpetual law, that in the future no one shall be so rash as to venture to

Regulation concerning the collection of debts

inflict any injury on scholars, or to occasion any loss to them on account of a debt owed by an inhabitant of their province—a thing which we have learned is sometimes done by an evil custom.[2] And let it be known to the violators of this constitution, and also to those who shall at the time be the rulers of the places, that a fourfold restitution of property shall be exacted from all and that, the mark of infamy being affixed to them by the law itself, they shall lose their office forever.

Moreover, if any one shall presume to bring a suit against them on account of any business, the choice in this matter shall be

Judicial privileges of scholars

given to the scholars, who may summon the accusers to appear before their professors or the bishop of the city, to whom we have given jurisdiction in this matter.[3] But if, indeed, the accuser shall attempt

[1] Evidently, from other passages, including students of law as well as teachers.

[2] Greedy creditors sometimes compelled students to pay debts owed by the fellow-countrymen of the latter—a very thinly disguised form of robbery. This abuse was now to be abolished.

[3] That is, in any legal proceedings against a scholar the defendant was to

to drag the scholar before another judge, even if his cause is a very just one, he shall lose his suit for such an attempt.

(b)

Concerning the safety of the students at Paris in the future, by the advice of our subjects we have ordained as follows:

We will cause all the citizens of Paris to swear that if any one sees an injury done to any student by any layman,[1] he will testify truthfully to this, nor will any one withdraw in order not to see [the act]. And if it shall happen that any one strikes a student, except in self-defense, especially if he strikes the student with a weapon, a club, or a stone, all laymen who see [the act] **Protection for scholars against crimes of violence** shall in good faith seize the malefactor, or malefactors, and deliver them to our judge; nor·shall they run away in order not to see the act, or seize the malefactor, or testify to the truth. Also, whether the malefactor is seized in open crime or not, we will make a legal and full examination through clerks, or laymen, or certain lawful persons; and our count and our judges shall do the same. And if by a full examination we, or our judges, are able to learn that he who is accused, is guilty of the crime, then we, or our judges, shall immediately inflict a penalty, according to the quality and nature of the crime; notwithstanding the fact that the criminal may deny the deed and say that he is ready to defend himself in single combat, or to purge himself by the ordeal by water.[2]

Also, neither our provost nor our judges shall lay hands on a student for any offense whatever; nor shall they place him in

choose whether he would be tried before his own master or before the bishop. In later times this right of choice passed generally to the plaintiff.

[1] The students of the French universities were regarded as, for all practical purposes, members of the clergy (*clerici*) and thus to be distinguished from laymen. They were not clergy in the full sense, but were subject to a special sort of jurisdiction closely akin to that applying to the clergy.

[2] The law on this point was exceptionally severe. The privilege of establishing innocence by combat or the ordeal by water was denied, though even the provost and his subordinates who had played false in the riot of 1200 had been given the opportunity of clearing themselves by such means if they chose and could do so.

our prison, unless such a crime has been committed by the student, that he ought to be arrested. And in that case, our judge shall arrest him on the spot, without striking him at all, unless he resists, and shall hand him over to the ecclesiastical judge,[1] who ought to guard him in order to satisfy us and the one suffering the injury. And if a serious crime has been committed, our judge shall go or shall send to see what is done with the student. If, indeed, the student does not resist arrest and yet suffers any injury, we will exact satisfaction for it, according to the aforesaid examination and the aforesaid oath. Also our judges shall not lay hands on the chattels of the students of Paris for any crime whatever. But if it shall seem that these ought to be sequestrated, they shall be sequestrated and guarded after sequestration by the ecclesiastical judge, in order that whatever is judged legal by the Church may be done with the chattels.[2] But if students are arrested by our count at such an hour that the ecclesiastical judge cannot be found and be present at once, our provost shall cause the culprits to be guarded in some student's house without any ill-treatment, as is said above, until they are delivered to the ecclesiastical judge.

Scholars to be tried and punished under ecclesiastical authority

In order, moreover, that these [decrees] may be kept more carefully and may be established forever by a fixed law, we have decided that our present provost and the people of Paris shall affirm by an oath, in the presence of the scholars, that they will carry out in good faith all the above-mentioned [regulations]. And always in the future, whosoever receives from us the office of provost in Paris, among the inaugural acts of his office, namely, on the first or second Sunday, in one of the churches of Paris—after he has been summoned for the purpose—shall affirm by an oath, publicly in the presence of the scholars, that he will keep in good

The oath required of the provost and people of Paris

---

[1] A further recognition of the clerical character of the students.
[2] The property, as the persons, of the scholars was protected from seizure except by the church authorities.

faith all the above-mentioned [regulations].[1] And that these decrees may be valid forever, we have ordered this document to be confirmed by the authority of our seal and by the characters of the royal name signed below.

61. The Foundation of the University of Heidelberg (1386)

UNTIL the middle of the fourteenth century Germany possessed no university. In the earlier mediæval period, when palace and monastic schools were multiplying in France, Italy, and England, German culture was too backward to permit of a similar movement beyond the Rhine; and later, when in other countries universities were springing into prosperity, political dissensions long continued to thwart such enterprises among the Germans. Germany was not untouched by the intellectual movements of the twelfth and thirteenth centuries, but her young men were obliged to seek their learning at Oxford or Paris or Bologna. The first German university was that of Prague, in Bohemia, founded by Emperor Charles IV., a contemporary of Petrarch, and chartered in 1348. Once begun, the work of establishing such institutions went on rapidly, until ere long every principality of note had its own university. Vienna was founded in 1365, Erfurt was given papal sanction in 1379, Heidelberg was established in 1386, and Cologne followed in 1388. The document given below is the charter of privileges issued for Heidelberg in October, 1386, by the founder, Rupert I., Count Palatine of the Rhine. Marsilius Inghen became the first rector of the university. He and two other masters began lecturing October 19, 1386—one on logic, another on the epistle to Titus, the third on the philosophy of Aristotle. Within four years over a thousand students had been in attendance at the university.

Source—Text in Edward Winkelmann, *Urkundenbuch der Universität Heidelberg* ["Cartulary of the University of Heidelberg"], Heidelberg, 1886, Vol. I., pp. 5–6. Translated in Ernest F. Henderson, *Select Historical Documents of the Middle Ages* (London, 1896), pp. 262–266.

1. We, Rupert the elder, by the grace of God count palatine of the Rhine, elector of the Holy Empire,[2] and duke of Bavaria,

[1] In this capacity the provost of Paris came to be known as the "Conservator of the Royal Privileges of the University."

[2] For an explanation of the phrase "elector of the Holy Empire" see p. 409.

—lest we seem to abuse the privilege conceded to us by the apostolic see of founding a place of study at Heidelberg similar to that at Paris, and lest, for this reason, being subjected to the divine judgment, we should deserve to be deprived of the privilege granted—do decree, with provident counsel (which decree is to be observed unto all time), that the University of Heidelberg shall be ruled, disposed, and regulated according to the modes and manners accustomed to be observed in the University **The university** of Paris.[1] Also that, as a handmaid of Paris— **to be organized on the** a worthy one let us hope—the latter's steps shall **ized on the** **model of Paris** be imitated in every way possible; so that, namely, there shall be four faculties in it: the first, of sacred theology and divinity; the second, of canon and civil law, which, by reason of their similarity, we think best to comprise under one faculty; the third, of medicine; the fourth, of liberal arts— of the three-fold philosophy, namely, primal, natural, and moral, three mutually subservient daughters.[2] We wish this institution to be divided and marked out into four nations, as it is at Paris;[3] and that all these faculties shall make one university, and that to it the individual students, in whatever of the said faculties they are, shall unitedly belong like lawful sons to one mother.

Likewise [we desire] that this university shall be governed by one rector,[4] and that the various masters and teachers, before they are admitted to the common pursuits of our institution,

[1] Rupert had sent sums of money to Rome to induce Pope Urban VI. to approve the foundation of the university. The papal bull of 1385, which was the reward of his effort, specifically enjoined that the university be modeled closely after that of Paris.

[2] The mediæval "three philosophies" were introduced by the rediscovery of some of Aristotle's writings in the twelfth century. Primal philosophy was what we now know as metaphysics; natural philosophy meant the sciences of physics, botany, etc.; and moral philosophy denoted ethics and politics.

[3] At Paris the students were divided into four groups, named from the nationality which predominated in each of them at the time of its formation—the French, the Normans, the Picards, and the English.

[4] The rector at Paris was head of the faculty of arts.

shall swear to observe the statutes, laws, privileges, liberties, and franchises of the same, and not reveal its secrets, to whatever grade they may rise. Also that they will uphold the honor of the rector and the rectorship of our university, and will obey **The obligations** the rector in all things lawful and honest, what-**of the masters** ever be the grade to which they may afterwards happen to be promoted. Moreover, that the various masters and bachelors shall read their lectures and exercise their scholastic functions and go about in caps and gowns of a uniform and similar nature, according as has been observed at Paris up to this time in the different faculties.

And we will that if any faculty, nation, or person shall oppose the aforesaid regulations, or stubbornly refuse to obey them, or any one of them—which God forbid—from that time forward that same faculty, nation, or person, if it do not desist upon being warned, shall be deprived of all connection with our aforesaid institution, and shall not have the benefit of our defense or **Internal gov-** protection. Moreover, we will and ordain that **ernment of the** as the university as a whole may do for those **university fur-** **ther provided** assembled here and subject to it, so each faculty, **for** nation, or province of it may enact lawful statutes, such as are suitable to its needs, provided that through them, or any one of them, no prejudice is done to the above regulations and to our institution, and that no kind of impediment arise from them. And we will that when the separate bodies shall have passed the statutes for their own observance, they may make them perpetually binding on those subject to them and on their successors. And as in the University of Paris the various servants of the institution have the benefit of the various privileges which its masters and scholars enjoy, so in starting our institution in Heidelberg, we grant, with even greater liberality, through these presents, that all the servants, i.e., its pedells,[1] librarians, lower officials, preparers of parchment,

---

[1] Equivalent to bedel. All mediæval universities had their bedels, who

scribes, illuminators and others who serve it, may each and all, without fraud, enjoy in it the same privileges, franchises, immunities and liberties with which its masters or scholars are now or shall hereafter be endowed.

2. Lest in the new community of the city of Heidelberg, their misdeeds being unpunished, there be an incentive to the scholars of doing wrong, we ordain, with provident counsel, by these presents, that the bishop of Worms, as judge ordinary of the clerks of our institution, shall have and possess, now and hereafter while our institution shall last, prisons, and an office in our town of Heidelberg for the detention of criminal clerks. These

The jurisdiction of the bishop of Worms things we have seen fit to grant to him and his successors, adding these conditions: that he shall permit no clerk to be arrested unless for a misdemeanor; that he shall restore any one detained for such fault, or for any light offense, to his master, or to the rector if the latter asks for him, a promise having been given that the culprit will appear in court and that the rector or master will answer for him if the injured parties should go to law about the matter. Furthermore, that, on being requested, he will restore a clerk arrested for a crime on slight evidence, upon receiving a sufficient pledge—sponsors if the prisoner can obtain them, otherwise an oath if he cannot obtain sponsors—to the effect that he will answer in court the charges against him; and in all these things there shall be no pecuniary exactions, except that the clerk shall give satis-

Conditions of imprisonment faction, reasonably and according to the rule of the aforementioned town, for the expenses which he incurred while in prison. And we desire that he will detain honestly and without serious injury a criminal clerk thus arrested for a crime where the suspicion is grave and strong, until the truth can be found out concerning the deed of which he is

bore the mace of authority before the rectors on public occasions, made announcements of lectures, book sales, etc., and exercised many of the functions of the modern bedel of European universities.

suspected. And he shall not for any cause, moreover, take away any clerk from our aforesaid town, or permit him to be taken away, unless the proper observances have been followed, and he has been condemned by judicial sentence to perpetual imprisonment for a crime.

We command our advocate and bailiff and their servants in our aforesaid town, under pain of losing their offices and our favor, not to lay a detaining hand on any master or scholar of our said institution, nor to arrest him or allow him to be **Limitations upon power to arrest students** arrested, unless the deed be such that that master or scholar ought rightly to be detained. He shall be restored to his rector or master, if he is held for a slight cause, provided he will swear and promise to appear in court concerning the matter; and we decree that a slight fault is one for which a layman, if he had committed it, ought to have been condemned to a light pecuniary fine. Likewise, if the master or scholar detained be found gravely or strongly suspected of the crime, we command that he be handed over by our officials to the bishop or to his representative in our said town, to be kept in custody.

3. By the tenor of these presents we grant to each and all the masters and scholars that, when they come to the said institution, while they remain there, and also when they return from it to their homes, they may freely carry with them, both coming and going, throughout all the lands subject to us, all things which they need while pursuing their studies, and all the **Students exempted from various imposts** goods necessary for their support, without any duty, levy, imposts, tolls, excises, or other exactions whatever. And we wish them and each one of them, to be free from the aforesaid imposts when purchasing corn, wines, meat, fish, clothes and all things necessary for their living and for their rank. And we decree that the scholars from their stock in hand of provisions, if there remain over one or two wagonloads of wine without their having practised deception, may, after the feast of Easter of that year, sell it at wholesale without paying impost. We grant to them, moreover, that each day the scholars, of themselves or through their servants, may be allowed to buy in the town of Heidelberg, at the accustomed hour, freely and without impediment or hurtful delay, any eatables or other necessaries of life.

4. Lest the masters and scholars of our institution of Heidelberg may be oppressed by the citizens, moved by avarice, through extortionate prices of lodgings, we have seen fit to decree that henceforth each year, after Christmas, one expert from the university on the part of the scholars, and one prudent, **How rates for lodgings should be fixed** pious, and circumspect citizen on the part of the citizens, shall be authorized to determine the price of the students' lodgings. Moreover, we will and decree that the various masters and scholars shall, through our bailiff, our judge and the officials subject to us, be defended and maintained in the quiet possession of the lodgings given to them free or of those for which they pay rent. Moreover, by the tenor of these presents, we grant to the rector and the university, or to those designated by them, entire jurisdiction concerning the payment of rents for the lodgings occupied by the students, concerning the making and buying of books, and the borrowing of money for other purposes by the scholars of our institution; also concerning the payment of assessments, together with everything that arises from, depends upon, and is connected with these.

In addition, we command our officials that, when the rector requires our and their aid and assistance for carrying out his sentences against scholars who try to rebel, they shall assist our clients and servants in this matter; first, however, obtaining lawful permission to proceed against clerks from the lord bishop of Worms, or from one deputed by him for this purpose.

62. Mediæval Students' Songs

"WHEN we try to picture to ourselves," says Mr. Symonds in one of his felicitous passages, "the intellectual and moral state of Europe in the Middle Ages, some fixed and almost stereotyped ideas immediately suggest themselves. We think of the nations immersed in a gross mental lethargy; passively witnessing the gradual extinction of arts and sciences which Greece and Rome had splendidly inaugurated; allowing libraries and monuments of antique civilization to crumble into dust; while they trembled under a dull and brooding terror of coming judgment, shrank from natural enjoyment as from deadly sin, or yielded themselves with brutal eagerness to the satisfaction of vulgar appetites. Preoccupation with the other world in this long period weakens man's hold upon the things that make his life desirable. . . . Prolonged habits of extra-mundane contemplation, combined with the decay of real knowledge, volatilize the thoughts and aspirations of the best and wisest into dreamy unrealities, giving a false air of mysticism to love, shrouding art in allegory, reducing the interpretation of texts to an exercise of idle ingenuity, and the study of nature to an insane system of grotesque and pious quibbling. The conception of man's fall and of the incurable badness of this world bears poisonous fruit of cynicism and asceticism, that two-fold bitter almond hidden in the harsh monastic shell. Nature is regarded with suspicion and aversion; the flesh, with shame and loathing, broken by spasmodic outbursts of lawless self-indulgence."[1]

All of these ideas are properly to be associated with the Middle Ages, but it must be borne in mind that they represent only one side of the picture. They are drawn very largely from the study of monastic literature and produce a somewhat distorted impression. Though many conditions prevailing in mediæval times operated strongly to paralyze the intellects and consciences of men, the fundamental manifestations and expressions of human instinct and vitality were far from crushed out. The life of many people was full and varied and positive—not so different, after all, from that of men and women to-day. That this was true is demonstrated by a wealth of literature reflecting the jovial and exuberant aspects of mediæval life, which has come down to us

[1] John Addington Symonds, *Wine, Women and Song: Mediæval Latin Students' Songs* (London, 1884), pp. 1–3.

chiefly in two great groups—the poetry of the troubadours and the songs of the wandering students. "That so bold, so fresh, so natural, so pagan a view of life," continues Mr. Symonds in the passage quoted, "as the Latin songs of the Wandering Students exhibit, should have found clear and artistic utterance in the epoch of the Crusades, is indeed enough to bid us pause and reconsider the justice of our stereotyped ideas about that period. This literature makes it manifest that the ineradicable appetites and natural instincts of men and women were no less vigorous in fact, though less articulate and self-assertive, than they had been in the age of Greece and Rome, and than they afterwards displayed themselves in what is known as the Renaissance. The songs of the Wandering Students were composed for the most part in the twelfth century. Uttering the unrestrained emotions of men attached by a slender tie to the dominant clerical class and diffused over all countries, they bring us face to face with a body of opinion which finds in studied chronicle or labored dissertation of the period no echo. On the one side, they express that delight in life and physical enjoyment which was a main characteristic of the Renaissance; on the other, they proclaim that revolt against the corruption of Papal Rome which was the motive force of the Reformation. Who were these Wandering Students? As their name implies, they were men, and for the most part young men, traveling from university to university in search of knowledge. Far from their homes, without responsibilities, light of purse and light of heart, careless and pleasure-seeking, they ran a free, disreputable course, frequenting taverns at least as much as lecture-rooms, more capable of pronouncing judgment upon wine or woman than upon a problem of divinity or logic. These pilgrims to the shrines of knowledge formed a class apart. According to tendencies prevalent in the Middle Ages, they became a sort of guild, and with pride proclaimed themselves an Order." [1]

Our knowledge of the mediæval students' songs is derived from two principal sources: (1) a richly illuminated thirteenth-century manuscript now preserved at Munich and edited in 1847 under the title *Carmina Burana;* and (2) another thirteenth-century manuscript published (with other materials) in 1841 under the title *Latin Poems commonly attributed to Walter Mapes.* Many songs occur in both collections. The half-

[1] Symonds, *Wine, Women, and Song,* pp. 5–20 *passim.*

dozen given in translation below very well illustrate the subjects, tone, and style of these interesting bits of literature.

Source—Texts in Edélestand du Méril, *Poésies Populaires Latines du Moyen Age* ["Popular Latin Poetry of the Middle Ages"], Paris, 1847, *passim*. Translated in John Addington Symonds, *Wine, Women, and Song: Mediæval Latin Students' Songs* (London, 1884), pp. 12–136, *passim*.

The first is a tenth century piece, marked by an element of tenderness in sentiment which is essentially modern. It is the invitation of a young man to his mistress, bidding her to a little supper at his home.

"Come therefore now, my gentle fere,
Whom as my heart I hold full dear;
Enter my little room, which is
Adorned with quaintest rarities:
There are the seats with cushions spread,
The roof with curtains overhead:
The house with flowers of sweetest scent
And scattered herbs is redolent:
A table there is deftly dight
With meats and drinks of rare delight;
There too the wine flows, sparkling, free;
And all, my love, to pleasure thee.
There sound enchanting symphonies;
The clear high notes of flutes arise;
A singing girl and artful boy
Are chanting for thee strains of joy;
He touches with his quill the wire,
She tunes her note unto the lyre:
The servants carry to and fro
Dishes and cups of ruddy glow;
But these delights, I will confess,
Than pleasant converse charm me less;
Nor is the feast so sweet to me
As dear familiarity.

Then come now, sister of my heart,
That dearer than all others art,
Unto mine eyes thou shining sun,
Soul of my soul, thou only one!
I dwelt alone in the wild woods,
And loved all secret solitudes;
Oft would I fly from tumults far,
And shunned where crowds of people are.
O dearest, do not longer stay!
Seek we to live and love to-day!
I cannot live without thee, sweet!
Time bids us now our love complete."

The next is a begging petition, addressed by a student on the road to some resident of the place where he was temporarily staying. The supplication for alms, in the name of learning, is cast in the form of a sing-song doggerel.

I, a wandering scholar lad,
    Born for toil and sadness,
Oftentimes am driven by
    Poverty to madness.

Literature and knowledge I
    Fain would still be earning,
Were it not that want of pelf
    Makes me cease from learning.

These torn clothes that cover me
    Are too thin and rotten;
Oft I have to suffer cold,
    By the warmth forgotten.

Scarce I can attend at church,
    Sing God's praises duly;
Mass and vespers both I miss,
    Though I love them truly.

Oh, thou pride of N——,[1]
    By thy worth I pray thee
Give the suppliant help in need,
    Heaven will sure repay thee.

Take a mind unto thee now
    Like unto St. Martin;[2]
Clothe the pilgrim's nakedness,
    Wish him well at parting.

So may God translate your soul
    Into peace eternal,
And the bliss of saints be yours
    In His realm supernal.

The following jovial *Song of the Open Road* throbs with exhilaration and even impudence. Two vagabond students are drinking together before they part. One of them undertakes to expound the laws of the brotherhood which bind them together. The refrain is intended apparently to imitate a bugle call.

We in our wandering,
Blithesome and squandering,
    Tara, tantara, teino!

Eat to satiety,
Drink to propriety;
    Tara, tantara, teino!

Laugh till our sides we split,
Rags on our hides we fit;
    Tara, tantara, teino!

[1] This is the only indication of the name of the place where the suppliant student was supposed to be making his petition.
[2] St. Martin was the founder of the monastery at Tours [see p. 48].

Jesting eternally,
Quaffing infernally.
    Tara, tantara, teino!

Craft's in the bone of us,
Fear 'tis unknown of us;
    Tara, tantara, teino!

When we're in neediness,
Thieve we with greediness:
    Tara, tantara, teino!

Brother catholical,
Man apostolical,
    Tara, tantara, teino!

Say what you will have done,
What you ask 'twill be done!
    Tara, tantara, teino!

Folk, fear the toss of the
Horns of philosophy!
    Tara, tantara, teino!

Here comes a quadruple
Spoiler and prodigal! [1]
    Tara, tantara, teino!

License and vanity
Pamper insanity:
    Tara, tantara, teino!

---

[1] "Honest folk are jeeringly bidden to beware of the *quadrivium* [see p. 339], which is apt to form a fourfold rogue instead of a scholar in four branches of knowledge."—Symonds, *Wine, Women, and Song*, p. 57.

As the Pope bade us do,
Brother to brother's true:
   Tara, tantara, teino!

Brother, best friend, adieu!
Now, I must part from you!
   Tara, tantara, teino!

When will our meeting be?
Glad shall our greeting be!
   Tara, tantara, teino!

Vows valedictory
Now have the victory:
   Tara, tantara, teino!

Clasped on each other's breast,
Brother to brother pressed,
   Tara, tantara, teino!

———

Here is a song entitled *The Vow to Cupid*.

Winter, now thy spite is spent,
Frost and ice and branches bent!
Fogs and furious storms are o'er,
Sloth and torpor, sorrow frore,
Pallid wrath, lean discontent.

Comes the graceful band of May!
Cloudless shines the limpid day,
Shine by night the Pleiades;
While a grateful summer breeze
Makes the season soft and gay.

Golden Love! shine forth to view!
Souls of stubborn men subdue!
See me bend! what is thy mind?
Make the girl thou givest kind,
And a leaping ram's thy due! [1]

O the jocund face of earth,
Breathing with young grassy birth!
Every tree with foliage clad,
Singing birds in greenwood glad,
Flowering fields for lovers' mirth!

Here is another song of exceedingly delicate sentiment. It is entitled
The Love-Letter in Spring.

Now the sun is streaming,
    Clear and pure his ray;
April's glad face beaming
    On our earth to-day.
Unto love returneth
    Every gentle mind;
And the boy-god burneth
    Jocund hearts to bind.

All this budding beauty,
    Festival array,
Lays on us the duty
    To be blithe and gay.
Trodden ways are known, love!
    And in this thy youth,
To retain thy own love
    Were but faith and truth.

[1] That is, as a sacrifice.

In faith love me solely,
  Mark the faith of me,
From thy whole heart wholly,
  From the soul of thee.
At this time of bliss, dear,
  I am far away;
Those who love like this, dear,
  Suffer every day!

Next to love and the springtime, the average student set his affections principally on the tavern and the wine-bowl. From his proneness to frequent the tavern's jovial company of topers and gamesters naturally sprang a liberal supply of drinking songs. Here is a fragment from one of them.

Some are gaming, some are drinking,
Some are living without thinking;
And of those who make the racket,
Some are stripped of coat and jacket;
Some get clothes of finer feather,
Some are cleaned out altogether;
No one there dreads death's invasion,
But all drink in emulation.

Finally may be given, in the original Latin, a stanza of a drinking song which fell to such depths of irreverence as to comprise a parody of Thomas Aquinas's hymn on the Lord's Supper.

Bibit hera, bibit herus,
Bibit miles, bibit clerus,
Bibit ille, bibit illa,
Bibit servus cum ancilla,
Bibit velox, bibit piger,
Bibit albus, bibit niger,
Bibit constans, bibit vagus,
Bibit rudis, bibit magus.

CHAPTER XXII.

THE FRIARS

FROM the twelfth century onwards one of the most conspicuous features of the internal development of the mediæval Church was the struggle to combat worldliness among ecclesiastics and to preserve the purity of doctrine and uprightness of living which had characterized the primitive Christian clergy. As the Middle Ages advanced to their close, unimpeachable evidence accumulates that the Church was increasingly menaced by grave abuses. This evidence appears not only in contemporary records and chronicles but even more strikingly in the great protesting movements which spring up in rapid succession—particularly the rise of heretical sects, such as the Waldenses and the Albigenses, and the inauguration of systematic efforts to regenerate the church body without disrupting its unity. These latter efforts at first took the form of repeated revivals of monastic enthusiasm and self-denial, marked by the founding of a series of new orders on the basis of the Benedictine Rule—the Cluniacs, the Carthusians, the Cistercians, and others of their kind [see p. 245]. This resource proving ineffective, the movement eventually came to comprise the establishment of wholly new and independent organizations—the mendicant orders—on principles better adapted than were those of monasticism to the successful propagation of simplicity and purity of Christian living. The chief of these new orders were the Franciscans, known also as Gray Friars and as Minorites, and the Dominicans, sometimes called Black Friars or Preaching Friars. Both were founded in the first quarter of the thirteenth century, the one by St. Francis of Assisi; the other by the Span-ish nobleman, St. Dominic.

The friars, of whatsoever type, are clearly to be distinguished from the monks. In the first place, their aims were different. The monks, in so far as they were true to their principles, lived in more or less seclusion from the rest of the world and gave themselves up largely to prayer and meditation; the fundamental purpose of the friars, on the other hand, was to mingle with their fellow-men and to spend their lives in active religious work among them. Whereas the old monasticism had been essentially selfish, the new movement was above all of a missionary and philanthropic character. In the second place, the friars were even more strongly committed to a life of poverty than were the monks, for they renounced not only individual property, as did the monks, but also collective property, as the monks did not. They were expected to get their living either by their own labor or by begging. They did not dwell in fixed abodes, but wandered hither and thither as inclination and duty led. Their particular sphere of activity was the populous towns; unlike the monks, they had no liking for rural solitudes. As one writer has put it, "their houses were built in or near the great towns; and to the majority of the brethren the houses of the orders were mere temporary resting-places from which they issued to make their journeys through town and country, preaching in the parish churches, or from the steps of the market-crosses, and carrying their ministrations to every castle and every cottage."

Both the Franciscans and the Dominicans were exempt from control by the bishops in the various dioceses and were ardent supporters of the papacy, which showered privileges upon them and secured in them two of its strongest allies. The organization of each order was elaborate and centralized. At the head was a master, or general, who resided at Rome and was assisted by a "chapter." All Christendom was divided into provinces, each of which was directed by a prior and provincial chapter. And over each individual "house" was placed a prior, or warden, appointed by the provincial chapter. In their earlier history the zeal and achievements of the friars were remarkable. Nearly all of the greatest men of the thirteenth and early fourteenth centuries—as Roger Bacon, Thomas Aquinas, Dun Scotus, and Albertus Magnus—were members of one of the mendicant orders. Unfortunately, with the friars as with the monks, prosperity brought decadence; and by the middle of the fourteenth century their ardor had cooled and their boasted self-denial had pretty largely given place to self-indulgence.

63. The Life of St. Francis

SAINT FRANCIS, the founder of the Franciscan order, was born, probably in 1182, at Assisi, a small town in central Italy. His boyhood was unpromising, but when he was about twenty years of age a great change came over him, the final result of which was the making of one of the most splendid and altogether lovable characters of the entire Middle Ages. From a wild, reckless, although cultured, youth he developed into a sympathetic, self-denying, sweet-spirited saint. Finding himself, after his conversion, possessed of a natural loathing for the destitute and diseased, especially lepers, he disciplined himself until he could actually take a certain sort of pleasure in associating with these outcasts of society. When his father, a wealthy and aristocratic cloth-merchant, protested against this sort of conduct, the young man promptly cast aside his gentlemanly raiment, clad himself in the worn-out garments of a gardener, and adopted the life of the wandering hermit. In 1209, in obedience to what he conceived to be a direct commission from heaven, he began definitely to imitate the early apostles in his manner of living and to preach the gospel of the older and purer Christianity. By 1210 he had a small body of followers, and in that year he sought and obtained Pope Innocent III.'s sanction of his work, though the papal approval was expressed only orally and more than a decade was to elapse before the movement received formal recognition. About 1217 Francis and his companions took up missionary work on a large scale. Members of the brotherhood were dispatched to England, Germany, France, Spain, Hungary, and several other countries, with instructions to spread the principles which by this time were coming to be recognized as peculiarly Franciscan. The success of these efforts was considerable, though in some places the brethren were ill treated and an appeal had to be made to the Pope for protection.

The several selections given below have been chosen to illustrate the principal features of the life and character of St. Francis. We are fortunate in possessing a considerable amount of literature, contemporary or nearly so, relating to the personal career of this noteworthy man. In the first place, we have some writings of St. Francis himself— the Rule (p. 373), the Will (p. 376), some poems, some reported sermons, and fragments of a few letters. Then we have several biographies, of which the most valuable, because not only the earliest but also the least conventional, are the *Mirror of Perfection* and the *Legend of the Three Companions*. These were written by men who knew St. Francis intimately and who could avow "we who were with him have heard him say" or "we who were with him have seen," such and such things. The "three companions" were Brothers Leo, Rufinus, and Angelo—all men of noble birth, the last-named being the first soldier to be identified with the order. The *Mirror of Perfection* was written in 1227 by Brother Leo, who of all men probably knew St. Francis best. It is a vivid and fascinating portrait drawn from life. The *Legend of the Three Companions* was written in 1246. The later biographies, such as the official *Life* by St. Bonaventura (1261) and the *Little Flowers of St. Francis* (written probably in the fourteenth century), though until recently the best known of the group, are relatively inferior in value. In them the real St. Francis is conventionalized and much obscured.

The first passage here reproduced (a) comes from the *Legend of the Three Companions;* the others (b) are taken from the *Mirror of Perfection.*

Sources—(a) *Legenda S. Francisci Assisiensis quæ dicitur Legenda trium sociorum.* Adapted from translation by E. G. Salter, under title of "The Legend of the Three Companions," in the Temple Classics (London, 1902), pp. 8–24, *passim.*

(b) *Speculum Perfectionis.* Translated by Constance, Countess de la Warr, under title of "The Mirror of Perfection" (London, 1902), *passim.*

(a)

Francis, born in the city of Assisi, which lies in the confines of the Vale of Spoleto, was at first named John by his mother. Then, when his father, in whose absence he had been born, returned from France, he was afterward named Francis.[1] After he was grown up, and had become of a subtle wit, he practiced the art of his father, that is, trade. But [he did so] in a very different manner, for he was a merrier man than was his father,

[1] The father's name was Pietro Bernardone. As a cloth-merchant he was probably accustomed to make frequent journeys to northern France, particularly Champagne, which was the principal seat of commercial exchange between northern and southern Europe.

and more generous, given to jests and songs, going about the city of Assisi day and night in company with his kind, most free-handed in spending; insomuch that he consumed all his income and his profits in banquets and other matters. On this **His youthful vanities and waywardness** account he was often rebuked by his parents, who told him he ran into so great expense on himself and on others that he seemed to be no son of theirs, but rather of some mighty prince. Nevertheless, because his parents were rich and loved him most tenderly, they bore with him in such matters, not being disposed to chastise him. Indeed, his mother, when gossip arose among the neighbors concerning his prodigal ways, made answer: "What think ye of my son? He shall yet be the son of God by grace." But he himself was free-handed, or rather prodigal, not only in these things, but even in his clothes he was beyond measure sumptuous, using stuffs more costly than it befitted him to wear. So wayward was his fancy that at times on the same coat he would cause a costly cloth to be matched with one of the meanest sort.

Yet he was naturally courteous, in manner and word, after the purpose of his heart, never speaking a harmful or shameful word to any one. Nay, indeed, although he was so gay and wanton a youth, yet of set purpose would he make no reply to those who said shameful things to him. And hence was his fame so spread abroad throughout the whole neighborhood that **His redeeming qualities** it was said by many who knew him that he would do something great. By these steps of godliness he progressed to such grace that he would say in communing with himself: "Seeing that thou art bountiful and courteous toward men, from whom thou receivest naught save a passing and empty favor, it is just that thou shouldst be courteous and bountiful toward God, who is Himself most bountiful in rewarding His poor." Wherefore thenceforward did he look with goodwill upon the poor, bestowing alms upon them abundantly. And although he was a merchant, yet was he a most lavish dispenser of this world's riches. One day, when he was standing in the warehouse in which he sold goods, and was intent on business, a certain poor man came to him asking alms for the love of God. Nevertheless, he was held back by the covetousness of wealth and the cares of merchandise, and **A lesson in** denied him the alms. But forthwith, being looked **charity** upon by the divine grace, he rebuked himself of great churlishness, saying, "Had this poor man asked thee aught in the name of a great count or baron, assuredly thou wouldst have given him what he had asked. How much more then oughtest thou to have done it for the King of Kings and Lord of all?" By reason whereof he thenceforth determined in his heart never again to deny anything asked in the name of so great a Lord. . . .

Now, not many days after he returned to Assisi,[1] he was chosen one evening by his comrades as their master of the revels, to spend the money collected from the company after his own fancy. So he caused a sumptuous banquet to be made ready, as he had often done before. And when they came forth from the house, and his comrades together went before him, going through the city singing while he carried a wand in his hand as their master, he was walking behind them, not singing, but meditating very earnestly. And lo! suddenly he was visited by the Lord, and his heart was filled with such sweetness that he could neither speak nor move; nor was he able to feel and **A vision in** hear anything except that sweetness only, which **the midst of** so separated him from his physical senses that **revelry** —as he himself afterward said—had he then been pricked with knives all over at once, he could not have moved

[1] Aspiring to become a knight and to win distinction on the field of battle, Francis had gone to Spoleto with the intention of joining an expedition about to set out for Apulia. While there he was stricken with fever and compelled to abandon his purpose. Returning to Assisi, he redoubled his works of charity and sought to keep aloof from the people of the town. His old companions, however, flocked around him, expecting still to profit by his prodigality, and for a time, being himself uncertain as to the course he would take, he acceded to their desires.

from the spot. But when his comrades looked back and saw him thus far off from them, they returned to him in fear, staring at him as one changed into another man. And they asked him, "What were you thinking about, that you did not come along with us? Perchance you were thinking of taking a wife." To them he replied with a loud voice: "Truly have you spoken, for I thought of taking to myself a bride nobler and richer and fairer than ever you have seen." And they mocked at him. But this he said not of his own accord, but inspired of God; for the bride herself was true Religion, whom he took unto him, nobler, richer, and fairer than others in her poverty.

And so from that hour he began to grow worthless in his own eyes, and to despise those things he had formerly loved, although not wholly so at once, for he was not yet entirely freed from the vanity of the world. Nevertheless, withdrawing himself little by little from the tumult of the world, he made it his study to treasure up Jesus Christ in his inner man, and, hiding from the eyes of mockers the pearl that he would fain buy at the price of selling his all, he went oftentimes, and as it were in secret, daily to prayer, being urged thereto by the foretaste of that sweetness that had visited him more and more often, and compelled him to come from the streets and other public places to prayer. Although he had long done good unto the poor, yet from this time forth he determined still more firmly in his heart never **His increasing** again to deny alms to any poor man who should **zeal in charity** ask it for the love of God, but to give alms more willingly and bountifully than had been his practice. Whenever, therefore, any poor man asked of him an alms out of doors, he would supply him with money if he could; if he had no ready money, he would give him his cap or girdle rather than send the poor man away empty. And if it happened that he had nothing of this kind, he would go to some hidden place, and strip off his shirt, and send the poor man thither that he might take it, for the sake of God. He also would buy vessels

for the adornment of churches, and would send them in all
secrecy to poor priests. . . .

So changed, then, was he by divine grace (although still in
the secular garb) that he desired to be in some city where he
might, as one unknown, strip off his own clothes and exchange
them for those of some beggar, so that he might wear his instead
and make trial of himself by asking alms for the love of God.
Now it happened that at that time he had gone to Rome on a
pilgrimage. And entering the church of St. Peter, he reflected
on the offerings of certain people, seeing that they were small,
and spoke within himself: "Since the Prince of the Apostles
should of right be magnificently honored, why do these folk
make such sorry offerings in the church wherein his body rests?"
And so in great fervency he put his hand into his purse and drew
it forth full of money, and flung it through the grating of the
altar with such a crash that all who were standing by marveled
greatly at so splendid an offering. Then, going forth in front
of the doors of the church, where many beggars were gathered
to ask alms, he secretly borrowed the rags of one among the
He begs alms neediest and donned them, laying aside his own
at Rome clothing. Then, standing on the church steps
with the other beggars, he asked an alms in French, for he loved
to speak the French tongue, although he did not speak it correctly. Thereafter, putting off the rags, and taking again his
own clothes, he returned to Assisi, and began to pray the Lord
to direct his way. For he revealed unto none his secret, nor
took counsel of any in this matter, save only of God (who had
begun to direct his way) and at times of the bishop of Assisi.
For at that time no true Poverty was to be found anywhere, and
she it was that he desired above all things of this world, being
minded in her to live—yea, and to die. . . .

Now when on a certain day he was praying fervently unto the
Lord, answer was made unto him: "Francis, all those things that
thou hast loved after the flesh, and hast desired to have, thou

must needs despise and hate, if thou wouldst do My will, and
after thou shalt have begun to do this the things that aforetime
seemed sweet unto thee and delightful shall be unbearable unto
thee and bitter, and from those that aforetime thou didst loathe
thou shalt drink great sweetness and delight unmeasured."
Rejoicing at these words, and consoled in the Lord, when he
Francis and   had ridden nigh unto Assisi, he met one that was
the leper   a leper. And because he had been accustomed
greatly to loathe lepers, he did violence to himself, and dis-
mounted from his horse, gave him money, and kissed his hand.
And receiving from him the kiss of peace, he remounted his
horse and continued his journey. Thenceforth he began more
and more to despise himself, until by the grace of God he had
attained perfect mastery over himself.

A few days later, he took much money and went to the quarter
of the lepers, and, gathering all together, gave to each an alms,
kissing his hand. As he departed, in very truth that which had
aforetime been bitter to him, that is, the sight and touch of
lepers, was changed into sweetness. For, as he confessed, the
sight of lepers had been so grievous to him that he had been
accustomed to avoid not only seeing them, but even going near
their dwellings. And if at any time he happened to pass their
abodes, or to see them, although he was moved by compassion
to give them an alms through another person, yet always would
he turn aside his face, stopping his nostrils with his hand. But,
through the grace of God, he became so intimate a friend of the
lepers that, even as he recorded in his Will,[1] he lived with them
and did humbly serve them.

(b)

A very spiritual friar, who was familiar with Blessed Francis,
erected at the hermitage where he lived a little cell in a solitary
spot, where Blessed Francis could retire and pray when he came

[1] See p. 376.

thither. When he arrived at this place the friar took him to the cell, and Blessed Francis said, "This cell is too splendid"—it **How St. Francis would not dwell in an adorned cell** was, indeed, built only of wood, and smoothed with a hatchet—"if you wish me to remain here, make it within and without of branches of trees and clay." For the poorer the house or cell, the more was he pleased to live therein. When the friar had done this, Blessed Francis remained there several days. One day he was out of the cell when a friar came to see him, who, coming thereafter to the place where Blessed Francis was, was asked, "Whence came you, Brother?" He answered, "I come from your cell." Then said Blessed Francis: "Since you have called it mine, let another dwell there and not I." And, in truth, we who were with him often heard him say: "The foxes have holes, and the birds of the **Or in a cell called his own** air have their nests, but the Son of Man hath not where to lay His head." And again he would say: "When the Lord remained in the desert, and fasted forty days and forty nights, He did not make for Himself a cell or a house, but found shelter amongst the rocks of the mountain." For this reason, and to follow His example, he would not have it said that a cell or house was his, nor would he allow such to be constructed. . . . When he was nigh unto death he caused it to be written in his Testament [1] that all the cells and houses of the friars should be of wood and clay, the better to safeguard poverty and humility.

At the beginning of the Order, when the friars were at Rivo-Torto,[2] near Assisi, there was among them one friar who would **A lazy friar** not pray, work, nor ask for alms, but only eat. Considering this, Blessed Francis knew by the Holy Spirit that he was a carnal man, and said to him, "Brother Fly, go

---

[1] Brief portions of this testament, or will, are given on p. 376.
[2] This was in the latter part of 1210 and the early part of 1211. Rivo-Torto was an abandoned cottage in the plain of Assisi, an hour's walk from the town and near the highway between Perugia and Rome. The building

your way, since you consume the labor of the brethren, and are slothful in the work of the Lord, like the idle and barren drone who earns nothing and does not work, but consumes the labor and earnings of the working bee." He, therefore, went his way, and as he was a carnally-minded man he neither sought for mercy nor obtained it.

Having at a time suffered greatly from one of his serious attacks of illness, when he felt a little better he began to think that during his sickness he had exceeded his usual allowance of food, whereas he had really eaten very little. Though not quite recovered from the ague, he caused the people of Assisi to be called together in the public square to listen to a sermon. When he had finished preaching, he told the people to remain where they were until he came back to them, and entered the cathedral of St. Rufinus with many friars and Brother Peter of Catana, who had been a canon of that church, and was now the first Minister-General[1] appointed by Blessed Francis. To Brother

Public humiliation inflicted upon himself Peter Francis spoke, enjoining him under obedience not to contradict what he was about to say. Brother Peter replied: "Brother, neither is it possible, as between you and me, nor do I wish to do anything save what is pleasing to you." Then, taking off his tunic, Blessed Francis bade him place a rope around his neck and drag him thus before the people to the place where he had preached. At the same time he ordered another friar to carry a bowlful of ashes to the place, and when he got there to throw the ashes

had once served as a leper hospital. Francis and his companions selected it as a temporary place of abode, probably because of its proximity to the *carceri*, or natural grottoes, of Mount Subasio to which the friars resorted for solitude, and because it was at the same time sufficiently near the Umbrian towns to permit of frequent trips thither for preaching and charity.

[1] Practically, St. Francis's successor in the headship of the order. With the idea of realizing entire humility in his own life, St. Francis had resigned his position of authority into the hands of Brother Peter and had pledged the implicit obedience of himself and the others to the new prelate.

into his face. But this order was not obeyed by the friar out of the pity and compassion he felt for him.

Brother Peter, taking the rope, did as he had been told; but he and all the other friars shed tears of compassion and bitterness. When he [Francis] stood thus bared before the people in the place where he had preached, he cried: "You, and all those who by my example have been induced to abandon the world and enter Religion to lead the lives of friars, I confess before God and you that in my illness I have eaten meat and broths made of meat." And all the people could not refrain from weeping, especially as at that time it was very cold and he had scarcely recovered from the fever. Beating their breasts where they stood, they exclaimed, "If this saint, for just and manifest necessity, with shame of body thus accuses himself, whose life we know to be holy, and who has imposed on himself such great abstinence and austerity since his first conversion to Christ (whom we here, as it were, see in the flesh), what will become of us sinners who all our lifetime seek to follow our carnal appetites?"

Blessed Francis, wholly wrapped up in the love of God, discerned perfectly the goodness of God not only in his own soul, now adorned with the perfection of virtue, but in every creature. On account of which he had a singular and intimate love of **St. Francis** creatures, especially of those in which was figured **and the larks** anything pertaining to God or the Order. Wherefore above all other birds he loved a certain little bird which is called the lark, or by the people, the cowled lark. And he used to say of it: "Sister Lark hath a cowl like a Religious; and she is a humble bird, because she goes willingly by the road to find there any food. And if she comes upon it in foulness, she draws it out and eats it. But, flying, she praises God very sweetly, like a good Religious, despising earthly things, whose conversation is always in the heavens, and whose intent is always to the praise of God. Her clothes (that is, her feathers), are like to the earth and she gives an example to Religious that they should not have delicate and colored garments, but common in price and color, as earth is commoner than the other elements." And because he perceived this in them, he looked on them most willingly. Therefore it pleased the Lord, that these most holy little birds should show some sign of affection towards him in the hour of his death. For late in the Sabbath day after vespers, before the night in which he passed away to the Lord, a great multitude of that kind of birds called larks came on the roof of the house where he was lying, and, flying about, made a wheel like a circle around the roof, and, sweetly singing, seemed likewise to praise the Lord.

We who were with Blessed Francis and write these things, testify that many times we heard him say: "If I could speak with the Emperor,[1] I would supplicate and persuade him that, for the love of God and me, he would make a special law that no man should snare or kill our sisters, the larks, nor do them any harm. Also, that all chief magistrates of cities and lords of castles and villages should, every year, on the day of the Lord's **His desire that** Nativity, compel men to scatter wheat and other **birds and animals be fed on** grain on the roads outside cities and castles, that **Christmas day** our Sister Larks and all other birds might have to eat on that most solemn day; and that, out of reverence for the Son of God, who on that night was laid by the most Blessed Virgin Mary in a manger between an ox and an ass, all who have oxen and asses should be obliged on that night to provide them with abundant and good fodder; and also that on that day the poor should be most bountifully fed by the rich."

For Blessed Francis held in higher reverence than any other the Feast of the Lord's Nativity, saying, "After the Lord was born, our salvation became a necessity." Therefore he desired that on this day all Christians should rejoice in the Lord, and,

---

[1] That is, the sovereign of the Holy Roman Empire.

for the love of Him who gave Himself for us, should generously provide not only for the poor, but also for the beasts and birds.

Next to fire he most loved water, which is the symbol of holy penance and tribulation, whereby the stains are washed from the soul, and by which the first cleansing of the soul takes place in holy baptism. Hence, when he washed his hands, he would select a place where he would not tread the water underfoot. **His regard for trees, stones, and all created things** When he walked over stones he would tread on them with fear and reverence, for the love of Him who is called the Rock, and when reciting the words of the Psalm, *Thou hast exalted me on a rock*, would add with great reverence and devotion, "beneath the foot of the rock hast thou exalted me."

In the same way he would tell the friars who cut and prepared the wood not to cut down the whole tree, but only such branches as would leave the tree standing, for love of Him who died for us on the wood of the Cross. So, also, he would tell the friar who was the gardener not to cultivate all the ground for vegetables and herbs for food, but to set aside some part to produce green plants which should in their time bear flowers for the friars, for love of Him who was called "The Flower of the Field," and "The Lily of the Valley." Indeed he would say the Brother Gardener should always make a beautiful little garden in some part of the land, and plant it with sweet-scented herbs bearing lovely flowers, which in the time of their blossoming invited men to praise Him who made all herbs and flowers. For every creature cries aloud: "God has made me for thee, O man!"

64. The Rule of St. Francis

THERE is every reason for believing that St. Francis set out upon his mission with no idea whatever of founding a new religious order. His fundamental purpose was to revive what he conceived to be the purer Christianity of the apostolic age, and so far as this involved the announce-

ment of any definite principles or rules he was quite content to draw
them solely from the Scriptures. We have record, for example, of how
when (in 1209) St. Francis had yet but two followers, he led them to the
steps of the church of St. Nicholas at Assisi and there read to them
three times the words of Jesus sending forth his disciples,[1] adding,
"This, brethren, is our life and our rule, and that of all who may join us.
Go, then, and do as you have heard." As his field of labor expanded,
however, and the number of the friars increased, St. Francis decided to
write out a definite Rule for the brotherhood and go to Rome to procure
its approval by the Pope. The Rule as thus formulated, in 1210, has not
come down to us. We know only that it was extremely simple and that
it was composed almost wholly of passages from the Bible (doubtless
those read to the companions at Assisi), with a few precepts about the
occupations and manner of living of the brethren. This first Rule indeed
proved too simple and brief to satisfy the demands of the growing order.
A general injunction, such as "be poor," was harder to apply and to
live up to than a more specific set of instructions explaining just what
was to be considered poverty and what was not. The brethren, moreover, were soon preaching and laboring in all the countries of western
Europe and questions were continually coming up regarding their relations with the temporal powers in those countries, with the local clergy,
with the papal government, and also among themselves.

Reluctantly, and with a heart-felt warning against the insidious
influences of ambition and organization, the founder finally brought himself to the task of drawing up a constitution for the order which had surprised him, and in a certain sense grieved him, by the very elaborateness
of its development. During the winter of 1220–21, when physical infirmities were foreshadowing the end, Francis worked out the document generally known as the Rule of 1221, which became the basis for the Rule of
1223, quoted in part below. Before the Rule took its final form, the in-

---

[1] The passage (Luke ix. 1–6) is as follows: "Jesus, having called to Him
the Twelve, gave them power and authority over all devils and to cure
diseases. And He sent them to preach the Kingdom of God and to heal the
sick. And He said unto them, Take nothing for your journey, neither staves,
nor scrip, neither bread, neither money; neither have two coats apiece. And
whatsoever house ye enter into, there abide, and thence depart. And whosoever will not receive you, when ye go out of that city shake off the very
dust from your feet for a testimony against them. And they departed and
went through the towns, preaching the gospel and healing everywhere."

fluence of the Church was brought to bear through the papacy, with the result that most of the freshness and vigor that St. Francis put into the earlier effort was crushed out in the interest of ecclesiastical regularity. Only a small portion of the document can be reproduced here, but enough, perhaps, to show something as to what the manner of life of the Franciscan friar was expected to be. The extract may profitably be compared with the Benedictine Rule governing the monks [see p. 83].

Source—*Bullarium Romanum* [" Collection of Papal Bulls "], editio Taurinensis, Vol. III., p. 394. Adapted from translation in Ernest F. Henderson, *Select Historical Documents of the Middle Ages* (London, 1896), pp. 344–349 *passim*.

1. This is the rule and way of living of the Minorite brothers, namely, to observe the holy Gospel of our Lord Jesus Christ, living in obedience, without personal possessions, and in chastity. Brother Francis promises obedience and reverence to our lord Pope Honorius,[1] and to his successors who canonically enter upon their office, and to the Roman Church. And the other brothers shall be bound to obey Brother Francis and his successors.

4. I firmly command all the brothers by no means to receive coin or money, of themselves or through an intervening person. **Money in no case to be received by the brothers** But for the needs of the sick and for clothing the other brothers, the ministers alone and the guardians shall provide through spiritual friends, as it may seem to them that necessity demands, according to time, place and the coldness of the temperature. This one thing being always borne in mind, that, as has been said, they receive neither coin nor money.

5. Those brothers to whom God has given the ability to labor shall labor faithfully and devoutly, in such manner that idleness, the enemy of the soul, being averted, they may not extinguish **The obligation to labor** the spirit of holy prayer and devotion, to which other temporal things should be subservient. As a reward, moreover, for their labor, they may receive for them-

[1] Honorius III., 1216–1227.

selves and their brothers the necessities of life, but not coin or money; and this humbly, as becomes the servants of God and the followers of most holy poverty.

6. The brothers shall appropriate nothing to themselves, neither a house, nor a place, nor anything; but as pilgrims and strangers in this world, in poverty and humility serving God, they shall confidently go seeking for alms. Nor need they be ashamed, for the Lord made Himself poor for us in this world.

65. The Will of St. Francis

THE will which St. Francis prepared just before his death (1226) contains an admirable statement of the principles for which he labored, as well as a notable warning to his successors not to allow the order to fall away from its original high ideals. Among the later Franciscans the Will acquired a moral authority superior even to that of the Rule.

Source—Text in Amoni, *Legenda Trium Sociorum* ["Legend of the Three Companions"], Appendix, p. 110. Translation adapted from Paul Sabatier, *Life of St. Francis of Assisi* (New York, 1894), pp. 337–339.

God gave it to me, Brother Francis, to begin to do penance in the following manner: when I was yet in my sins it seemed to me too painful to look upon the lepers, but the Lord Himself led me among them, and I had compassion upon them. When I left them, that which had seemed to me bitter had become sweet and easy. A little while after, I left the world,[1] and God gave me such faith that I would kneel down with simplicity in any of his churches, and I would say, "We adore thee, Lord Jesus Christ, here and in all thy churches which are in the world, and we bless thee that by Thy holy cross Thou hast ransomed the world."

Afterward the Lord gave me, and still gives me, so great a faith in priests who live according to the form of the holy Roman Church, because of their sacerdotal character, that even if they

[1] That is, abandoned the worldly manner of living.

persecuted me I would have recourse to them, and even though
I had all the wisdom of Solomon, if I should find poor secular

**St. Francis not
hostile to the
existing Church**
priests, I would not preach in their parishes
against their will.[1] I desire to respect them like
all the others, to love them and honor them as
my lords. I will not consider their sins, for in them I see the
Son of God, and they are my lords. I do this because here below
I see nothing, I perceive nothing physically of the most high
Son of God, except His most holy body and blood, which the
priests receive and alone distribute to others.[2]

I desire above all things to honor and venerate all these most
holy mysteries and to keep them precious. Wherever I find the
sacred name of Jesus, or his words, in unsuitable places, I desire
to take them away and put them in some decent place; and I
pray that others may do the same. We ought to honor and
revere all the theologians and those who preach the most holy
word of God, as dispensing to us spirit and life.

When the Lord gave me the care of some brothers, no one
showed me what I ought to do, but the Most High himself revealed to me that I ought to live according to the model of the
holy gospel. I caused a short and simple formula to be written
and the lord Pope confirmed it for me.[3]

Those who volunteered to follow this kind of life distributed
all they had to the poor. They contented themselves with

**Poverty and
labor enjoined**
one tunic, patched within and without, with
the cord and breeches, and we desired to have
nothing more. . . . We loved to live in poor and aban-

---

[1] Despite the willingness of St. Francis here expressed to get on peaceably
with the secular clergy, i. e., the bishops and priests, the history of the
mendicant orders is filled with the records of strife between the seculars and
friars. This was inevitable, since such friars as had taken priestly orders
were accustomed to hear confessions, preside at masses, preach in parish
churchyards, bury the dead, and collect alms—all the proper functions of
the parish priests but permitted to the friars by special papal dispensations.
The priests very naturally regarded the friars as usurpers.

[2] That is, in the sacrament of the Lord's Supper.

[3] The Rule of 1210, approved by Innocent III., is here meant [see p. 374].

doned churches, and we were ignorant and were submissive to all.
I worked with my hands and would still do so, and I firmly
desire also that all the other brothers work, for this makes for
goodness. Let those who know no trade learn one, not for the
purpose of receiving wages for their toil, but for their good
example and to escape idleness. And when we are not given the
price of our work, let us resort to the table of the Lord, begging
our bread from door to door. The Lord revealed to me the
salutation which we ought to give: "God give you peace!"

Let the brothers take great care not to accept churches,
dwellings, or any buildings erected for them, except as all is
in accordance with the holy poverty which we have vowed in
the Rule; and let them not live in them except as strangers and
pilgrims. I absolutely forbid all the brothers, in whatsoever
place they may be found, to ask any bull from the court of
No further Rome, whether directly or indirectly, in the in-
privileges
to be sought terest of church or convent, or under pretext of
from the Pope preaching, or even for the protection of their
bodies. If they are not received anywhere, let them go of themselves elsewhere, thus doing penance with the benediction of
God. . . .

And let the brothers not say, "This is a new Rule"; for this is
only a reminder, a warning, an exhortation. It is my last will
and testament, that I, little Brother Francis, make for you, my
blessed brothers, in order that we may observe in a more Catholic
way the Rule which we promised the Lord to keep.

Let the ministers-general, all the other ministers, and the
custodians be held by obedience to add nothing to and take
No additions nothing away from these words. Let them always
to be made to keep this writing near them beside the Rule; and
the Rule or
the Will in all the assemblies which shall be held, when
the Rule is read, let these words be read also.

I absolutely forbid all the brothers, clerics and laymen, to
introduce comments in the Rule, or in this Will, under pretext

of explaining it. But since the Lord has given me to speak and to write the Rule and these words in a clear and simple manner, so do you understand them in the same way without commentary, and put them in practice until the end.

And whoever shall have observed these things, may he be crowned in heaven with the blessings of the heavenly Father, and on earth with those of his well-beloved Son and of the Holy Spirit, the Consoler, with the assistance of all the heavenly virtues and all the saints.

And I, little Brother Francis, your servant, confirm to you, so far as I am able, this most holy benediction. Amen.

CHAPTER XXIII.

THE PAPACY AND THE TEMPORAL POWERS IN THE LATER MIDDLE AGES

66. The Interdict Laid on France by Innocent III. (1200)

Two of the most effective weapons at the service of the mediæval Church were excommunication and the interdict. By the ban of excommunication the proper ecclesiastical authorities could exclude a heretic or otherwise objectionable person from all religious privileges, thereby cutting him off from association with the faithful and consigning him irrevocably (unless he repented) to Satan. The interdict differed from excommunication in being less sweeping in its condemnatory character, and also in being applied to towns, provinces, or countries rather than to individuals. As a rule the interdict undertook to deprive the inhabitants of a specified region of the use of certain of the sacraments, of participation in the usual religious services, and of the right of Christian burial. It did not expel men from church membership, as did excommunication, but it suspended most of the privileges and rights flowing from such membership. The interdict was first employed by the clergy of north France in the tenth and eleventh centuries. In the twelfth it was adopted by the papacy on account of its obvious value as a means of disciplining the monarchs of western Europe. Because of its effectiveness in stirring up popular indignation against sovereigns who incurred the papal displeasure, by the time of Innocent III. (1198-1216) it had come to be employed for political as well as for purely religious purposes, though generally the two considerations were closely intertwined. A famous and typical instance of its use was that of the year 1200, described below.

In August, 1193, Philip Augustus, king of France, married Ingeborg, second sister of King Knut VI. of Denmark. At the time Philip was

contemplating an invasion of England and hoped through the marriage
to assure himself of Danish aid. Circumstances soon changed his plans,
however, and almost immediately he began to treat his new wife coldly,
with the obvious purpose of forcing her to return to her brother's court.
Failing in this, he convened his nobles and bishops at Compiègne and
got from them a decree of divorce, on the flimsy pretext that the marriage with Ingeborg had been illegal on account of the latter's distant
relationship to Elizabeth of Hainault, Philip's first wife. Ingeborg
and her brother appealed to Rome, and Pope Celestine III. dispatched
letter after letter and legate after legate to the French court, but without result. Indeed, after three years, Philip, to clinch the matter, as he
thought, married Agnes of Meran, daughter of a Bavarian nobleman,
and shut up Ingeborg in a convent at Soissons. In 1198, while the
affair stood thus, Celestine died and was succeeded by Innocent III.,
under whom the papal power was destined to attain a height hitherto
unknown. Innocent flatly refused to sanction the divorce or to recognize the second marriage, although he was not pope, of course, until
some years after both had occurred. On the ground that the whole
subject of marriage lay properly within the jurisdiction of the Church,
Innocent demanded that Philip cast off the beautiful Agnes and
restore Ingeborg to her rightful place. This Philip promptly refused
to do.

The threat of an interdict failing to move him, the Pope proceeded to
put his threat into execution. In January, 1200, the interdict was pronounced and, though the king's power over the French clergy was so
strong that many refused to heed the voice from Rome, gradually
the discontent and indignation of the people grew until after nine
months it became apparent that the king must yield. He did so as
gracefully as he could, promising to take back Ingeborg and submit
the question of a divorce to a council presided over by the papal legate.
This council, convened in 1201 at Soissons, decided against the king and
in favor of Ingeborg; but Philip had no intention to submit in good
faith and, until the death of Agnes in 1204, he maintained his policy of
procrastination and double-dealing. Even in the later years of the reign
the unfortunate Ingeborg had frequent cause to complain of harshness
and neglect at the hand of her royal husband.

The following are the principal portions of Innocent's interdict.

Source—Martène, Edmond, and Durand, Ursin, *Thesaurus novus Anecdotorum* ["New Collection of Unpublished Documents"], Paris, 1717, Vol. IV., p. 147.   Adapted from translation by Arthur C. Howland in *Univ. of Pa. Translations and Reprints*, Vol. IV., No. 4, pp. 29–30.

Let all the churches be closed; let no one be admitted to them, except to baptize infants; let them not be otherwise opened, except for the purpose of lighting the lamps, or when the priest shall come for the Eucharist and holy water for the use of the sick.   We permit Mass to be celebrated once a week, on Friday, early in the morning, to consecrate the Host [1] for the use of the sick, but only one clerk is to be admitted to assist the priest.

Partial suspension of the services and offices of the Church   Let the clergy preach on Sunday in the vestibules of the churches, and in place of the Mass let them deliver the word of God.   Let them recite the canonical hours [2] outside the churches, where the people do not hear them; if they recite an epistle or a gospel, let them beware lest the laity hear them; and let them not permit the dead to be interred, nor their bodies to be placed unburied in the cemeteries.   Let them, moreover, say to the laity that they sin and transgress grievously by burying bodies in the earth, even in unconsecrated ground, for in so doing they assume to themselves an office pertaining to others.

Let them forbid their parishioners to enter churches that may be open in the king's territory, and let them not bless the wallets of pilgrims, except outside the churches.   Let them not cele-

How Easter should be observed   brate the offices in Passion week, but refrain even until Easter day, and then let them celebrate in private, no one being admitted except the assisting priest, as above directed; let no one communicate, even at Easter, unless he be sick and in danger of death.   During the same week, or on Palm Sunday, let them announce to their

[1] The consecrated wafer, believed to be the body of Christ, which in the Mass is offered as a sacrifice; also the bread before consecration.

[2] Certain periods of the day, set apart by the laws of the Church, for the duties of prayer and devotion; also certain portions of the Breviary to be used at stated hours.   The seven canonical hours are matins and lauds, the first, third, sixth, and ninth hours, vespers, and compline.

parishioners that they may assemble on Easter morning before
the church and there have permission to eat flesh and consecrated bread. . . . Let the priest confess all who desire
it in the portico of the church; if the church have no portico,
Arrangements we direct that in bad or rainy weather, and not
for confession otherwise, the nearest door of the church may
be opened and confessions heard on its threshold (all being excluded except the one who is to confess), so that the priest and
the penitent can be heard by those who are outside the church.
If, however, the weather be fair, let the confession be heard in
front of the closed doors. Let no vessels of holy water be placed
outside the church, nor shall the priests carry them anywhere; for all the sacraments of the Church beyond these two
which are reserved [1] are absolutely prohibited. Extreme unction,
which is a holy sacrament, may not be given.[2]

67. The Bull "Unam Sanctam" of Boniface VIII. (1302)

IN the history of the mediæval Church at least three great periods of
conflict between the papacy and the temporal powers can be distinguished. The first was the era of Gregory VII. and Henry IV. of Germany [see p. 261]; the second was that of Innocent III. and John of
England and Philip Augustus of France [see p. 380]; the third was that
of Boniface VIII. and Philip the Fair of France. In many respects the
most significant document pertaining to the last of these struggles is
the papal bull, given below, commonly designated by its opening words,
Unam Sanctam.

The question at issue in the conflict of Boniface VIII. and Philip the
Fair was the old one as to whether the papacy should be allowed to
dominate European states in temporal as well as in spiritual matters.
The Franconian emperors, in the eleventh century, made stubborn
resistance to such domination, but the immediate result was only partial

[1] That is, infant baptism and the *viaticum* (the Lord's Supper when administered to persons in immediate danger of death).

[2] Extreme unction is the sacrament of anointing in the last hours,—the
application of consecrated oil by a priest to all the senses, i. e., to eyes, ears,
nostrils, etc., of a person when in immediate danger of death. The sacrament is performed for the remission of sins.

success, while later efforts to keep up the contest practically ruined the power of the house of Hohenstaufen. Even Philip Augustus, at the opening of the thirteenth century, had been compelled to yield, at least outwardly, to the demands of the papacy respecting his marriages and his national policies. With the revival of the issue under Boniface and Philip, however, the tide turned, for at last there had arisen a nation whose sovereign had so firm a grip upon the loyalty of his subjects that he could defy even the power of Rome with impunity.

The quarrel between Boniface and Philip first assumed importance in 1296—two years after the accession of the former and eleven after that of the latter. The immediate subject of dispute was the heavy taxes which Philip was levying upon the clergy of France and the revenues from which he was using in the prosecution of his wars with Edward I. of England; but royal and papal interests were fundamentally at variance and as both king and pope were of a combative temper, a conflict was inevitable, irrespective of taxes or any other particular cause of controversy. In 1096 Boniface issued the famous bull *Clericis Laicos*, forbidding laymen (including monarchs) to levy subsidies on the clergy without papal consent and prohibiting the clergy to pay subsidies so levied. Philip the Fair was not mentioned in the bull, but the measure was clearly directed primarily at him. He retaliated by prohibiting the export of money, plate, etc., from the realm, thereby cutting off the accustomed papal revenues from France. In 1297 an apparent reconciliation was effected, the Pope practically suspending the bull so far as France was concerned, though only to secure relief from the conflict with Philip while engaged in a struggle with the rival Colonna family at Rome.

In 1301 the contest was renewed, mainly because of the indiscretion of a papal legate, Bernard Saisset, bishop of Pamiers, who vilified the king and was promptly imprisoned for his violent language. Boniface took up the cause of Saisset and called an ecclesiastical council to regulate the affairs of church and state in France and to rectify the injuries wrought by King Philip. The claim to papal supremacy in temporal as well as spiritual affairs, which Boniface proposed thus to make good, was boldly stated in a new bull—that of *Ausculta Fili*—in 1301. At the same time the bull *Clericis Laicos* was renewed for France. Philip knew that the Franconians and his own Capetian predecessors had failed in their struggles with Rome chiefly for the reason that they had been lacking in consistent popular support. National feeling was unquestionably stronger in the France of 1301 than in the Germany of 1077, or even in the France of 1200; but to make doubly sure, Philip, in 1302, caused the first meeting of a complete States General to be held, and from this body, representing the various elements of the French people, he got reliable pledges of support in his efforts to resist the temporal aggressions of the papacy. It was at this juncture that Boniface issued the bull *Unam Sanctam*, which has well been termed the classic mediæval expression of the papal claims to universal temporal sovereignty.

In 1303 an assembly of French prelates and magnates, under the inspiration of Philip, brought charges of heresy and misconduct against Boniface and called for a meeting of a general ecclesiastical council to depose him. Boniface decided to issue a bull excommunicating and deposing Philip. But before the date set for this step (September, 1303) a catastrophe befell the papacy which resulted in an unexpected termination of the episode. On the day before the bull of deposition was to be issued William of Nogaret, whom Philip had sent to Rome to force Boniface to call a general council to try the charges against himself, led a band of troops to Anagni and took the Pope prisoner with the intention of carrying him to France for trial. After three days the inhabitants of Anagni attacked the Frenchmen and drove them out and Boniface, who had barely escaped death, returned to Rome. The unfortunate Pope never recovered, however, from the effects of the outrage and his death in October (1303) left Philip, by however unworthy means, a victor. From this point the papacy passes under the domination of the French court and in 1309 began the dark period of the so-called Babylonian Captivity, during most of which the popes dwelt at Avignon under conditions precisely the reverse of the ideal which Boniface so clearly asserted in *Unam Sanctam*.

Source—Text based upon the papal register published by P. Mury in *Revue des Questions Historiques*, Vol. XLVI. (July, 1889), pp. 255–256. Translated in Oliver J. Thatcher and Edgar H. McNeal, *Source Book for Mediæval History* (New York), 1905, pp. 314–317.

The true faith compels us to believe that there is one holy Catholic Apostolic Church, and this we firmly believe and plainly

confess. And outside of her there is no salvation or remission of sins, as the Bridegroom says in the Song of Solomon: "My dove, my undefiled, is but one; she is the only one of her mother, she is the choice one of her that bare her" [Song of Sol., vi. 9]; which represents the one mystical body, whose head is Christ, but the head of Christ is God [1 Cor., xi. 3]. In this Church there
An assertion of the unity of the Church is "one Lord, one faith, one baptism" [Eph., iv. 5]. For in the time of the flood there was only one ark, that of Noah, prefiguring the one Church, and it was "finished above in one cubit" [Gen., vi. 16], and had but one helmsman and master, namely, Noah. And we read that all things on the earth outside of this ark were destroyed. This Church we venerate as the only one, since the Lord said by the prophet: "Deliver my soul from the sword; my darling from the power of the dog" [Ps., xxii. 20]. He prayed for his soul, that is, for himself, the head; and at the same time for the body, and he named his body, that is, the one Church, because there is but one Bridegroom [John, iii. 29], and because of the unity of the faith, of the sacraments, and of his love for the Church. This is the seamless robe of the Lord which was not rent but parted by lot [John, xix. 23].

Therefore there is one body of the one and only Church, and one head, not two heads, as if the Church were a monster. And this head is Christ, and his vicar, Peter and his successor; for the Lord himself said to Peter: "Feed my sheep" [John, xxi. 16]. And he said "my sheep," in general, not these or those sheep in particular; from which it is clear that all were committed to him.
An allusion to the Petrine Supremacy If, therefore, Greeks [i.e., the Greek Church] or any one else say that they are not subject to Peter and his successors, they thereby necessarily confess that they are not of the sheep of Christ. For the Lord says, in the Gospel of John, that there is one fold and only one shepherd [John, x. 16]. By the words of the gospel we are taught that the two swords, namely, the spiritual authority and the temporal,

are in the power of the Church.   For when the apostles said
"Here are two swords" [Luke, xxii. 38]—that is, in the Church,
since it was the apostles who were speaking—the Lord did not
answer, "It is too much," but "It is enough."   Whoever denies
that the temporal sword is in the power of Peter does not properly
understand the word of the Lord when He said: "Put up thy
sword into the sheath" [John, xviii. 11].   Both swords, therefore,
The proper re- the spiritual and the temporal, are in the power
lation of spir- of the Church.   The former is to be used by the
itual and tem-
poral powers Church, the latter for the Church; the one by the
hand of the priest, the other by the hand of kings and knights,
but at the command and permission of the priest.   Moreover, it
is necessary for one sword to be under the other, and the temporal authority to be subjected to the spiritual; for the apostle
says, "For there is no power but of God: and the powers that be
are ordained of God" [Rom., xiii. 1]; but they would not be ordained unless one were subjected to the other, and, as it were,
the lower made the higher by the other.

For, according to St. Dionysius,[1] it is a law of divinity that
the lowest is made the highest through the intermediate.   According to the law of the universe all things are not equally and
directly reduced to order, but the lowest are fitted into their
order through the intermediate, and the lower through the
higher.   And we must necessarily admit that the spiritual power
The superi- surpasses any earthly power in dignity and honor,
ority of the because spiritual things surpass temporal things.
spiritual
We clearly see that this is true from the paying
of tithes, from the benediction, from the sanctification, from the
receiving of the power, and from the governing of these things.
For the truth itself declares that the spiritual power must
establish the temporal power and pass judgment on it if it is
not good.   Thus the prophecy of Jeremiah concerning the Church

---

[1] St. Dionysius was bishop of Alexandria about the middle of the third
century.   He was a pupil of the great theologian Origen and himself a writer
of no small ability on the doctrinal questions which vexed the early Church.

and the ecclesiastical power is fulfilled: "See, I have this day set thee over the nations and over the kingdoms, to root out, and to pull down, and to destroy, and to throw down, to build, and to plant" [Jer., i. 10].

Therefore if the temporal power errs, it will be judged by the spiritual power, and if the lower spiritual power errs, it will be **The highest** judged by its superior. But if the highest **spiritual pow-** spiritual power errs, it cannot be judged by **er (the papacy)** men, but by God alone. For the apostle says: **responsible to** men, but by God alone. For the apostle says: **God alone** "But he that is spiritual judgeth all things, yet he himself is judged of no man" [1 Cor., ii. 15]. Now this authority, although it is given to man and exercised through man, is not human, but divine. For it was given by the word of the Lord to Peter, and the rock was made firm to him and his successors, in Christ himself, whom he had confessed. For the Lord said to Peter: "Whatsoever thou shalt bind on earth shall be bound in heaven; and whatsoever thou shalt loose on earth shall be loosed in heaven" [Matt., xvi. 19].

Therefore, whosoever resisteth this power thus ordained of God resisteth the ordinance of God [Rom., xiii. 2], unless there are two principles [beginnings], as Manichæus [1] pretends there are. But this we judge to be false and heretical. For Moses says that, not in the beginnings, but in the beginning, God created **Submission to** the heaven and the earth [Gen., i. 1]. We there- **the papacy es-** fore declare, say, and affirm that submission on **sential to sal-** fore declare, say, and affirm that submission on **vation** the part of every man to the bishop of Rome is altogether necessary for his salvation.

---

[1] Manichæus was a learned Persian who, in the third century, worked out a system of doctrine which sought to combine the principles of Christianity with others taken over from the Persian and kindred Oriental religions. The most prominent feature of the resulting creed was the conception of an absolute dualism running throughout the universe—light and darkness, good and evil, soul and body—which existed from the beginning and should exist forever. The Manichæan sect spread from Persia into Asia Minor North Africa, Sicily, and Italy. Though persecuted by Diocletian, and afterwards by some of the Christian emperors, it had many adherents as late as the sixth century, and certain of its ideas appeared under new names at still later times, notably among the Albigenses in southern France in the twelfth century.

68. The Great Schism and the Councils of Pisa and Constance

THE "Babylonian Captivity"—begun in 1305, or perhaps more properly in 1309, when the French Pope, Clement V., took up his residence regularly at Avignon—lasted until 1377. During these sixty or seventy years the College of Cardinals consisted chiefly of Frenchmen, all of the seven popes were of French nationality, and for the most part the papal authority was little more than a tool in the hands of the aggressive French sovereigns. In 1377, at the solicitation of the Italian clergy and people, Pope Gregory XI. removed to Rome, where he died in 1378. In the election that followed the Roman populace, determined to bring the residence of the popes at Avignon to an end once for all, demanded a Roman, or at least an Italian, pope. The majority of the cardinals were French, but they could not agree upon a French candidate and, intimidated by the threats of the mob, they at last chose a Neapolitan who took the name Urban VI. A few months of Urban's obstinate administration convinced the cardinals that they had made a serious mistake, and, on the ground that their choice had been unduly influenced by popular clamor, they sought to nullify the election and to replace Urban by a Genevan who took the title Clement VII. Urban utterly refused thus to be put aside, so that there were now two popes, each duly elected by the College of Cardinals and each claiming the undivided allegiance of Christendom. This was the beginning of the Great Schism, destined to work havoc in the Church for a full generation, or until finally ended in 1417. Clement VII. fixed his abode at Avignon and French influence secured for him the support of Spain, Scotland, and Sicily. The rest of Europe, displeased with the subordination of the papacy to France and French interests, declared for Urban, who was pledged to maintain the papal capital at Rome.

France must be held responsible in the main for the evils of the Great Schism—a breach in the Church which she deliberately created and for many years maintained; but she herself suffered by it more than any other nation of Europe because of the annates,[1] the *décime*,[2] and other

---

[1] Annates were payments made to the pope by newly elected or appointed ecclesiastical officials of the higher sort. They were supposed to comprise the first year's income from the bishop's or abbot's benefice.

[2] The *décime* was an extraordinary royal revenue derived from the payment by the clergy of a tenth of the annual income from their benefices. Its

taxes which were imposed upon the French clergy and people to support
the luxurious and at times extravagant papal court at Avignon, or which
were exacted by ambitious monarchs under the cover of papal license.
In the course of time the impossible situation created by the Schism
demanded a remedy and in fairness it should be observed that in the
work of adjustment the leading part was taken by the French.   After
the death of Clement VII., in 1394, the French court sincerely desired
to bring the Schism to an end on terms that would be fair to all.   Already in 1393 King Charles VI. had laid the case before the University
of Paris and asked for an opinion as to the best course to be pursued.
The authorities of the university requested each member of the various
faculties to submit his idea of a solution of the problem and from the
mass of suggestions thus brought together a committee of fifty-four
professors, masters, and doctors worked out the three lines of action
set forth in selection (a) below.   The first plan, i.e., that both popes
should resign as a means of restoring harmony, was accepted as the
proper one by an assembly of the French clergy convened in 1395.   It
was doomed to defeat, however, by the vacillation of both Benedict
XIII. at Avignon and Boniface IX. at Rome, and in the end it was
agreed to fall back upon the third plan which the University of Paris had
proposed, i.e., the convening of a general council.   There was no doubt
that such a council could legally be summoned only by the pope, but
finally the cardinals attached to both popes deserted them and united
in issuing the call in their own name.

The council met at Pisa in 1409 and proceeded to clear up the question
of its own legality and authority by issuing the unequivocal declaration
comprised in (b) below.   It furthermore declared both popes deposed and
elected a new one, who took the name Alexander V.   Neither of the
previous popes, however, recognized the council's action, so now there
were three rivals instead of two and the situation was only so much
worse than before.   In 1410 Alexander V. died and the cardinals chose
as his successor John XXIII., a man whose life was notoriously wicked,

prototype was the Saladin tithe, imposed by Philip Augustus (1180–1223)
for the financing of his crusade.   In the latter half of the thirteenth century,
and throughout the fourteenth, the *décime* was called for by the kings with
considerable frequency, often ostensibly for crusading purposes, and it was
generally obtained by a more or less compulsory vote of the clergy, or without their consent at all.

but who was far from lacking in political sagacity. Three years later the capture of Rome by the king of Naples forced John to appeal for assistance to the Emperor Sigismund; and Sigismund demanded, before extending the desired aid, that a general church council be summoned to meet on German soil for the adjustment of the tangled papal situation. The result was the Council of Constance, whose sessions extended from November, 1414, to April, 1418, and which, because of its general European character, was able to succeed where the Council of Pisa had failed. In the decree *Sacrosancta* given below (c), issued in April, 1415, we have the council's notable assertion of its supreme authority in ecclesiastical matters, even as against the pope himself. The Schism was healed with comparative facility. Gregory XII., who had been the pope at Rome, but who was now in exile, sent envoys to offer his abdication. Benedict XIII., likewise a fugitive, was deposed and found himself without supporters. John XXIII. was deposed for his unworthy character and had no means of offering resistance. The cardinals, together with representatives of the five "nations" into which the council was divided, harmoniously selected for pope a Roman cardinal, who assumed the name of Martin V. This was in 1417. The Schism was at an end, though the work of combating heresy and of propagating reform within the Church went on in successive councils, notably that of Basel (1431–1449).

Sources—(a) Lucæ d'Achery, *Spicilegium, sive Collectio veterum aliquot Scriptorum qui in Galliæ Bibliothecis Delituerant* ["Gleanings, or a Collection of some Early Writings, which survive in Gallic Libraries"], Paris, 1723, Vol. I., p. 777. Translated in Thatcher and McNeal, *Source Book for Mediæval History* (New York, 1905), pp. 326–327.

(b) Raynaldus, *Annales, anno 1409* ["Annals, year 1409"], § 71.

(c) Von der Hardt, *Magnum Constantiense Concilium* ["Great Council of Constance"], Vol. II., p. 98.

(a)

The first way. Now the first way to end the Schism is that both parties should entirely renounce and resign all rights which they may have, or claim to have, to the papal office.

The second way. But if both cling tenaciously to their rights and refuse to resign, as they have thus far done, we would propose a resort to arbitration. That is, that they should together choose worthy and suitable men, or permit such to be chosen in a **Three possible** regular and canonical way, and these should have **solutions of the** full power and authority to discuss the case and **Schism offered** **by the Univer-** decide it, and if necessary and expedient and **sity of Paris** approved by those who, according to the canon law, have the authority [i.e., the cardinals], they might also have the right to proceed to the election of a pope.

The third way. If the rival popes, after being urged in a brotherly and friendly manner, will not accept either of the above ways, there is a third way which we propose as an excellent remedy for this sacrilegious schism. We mean that the matter should be left to a general council. This general council might be composed, according to canon law, only of prelates; or, since many of them are very illiterate, and many of them are bitter partisans of one or the other pope, there might be joined with the prelates an equal number of masters and doctors of theology and law from the faculties of approved universities. Or, if this does not seem sufficient to any one, there might be added, besides, one or more representatives from cathedral chapters and the chief monastic orders, to the end that all decisions might be rendered only after most careful examination and mature deliberation.

(b)

This holy and general council, representing the universal Church, decrees and declares that the united college of cardinals was empowered to call the council, and that the power to call **Declarations** such a council belongs of right to the aforesaid **of the Council** holy college of cardinals, especially now when **of Pisa (1409)** there is a detestable schism. The council further declares that this holy council, representing the universal Church, caused both claimants of the papal throne to be cited in the gates and doors of the churches of Pisa to come and hear the final decision [in the matter of the Schism] pronounced, or to give a good and sufficient reason why such sentence should not be rendered.

(c)

This holy synod of Constance, being a general council, and legally assembled in the Holy Spirit for the praise of God and for ending the present schism, and for the union and reformation of the Church of God in its head and in its members, in order more easily, more securely, more completely, and more fully to bring about the union and reformation of the Church of God, ordains, declares, and decrees as follows: First it declares that this synod, legally assembled, is a general council, and represents the Catholic church militant and has its authority directly

The Council of Constance asserts its superiority to even the papacy

from Christ; and everybody, of whatever rank or dignity, including also the pope, is bound to obey this council in those things which pertain to the faith, to the ending of this schism, and to a general reformation of the Church in its head and members. Likewise it declares that if any one, of whatever rank, condition, or dignity, including also the pope, shall refuse to obey the commands, statutes, ordinances, or orders of this holy council, or of any other holy council properly assembled, in regard to the ending of the Schism and to the reformation of the Church, he shall be subject to the proper punishment, and, unless he repents, he shall be duly punished, and, if necessary, recourse shall be had to other aids of justice.

69. The Pragmatic Sanction of Bourges (1438)

THE Council of Basel, convened in 1431, had for its object a thoroughgoing reformation of the Church, "in its head and its members," from papacy to parish priest. Like all of the councils of the period, its spirit was distinctly anti-papal and for this reason Pope Eugene IV. sought to bring it under his control by transferring it to Bologna and, failing in this, to turn its deliberations into channels other than criticism of the papacy. While the negotiations of Eugene and the council were in progress a step fraught with great significance was taken in France in the promulgation of the Pragmatic Sanction of Bourges.[1] France was the only country in which the principles laid down by the councils— Pisa, Constance, Basel, and the rest—had taken firm hold. In 1438 Charles VII. convened at Bourges an assembly composed of leading prelates, councillors, and princes of the royal blood, to which the Pope and the Council of Basel both sent delegates. This assembly proceeded to adapt the decrees of the council to the conditions and needs of France, on the evident assumption that the will of the French magnates in such matters was superior to that of both pope and council, so far as France was concerned. The action at Bourges well illustrates the growing spirit of French nationality which had sprung up since the recent achievements of Joan of Arc.

The Pragmatic Sanction dealt in the main with four subjects— the authority of church councils, the diminishing of papal patronage, the restriction of papal taxation, and the limitation of appeals to Rome. Together these matters are commonly spoken of as the "Gallican liberties," i.e., the liberties of the Gallic or French church, and they implied the right of the national church to administer its own affairs with only the slightest interference from the pope or other outside powers; in other words, they were essentially anti-papal. Louis XI., the successor of Charles VII., for diplomatic reasons, sought to revoke the Pragmatic Sanction, but the Parlement of Paris refused to register the ordinance and for all practical purposes the Pragmatic was maintained until 1516. In that year Francis I. established the relations of the papacy and the French clergy on the basis of a new "concordat," which, however, was not very unlike the Pragmatic. The Pragmatic is of interest to the student of French history mainly because of the degree in which it enhanced the power of the crown, particularly in respect to the ecclesiastical affairs of the realm, and because of the testimony it bears to the declining influence of the papacy in the stronger nations like France and England. The text printed below represents only an abstract of the document, which in all included thirty-three chapters.

---

[1] Pragmatic, in the general sense, means any sort of decree of public importance; in its more special usage it denotes an ordinance of the crown regulating the relations of the national clergy with the papacy. The modern equivalent is "concordat."

Source.—Text in Vilevault et Bréquigny, *Ordonnances des Rois de France de la Troisième Race* (Paris, 1772), Vol. XIII., pp. 267–291.

The king declares that, according to the oath taken at their coronation, kings are bound to defend and protect the holy

Charles VII. recognizes the obligations of the king to the Church

Church, its ministers and its sacred offices, and zealously to guard in their kingdoms the decrees of the holy fathers. The general council assembled at Basel to continue the work begun by the councils of Constance and Siena,[1] and to labor for the reform of the Church, in both its head and members, having had presented to it numerous decrees and regulations, with the request that it accept them and cause them to be observed in the kingdom, the king has convened an assembly composed of prelates and other ecclesiastics representing the clergy of France and of the Dauphiné.[2] He has presided in person over its deliberations, surrounded by his son, the princes of the blood, and the principal lords of the realm. He has listened to the ambassadors of the Pope and the council. From the examination of prelates and

Abuses prevalent in the French church

the most renowned doctors, and from the thoroughgoing discussions of the assembly, it appears that, from the falling into decay of the early discipline, the churches of the kingdom have been made to suffer from all sorts of insatiable greed; that the *réserve* and the *grâce*

[1] When the Council of Constance came to an end, in April, 1418, it was agreed between this body and Pope Martin V. that a similar council should be convened at Pavia in 1423. When the time arrived, conditions were far from favorable, but the University of Paris pressed the Pope to observe his pledge in the matter and the council was duly convened. Very few members appeared at Pavia, and, the plague soon breaking out there, the meeting was transferred to Siena. Even there only five German prelates were present, six French, and not one Spanish. Small though it was, the council entered upon a course so independent and self-assertive that in the following year the Pope was glad to take advantage of its paucity of numbers to declare it dissolved.

[2] The Dauphiné was a region on the east side of the Rhone which, in 1349, was purchased of Humbert, Dauphin of Vienne, by Philip VI., and ceded by the latter to his grandson Charles, the later Charles V. (1364–1380). Charles assumed the title of "the Dauphin," which became the established designation of the heir-apparent to the French throne.

expectative [1] have given rise to grievous abuses and unbearable burdens; that the most notable and best endowed benefices have fallen into the hands of unknown men, who do not conform at all to the requirement of residence and who do not understand the speech of the people committed to their care, and consequently are neglectful of the needs of their souls, like mercenaries who dream of nothing whatever but temporal gain; that thus the worship of Christ is declining, piety is enfeebled, the laws of the Church are violated, and buildings for religious uses are falling in ruin. The clergy abandon their theological studies, because there is no hope of advancement. Conflicts without number rage over the possession of benefices, plurality of which is coveted by an execrable ambition. Simony is everywhere glaring; the prelates and other collators [2] are pillaged of their rights and their ministry; the rights of patrons are impaired; and the wealth of the kingdom goes into the hands of foreigners, to the detriment of the clergy.

Since, in the judgment of the prelates and other ecclesiastics, the decrees of the holy council of Basel seemed to afford a suitable

The decrees of Basel accepted with some modifications remedy for all these evils, after mature deliberation, we have decided to accept them—some without change, others with certain modifications—without wishing to cast doubt upon the power and authority of the council, but at the same time taking account of the necessities of the occasion and of the customs of the nation.

1. General councils shall be held every ten years, in places to be designated by the pope.

[1] Under the *grâce expectative* the pope conferred upon a prelate a benefice which at the time was filled, to be assumed as soon as it should fall vacant. Benefices of larger importance, such as the offices of bishop and abbot, were often subject to the *réserve;* that is, the pope regularly reserved to himself the right of filling them, sometimes before, sometimes after, the vacancy occurred. These acts constituted clear assumptions by the popes of power which under the law of the Church was not theirs, and, though the framers of the Pragmatic Sanction had motives which were more or less selfish for combatting the *réserve* and the *grâce expectative*, there can be no question that the abuses aimed at were as real as they were represented to be.

[2] Those who presented and installed men in benefices.

2. The authority of the general council is superior to that of the pope in all that pertains to the faith, the extirpation of schism, and the reform of the Church in both head and members.[1]

3. Election is reëstablished for ecclesiastical offices; but the king, or the princes of his kingdom, without violating the canonical rules, may make recommendations when elections are to occur in the chapters or the monasteries.[2]

4. The popes shall not have the right to reserve the collation of benefices, or to bestow any benefice before it becomes vacant.

5. All grants of benefices made by the pope in virtue of the *droit d'expectative* are hereby declared null. Those who shall have received such benefices shall be punished by the secular power. The popes shall not have the right to interfere by the creation of canonships.[3]

6. Appeals to Rome are prohibited until every other grade of jurisdiction shall have been exhausted.

7. Annates are prohibited.[4]

[1] These first two chapters reproduce without change the decrees of the Council of Basel. The second reiterates, in substance, the declaration of the Council of Constance [see p. 393].

[2] That is, the "canonical" system of election of bishops by the chapters and of abbots by the monks. The Pragmatic differs in this clause from the decree of the Council of Basel in allowing temporal princes to recommend persons for election.

[3] This means that the pope is not to add to the number of canons in any cathedral chapter as a means of influencing the composition and deliberations of that body.

[4] Annates were ordinarily the first year's revenues of a benefice which, under the prevailing system, were supposed to be paid by the incumbent to the pope. The Pragmatic goes on to provide that during the lifetime of Pope Eugene one-fifth of the accustomed annates should continue to be paid.

CHAPTER XXIV.

THE EMPIRE IN THE TWELFTH, THIRTEENTH, AND FOUR-TEENTH CENTURIES

70. The Peace of Constance (1183)

With the election of Frederick Barbarossa as emperor, in 1152, a new stage of the great papal-imperial combat was entered upon, though under conditions quite different from those surrounding the contest in the preceding century [see Chap. XVI]. The Empire was destined to succumb in the end to the papacy, but with a sovereign of Frederick's energy and ability at its head it was able at least to make a stubborn fight and to meet defeat with honor. The new reign was inaugurated by a definite announcement of the Emperor's intention to consolidate and strengthen the imperial government throughout all Germany and Italy. The task in Germany was far from simple; in Italy it was the most formidable that could have been conceived, and this for the reason that the Italian population was largely gathered in cities with strong political and military organization, with all the traditions of practical independence, and with no thought of submitting to the government of an emperor or any other claimant to more than merely nominal sovereignty.

Trouble began almost at once between Frederick and the free commune of Milan, though war was averted for a time by the oaths taken to the Emperor on the occasion of his first expedition across the Alps in 1154. Between that date and 1158 the consuls of the city were detected in treacherous conduct and, the people refusing to disavow them, in the latter year the Emperor again crossed the Alps, bent on nothing less than the annihilation of the commune and the dispersion of its inhabitants. He carried with him a larger army than a head of the Holy Roman Empire had ever led into Italy. The Milanese submitted, under conditions extremely humiliating, and Frederick, after being assured by the doctors of law at the new university of Bologna that he was acting

398

quite within the letter of the Roman law, proceeded to lay claim to the *regalia* (royal rights, such as tolls from roads and rivers, products of mines, and the estates of criminals), to the right to levy an extraordinary war tax, and to that of appointing the chief civic magistrates. Disaffection broke out at once in many of the communes, but chiefly at Milan; whereupon Frederick came promptly to the conclusion that the time had arrived to rid himself of this irreconcilable opponent of his measures. The city was besieged and, after its inhabitants had been starved into surrender, almost completely destroyed (1162).

Only temporarily did the barbarous act have its intended effect; the net result was a widespread revival of the communal spirit, which expressed itself in the formation of a sturdy confederacy known as the Lombard League. One of the League's first acts was to rebuild Milan, under whose leadership the struggle with the Emperor was actively renewed. In 1168 a new city was founded at the foot of the Alps near Pavia to serve as a base of operations in the campaign which the League proposed to wage against the common enemy. It was given the name Alessandria (or Alexandria) in honor of Pope Alexander III., who was friendly to the cause of the cities. In 1174 Frederick began an open attack on the League, but in 1176, at Legnano, he suffered an overwhelming defeat, due largely to his failure to receive reinforcements from Germany. The adjustment of peace was intrusted to an assembly at Venice in which all parties were represented. The result was the treaty of Venice (1177), the advantages of which were wholly against the Empire. A truce of six years was granted the cities, with the understanding that all details were to be arranged within, or at the expiration of, that time.

When the close of the period arrived, in 1183, Frederick no longer dreamed of subduing and punishing the rebellious Italians, but instead was quite ready to agree to a permanent peace. The result was the Peace of Constance, which has been described as the earliest international agreement of the kind in modern history. By this instrument the theoretical overlordship of the Emperor in Italy was reasserted, though in fact it had never been denied. Beyond this, however, the communes were recognized as essentially independent. Those who had enjoyed the right to choose their own magistrates retained it; their financial obligations to the Emperor were clearly defined; and the

League was conceded to be a legitimate and permanent organization. By yielding on numerous vital points the Empire had vindicated its right to exist, but its administrative machinery, so far as Italy was concerned, was still further impaired. This machinery, it must be said, had never been conspicuously effective south of the Alps. As for Frederick, he set out in 1189 upon the Third Crusade, during the course of which he met his death in Asia Minor without being permitted to see the Holy Land.

Source—Text in *Monumenta Germaniæ Historica,* Legum Sectio IV. (Weiland ed.), Vol. I., pp. 411–418. Adapted from translation in Oliver J. Thatcher and Edgar H. McNeal, *Source Book for Mediæval History* (New York, 1905,) pp. 199–202.

1. We, Frederick, emperor of the Romans, and our son Henry, king of the Romans,[1] hereby grant to you, the cities, territories,

Concessions to the cities of the League

and persons of the League, the *regalia* and other rights within and without the cities, as you have been accustomed to hold them; that is, each member of the League shall have the same rights as the city of Verona has had in the past, or has now.

2. The members of the League shall exercise freely and without interference from us all the rights which they have exercised of old.

3. These are the rights which are guaranteed to you: the *fodrum,*[2] forests, pastures, bridges, streams, mills, fortifications of the cities, criminal and civil jurisdiction, and all other rights which concern the welfare of the city.

4. The *regalia* which are not to be granted to the members of the League shall be determined in the following manner: in

How the regalia remaining to the Emperor were to be determined

the case of each city, certain men shall be chosen for this purpose from both the bishopric and the city; these men shall be of good repute, capable of deciding these questions, and such as are not prejudiced against either party. Acting with the bishop of the

---

[1] Henry VI. succeeded his father as emperor, reigning from 1190 to 1197.

[2] The term (meaning literally "fodder") designates the obligation to furnish provisions for the royal army. The right of demanding such provisions was now given up by the Emperor.

diocese, they shall swear to inquire into the questions of the *regalia* and to set aside those that by right belong to us. If, however, the cities do not wish to submit to this inquisition, they shall pay to us an annual tribute of 2,000 marks in silver as compensation for our *regalia*. If this sum seems excessive, it may be reduced.

5. If anyone appeals to us in regard to matters which are by this treaty admitted to be under your jurisdiction, we agree not to hear such an appeal.

8. All privileges, gifts, and concessions made in the time of the war by us or our representatives to the prejudice or injury of the cities, territories, or members of the League are to be null and void.

9. Consuls [1] of cities where the bishop holds the position of count from the king or emperor shall receive their office from the bishop, if this has been the custom before. In all other cities **The consuls** the consuls shall receive their office from us, in the following manner: after they have been elected by the city they shall be invested with office by our representative in the city or bishopric, unless we are ourselves in Lombardy, in which case they shall be invested by us. At the end of every five years each city shall send its representative to us to receive the investiture.

10. This arrangement shall be observed by our successor, and all such investitures shall be free.

11. After our death, the cities shall receive investiture in the same way from our son and from his successors.

12. The Emperor shall have the right of hearing appeals in cases involving more than 25 pounds, saving the right of the **Appeals to the Emperor** church of Brescia to hear appeals. The appellant shall not, however, be compelled to come to Germany, but he shall appeal to the representative of the Emperor in the city or bishopric. This representative shall examine

[1] The consuls—often twelve in number—were the chief magistrates of the typical Italian commune.

the case fairly and shall give judgment according to the laws and customs of that city. The decision shall be given within two months from the time of appeal, unless the case shall have been deferred by reason of some legal hindrance or by the consent of both parties.

13. The consuls of cities shall take the oath of allegiance to the Emperor before they are invested with office.

14. Our vassals shall receive investiture from us and shall take the vassal's oath of fidelity. All other persons between the

The oath of fidelity

ages of 15 and 70 shall take the ordinary oath of fidelity to the Emperor unless there be some good reason why this oath should be omitted.

17. All injuries, losses, and damages which we or our followers have sustained from the League, or any of its members or allies, are hereby pardoned, and all such transgressors are hereby received back into our favor.

18. We will not remain longer than is necessary in any city or bishopric.

19. It shall be permitted to the cities to erect fortifications within or without their boundaries.

Recognition of the League's right to exist

20. It shall be permitted to the League to maintain its organization as it now is, or to renew it as often as it desires.

71. Current Rumors Concerning the Life and Character of Frederick II.

FREDERICK II. (1194–1250), king of Naples and Sicily and emperor of the Holy Roman Empire, was a son of Emperor Henry VI. and a grandson of Frederick Barbarossa. When his father died (1197) it was intended that the young child's uncle, Philip of Hohenstaufen, should occupy the imperial throne temporarily as regent. Philip, however, proceeded to assume the position as if in his own right and became engaged in a deadly conflict with a rival claimant, Otto IV., during which the Pope, Innocent III., fanned the flames of civil war and made the situation contribute chiefly to the aggrandizement of papal authority in tem-

Source—Matthæus Parisiensis, *Chronica Majora* [Matthew Paris, "Greater Chronicle"]. Adapted from translation by J. A. Giles (London, 1852), Vol. I., pp. 157–158, 166–167, 169–170; Vol. II., pp. 84–85, 103.

In the course of the same year [1238] the fame of the Emperor Frederick was clouded and marred by his jealous enemies and rivals; for it was imputed to him that he was wavering in the Catholic faith, or wandering from the right way, and had given

Frederick suspected of heresy

utterance to some speeches, from which it could be inferred and suspected that he was not only weak in the Catholic faith, but—what was a much greater and more serious crime—that there was in him an enormity of heresy, and the most dreadful blasphemy, to be detested and execrated by all Christians. For it was reported that the Emperor Frederick had said (although it may not be proper to mention it) that three imposters had so craftily deceived their contemporaries as to gain for themselves the mastery of the world: these were Moses, Jesus, and Mahomet [Mohammed]; and that he had impiously given expression to some wicked and incredible ravings and blasphemies respecting the most holy Eucharist. Far be it from any discreet man, much less a Christian, to employ his tongue in such raving blasphemy. It was also said by his rivals that the Emperor agreed with and believed in the law of Mahomet more than that of Jesus Christ. A rumor

Accusation of friendly relations with the Saracens

also crept amongst the people (which God forbid to be true of such a great prince) that he had been for a long time past in alliance with the Saracens, and was more friendly to them than to the Christians; and his rivals, who were endeavoring to blacken his fame, attempted to establish this by many proofs. Whether they sinned or not, He alone knows who is ignorant of nothing. . . .

In Lent, of the same year [1239], seeing the rash proceedings of the Emperor, and that his words pleaded excuse for his sins,—namely, that by the assistance of some of the nobles and judges of Sardinia he had taken into his own possession, and still held, the land and castles of the bishop of Sardinia, and constantly declared that they were a portion of the Empire, and

Frederick's seizure of the lands belonging to a bishop that he by his first and chief oath would preserve the rights of the Empire to the utmost of his power, and would also collect the scattered portions of it,—the Pope[1] was excited to the most violent anger against him.   He set forth some very serious complaints and claims against the Emperor and wrote often boldly and carefully to him, advising him repeatedly by many special messengers, whose authority ought to have obtained from him the greatest attention, to restore the possessions he had seized, and to desist from depriving the Church of her possessions, of which she was endowed by long prescription.   And, like a skilful physician, who at one time makes use of medicines, at another of the knife, and at another of the cauterizing instrument, he mixed threats with entreaties, friendly messages with fearful denunciations. As the Emperor, however, scornfully rejected his requests, and

Refusing to restore them, he is excommunicated excused his actions by arguments founded on reason, his holiness the Pope, on Palm Sunday, in the presence of a great many of the cardinals, in the spirit of glowing anger, solemnly excommunicated the said Emperor Frederick, as though he would at once have hurled him from his imperial dignity, consigning him with terrible denunciations to the possession of Satan at his death; and, as it were, thundering forth the fury of his anger, he excited terror in all his hearers.[2]   .   .   .

The Emperor, on hearing of this, was inflamed with violent anger, and with oft-repeated reproaches accused the Church and its rulers of ingratitude to him, and of returning evil for good. He recalled to their recollection how he had exposed himself and his property to the billows and to a thousand kinds of danger

---

[1] Gregory IX., (1227–1241).

[2] Frederick was excommunicated and anathematized on sixteen different charges, which the Pope carefully enumerated.   All who were bound to him by oath of fealty were declared to be absolved from their allegiance.

for the advancement of the Church's welfare and the increase of the Catholic faith, and affirmed that whatever honors the Church possessed in the Holy Land had been acquired by his toil and **Frederick ac-** industry. "But," said he, "the Pope, jealous at **cuses the Pope** such a happy increase being acquired for the **of ingratitude** **and jealousy** Church by a layman, and who desires gold and silver rather than an increase of the faith (as witness his proceedings), and who extorts money from all Christendom in the name of tithes, has, by all the means in his power, done his best to supplant me, and has endeavored to disinherit me while fighting for God, exposing my body to the weapons of war, to sickness, and to the snares of his enemies, after encountering the dangers of the unsparing billows. See what sort of protection is this of our father's! What kind of assistance in difficulties is this afforded by the vicar of Jesus Christ"! . . .[1]

" Besides, he is united by a detestable alliance with the Saracens,—has ofttimes sent messages and presents to them, and in turn received the same from them with respect and alacrity . . .; and what is a more execrable offense, he, when formerly in the country beyond sea, made a kind of arrangement, or rather collusion, with the sultan, and allowed the name of Mahomet to be publicly proclaimed in the temple of the Lord day and **Further accu-** night; and lately, in the case of the sultan of Baby- **sation of an** lon [Cairo], who, by his own hands, and through his **alliance with** **the Saracens** agents, had done irreparable mischief and injury to the Holy Land and its Christian inhabitants, he caused that sultan's ambassadors, in compliment to their master, as is reported, to be honorably received and nobly entertained in his kingdom of Sicily. He also, in opposition to the Christians, abuses the pernicious and horrid rites of other infidels, and, entering into an alliance of friendship with those who wickedly pay little respect to and despise the Apostolic See, and have

[1] At the Council of Lyons, in 1245, the Emperor was again excommunicated. The ensuing paragraph comprises a portion of Pope Innocent IV.'s denunciation of him upon that occasion.

seceded from the unity of the Church, he, laying aside all respect
for the Christian religion, caused, as is positively asserted, the
duke of Bavaria, of illustrious memory, a special and devoted
ally of the Roman Church, to be murdered by the assassins. He
has also given his daughter in marriage to Battacius, an enemy
of God and the Church, who, together with his aiders, counsel-
lors, and abettors, was solemnly expelled from the communion
of the Christians by sentence of excommunication. Rejecting
the proceedings and customs of Catholic princes, neglecting
his own salvation and the purity of his fame, he does not employ
himself in works of piety; and what is more (to
be silent on his wicked and dissolute practices),
although he has learned to practice oppression to
such a degree, he does not trouble himself to relieve those oppressed by injuries, by extending his hand, as a Christian prince
ought, to bestow alms, although he has been eagerly aiming at
the destruction of the churches, and has crushed religious men
and other ecclesiastical persons with the burden and persecution
of his yoke. And it is not known that he ever built or founded
either churches, monasteries, hospitals, or other pious places.
Now these are not light, but convincing, grounds for suspicions
of heresy being entertained against him." . . .

His neglect of pious and char-itable works

When the Emperor Frederick was made fully aware of all
these proceedings [i.e., his excommunication at Lyons] he could
not contain himself, but burst into a violent rage and, darting a
scowling look on those who sat around him, he thundered forth:
"The Pope in his synod has disgraced me by depriving me of
my crown. Whence arises such great audacity? Whence proceeds such rash presumption? Where are my chests which
contain my treasures?" And on their being
brought and unlocked before him, by his order,
he said, "See if my crowns are lost now;" then
finding one, he placed it on his head and, being thus crowned,
he stood up, and, with threatening eyes and a dreadful voice, un-

Frederick's wrath at his excommuni-cation

restrainable from passion, he said aloud, "I have not yet lost my crown, nor will I be deprived of it by any attacks of the Pope or the council, without a bloody struggle.   Does his vulgar pride raise him to such heights as to enable him to hurl from the imperial dignity me, the chief prince of the world, than whom none is greater—yea, who am without an equal?   In this matter my condition is made better: in some things I *was* bound to obey, at least to respect, him; but now I am released from all ties of affection and veneration, and also from the obligation of any kind of peace with him."   From that time forth, therefore, he, in order to injure the Pope more effectually and perseveringly, did all kinds of harm to his Holiness, in his money, as well as in his friends and relatives.

72. The Golden Bull of Charles IV. (1356)

THE century following the death of Frederick II. (1250) was a period of unrest and turbulence in German history, the net result of which politically was the almost complete triumph of the princes, lay and clerical, over the imperial power.   By 1350 the local magnates had come to be virtually sovereign throughout their own territories.   They enjoyed the right of legislation and the privileges of coining money and levying taxes, and in many cases they had scarcely so much as a feudal bond to remind them of their theoretical allegiance to the Empire.   The one principle of action upon which they could agree was that the central monarchy should be kept permanently in the state of helplessness to which it had been reduced.   The power of choosing a successor when a vacancy arose in the imperial office had fallen gradually into the hands of seven men, who were known as the "electors" and who were recognized in the fourteenth century as possessing collective importance far greater than that of the emperor.   Three of these seven—the archbishops of Mainz, Trier, and Cologne—were great ecclesiastics; the other four—the king of Bohemia, the margrave of Brandenburg, the duke of Saxony, and the count palatine of the Rhine—were equally influential laymen.   This electoral college first came into prominence at the election of Rudolph I. (of the House of Hapsburg) at the end of the Interregnum in 1273.

From that time until the termination of the Holy Roman Empire in 1806 these seven men (eight after 1648 and nine after 1692) played a part in German history not inferior to that of the emperors. They imposed upon their candidates such conditions as they chose, and when the bearer of the imperial title grew restive and difficult to control they did not hesitate to make war upon him, or even in extreme cases to depose him. It has been well said that never in all history have worse scandals been connected with any sort of elections than were associated repeatedly with the actions of these German electors.

The central document in German constitutional history in the Middle Ages is the Golden Bull of Emperor Charles IV. (1347–1378), promulgated in 1356. For a century prior to the reign of Charles the question of the imperial succession had been one of extreme perplexity. The electoral college had grown up to assume the responsibility, but this body rested on no solid legal basis and its acts were usually regarded as null by all whom they displeased, with the result that a civil war succeeded pretty nearly every election. Charles was shrewd enough to see that the existing system could not be set aside; the electors were entirely too powerful to permit of that. But he also saw that it might at least be improved by giving it the quality of legality which it had hitherto lacked. The result of his efforts in this direction was the Golden Bull, issued and confirmed at the diets of Nürnberg (Nuremberg) and Metz in 1356. The document, thenceforth regarded as the fundamental law of the Empire, dealt with a wide variety of subjects. It confirmed the electorship in the person of the king of Bohemia which had long been disputed by a rival branch of the family;[1] it made elaborate provision for the election of the emperor by the seven magnates; it defined the social and political prerogatives of these men and prescribed the relations which they should bear to their subjects, to other princes, and to the emperor; and it made numerous regulations regarding conspiracies, coinage, immunities, the forfeiture of fiefs, the succession of electoral princes, etc. In a word, as Mr. Bryce has put it, the document "confessed and legalized the independence of the Electors and the powerlessness of the crown."[2] Only a few selections from it can be given here, particularly those bearing on the methods of electing the emperor.

[1] Charles IV. was himself king of Bohemia, so that for the present the Emperor was also one of the seven imperial electors.

[2] James Bryce, *The Holy Roman Empire* (new ed., New York, 1904), p. 234.

Source—Text in Wilhelm Altmann und Ernst Bernheim, *Ausgewählte Urkunden zur Erläuterung der Verfassungsgeschichte Deutschlands im Mittelalter* ["Select Documents Illustrative of the Constitutional History of Germany in the Middle Ages"], 3rd ed., Berlin, 1904, pp. 54–83. Adapted from translation in Oliver J. Thatcher and Edgar H. McNeal, *Source Book for Mediæval History* (New York, 1905), pp. 284–295 *passim*.

I. 1. We decree and determine by this imperial edict that, whenever the electoral princes are summoned according to the ancient and praiseworthy custom to meet and elect a king of the Romans and future emperor, each one of them shall be bound **Guarantee of safety of travel for the electors** to furnish on demand an escort and safe-conduct to his fellow electors or their representatives, within his own lands and as much farther as he can, for the journey to and from the city where the election is to be held. Any electoral prince who refuses to furnish escort and safe-conduct shall be liable to the penalties for perjury and to the loss of his electoral vote for that occasion.

2. We decree and command also that all other princes who hold fiefs from the Empire, by whatever title, and all counts, barons, knights, clients, nobles, commoners, citizens, and all corporations of towns, cities, and territories of the Empire, shall furnish escort and safe-conduct for this occasion to every electoral prince or his representatives, on demand, within their own lands and as much farther as they can. Violators of this decree shall be punished as follows: princes, counts, barons, knights, **Penalties for violation of the safe-conduct of the electors** clients, and all others of noble rank, shall suffer the penalties of perjury, and shall lose the fiefs which they hold of the emperor or any other lord, and all their possessions; citizens and corporations shall also suffer the penalty for perjury, shall be deprived of all the rights, liberties, privileges, and graces which they have received from the Empire, and shall incur the ban of the Empire against their persons and property. Those whom we deprive of their rights for this offense may be attacked by any man without appealing to a magistrate, and without danger of reprisal; for they are rebels

against the state and the Empire, and have attacked the honor and security of the prince, and are convicted of faithlessness and perfidy.

3. We also command that the citizens and corporations of cities shall furnish supplies to the electoral princes and their

Supplies for the use of the electors

representatives on demand at the regular price and without fraud, whenever they arrive at, or depart from, the city on their way to or from the election. Those who violate this decree shall suffer the penalties described in the preceding paragraph for citizens and corporations. If any prince, count, baron, knight, client, noble, commoner, citizen, or city shall attack or molest in person or goods any of the electoral princes or their representatives, on their way to or from an election, whether they have safe-conduct or not, he and his accomplices shall incur the penalties above described, according to his position and rank.

16. When the news of the death of the king of the Romans has been received at Mainz, within one month from the date of

The electors to be summoned by the archbishop of Mainz

receiving it the archbishop of Mainz shall send notices of the death and the approaching election to all the electoral princes. But if the archbishop neglects or refuses to send such notices, the electoral princes are commanded on their fidelity to assemble on their own motion and without summons at the city of Frankfort,[1] within three months from the death of the emperor, for the purpose of electing a king of the Romans and future emperor.

17. Each electoral prince or his representatives may bring with him to Frankfort at the time of the election a retinue of 200 horsemen, of whom not more than 50 shall be armed.

---

[1] Frankfort lay on the river Main, a short distance east of Mainz. "It was fixed as the place of election, as a tradition dating from East Frankish days preserved the feeling that both election and coronation ought to take place on Frankish soil."—James Bryce, *The Holy Roman Empire* (new ed., New York, 1904), p. 243.

18. If any electoral prince, duly summoned to the election, fails to come, or to send representatives with credentials containing full authority, or if he (or his representatives) withdraws from the place of the election before the election has been completed, without leaving behind substitutes fully accredited and empowered, he shall lose his vote in that election.

How a vote might be forfeited

II. **2.**[1] "I, archbishop of Mainz, archchancellor of the Empire for Germany,[2] electoral prince, swear on the holy gospels here before me, and by the faith which I owe to God and to the Holy Roman Empire, that with the aid of God, and according to my best judgment and knowledge, I will cast my vote, in this election of the king of the Romans and future emperor, for a person fitted to rule the Christian people. I will give my voice and vote freely, uninfluenced by any agreement, price, bribe, promise, or anything of the sort, by whatever name it may be called. So help me God and all the saints."

The oath taken by the electors

3. After the electors have taken this oath, they shall proceed to the election, and shall not depart from Frankfort until the majority have elected a king of the Romans and future emperor, to be ruler of the world and of the Christian people. If they have not come to a decision within thirty days from the day on which they took the above oath, after that they shall live upon bread and water and shall not leave the city until the election has been decided.

Provision to ensure an election

III. **1.** To prevent any dispute arising between the archbishops of Trier, Mainz, and Cologne, electoral princes of the

---

1 The preceding section specifies that Mass should be celebrated the day following the arrival of the electors at Frankfort, and that the archbishop of Mainz should administer to his six colleagues the oath which he himself has taken, as specified in section 2.

2 The three archbishops were "archchancellors" of the Empire for Germany, Gaul and Burgundy, and Italy respectively. The king of Bohemia was designated as cupbearer, the margrave of Brandenburg as chamberlain, the count palatine as seneschal, and the duke of Saxony as marshal.

Empire, as to their priority and rank in the diet,[1] it has been decided and is hereby decreed, with the advice and consent of all
the electoral princes, ecclesiastical and secular, that the archbishop of Trier shall have the seat directly opposite and facing the
Order of prece- emperor; that the archbishop of Mainz shall have
dence of the
three arch- the seat at the right of the emperor when the diet
bishops is held in the diocese or province of Mainz, or
anywhere in Germany except in the diocese of Cologne; that the
archbishop of Cologne shall have the seat at the right of the
emperor when the diet is held in the diocese or province of
Cologne, or anywhere in Gaul or Italy. This applies to all public
ceremonies—court sessions, conferring of fiefs, banquets, councils, and all occasions on which the princes meet with the emperor for the transaction of imperial business. This order of
seating shall be observed by the successors of the present archbishops of Cologne, Trier, and Mainz, and shall never be questioned.

IV. **1.** In the imperial diet, at the council-board, table, and
all other places where the emperor or king of the Romans meets
with the electoral princes, the seats shall be arranged as follows:
Seating On the right of the emperor, first, the archbishop
arrangement of Mainz, or of Cologne, according to the province
at table in which the meeting is held, as arranged above;
second, the king of Bohemia, because he is a crowned and
anointed prince; third, the count palatine of the Rhine; on the
left of the emperor, first, the archbishop of Cologne, or of Mainz;
second, the duke of Saxony; third, the margrave of Brandenburg.

2. When the imperial throne becomes vacant, the archbishop
of Mainz shall have the authority, which he has had from of old,
to call the other electors together for the election. It shall be
his peculiar right also, when the electors have convened for the

[1] The diet was the Empire's nearest approach to a national assembly. It
was made up of three orders—the electors, the princes, and the representatives of the cities.

election, to collect the votes, asking each of the electors separately in the following order: first, the archbishop of Trier, who
shall have the right to the first vote, as he has had from of old;
The order then the archbishop of Cologne, who has the office
of voting of first placing the crown upon the head of the
king of the Romans; then the king of Bohemia, who has the priority among the secular princes because of his royal title; fourth,
the count palatine of the Rhine; fifth, the duke of Saxony;
sixth, the margrave of Brandenburg. Then the princes shall ask
the archbishop of Mainz in turn to declare his choice and vote.
At the diet, the margrave of Brandenburg shall offer water to
the emperor or king, to wash his hands; the king of Bohemia
shall have the right to offer him the cup first, although, by reason of his royal dignity, he shall not be bound to do this unless
he desires; the count palatine of the Rhine shall offer him food;
and the duke of Saxony shall act as his marshal in the accustomed
manner.

XI. **1.** We decree also that no count, baron, noble, vassal,
burggrave,[1] knight, client, citizen, burgher, or other subject of
the churches of Cologne, Mainz, or Trier, of whatever status,
condition, or rank, shall be cited, haled, or summoned to any
authority before any tribunal outside of the territories, boundaries, and limits of these churches and their dependencies, or
before any judge, except the archbishop and their judges. . . .
We refuse to hear appeals based upon the authority of others
Judicial over the subjects of these princes; if these princes
privileges of are accused by their subjects of injustice, ap-
the electors peal shall lie to the imperial diet, and shall be
confirmed and heard there and nowhere else.
enlarged

2. We extend this right by the present law to the secular
electoral princes, the count palatine of the Rhine, the duke of
Saxony, and the margrave of Brandenburg, and to their heirs,
successors, and subjects forever.

---

[1] An official representative of a king or overlord in a city.

XII. 1. It has been decided in the general diet held at Nürnberg [1] with the electoral princes, ecclesiastical and secular, and
other princes and magnates, by their advice and with their consent, that in the future, the electoral princes shall meet every
The electors to year in some city of the Empire four weeks after
meet annually Easter. This year they are to meet at that date
in the imperial city of Metz.[2]   On that occasion, and on every
meeting thereafter, the place of assembling for the following
year shall be fixed by us, with the advice and consent of the
princes.   This ordinance shall remain in force as long as it shall
be pleasing to us and to the princes; and as long as it is in effect,
we shall furnish the princes with safe-conduct for that assembly,
going, staying, and returning.

[1] Nürnberg (or Nuremberg) is situated in Bavaria, in south central Germany.
[2] Metz lay on the Moselle, above Trier.   Apparently this clause providing
for a regular annual meeting of the electors was inserted by Charles in the
hope that he might be able to make use of the body as an advisory council in
the affairs of the Empire.   The provision remained a dead letter, for the reason that the electors were indifferent to the Emperor's purposes in the matter.

CHAPTER XXV.

THE HUNDRED YEARS' WAR

Our chief contemporary source of information on the history of the Hundred Years' War is Jean Froissart's *Chronicles of England, France, and the Adjoining Countries, from the Latter Part of the Reign of Edward II. to the Coronation of Henry IV.*,[1] and it is from this important work that all of the extracts (except texts of treaties) which are included in this chapter have been selected. Froissart was a French poet and historian, born at Beaumont, near Valenciennes in Hainault, in 1337, when the Hundred Years' War was just beginning. He lived until the early part of the fifteenth century, 1410 being one of the conjectural dates of his death. He was a man of keen mental faculties and had enjoyed the advantages of an unusually thorough education during boyhood. This native ability and training, together with his active public life and admirable opportunities for observation, constituted his special qualification for the writing of a history of his times. Froissart represents a type of mediæval chronicler which was quite rare, in that he was not a monk living in seclusion but a practical man of affairs, accustomed to travel and intercourse with leading men in all the important countries of western Europe. He lived for five years at the English court as clerk of the Queen's Chamber; many times he was sent by the French king on diplomatic missions to Scotland, Italy, and other countries; and he made several private trips to various parts of Europe for the sole purpose of acquiring information. Always and everywhere he was observant and quick to take advantage of opportunities to ascertain facts which he could use, and we are told that after it came to be generally known that he was preparing to write an extended history of his times not a few kings and princes took pains to send him details regarding events which they desired to have recorded. The writing of the *Chronicles* was a life work.

[1] This is the title employed by Thomas Johnes in his translation of the work a hundred years ago. Froissart himself called his book, in the French of his day, *Chroniques de France, d'Engleterre, d'Escoce, de Bretaigne, d'Espaigne, d'Italie, de Flandres et d'Alemaigne.*

When only twenty years of age Froissart submitted to Isabella, wife of King Edward III. of England, an account of the battle of Poitiers, in which the queen's son, the famous Black Prince, had won distinction in the previous year. Thereafter the larger history was published book by book, until by 1373 it was complete to date. Subsequently it was extended to the year 1400 (it had begun with the events of 1326), while the earlier portions were rewritten and considerably revised. And, indeed, when death came to the author he was still working at his arduous but congenial task. "As long as I live," he wrote upon one occasion, "by the grace of God I shall continue it; for the more I follow it and labor thereon, the more it pleases me. Even as a gentle knight or esquire who loves arms, while persevering and continuing develops himself therein, thus do I, laboring and striving with this matter, improve and delight myself."

The *Chronicles* as they have come down to us are written in a lively and pleasing style. It need hardly be said that they are not wholly accurate; indeed, on the whole, they are quite inaccurate, measured even by mediæval standards. Froissart was obliged to rely for a large portion of his information upon older chronicles and especially upon conversations and interviews with people in various parts of Europe. Such sources are never wholly trustworthy and it must be admitted that our author was not as careful to sift error from truth as he should have been. His credulity betrayed him often into accepting what a little investigation would have shown to be false, and only very rarely did he make any attempt, as a modern historian would do, to increase and verify his knowledge by a study of documents. Still, the *Chronicles* constitute an invaluable history of the period they cover. The facts they record, the events they explain, the vivid descriptions they contain, and the side-lights they throw upon the life and manners of an interesting age unite to give them a place of peculiar importance among works of their kind. And, wholly aside from their historical value, they constitute one of the monuments of mediæval French literature.

73. An Occasion of War between the Kings of England and France

THE causes, general and specific, of the Hundred Years' War were numerous. The most important were: (1) The long-standing bad feeling between the French and English regarding the possession of Normandy and Guienne. England had lost the former to France and she had never ceased to hope for its recovery; on the other hand, the French were resolved upon the eventual conquest of the remaining English continental possession of Guienne and were constantly asserting themselves there in a fashion highly irritating to the English; (2) the assistance and general encouragement given the rebellious Scots by the French; (3) the pressure brought to bear upon the English crown by the popular party in Flanders to claim the French throne and to resort to war to obtain it. The Flemish wool trade was a very important item in England's economic prosperity and it was felt to be essential at all hazards to prevent the extension of French influence in Flanders, which would inevitably mean the checking, if not the ruin, of the commercial relations of the Flemish and the English; and (4) the claim to the throne of France which Edward III., king of England, set up and prepared to defend. It is this last occasion of war that Froissart describes in the passage below.

Source—Text in Siméon Luce (ed.), *Chroniques de Jean Froissart* [published for the Société de l'Histoire de France], Paris, 1869, Chap. I. Translated in Thomas Johnes, *Froissart's Chronicles* (London, 1803), Vol. I., pp. 6–7.

History tells us that Philip, king of France, surnamed the Fair,[1] had three sons, besides his beautiful daughter Isabella, married to the king of England.[2] These three sons were very handsome. The eldest, Louis, king of Navarre, during the lifetime of his father, was called Louis Hutin; the second was named Philip the Great, or the Long; and the third, Charles. All these were kings of France, after their father Philip, by legitimate succession, one after the other, without having by marriage any male heirs.[3] Yet on the death of the last king, Charles, the twelve peers and barons of France [4] did not give the kingdom

[1] Philip IV., king of France, 1285–1314.

[2] Isabella was the wife of Edward II., who reigned in England from 1307 until his deposition in 1327.

[3] Louis X. (the Quarrelsome) reigned 1314–1316; Philip V. (the Long), 1316–1322; and Charles IV. (the Fair), 1322–1328. Louis and Charles were very weak kings, though Philip was vigorous and able.

[4] The French Court of Twelve Peers did not constitute a distinct organization, but was merely a high rank of baronage. In the earlier Middle Ages,

to Isabella, the sister, who was queen of England, because they
said and maintained, and still insist, that the kingdom of

**The succession
to the French
throne in 1328**

France is so noble that it ought not to go to a
woman; consequently neither to Isabella nor to
her son, the king of England; for they held that
the son of a woman cannot claim any right of succession where
that woman has none herself.[1] For these reasons the twelve
peers and barons of France unanimously gave the kingdom of
France to the lord Philip of Valois, nephew of King Philip,[2] and
thus put aside the queen of England (who was sister to Charles,
the late king of France) and her son. Thus, as it seemed to
many people, the succession went out of the right line, which has
been the occasion of the most destructive wars and devastations
of countries, as well in France as elsewhere, as you will learn

the number of peers was generally twelve, including the most powerful lay
vassals of the king and certain influential prelates. In later times the number was frequently increased by the creation of peers by the crown.

[1] In 1317, after the accession of Philip IV., an assembly of French magnates (such as that which disposed of the crown in 1328) laid down the
general rule that no woman should succeed to the throne of France. This
rule has come to be known as the Salic Law of France, though it has no
historical connection with the law of the Salian Franks against female inheritance of property, with which older writers have generally confused it
[see p. 67, note 1].   The rule of 1317 was based purely on grounds of political
expediency. It was announced at this particular time because the death of
Louis X. had left France without a male heir to the throne for the first time
since Hugh Capet's day and the barons thought it not best for the realm that
a woman reign over it.   Between 1316 and 1328 daughters of kings were
excluded from the succession three times, and though in 1328, when Charles
IV. died, there had been no farther legislation on the subject, the principle of
the misnamed Salic Law had become firmly established in practice.   In
1328, however, when the barons selected Philip of Valois to be regent first
and then king, they went a step farther and declared not only that no
woman should be allowed to inherit the throne of France but that the inheritance could not pass through a woman to her son; in other words, she
could not transmit to her descendants a right which she did not herself
possess. This was intended to cover any future case such as that of Edward
III.'s claim to inherit through his mother Isabella, daughter of Philip IV.
The action of the barons was supported by public opinion in practically all
France—especially since it appeared that only through this expedient could
the realm be saved from the domination of an alien sovereign.

[2] Philip of Valois was a son of Charles of Valois, who was a brother of
Philip IV. The line of direct Capetian descent was now replaced by the
branch line of the Valois.   The latter occupied the French throne until the
death of Henry III. in 1589.

hereafter; the real object of this history being to relate the great enterprises and deeds of arms achieved in these wars, for from the time of good Charlemagne, king of France, never were such feats performed.

74. Edward III. Assumes the Arms and Title of the King of France

Due to causes which have been mentioned, the relations of England and France at the accession of Philip VI. in 1328 were so strained that only a slight fanning of the flames was necessary to bring on an open conflict. Edward III.'s persistent demand to be recognized as king of France sufficed to accomplish this result. The war did not come at once, for neither king felt himself ready for it; but it was inevitable and preparations for it were steadily pushed on both sides from 1328 until its formal declaration by Edward nine years later. These preparations were not merely military and naval but also diplomatic. The primary object of both sovereigns was to secure as many and as strong foreign alliances as possible. In pursuit of this policy Philip soon assured himself of the support of Louis de Nevers, count of Flanders, King John of Bohemia, Alphonso XI. of Castile, and a number of lesser princes of the north. Edward was even more successful. In Spain and the Scandinavian countries many local powers allied themselves with him; in the Low Countries, especially Flanders and Brabant, the people and the princes chose generally to identify themselves with his cause; and the climax came in July, 1337, when a treaty of alliance was concluded with the Emperor, Louis of Bavaria. War was begun in this same year, and in 1338 Edward went himself to the continent to undertake a direct attack on France from Flanders as a base. The years 1338 and 1339 were consumed with ineffective operations against the walled cities of the French frontier, Philip steadily refusing to be drawn into an open battle such as Edward desired. The following year the English king resolved to declare himself sovereign of France. The circumstances attending this important step are detailed in the passage from Froissart given below.

Heretofore Edward had merely protested that by reason of his being a grandson of Philip the Fair he should have been awarded the throne by the French barons in 1328; now, at the instigation of his German and Flemish allies, he flatly announces that he *is* of right the king and that Philip VI. is to be deposed as an usurper. Of course this was a declaration which Edward could make good only by victory in the war upon which he had entered. But the claim thus set up rendered it inevitable that the war should be waged to the bitter end on both sides.

Source--*Chroniques de Jean Froissart* (Société de l'Histoire de France edition), Chap. XXXI. Translated in Thomas Johnes, *Froissart's Chronicles*, Vol. I., pp. 110–112.

When King Edward had departed from Flanders and arrived at Brabant he set out straight for Brussels, whither he was attended by the duke of Gueldres, the duke of Juliers, the marquis of Blanckenburg, the earl of Mons, the lord John of Hainault, the **The conference at Brussels** lord of Fauquemont, and all the barons of the Empire who were allied to him, as they wished to consider what was next to be done in this war which they had begun. For greater expedition, they ordered a conference to be held in the city of Brussels, and invited James van Arteveld[1] to attend it, who came thither in great array, and brought with him all the councils from the principal towns of Flanders.

At this parliament the king of England was advised by his allies of the Empire to solicit the Flemings to give him their aid and assistance in this war, to challenge the king of France, and to follow King Edward wherever he should lead them, and in return he would assist them in the recovery of Lisle, Douay, and Bethune.[2] The Flemings heard this proposal with pleasure; but they requested of the king that they might consider it among themselves and in a short time they would give their answer.

The king consented and soon after they made this reply:

[1] James van Arteveld, a brewer of Ghent, was the leader of the popular party in Flanders—the party which hated French influence, which had expelled the count of Flanders on account of his services to Philip VI., and which was the most valuable English ally on the continent. Arteveld was murdered in 1345 during the civil discord which prevailed in Flanders throughout the earlier part of the Hundred Years' War.

[2] These were towns situated near the Franco-Flemish frontier. They had been lost by Flanders to France and assistance in their recovery was rightly considered by the German advisers of Edward as likely to be more tempting to the Flemish than any other offer he could make them.

"Beloved sire, you formerly made us a similar request; and we are willing to do everything in reason for you without prejudice to our honor and faith.   But we are pledged by promise on oath, under a penalty of two millions of florins, to the apostolical **Proposition** chamber,[1] not to act offensively against the king **made by the** of France in any way, whoever he may be, with- **Flemings to** **King Edward** out forfeiting this sum, and incurring the sentence of excommunication.   But if you will do what we will tell you, you will find a remedy, which is, that you take the arms of France, quarter them with those of England, and call yourself king of France.   We will acknowledge your title as good, and we will demand of you quittance for the above sum, which you will grant us as king of France.   Thus we shall be absolved and at liberty to go with you wherever it pleases you."

The king summoned his council, for he was loath to take the title and arms of France, seeing that at present he had not con- quered any part of that kingdom and that it was uncertain whether he ever should.   On the other hand, he was unwilling to lose the aid and assistance of the Flemings, who could be of greater service to him than any others at that period.   He consulted, therefore, with the lords of the Empire, the lord Robert d'Artois,[2] and his most privy councilors, who, after having duly weighed the good and bad, advised him to make for answer to the Flem- **The agreement** ings, that if they would bind themselves under **concluded** their seals, to an agreement to aid him in carry- ing on the war, he would willingly comply with their conditions, and would swear to assist them in the recovery of Lisle, Douay, and Bethune.   To this they willingly consented.   A day was fixed for them to meet at Ghent,[3] where the king and the greater

[1] That is, the papal court.
[2] Robert of Artois was a prince who had not a little to do with the outbreak of the Hundred Years' War.   After having lost a suit for the inheritance of the county of Artois (the region about the Somme River) and having been proved guilty of fabricating documents to support his claims, he had fled to England and there as an exile had employed every resource to influence Edward to claim the French throne and to go to war to secure it.
[3] In northeastern Flanders.

part of the lords of the Empire, and in general the councils from the different towns in Flanders, assembled. The above-mentioned proposals and answers were then repeated, sworn to, and sealed; and the king of England bore the arms of France, quartering them with those of England. He also took the title of king of France from that day forward.

75. The Naval Battle of Sluys (1340)

IN the spring of 1340 Edward returned to England to secure money and supplies with which to prosecute the war. The French king thought he saw in this temporary withdrawal of his enemy an opportunity to strike him a deadly blow. A fleet of nearly two hundred vessels was gathered in the harbor of Sluys, on the Flemish coast, with a view to attacking the English king on his return to the continent and preventing him from again securing a foothold in Flanders. Edward, however, accepted the situation and made ready to fight his way back to the country of his allies. June 24, 1340, he boldly attacked the French at Sluys. The sharp conflict which ensued resulted in a brilliant victory for the English. Philip's fleet found itself shut up in the harbor and utterly unable to withstand the showers of arrows shot by the thousands of archers who crowded the English ships. The French navy was annihilated, England was relieved from the fear of invasion, and the whole French coast was laid open to attack.

Source—*Chroniques de Jean Froissart* (Société de l'Histoire de France edition), Chap. XXXVII. Translated in Thomas Johnes, *Froissart's Chronicles*, Vol. I., pp. 141–143.

He [King Edward] and his whole navy sailed from the Thames the day before the eve of St. John the Baptist, 1340,[1] and made straight for Sluys.

Sir Hugh Quiriel, Sir Peter Bahucet, and Barbenoir, were at that time lying between Blankenburg and Sluys with upwards of one hundred and twenty large vessels, without counting others. These were manned with about forty thousand men,

[1] That is, June 23. The English fleet was composed of two hundred and fifty vessels, carrying 11,000 archers and 4,000 men-at-arms.

Genoese and Picards, including mariners. By the orders of the king of France, they were there at anchor, awaiting the return of the king of England, to dispute his passage.

When the king's fleet had almost reached Sluys, they saw so many masts standing before it that they looked like a wood. The king asked the commander of his ship what they could be. The latter replied that he imagined they must be that armament of Normans which the king of France kept at sea, and which had so frequently done him much damage, had burned his good town of Southampton and taken his large ship

Edward determines to fight at Sluys
the *Christopher*. The king replied, "I have for a long time desired to meet them, and now, please God and St. George, we will fight with them; for, in truth, they have done me so much mischief that I will be revenged on them if it be possible."

The king then drew up all his vessels, placing the strongest in front, and his archers on the wings. Between every two vessels with archers there was one of men-at-arms. He stationed some detached vessels as a reserve, full of archers, to assist and help such as might be damaged. There were in this fleet a great many ladies from England, countesses, baronesses, and knights' and gentlemen's wives, who were going to attend on the queen at Ghent.[1] These the king had guarded most carefully by three hundred men-at-arms and five hundred archers.

When the king of England and his marshals had properly divided the fleet, they hoisted their sails to have the wind on their quarter, as the sun shone full in their faces (which they considered might be of disadvantage to them) and stretched out a little, so that at last they got the wind as they wished. The Normans, who saw them tack, could not help wondering why they

The French make ready
did so, and remarked that they took good care to turn about because they were afraid of meddling with them. They perceived, however, by his banner, that the king

[1] Edward III.'s queen was Philippa, daughter of the count of Hainault.

was on board, which gave them great joy, as they were eager to fight with him. So they put their vessels in proper order, for they were expert and gallant men on the seas. They filled the *Christopher*, the large ship which they had taken the year before from the English, with trumpets and other warlike instruments, and ordered her to fall upon the English.

The battle then began very fiercely. Archers and crossbowmen shot with all their might at each other, and the men-at-arms engaged hand to hand. In order to be more successful, they had large grapnels and iron hooks with chains, which they flung from ship to ship to moor them to each other. There were many valiant deeds performed, many prisoners made, and many rescues. The *Christopher*, which led the van, was recaptured by the English, and all in her taken or killed. There were then great shouts and cries, and the English manned her again with archers, and sent her to fight against the Genoese.

The battle rages

This battle was very murderous and horrible. Combats at sea are more destructive and obstinate than upon land, for it is not possible to retreat or flee—every one must abide his fortune, and exert his prowess and valor. Sir Hugh Quiriel and his companions were bold and determined men; they had done much mischief to the English at sea and destroyed many of their ships. The combat, therefore, lasted from early in the morning until noon,[1] and the English were hard pressed, for their enemies were four to one, and the greater part men who had been used to the sea.

The king, who was in the flower of his youth, showed himself on that day a gallant knight, as did the earls of Derby, Pembroke, Hereford, Huntingdon, Northampton, and Gloucester; the lord Reginald Cobham, lord Felton, lord Bradestan, sir Richard Stafford, the lord Percy, sir Walter Manny, sir Henry de Flanders, sir John Beauchamp, sir John Chandos, the lord

---

[1] In reality, until five o'clock in the evening, or about nine hours in all.

Delaware, Lucie lord Malton, and the lord Robert d'Artois, now called earl of Richmond. I cannot remember the names of **The English** all those who behaved so valiantly in the combat. **triumph** But they did so well that, with some assistance from Bruges and those parts of the country, the French were completely defeated, and all the Normans and the others were killed or drowned, so that not one of them escaped.[1]

After the king had gained this victory, which was on the eve of St. John's day,[2] he remained all that night on board his ship before Sluys, and there were great noises with trumpets and all kinds of other instruments.

76. The Battle of Crécy (1346)

IN July, 1346, Edward III. landed on the northwest coast of Normandy with a splendid army of English, Irish, and Welsh, including ten thousand men skilled in the use of the long bow. He advanced eastward, plundering and devastating as he went, probably with the ultimate intention of besieging Calais. Finding the passage of the Seine impossible at Rouen, he ascended the river until he came into the vicinity of Paris, only to learn that Philip with an army twice the size of that of the English had taken up a position on the Seine to turn back the invasion. The French king allowed himself to be outwitted, however, and Edward got out of the trap into which he had fallen by marching northward to the village of Crécy in Ponthieu. With an army that had grown to outnumber the English three to one Philip advanced in the path of the enemy, first to Abbeville on the Somme, and later to Crécy, slightly to the east of which Edward had taken his stand for battle. The English arrived at Crécy about noon on Friday, August 25. The French were nearly a day behind, having spent the night at Abbeville and set out thence over the roads to Crécy before sunrise Saturday morning. The

---

[1] The tide of battle was finally turned in favor of the English by the arrival of reinforcements in the shape of a squadron of Flemish vessels. The contest was not so one-sided or the French defeat so complete as Froissart represents, yet it was decisive enough, as is indicated by the fact that only thirty of the French ships survived and 20,000 French and Genoese were slain or taken prisoners, as against an English loss of about 10,000.

[2] June 24, 1340.

army of the English numbered probably about 14,000, besides an uncertain reserve of Welsh and Irish troops; that of the French numbered about 70,000, including 15,000 Genoese cross-bowmen. The course of the battle is well described by Froissart in the passage below. Doubtless the account is not accurate in every particular, yet it must be correct in the main and it shows very vividly the character of French and English warfare in this period. Despite the superior numbers of the French, the English had small difficulty in winning a decisive victory. This was due to several things. In the first place, the French army was a typical feudal levy and as such was sadly lacking in discipline and order, while the English troops were under perfect control. In the next place, the use of the long-bow gave the English infantry a great advantage over the French knights, and even over the Genoese mercenaries, who could shoot just once while an English long-bowman was shooting twelve times. In the third place, Philip's troops were exhausted before entering the battle and it was a grievous error on the part of the king to allow the conflict to begin before his men had an opportunity for rest.[1] The greatest significance of the English victory lay in the blow it struck at feudalism, and especially the feudal type of warfare. It showed very clearly that the armored knight was no match for the common foot-soldier, armed simply with his long-bow, and that feudal methods and ideals had come to be inconsistent with success in war.

Source—*Chroniques de Jean Froissart* (Société de l'Histoire de France edition), Chap. LX. Translated in Thomas Johnes, *Froissart's Chronicles*, Vol. I., pp. 320–329 *passim*.

The king of England, as I have mentioned before, encamped this Friday in the plain,[2] for he found the country abounding in provisions; but if they should have failed, he had an abundance in the carriages which attended him. The army set about furbishing and repairing their armor; and the king gave a supper that

---

[1] As appears from Froissart's account (see p. 431), the king, on the advice of some of his knights, decided at one time to postpone the attack until the following day; but, the army falling into hopeless confusion and coming up unintentionally within sight of the English, he recklessly gave the order to advance to immediate combat. Perhaps, however, it is only fair to place the blame upon the system which made the army so unmanageable, rather than upon the king personally.

[2] That is, the plain east of the village of Crécy.

evening to the earls and barons of his army, where they made good cheer. On their taking leave, the king remained alone with the lord of his bed-chamber. He retired into his oratory and, falling on his knees before the altar, prayed to God, that if he should fight his enemies on the morrow he might come off with honor. About midnight he went to his bed and, rising early the next day, he and the Prince of Wales [1] heard Mass and communicated. The greater part of his army did the same, confessed, and made proper preparations.

After Mass the king ordered his men to arm themselves and assemble on the ground he had before fixed on. He had enclosed a large park near a wood, on the rear of his army, in which he placed all his baggage-wagons and horses; and this park had but one entrance. His men-at-arms and archers remained on foot. The king afterwards ordered, through his constable and his two marshals, that the army should be divided into three battalions. . . .

The English prepare for battle

The king then mounted a small palfrey, having a white wand in his hand and, attended by his two marshals on each side of him, he rode through all the ranks, encouraging and entreating the army, that they should guard his honor. He spoke this so gently, and with such a cheerful countenance, that a l who had been dejected were immediately comforted by seeing and hearing him.

When he had thus visited all the battalions, it was near ten o'clock. He retired to his own division and ordered them all to eat heartily afterwards and drink a glass. They ate and drank at their ease; and, having packed up pots, barrels, etc., in the carts, they returned to their battalions, according to the marshals' orders, and seated themselves on the ground, placing their helmets and bows before them, that they might be the fresher when their enemies should arrive.

[1] The king's eldest son, Edward, generally known as the Black Prince.

That same Saturday, the king of France arose betimes and heard Mass in the monastery of St. Peter's in Abbeville,[1] where he was lodged. Having ordered his army to do the same, he left that town after sunrise. When he had marched about two leagues from Abbeville and was approaching the enemy, he was advised to form his army in order of battle, and to let those on foot march forward, that they might not be trampled on by the horses. The king, upon this, sent off four knights—the lord

The French advance from Abbeville to Crécy   Moyne of Bastleberg, the lord of Noyers, the lord of Beaujeu, and the lord of Aubigny—who rode so near to the English that they could clearly distinguish their position. The English plainly perceived that they were come to reconnoitre. However, they took no notice of it, but suffered them to return unmolested. When the king of France saw them coming back, he halted his army, and the knights, pushing through the crowds, came near the king, who said to them, "My lords, what news?" They looked at each other, without opening their mouths; for no one chose to speak first. At last the king addressed himself to the lord Moyne, who was attached to the king of Bohemia, and had performed very many gallant deeds, so that he was esteemed one of the most valiant knights in Christendom. The lord Moyne said, "Sir, I will speak, since it pleases you to order me, but with the assistance of my companions. We have advanced far enough to reconnoitre your enemies. Know, then, that they are drawn up in three battalions and are awaiting you. I would advise, for my part (submitting, however, to better counsel), that you halt your army here and quarter them for the night; for before the rear shall come up and the army be properly drawn out, it

Philip's knights advise delay   will be very late. Your men will be tired and in disorder, while they will find your enemies fresh and properly arrayed. On the morrow, you may draw up your army more at your ease and may reconnoitre at

---

[1] Abbeville was on the Somme about fifteen miles south of Crécy.

leisure on what part it will be most advantageous to begin the attack; for, be assured, they will wait for you."

The king commanded that it should be so done; and the two marshals rode, one towards the front, and the other to the rear, crying out, "Halt banners, in the name of God and St. Denis." Those that were in the front halted; but those behind said they would not halt until they were as far forward as the front. When the front perceived the rear pushing on, they pushed forward; and neither the king nor the marshals could stop them, **Confusion in the French ranks** but they marched on without any order until they came in sight of their enemies.[1] As soon as the foremost rank saw them, they fell back at once in great disorder, which alarmed those in the rear, who thought they had been fighting. There was then space and room enough for them to have passed forward, had they been willing to do so. Some did so, but others remained behind.

All the roads between Abbeville and Crécy were covered with common people, who, when they had come within three leagues of their enemies, drew their swords, crying out, "Kill, kill;" and with them were many great lords who were eager to make show of their courage. There is no man, unless he had been present, who can imagine, or describe truly, the confusion of that day; especially the bad management and disorder of the French, whose troops were beyond number.

The English, who were drawn up in three divisions and seated on the ground, on seeing their enemies advance, arose boldly **The English prepare for battle** and fell into their ranks. That of the prince[2] was the first to do so, whose archers were formed in the manner of a portcullis, or harrow, and the men-at-arms in the rear. The earls of Northampton and Arundel, who commanded the second division, had posted them-

---

[1] This incident very well illustrates the confusion and lack of discipline prevailing in a typical feudal army.

[2] Edward, the Black Prince, eldest son of the English king.

selves in good order on his wing to assist and succor the prince, if necessary.

You must know that these kings, dukes, earls, barons, and lords of France did not advance in any regular order, but one after the other, or in any way most pleasing to themselves. As soon as the king of France came in sight of the English his blood began to boil, and he cried out to his marshals, "Order the Genoese forward, and begin the battle, in the name of God and St. Denis."

There were about fifteen thousand Genoese cross-bowmen; but they were quite fatigued, having marched on foot that day six leagues, completely armed, and with their cross-bows. They told the constable that they were not in a fit condition to do any great things that day in battle. The earl of Alençon, hearing this, said, "This is what one gets by employing such scoundrels, who fail when there is any need for them."

During this time a heavy rain fell, accompanied by thunder and a very terrible eclipse of the sun; and before this rain a great flight of crows hovered in the air over all those battalions, making a loud noise. Shortly afterwards it cleared up and the sun shone very brightly; but the Frenchmen had it in their faces, and the English at their backs.

When the Genoese were somewhat in order they approached the English and set up a loud shout in order to frighten them; but the latter remained quite still and did not seem to hear it. They then set up a second shout and advanced a little forward; but the English did not move. They hooted a third time, advancing with their cross-bows presented, and began to shoot. The English archers then advanced one step forward and shot their arrows with such force and quickness that it seemed as if it snowed.

When the Genoese felt these arrows, which pierced their arms, heads, and through their armor, some of them cut the strings of their cross-bows, others flung them on the ground, and all turned about and retreated, quite discomfited. The French had a large body of men-at-arms on horseback, richly dressed, to

The Genoese mercenaries repulsed

support the Genoese. The king of France, seeing them thus fall back, cried out, "Kill me those scoundrels; for they stop up our road, without any reason." You would then have seen the above-mentioned men-at-arms lay about them, killing all that they could of these runaways.

The English continued shooting as vigorously and quickly as before. Some of their arrows fell among the horsemen, who were sumptuously equipped and, killing and wounding many, made them caper and fall among the Genoese, so that they were in such confusion they could never rally again. In the English army there were some Cornish and Welshmen on foot who had

Slaughter by the Cornish and Welsh

armed themselves with large knives. These, advancing through the ranks of the men-at-arms and archers, who made way for them, came upon the French when they were in this danger and, falling upon earls, barons, knights and squires, slew many, at which the king of England was afterwards much exasperated.

The valiant king of Bohemia was slain there. He was called Charles of Luxemburg, for he was the son of the gallant king and emperor, Henry of Luxemburg.[1]   Having heard the order of the battle, he inquired where his son, the lord Charles, was. His attendants answered that they did not know, but believed that he was fighting. The king said to them: "Sirs, you are all my people, my friends and brethren at arms this day; therefore, as I am blind, I request of you to lead me so far into the engagement that I may strike one stroke with my sword." The

Death of the king of Bohemia

knights replied that they would lead him forward immediately; and, in order that they might not lose him in the crowd, they fastened the reins of all their horses together, and put the king at their head,

[1] The Emperor Henry VII., 1308–1314.

that he might gratify his wish, and advanced towards the enemy. The king rode in among the enemy, and made good use of his sword; for he and his companions fought most gallantly They advanced so far that they were all slain; and on the morrow they were found on the ground, with their horses all tied together.

Early in the day, some French, Germans, and Savoyards had broken through the archers of the prince's battalion, and had engaged with the men-at-arms, upon which the second battalion came to his aid; and it was time, for otherwise he would have been hard pressed. The first division, seeing the danger they were in, sent a knight [1] in great haste to the king of England, who was posted upon an eminence, near a windmill. On the knight's arrival, he said, "Sir, the earl of Warwick, the lord Stafford, the lord Reginald Cobham, and the others who are about your son are vigorously attacked by the French; and they entreat that you come to their assistance with your battalion for, if the number of the French should increase, they fear he will have too much to do."

The king replied: "Is my son dead, unhorsed, or so badly wounded that he cannot support himself?" "Nothing of the sort, thank God," rejoined the knight; "but he is in so hot an engagement that he has great need of your help." The king

Edward gives the Black Prince a chance to win his spurs answered, "Now, Sir Thomas, return to those who sent you and tell them from me not to send again for me this day, or expect that I shall come, let what will happen, as long as my son has life; and say that I command them to let the boy win his spurs; for I am determined, if it please God, that all the glory and honor of this day shall be given to him, and to those into whose care I have entrusted him." The knight returned to his lords and related the king's answer, which greatly encouraged them and made them regret that they had ever sent such a message.

Late after vespers, the king of France had not more about him

---

[1] Sir Thomas Norwich.

than sixty men, every one included. Sir John of Hainault, who was of the number, had once remounted the king; for the latter's horse had been killed under him by an arrow. He said to the king, "Sir, retreat while you have an opportunity, and do not expose

King Philip abandons the field of battle yourself so needlessly. If you have lost this battle, another time you will be the conqueror." After he had said this, he took the bridle of the king's horse and led him off by force; for he had before entreated him to retire.

The king rode on until he came to the castle of La Broyes, where he found the gates shut, for it was very dark. The king ordered the governor of it to be summoned. He came upon the battlements and asked who it was that called at such an hour. The king answered, "Open, open, governor; it is the fortune of France." The governor, hearing the king's voice, immediately descended, opened the gate, and let down the bridge. The king and his company entered the castle; but he had with him only five barons—Sir John of Hainault, the lord Charles of Montmorency, the lord of Beaujeu, the lord of Aubigny, and the lord of Montfort. The king would not bury himself in such a place as that, but, having taken some refreshments, set out again with his attendants about midnight, and rode on, under the direction of guides who were well acquainted with the country, until, about daybreak, he came to Amiens, where he halted.

This Saturday the English never quitted their ranks in pursuit of any one, but remained on the field, guarding their position and defending themselves against all who attacked them. The battle was ended at the hour of vespers. When, on this Saturday night, the English heard no more hooting or shouting, nor any more crying out to particular lords, or their banners, they looked upon the field as their own and their enemies as beaten.

The English after the battle

They made great fires and lighted torches because of the darkness of the night. King Edward then came down from his post, who all that day had not put on his helmet, and, with his whole battalion, advanced to the Prince of Wales, whom he embraced in his arms and kissed, and said, "Sweet son, God give you good preference. You are my son, for most loyally have you acquitted yourself this day. You are worthy to be a sovereign." The prince bowed down very low and humbled himself, giving all honor to the king his father.

The English, during the night, made frequent thanksgivings to the Lord for the happy outcome of the day, and without rioting; for the king had forbidden all riot or noise.

77. The Sack of Limoges (1370)

As a single illustration of the devastation wrought by the Hundred Years' War, and of the barbarity of the commanders and troops engaged in it, Froissart's well-known description of the sack of Limoges in 1370 by the army of the Black Prince is of no small interest. In some respects, of course, circumstances in connection with this episode were exceptional, and we are not to imagine that such heartless and indiscriminate massacres were common. Yet the evidence which has survived all goes to show that the long course of the war was filled with cruelty and destruction in a measure almost inconceivable among civilized peoples in more modern times.

Source—*Chroniques de Jean Froissart* (Société de l'Histoire de France edition), Chap. XCVII. Translated in Thomas Johnes, *Froissart's Chronicles*, Vol. II., pp. 61–68 *passim*.

When word was brought to the prince that the city of Limoges [1] had become French, that the bishop, who had been his companion and one in whom he had formerly placed great confi-

---

[1] Limoges, besieged by the duke of Berry and the great French general, Bertrand du Guesclin, had just been forced to surrender. It was a very important town and its capture was the occasion of much elation among the French. Treaties were entered into between the duke of Berry on the one hand and the bishop and citizens of Limoges on the other, whereby the inhabitants recognized the sovereignty of the French king. It was the news of this surrender that so angered the Black Prince.

dence, was a party to all the treaties and had greatly aided and assisted in the surrender, he was in a violent passion and held **The Black Prince re-solves to re-take Limoges** the bishop and all other churchmen in very low estimation, in whom formerly he had put great trust. He swore by the soul of his father, which he had never perjured, that he would have it back again, that he would not attend to anything before he had done this, and that he would make the inhabitants pay dearly for their treach-ery. . . .[1]

All these men-at-arms were drawn out in battle-array and took the field, when the whole country began to tremble for the consequences. At that time the Prince of Wales was not able to mount his horse, but was, for his greater ease, carried in a litter. They followed the road to the Limousin,[2] in order to get to Limoges, where in due time they arrived and encamped all around it. The prince swore he would never leave the place until he had regained it.

The bishop of the place and the inhabitants found that they had acted wickedly and had greatly incensed the prince, for which they were very repentant, but that was now of no avail, as they were not the masters of the town.[3] When the prince and his marshals had well considered the strength and force of Limoges, and knew the number of people that were in it, they agreed that **The town to be undermined** they could never take it by assault, but said they would attempt it by another manner. The prince was always accustomed to carry with him on his expeditions a large body of miners. These were immediately set to work and made great progress. The knights who were in the town soon

---

[1] A force of 3,200 men was led by the Black Prince from the town of Cognac to undertake the siege of Limoges. Froissart here enumerates a large number of notable knights who went with the expedition.

[2] The Limousin was a district in south central France, southeast of Poitou.

[3] Limoges was now in the hands of three commanders representing the French king. Their names were John de Villemur, Hugh de la Roche, and Roger de Beaufort.

perceived that they were undermining them, and on that account began to countermine to prevent the effect. . . .

The Prince of Wales remained about a month, and not more, before the city of Limoges. He would not allow any assaults or skirmishing, but kept his miners steadily at work. The knights in the town perceived what they were about and made countermines to destroy them, but they failed in their attempt. When the miners of the prince (who, as they found themselves countermined, kept changing the line of direction of their own mine) had finished their business, they came to the prince and said, "My lord, we are ready, and will throw down, whenever it pleases you, a very large part of the wall into the ditch, through the breach of which you may enter the town at your ease and without danger."

This news was very agreeable to the prince, who replied: "I desire, then, that you prove your words to-morrow morning at six o'clock." The miners set fire to the combustibles in the mine, and on the morrow morning, as they had foretold the **The English** prince, they flung down a great piece of wall which **assault** filled the ditches. The English saw this with pleasure, for they were armed and prepared to enter the town. Those on foot did so and ran to the gate, which they destroyed, as well as the barriers, for there were no other defenses; and all this was done so suddenly that the inhabitants had not time to prevent it.

The prince, the duke of Lancaster, the earls of Cambridge and of Pembroke, sir Guiscard d'Angle and the others, with their men, rushed into the town. You would then have seen pillagers, active to do mischief, running through the town, slaying men, women, and children, according to their orders. It was a most melancholy business; for all ranks, ages, and sexes cast themselves on their knees before the prince, begging for mercy; but he was so inflamed with passion and revenge that he listened to none. But all were put to the sword, wherever they could be found, even those who were not guilty. For I know not why the poor were not spared, who could not have had any **Barbarity of the sack** part in the treason; but they suffered for it, and indeed more than those who had been the leaders of the treachery.

There was not that day in the city of Limoges any heart so hardened, or that had any sense of religion, that did not deeply bewail the unfortunate events passing before men's eyes; for upwards of three thousand men, women, and children were put to death that day. God have mercy on their souls, for they were truly martyrs. . . . The entire town was pillaged, burned, and totally destroyed. The English then departed, carrying with them their booty and prisoners.

78. The Treaties of Bretigny (1360) and Troyes (1420)

THE most important documents in the diplomatic history of the Hundred Years' War are the texts of the treaty of London (1359), the treaty of Bretigny (1360), the truce of Paris (1396), the treaty of Troyes (1420), the treaty of Arras (1435), and the truce of Tours (1444). Brief extracts from two of these are given below. The treaty of Bretigny was negotiated soon after the refusal of the French to ratify the treaty of London. In November, 1359, King Edward III., with his son, Edward, the Black Prince, and the duke of Lancaster, crossed the Channel, marched on Rheims, and threatened Paris. Negotiations for a new peace were actively opened in April, 1360, after the English had established themselves at Montlhéri, south from Paris. The French king, John II., who had been taken prisoner at Poitiers (1356), gave full powers of negotiation to his son Charles, duke of Normandy and regent of the kingdom. For some time no definite conclusions were reached, owing chiefly to Edward's unwillingness to renounce his claim to the French throne. Late in April the negotiations were transferred to Chartres, subsequently to Bretigny. Finally, on the eighth of May, representatives of the two parties signed the so-called treaty of Bretigny. Although the instrument was promptly ratified by the French regent and by the Black Prince (and, if we may believe Froissart, by the two kings themselves), it was afterwards revised and accepted in a somewhat different form by the monarchs and their following assembled at Calais (October 24, 1360). The most important respect in which the second document differed from the first was the omission of Article 12 of the first treaty, in which Edward renounced his claim to the throne of France and the sovereignty of Normandy, Maine, Anjou, Touraine, Brittany, and Flanders; nevertheless Edward, at Calais, made this renunciation in a separate convention, which for all practical purposes was regarded as a part of the treaty. The passages printed below are taken from the Calais text. Most of the thirty-nine articles composing the document are devoted to mere details. The war was renewed after a few years, and within two decades the English had lost all the territory guaranteed to them in 1360, except a few coast towns.

The treaty of Troyes (1420) belongs to one of the most stormy periods in all French history. The first two decades of the fifteenth century were marked by a cessation of the war with England (until its renewal in 1415), but also unfortunately by the outbreak of a desperate civil struggle between two great factions of the French people, the Burgundians and the Armagnacs. The Burgundians, led by Philip the Bold and John the Fearless (successive dukes of Burgundy), stood for a policy of friendship with England, while the Armagnacs, comprising the adherents of Charles, duke of Orleans, whose wife was a daughter of the count of Armagnac, advocated the continuation of the war with the English; though, in reality, the forces which kept the two factions apart were jealousy and ambition rather than any mere question of foreign relations. The way was prepared for a temporary Burgundian triumph by the notable victory of the English at Agincourt in 1415 and by the assassination of John the Fearless at Paris in 1419, which made peace impossible and drove the Burgundians openly into the arms of the English. Philip the Good, the new duke of Burgundy, became the avowed ally of the English king Henry V., who since 1417 had been slowly but surely conquering Normandy and now had the larger portion of it in his possession. Philip recognized Henry as the true heir to the French throne and in 1419 concluded with him two distinct treaties on that basis. Charles VI., the reigning king of France, was mentally unbalanced and the queen, who bitterly hated the Armagnacs (with whom her son, the Dauphin Charles, was actively identified), was easily persuaded by

Duke Philip to acquiesce in a treaty by which the succession should be vested in the English king upon the death of Charles VI. The result was the treaty of Troyes, signed May 21, 1420. According to agreements already entered into by Philip and Henry, the latter was to marry Catherine, daughter of Charles VI. (the marriage was not mentioned in the treaty of Troyes, but it was clearly assumed), and he was to act as regent of France until Charles VI.'s death and then become king in his own name. Most of the thirty-one articles of the treaty were taken up with a definition of Henry's position and obligations as regent and prospective sovereign of France.

In due time the marriage of Henry and Catherine took place and Henry assumed the regency, though the Armagnacs, led by the Dauphin, refused absolutely to accept the settlement. War broke out, in the course of which (in 1422) Henry V. died and was succeeded by his infant son, Henry VI. In the same year Charles VI. also died, which meant that the young Henry would become king of France. With such a prospect the future of the country looked dark. Nevertheless, the death of Charles VI. and of Henry V. came in reality as a double blessing. Henry V. might long have kept the French in subjection and his position as Charles VI.'s son-in-law gave him some real claim to rule in France. But with the field cleared, as it was in 1422, opportunity was given for the Dauphin Charles (Charles VII.) to retrieve the fallen fortunes of his country—a task which, with more or less energy and skill, he managed in the long run to accomplish.

Sources—(a) Text in Eugène Cosneau, *Les Grands Traités de la Guerre de Cent Ans* ["The Great Treaties of the Hundred Years' War"], Paris, 1889, pp. 39–68 *passim*.

(b) Text in Cosneau, *ibid.* pp. 102–115 *passim*.

(a)

1. The king of England shall hold for himself and his heirs, for all time to come, in addition to that which he holds in Guienne

Territories conceded to the English by the treaty of Bretigny and Gascony, all the possessions which are enumerated below, to be held in the same manner that the king of France and his sons, or any of their ancestors, have held them. . . .[1]

[1] Here follows a minute enumeration of the districts, towns, and castles

7. And likewise the said king and his eldest son[1] shall give order, by their letters patent to all archbishops and other prelates of the holy Church, and also to counts, viscounts, barons, nobles, citizens, and others of the cities, lands, countries, islands, and places before mentioned, that they shall be obedient to the king of England and to his heirs and at their ready command, in the same manner in which they have been obedient to the kings and to the crown of France. And by the same letters they shall liberate and absolve them from all homage, pledges, oaths, obligations, subjections, and promises made by any of them to the kings and to the crown of France in any manner.

13. It is agreed that the king of France shall pay to the king of England three million gold crowns, of which two are worth an obol of English money.[2]

30. It is agreed that honest alliances, friendships, and confederations shall be formed by the two kings of France and

Provision regarding alliances
England and their kingdoms, not repugnant to the honor or the conscience of one king or the other. No alliances which they have, on this side or that, with any person of Scotland or Flanders, or any other country, shall be allowed to stand in the way.[3]

---

conceded to the English. The most important were Poitou, Limousin, Rouergne, and Saintonge in the south, and Calais, Guines, and Ponthieu in the north.

[1] That is, King John II. and the regent Charles.

[2] The enormous ransom thus specified for King John was never paid. The three million gold crowns would have a purchasing power of perhaps forty or forty-five million dollars to-day. On the strength of the treaty provision John was immediately released from captivity. With curious disregard of the bad conditions prevailing in France as the result of foreign and civil war he began preparations for a crusade, which, however, he was soon forced to abandon. In 1364, attracted by the gayety of English life as contrasted with the wretchedness and gloom of his impoverished subjects, he went voluntarily to England, where he died before the festivities in honor of his coming were completed.

[3] Throughout the Hundred Years' War the English had maintained close relations with the Flemish enemies of France, just as France, in defiance of English opposition, had kept up her traditional friendship with Scotland. The treaty of Bretigny provided for a mutual reshaping of foreign policy, to the end that these obstacles to peace might be removed.

(b)

6. After our death,[1] and from that time forward, the crown

The Treaty of Troyes fixes the succession upon Henry V and kingdom of France, with all their rights and appurtenances, shall be vested permanently in our son [son-in-law], King Henry, and his heirs.

7. . . . The power and authority to govern and to control the public affairs of the said kingdom shall, during our life-time, be vested in our son, King Henry, with the advice of the nobles and the wise men who are obedient to us, and who have consideration for the advancement and honor of the said kingdom. . . .

22. It is agreed that during our life-time we shall designate our son, King Henry, in the French language in this fashion, *Notre*

Henry's title *très cher fils Henri, roi d'Angleterre, héritier de France;* and in the Latin language in this manner, *Noster præcarissimus filius Henricus, rex Angliæ, heres Franciæ.*

24. . . . [It is agreed] that the two kingdoms shall be governed from the time that our said son, or any of his heirs, shall assume the crown, not divided between different kings at

Union of France and England to be through the crown only the same time, but under one person, who shall be king and sovereign lord of both kingdoms; observing all pledges and all other things, to each kingdom its rights, liberties or customs, usages and laws, not submitting in any manner one kingdom to the other.[2]

29. In consideration of the frightful and astounding crimes and misdeeds committed against the kingdom of France by Charles, the said Dauphin, it is agreed that we, our son Henry, and also our very dear son Philip, duke of Burgundy, will never treat for peace or amity with the said Charles.[3]

---

[1] That is, the death of King Charles VI.

[2] France was not to be dealt with as conquered territory. This article comprises the only important provision in the treaty for safeguarding the interests of the French people.

[3] Charles VI., Henry V., and Philip the Good bind themselves not to come to any sort of terms with the Dauphin, which compact reveals the irreconcilable attitude characteristic of the factional and dynastic struggles of the period. Chapter 6 of the treaty disinherits the Dauphin; chapter 29 proclaims him an enemy of France.

CHAPTER XXVI.

THE BEGINNINGS OF THE ITALIAN RENAISSANCE

THE question as to when the Middle Ages came to an end cannot be answered with a specific date, or even with a particular century. The transition from the mediæval world to the modern was gradual and was accomplished at a much earlier period in some lines than in others. Roughly speaking, the change fell within the two centuries and a half from 1300 to 1550. This transitional epoch is commonly designated the Age of the Renaissance, though if the term is taken in its most proper sense as denoting the flowering of an old into a new culture it scarcely does justice to the period, for political and religious developments in these centuries were not less fundamental than the revival and fresh stimulus of culture. But in the earlier portion of the period, particularly the fourteenth century, the intellectual awakening was the most obvious feature of the movement and, for the time being, the most important.

The renaissance of the fourteenth and fifteenth centuries was not the first that Europe had known. There had been a notable revival of learning in the time of Charlemagne—the so-called Carolingian renaissance; another at the end of the tenth century, in the time of the Emperor Otto III. and Pope Sylvester II.; and a third in the twelfth century, with its center in northern France. The first two, however, had proved quite transitory, and even the third and most promising had dried up in the fruitless philosophy of the scholastics.

Before there could be a vital and permanent intellectual revival it was indispensable that the mediæval attitude of mind undergo a fundamental change. This attitude may be summed up in the one phrase, the absolute dominance of "authority"—the authority, primarily, of the Church, supplemented by the writings of a few ancients like Aristotle. The scholars of the earlier Middle Ages busied themselves, not with research and investigation whereby to increase knowledge, but rather with commenting on the Scriptures, the writings of the Church fathers, and Aristotle, and drawing conclusions and inferences by reasoning from these accepted authorities. There was no disposition to question what was found in the books, or to supplement it with fresh information. Only after about 1300 did human interests become sufficiently broadened to make men no longer altogether content with the mere process of threshing over the old straw. Gradually there began to appear scholars who suggested the idea, novel for the day, that the books did not contain all that was worth knowing, and also that perchance some things that had long gone unquestioned just because they were in the books were not true after all. In other words, they proposed to investigate things for themselves and to apply the tests of observation and impartial reason.

The most influential factor in producing this change of attitude was the revival of classical literature and learning. The Latin classics, and even some of the Greek, had not been unknown in the earlier Middle Ages, but they had not been read widely, and when read at all they had been valued principally as models of rhetoric rather than as a living literature to be enjoyed for the ideas that were contained in it and the forms in which they were expressed. These ideas were, of course, generally pagan, and that in itself was enough to cause the Church to look askance at the use of classical writings, except for grammatical or antiquarian purposes. In the fourteenth and fifteenth centuries, however, due to a variety of causes, the reading of the classics became commoner than since Roman days, and men, bringing to them more open minds, were profoundly attracted by the fresh, original, human ideas of life and the world with which Vergil and Horace and Cicero, for example, overflowed. It was all a new discovery of the world and of man, and from the *humanitas* which the scholars found set forth as the classical conception of culture they themselves took the name of "humanists," while the subjects of their studies came to be known as the *litteræ humaniores*. This first great phase of the Renaissance—the birth of humanism—found its finest expression in Dante and Petrarch, and it cannot be studied with better effect than in certain of the writings of these two men.

79. Dante's Defense of Italian as a Literary Language

DANTE ALIGHIERI was born at Florence in 1265. Of his early life little is known. His family seems to have been too obscure to have much part in the civil struggles with which Florence, and all Italy, in that day were vexed. The love affair with Beatrice, whose story Boccaccio relates with so much zest, is the one sharply-defined feature of Dante's youth and early manhood. It is known that at the age of eighteen the young Florentine was a poet and was winning wide recognition for his sonnets. Much time was devoted by him to study of literature and the arts, but the details of his employments, intellectual and otherwise, are impossible to make out. In 1290 occurred the death of Beatrice, which event marked an epoch in the poetical lover's life. In his sorrow he took refuge in the study of such books as Boëthius's *Consolations of Philosophy* and Cicero's *Friendship*, and became deeply interested in literary, and especially philosophical, problems. In 1295 he entered political life, taking from the outset a prominent part in the deliberations of the Florentine General Council and the Council of Consuls of the Arts. He assumed a firm attitude against all forms of lawlessness and in resistance to any external interference in Florentine affairs. Owing to conditions which he could not influence, however, his career in this direction was soon cut short and most of the remainder of his life was spent as a political exile, at Lucca, Verona, Ravenna, and other Italian cities, with a possible visit to Paris. He died at Ravenna, September 14, 1321, in his fifty-seventh year.

Dante has well been called "the Janus-faced," because he stood at the threshold of the new era and looked both forward and backward. His *Divine Comedy* admirably sums up the mediæval spirit, and yet it contains many suggestions of the coming age. His method was essentially that of the scholastics, but he knew many of the classics and had a genuine respect for them as literature. He was a mediævalist in his attachment to the Holy Roman Empire, yet he cherished the purely modern ambition of a united Italy. It is deeply significant that he chose to write his great poem—one of the most splendid in the world's literature—in the Italian tongue rather than the Latin. Aside from the fact that this, more than anything else, caused the Tuscan dialect, rather than the rival Venetian and Neapolitan dialects, to become the modern Italian, it evidenced the new desire for the popularization of literature which was a marked characteristic of the dawning era. Not content with putting his greatest effort in the vernacular, Dante undertook formally to defend the use of the popular tongue for literary purposes.   This he did in *Il Convito* ("The Banquet"), a work whose date is quite uncertain, but which was undoubtedly produced at some time while its author was in exile.   It is essentially a prose commentary upon three *canzoni* written for the honor and glory of the "noble, beautiful, and most compassionate lady, Philosophy."   In it Dante sought to set philosophy free from the schools and from the heavy disputations of the scholars and to render her beauty visible even to the unlearned.   It was the first important work on philosophy written in the Italian tongue, an innovation which the author rightly regarded as calling for some ex-planation and defense.   The passage quoted from it below comprises this defense.   Similar views on the nobility of the vulgar language, as com-pared with the Latin, were later set forth in fuller form in the treatise *De Vulgari Eloquentia*.

Source—Dante Alighieri, *Il Convito* ["The Banquet"], Bk. I., Chaps. 5–13
       passim.   Translated by Katharine Hillard (London, 1889), pp.
       17–47 *passim*.

V. 1. This bread being cleansed of its accidental impurities,[1] we have now but to free it from one [inherent] in its substance, that is, its being in the vulgar tongue, and not in Latin; so that we might metaphorically call it made of oats instead of wheat.

Reasons for using the Italian And this [fault] may be briefly excused by three reasons, which moved me to prefer the former rather than the latter [language].   The first arises from care to avoid an unfit order of things; the second, from a consummate liberality; the third, from a natural love of one's own tongue.   And I intend here in this manner to discuss, in due

[1] Dante represents the commentaries composing the *Convito* as in the nature of a banquet, the "meats" of which were to be set forth in fourteen courses, corresponding to the fourteen *canzoni*, or lyric poems, which were to be commented upon.   As a matter of fact, for some unknown reason, the "banquet" was broken off at the end of the third course.   "At the beginning of every well-ordered banquet" observes the author in an earlier passage (Bk. II., Chap. 1) "the servants are wont to take the bread given out for it, and cleanse it from every speck."   Dante has just cleansed his viands from the faults of egotism and obscurity,—the "accidental impurities"; he now proceeds to clear them of a less superficial difficulty, i. e., the fact that in serving them use is made of the Italian rather than the Latin language.

order, these things and their causes, that I may free myself from the reproach above named.

3. For, in the first place, had it [the commentary] been in Latin, it would have been sovereign rather than subject, by its nobility, its virtue, and its beauty. By its nobility, because Latin is enduring and incorruptible, and the vulgar tongue is unstable and corruptible. For we see that the ancient books of Latin tragedy and comedy cannot be changed from the form we

The Latin fixed, have to-day, which is not the case with the vulgar
the Italian tongue, as that can be changed at will. For we
changeable see in the cities of Italy, if we take notice of the past fifty years, how many words have been lost, or invented, or altered; therefore, if a short time can work such changes, how much more can a longer period effect! So that I think, should they who departed this life a thousand years ago return to their cities, they would believe them to be occupied by a foreign people, so different would the language be from theirs. Of this I shall speak elsewhere more fully, in a book which I intend to write, God willing, on *Vulgar Eloquence.*[1]

VII. **4.** . . . The Latin could only have explained them [the *canzoni*] to scholars; for the rest would not have understood it. Therefore, as among those who desire to understand them there are many more illiterate than learned, it follows that the Latin would not have fulfilled this behest as well as the vulgar tongue, which is understood both by the learned and the unlearned. Also the Latin would have explained them to people of other nations, such as Germans, English, and others; in doing which it would have exceeded their order.[2] For it would have

[1] The date of the composition of the *De Vulgari Eloquentia* is unknown, but there are reasons for assigning the work to the same period in the author's life as the *Convito*. Like the *Convito*, it was left incomplete; four books were planned, but only the first and a portion of the second were written. In it an effort was made to establish the dominance of a perfect and imperial Italian language over all the dialects. The work itself was written in Latin, probably to command the attention of scholars whom Dante hoped to convert to the use of the vernacular.

[2] The author conceives of the *canzoni* as masters and the commentaries as servants.

been against their will I say, speaking generally, to have explained their meaning where their beauty could not go with it.

Translations cannot preserve the literary splendor of the originals And, moreover, let all observe that nothing harmonized by the laws of the Muses[1] can be changed from its own tongue to another one without destroying all its sweetness and harmony. And this is the reason why Homer is not turned from
Greek into Latin like the other writings we have of theirs [the
Greeks]; [2] and this is why the verses of the Psalter [3] lack musical
sweetness and harmony; for they have been translated from
Hebrew to Greek, and from Greek to Latin, and in the first
translation all this sweetness perished.

IX. 1. . . . The Latin would not have served many; because, if we recall to mind what has already been said, scholars
in other languages than the Italian could not have availed themselves of its service.[4] And of those of this speech (if we should
care to observe who they are) we shall find that only to one in a
thousand could it really have been of use; because they would
not have received it, so prone are they to base desires, and thus
deprived of that nobility of soul which above all desires this
food. And to their shame I say that they are not worthy to be
called scholars, because they do not pursue learning for its own
sake, but for the money or the honors that they gain thereby;
just as we should not call him a lute-player who kept a lute in the
house to hire out, and not to play upon.

X. 5. Again, I am impelled to defend it [the vulgar tongue]
from many of its accusers, who disparage it and commend others,
above all the language of *Oco*,[5] saying that the latter is better and

---

[1] That is, any poetical composition.
[2] Some students of Dante hold that this phrase about Homer should be
rendered "does not admit of being turned"; but others take it in the absolute
sense and base on it an argument against Dante's knowledge of Greek literature.
[3] The Book of Psalms.
[4] The *canzoni* were in Italian and a Latin commentary would have been
useless to scholars of other nations, because they could not have understood
the *canzoni* to which it referred.
[5] The Provençal language—the peculiar speech of southeastern France,
whence comes the name Languedoc. *Oc* is the affirmative particle "yes."

more beautiful than the former, wherein they depart from the truth.   Wherefore by this commentary shall be seen the great

The Italian of more solid excellence than other tongues excellence of the vulgar tongue of *Si*,[1] because (although the highest and most novel conceptions can be almost as fittingly, adequately, and beautifully expressed in it as in the Latin) its excellence in rhymed pieces, on account of the accidental adornments connected with them, such as rhyme and rhythm, or ordered numbers, cannot be perfectly shown; as it is with the beauty of a woman, when the splendor of her jewels and her garments draw more admiration than her person.[2]   Wherefore he who would judge a woman truly looks at her when, unaccompanied by any accidental adornment, her natural beauty alone remains to her; so shall it be with this commentary, wherein shall be seen the facility of its language, the propriety of its diction, and the sweet discourse it shall hold; which he who considers well shall see to be full of the sweetest and most exquisite beauty.   But because it is most virtuous in its design to show the futility and malice of its accuser, I shall tell, for the confounding of those who attack the Italian language, the purpose which moves them to do this; and upon this I shall now write a special chapter, that their infamy may be the more notorious.

XI. 1.   To the perpetual shame and abasement of those wicked men of Italy who praise the language of others and disparage

Why people of Italy affect to despise their native tongue their own, I would say that their motive springs from five abominable causes.   The first is intellectual blindness; the second, vicious excuses; the third, greed of vain-glory; the fourth, an argument based on envy; the fifth and last, littleness of soul, that is, pusillanimity. And each of these vices has so large a following, that few are they who are free from them. . . .

---

[1] *Si* is the Italian affirmative particle.   In the *Inferno* Dante refers to Italy as "that lovely country where the *si* is sounded" (XXX., 80).

[2] That is, prose shows the true beauty of a language more effectively than poetry, in which the attention is distracted by the ornaments of verse.

3. The second kind work against our language by vicious excuses. These are they who would rather be considered masters than be such; and, to avoid the reverse (that is, not to be considered masters), they always lay the blame upon the materials prepared for their art, or upon their tools; as the bad **The unskilful** smith blames the iron given him, and the bad **attribute their** lute-player blames the lute, thinking thus to lay **faults to the language** the fault of the bad knife or the bad playing upon the iron or the lute, and to excuse themselves. Such are they (and they are not few) who wish to be considered orators; and in order to excuse themselves for not speaking, or for speaking badly, blame and accuse their material, that is, their own language, and praise that of others in which they are not required to work. And whoever wishes to see wherein this tool [the vulgar tongue] deserves blame, let him look at the work that good workmen have done with it, and he will recognize the viciousness of those who, laying the blame upon it, think they excuse themselves. Against such does Tullius exclaim, in the beginning of one of his books called *De Finibus*,[1] because in his time they blamed the Latin language and commended the Greek, for the same reasons that these people consider the Italian vile and the Provençal precious.

XII. **3.** That thing is nearest to a person which is, of all things of its kind, the most closely related to himself; thus of all men the son is nearest to the father, and of all arts medicine is nearest to the doctor, and music to the musician, because these are more closely related to them than any others; of all countries, **People should** the one a man lives in is nearest to him, because it **use their own** is most closely related to him. And thus a man's **language, as being most nat-** own language is nearest to him, because most **ural to them** closely related, being that one which comes alone and before all others in his mind, and not only of itself is it thus

[1] The author refers to Cicero's philosophical treatise *De Finibus Bonorum et Malorum*.

related, but by accident, inasmuch as it is connected with those nearest to him, such as his kinsmen, and his fellow-citizens, and his own people. And this is his own language, which is not only near, but the very nearest, to every one. Because if proximity be the seed of friendship, as has been stated above, it is plain that it has been one of the causes of the love I bear my own language, which is nearer to me than the others. The above-named reason (that is, that we are most nearly related to that which is first in our mind) gave rise to that custom of the people which makes the firstborn inherit everything, as the nearest of kin; and, because the nearest, therefore the most beloved.

4. And again, its goodness makes me its friend. And here we must know that every good quality properly belonging to a thing is lovable in that thing; as men should have a fine beard, and women should have the whole face quite free from hair; as the foxhound should have a keen scent, and the greyhound great speed. And the more peculiar this good quality, the more lovable it is, whence, although all virtue is lovable in man, that is most so which is most peculiarly human. . . . And we see that, of all things pertaining to language, the power of adequately expressing thought is the most loved and commended; therefore this is its peculiar virtue. And as this belongs to our own language, as has been proved above in another chapter, it is plain that this was one of the causes of my love for it; since, as we have said, goodness is one of the causes that engender love.

The Italian fulfils the highest requirement of a language

80. Dante's Conception of the Imperial Power

THE best known prose work of Dante, the *De Monarchia*, is perhaps the most purely idealistic political treatise ever written. Its quality of idealism is so pronounced, in fact, that there is not even sufficient mention of contemporary men or events to assist in solving the wholly unsettled problem of the date of its composition. The *De Monarchia* is composed of three books, each of which is devoted to a fundamental question in relation to the balance of temporal and spiritual authority. The first question is whether the temporal monarchy is necessary for the well-being of the world. The answer is that it is necessary for the preservation of justice, freedom, and unity and effectiveness of human effort. The second question is whether the Roman people took to itself this dignity of monarchy, or empire, by right. By a survey of Roman history from the days of Æneas to those of Cæsar it is made to appear that it was God's will that the Romans should rule the world. The third question is the most vital of all and its answer constitutes the pith of the treatise. In brief it is, does the authority of the Roman monarch, or emperor, who is thus by right the monarch of the world, depend immediately upon God, or upon some vicar of God, the successor of Peter? This question Dante answers first negatively by clearing away the familiar defenses of spiritual supremacy, and afterwards positively, by bringing forward specific arguments for the temporal superiority. The selection given below comprises the most suggestive portions of Dante's treatment of this aspect of his subject. The method, it will be observed, is quite thoroughly scholastic. Whenever the *De Monarchia* was composed, it remained all but unknown until after the author's death (1321); but with the renewal of conflict between papacy and imperial power the imperialists were not slow to make use of the treatise, and by the middle of the fourteenth century it had become known throughout Europe, being admired by one party as much as it was abhorred by the other. At various times copies of it were burned as heretical and in the sixteenth century it was placed by the Roman authorities upon the Index of Prohibited Books. Few literary productions of the later Middle Ages exercised greater influence upon contemporary thought and politics.

Source—Dante Alighieri, *De Monarchia* ["Concerning Monarchy"], Bk. III., Chaps. 1–16 *passim*. Translated by Aurelia Henry (Boston, 1904), pp. 137–206 *passim*.

I. 2. The question pending investigation, then, concerns two great luminaries, the Roman Pontiff [Pope] and the Roman Prince [Emperor]; and the point at issue is whether the authority **The problem to** of the Roman monarch, who, as proved in the **be considered** second book, is rightful monarch of the world, is derived from God directly, **or from some** vicar or minister of

God, by whom I mean the successor of Peter, indisputable keeper of the keys of the kingdom of heaven.

IV. 1. Those men to whom the entire subsequent discussion is directed assert that the authority of the Empire depends on the authority of the Church, just as the inferior artisan depends on the architect. They are drawn to this by divers opposing arguments, some of which they take from Holy Scripture, and some from certain acts performed by the chief pontiff, and by the Emperor himself; and they endeavor to make their conviction reasonable.

2. For, first, they maintain that, according to Genesis, God made two mighty luminaries, a greater and a lesser, the former to hold supremacy by day and the latter by night [Gen., i. 15, 16]. These they interpret allegorically to be the two rulers—spiritual and temporal.[1] Whence they argue that as the lesser luminary, the moon, has no light but that gained from the sun, so the temporal ruler has no authority but that gained from the spiritual ruler.

The analogy of the sun and moon

8. I proceed to refute the above assumption that the two luminaries of the world typify its two ruling powers. The whole force of their argument lies in the interpretation; but this we can prove indefensible in two ways. First, since these ruling powers are, as it were, accidents necessitated by man himself, God would seem to have used a distorted order in creating first accidents, and then the subject necessitating them. It is absurd to speak thus of God, but it is evident from the Word that the two lights were created on the fourth day, and man on the sixth.

9. Secondly, the two ruling powers exist as the directors of men toward certain ends, as will be shown further on. But had man remained in the state of innocence in which God made him, he would have required no such direction. These ruling powers

---

[1] For example, Pope Innocent IV. (1243–1254) declared: "Two lights, the sun and the moon, illumine the globe; two powers, the papal and the royal, govern it; but as the moon receives her light from the more brilliant star, so kings reign by the chief of the Church, who comes from God."

are therefore remedies against the infirmity of sin.   Since on
the fourth day man was not only not a sinner, but was not even

An abstruse bit of mediæval reasoning
existent, the creation of a remedy would have been
purposeless, which is contrary to divine goodness.
Foolish indeed would be the physician who
should make ready a plaster for the abscess of a man not yet born.
Therefore it cannot be asserted that God made the two ruling
powers on the fourth day; and consequently the meaning of
Moses cannot have been what it is supposed to be.

10. Also, in order to be tolerant, we may refute this fallacy
by distinction.   Refutation by distinction deals more gently with
an adversary, for it shows him to be not absolutely wrong, as
does refutation by destruction.   I say, then, that although the
moon may have abundant light only as she receives it from the
sun, it does not follow on that account that the moon herself
owes her existence to the sun.   It must be recognized that the
essence of the moon, her strength, and her function, are not one
and the same thing.   Neither in her essence, her strength, nor
her function taken absolutely, does the moon owe her existence
to the sun, for her movement is impelled by her own force and
her influence by her own rays.   Besides, she has a certain light
of her own, as is shown in eclipse.   It is in order to fulfill her
function better and more potently that she borrows from the
sun abundance of light, and works thereby more effectively.

11. In like manner, I say, the temporal power receives from
the spiritual neither its existence, nor its strength, which is its
authority, nor even its function, taken absolutely.   But well

Why the argument from the sun and moon fails
for her does she receive therefrom, through the
light of grace which the benediction of the chief
pontiff sheds upon it in heaven and on earth,
strength to fulfill her function more perfectly.   So the argument was at fault in form, because the predicate of the conclusion is not a term of the major premise, as is evident.   The
syllogism runs thus: The moon receives light from the sun, which

is the spiritual power; the temporal ruling power is the moon; therefore the temporal receives authority from the spiritual. They introduce "light" as the term of the major, but "authority" as predicate of the conclusion, which two things we have seen to be diverse in subject and significance.

VIII. 1. From the same gospel they quote the saying of Christ to Peter, "Whatsoever thou shalt loose on earth shall be loosed in heaven" [Matt., xvi. 19], and understand this saying to refer alike to all the Apostles, according to the text of Matthew and John [Matt., xviii. 18 and John, xx. 23]. They reason from

Argument from the prerogative of the keys committed to Peter
this that the successor of Peter has been granted of God power to bind and loose all things, and then infer that he has power to loose the laws and decrees of the Empire, and to bind the laws and decrees of the temporal kingdom. Were this true, their inference would be correct.

2. But we must reply to it by making a distinction against the major premise of the syllogism which they employ. Their syllogism is this: Peter had power to bind and loose all things; the successor of Peter has like power with him; therefore the successor of Peter has power to loose and bind all things. From this they infer that he has power to loose and bind the laws and decrees of the Empire.

3. I concede the minor premise, but the major only with distinction. Wherefore I say that "all," the symbol of the universal which is implied in "whatsoever," is never distributed beyond the scope of the distributed term. When I say, "All animals run," the distribution of "all" comprehends whatever comes under the genus "animal." But when I say, "All men run," the symbol of the universal refers only to whatever comes under the term "man." And when I say, "All grammarians run," the distribution is narrowed still further.

4. Therefore we must always determine what it is over which the symbol of the universal is distributed; then, from the recog-

nized nature and scope of the distributed term, will be easily apparent the extent of the distribution. Now, were "whatsoever" to be understood absolutely when it is said, "Whatsoever thou shalt bind," he would certainly have the power they claim; nay, he would have even greater power—he would be able to loose a wife from her husband, and, while the man still lived, bind her to another—a thing he can in nowise do. He would be able to absolve me, while impenitent—a thing which God Himself cannot do.

5. So it is evident that the distribution of the term under discussion is to be taken, not absolutely, but relatively to something else. A consideration of the concession to which the distribution is subjoined will make manifest this related something. **Dante's interpretation of the Scripture in question** Christ said to Peter, "I will give unto thee the keys of the kingdom of heaven;" that is, I will make thee doorkeeper of the kingdom of heaven. Then He adds, "and whatsoever," that is, "everything which," and He means thereby, "Everything which pertains to that office thou shalt have power to bind and loose." And thus the symbol of the universal which is implied in "whatsoever" is limited in its distribution to the prerogative of the keys of the kingdom of heaven. Understood thus, the proposition is true, but understood absolutely, it is obviously not. Therefore I conclude that, although the successor of Peter has authority to bind and loose in accordance with the requirements of the prerogative granted to Peter, it does not follow, as they claim, that he has authority to bind and loose the decrees or statutes of empire, unless they prove that this also belongs to the office of the keys. But further on we shall demonstrate that the contrary is true.

XIII. 1. Now that we have stated and rejected the errors on which those chiefly rely who declare that the authority of the Roman Prince is dependent on the Roman Pontiff,[1] we must

[1] The arguments disposed of by the author, in addition to those treated

return and demonstrate the truth of that question which we propounded for discussion at the beginning. The truth will be evident enough if it can be shown, under the principle of inquiry agreed upon, that imperial authority derives immediately from the summit of all being, which is God. And this will be shown, whether we prove that imperial authority does not derive from that of the Church (for the dispute concerns no other authority), or whether we prove simply that it derives immediately from God.

2. That ecclesiastical authority is not the source of imperial authority is thus verified. A thing non-existent, or devoid of active force, cannot be the cause of active force in a thing possessing that quality in full measure. But before the Church existed, or while it lacked power to act, the Empire had active force in **The Church (or papacy) is not the source of imperial authority** full measure. Hence the Church is the source, neither of acting power nor of authority in the Empire, where power to act and authority are identical. Let A be the Church, B the Empire, and C the power or authority of the Empire. If, A being non-existent, C is in B, the cause of C's relation to B cannot be A, since it is impossible that an effect should exist prior to its cause. Moreover, if, A being inoperative, C is in B, the cause of C's relation to B cannot be A, since it is indispensable for the production of effect that the cause should be in operation previously, especially the efficient cause which we are considering here.

3. The major premise of this demonstration is intelligible from its terms; the minor is confirmed by Christ and the Church. Christ attests it, as we said before, in His birth and death. The Church attests it in Paul's declaration to Festus in the Acts of

in the passages here presented, are: the precedence of Levi over Judah (Gen., xxix. 34, 35), the election and deposition of Saul by Samuel (1 Sam., x. 1; xv. 23; xv. 28), the oblation of the Magi (Matt., ii. 11), the two swords referred to by Peter (Luke, xxii. 38), the donation of Constantine, the summoning of Charlemagne by Pope Hadrian, and finally the argument from pure reason.

the Apostles: "I stand at Cæsar's judgment seat, where I ought
to be judged" [Acts, xxv. 10]; and in the admonition of God's

**Early Chris-
tian recogni-
tion of the au-
thority of the
Emperor**
angel to Paul a little later: "Fear not, Paul;
thou must be brought before Cæsar" [Acts, xxvii.
24]; and again, still later, in Paul's words to the
Jews dwelling in Italy: "And when the Jews spake
against it, I was constrained to appeal unto Cæsar; not that I
had aught to accuse my nation of," but "that I might deliver
my soul from death" [Acts, xxviii. 19]. If Cæsar had not
already possessed the right to judge temporal matters, Christ
would not have implied that he did, the angel would not have
uttered such words, nor would he who said, "I desire to depart
and be with Christ" [Phil., i. 23], have appealed to an un-
qualified judge.

XIV. 1. Besides, if the Church has power to confer authority
on the Roman Prince, she would have it either from God, or
from herself, or from some Emperor, or from the unanimous
consent of mankind, or, at least, from the consent of the most
influential. There is no other least crevice through which the
power could have diffused itself into the Church. But from
none of these has it come to her, and therefore the aforesaid
power is not hers at all.

XVI. 1. Although by the method of reduction to absurdity
it has been shown in the foregoing chapter that the authority of
empire has not its source in the Chief Pontiff, yet it has not been
fully proved, save by an inference, that its immediate source
is God, seeing that if the authority does not depend on the vicar
of God, we conclude that it depends on God Himself. For a
perfect demonstration of the proposition we must prove directly
that the Emperor, or Monarch, of the world has immediate
relationship to the Prince of the universe, who is God.

2. In order to realize this, it must be understood that man
alone of all beings holds the middle place between corruptibility
and incorruptibility, and is therefore rightly compared by phi-

losophers to the horizon which lies between the two hemispheres. Man may be considered with regard to either of his essential

Positive argument that the authority of the emperor is derived directly from God parts, body or soul. If considered in regard to the body alone, he is perishable; if in regard to the soul alone, he is imperishable. So the Philosopher [1] spoke well of its incorruptibility when he said in the second book, *On the Soul*, "And this only can be separated as a thing eternal from that which perishes."

3. If man holds a middle place between the perishable and the imperishable, then, inasmuch as every man shares the nature of the extremes, man must share both natures. And inasmuch as every nature is ordained for a certain ultimate end, it follows that there exists for man a two-fold end, in order that as he alone of all beings partakes of the perishable and the imperishable, so he alone of all beings should be ordained for two ultimate ends. One end is for that in him which is perishable, the other for that which is imperishable.

4. Omniscient Providence has thus designed two ends to be contemplated by man: first, the happiness of this life, which con-

Double aspect of human life sists in the activity of his natural powers, and is prefigured by the terrestrial Paradise; and then the blessedness of life everlasting, which consists in the enjoyment of the countenance of God, to which man's natural powers may not obtain unless aided by divine light, and which may be symbolized by the celestial Paradise.[2]

5. To these states of blessedness, just as to diverse conclusions, man must come by diverse means. To the former we come by the teachings of philosophy, obeying them by acting in conformity with the moral and intellectual virtues; to the latter, through spiritual teachings which transcend human reason, and which we obey by acting in conformity with the theological virtues,

---

[1] This was the common mediæval designation of Aristotle.
[2] For Dante's conception of the terrestrial and the celestial paradise see the *Paradiso* in the *Divina Commedia*.

faith, hope, and charity.   Now the former end and means are
made known to us by human reason, which the philosophers
have wholly explained to us; and the latter by the Holy Spirit,
which has revealed to us supernatural but essential truth through
the prophets and sacred writers, through Jesus Christ, the coëter-
nal Son of God, and through His disciples.   Nevertheless, human
passion would cast these behind, were not man, like horses
astray in their brutishness, held to the road by bit and rein.

6. Wherefore a twofold directive agent was necessary to man,
in accordance with the twofold end; the Supreme Pontiff to lead
the human race to life eternal by means of revelation, and the
Emperor to guide it to temporal well-being by means of philo-
sophic instruction.   And since none or few—and these with ex-

**The proper
functions of
Pope and Em-
peror**

ceeding difficulty—could attain this port, were
not the waves of seductive desire calmed, and
mankind made free to rest in the tranquillity of
peace, therefore this is the goal which he whom we call the
guardian of the earth and Roman Prince should most urgently
seek; then would it be possible for life on this mortal threshing-
floor to pass in freedom and peace.   The order of the world follows the order inherent in the revolution of the heavens.   To
attain this order it is necessary that instruction productive of
liberality and peace should be applied by the guardian of the
realm, in due place and time, as dispensed by Him who is the
ever-present Watcher of the whole order of the heavens.   And
He alone foreordained this order, that by it, in His providence,
He might link together all things, each in its own place.

7. If this is so, and there is none higher than He, only God
elects and only God confirms.   Whence we may further conclude that neither those who are now, nor those who in any way
whatsoever have been, called electors [1] have the right to be so

---

[1] These were the lay and ecclesiastical princes in whom was vested the
right of choosing the Emperor. The electoral college was first clearly defined
in the Golden Bull issued by Charles IV. in 1356 [see p. 409]. Its composition
in Dante's time is uncertain.

called; rather should they be entitled heralds of Divine Providence. Whence it is that those in whom is vested the dignity of proclamation suffer dissension among themselves at times, when, all or part of them being shadowed by the clouds of passion, they discern not the face of God's dispensation.

8. It is established, then, that the authority of temporal monarchy descends without mediation from the fountain of universal authority. And this fountain, one in its purity of source, flows into multifarious channels out of the abundance of its excellence.

9. I believe I have now approached sufficiently close to the goal I had set myself, for I have taken the kernels of truth from the husks of falsehood, in that question which asked whether the office of monarchy was essential to the welfare of the world, and in the next which made inquiry whether the Roman people rightfully appropriated the empire, and in the last which sought whether the authority of the monarch derived from God directly, or from some other. But the truth of this final question must not be restricted to mean that the Roman Prince shall not be subject in some degree to the Roman Pontiff, for well-being that is mortal is ordered in a measure after well-being that is immortal. Wherefore let Cæsar honor Peter as a first-born son should honor his father, so that, brilliant with the light of paternal grace, he may illumine with greater radiance the earthly sphere over which he has been set by Him who alone is Ruler of all things spiritual and temporal.[1]

The ideal relation of the two powers

81. Petrarch's Love of the Classics

FRANCESCO PETRARCA was born at Arezzo in northern Italy in July, 1304. His father was a Florentine notary who had been banished by the same decree with Dante in 1302, and who finally settled at Avignon

[1] Dante's ideal solution was the harmonious rule of the two powers by the acknowledgment of filial relationship between pope and emperor, on the basis of a recognition of the different and essentially irreconcilable character of their functions.

in 1313 to practice his profession in the neighborhood of the papal court. Petrarch was destined by his father for the law and was sent to study that subject at Montpellier and subsequently at Bologna. But from the moment when he first got hold of the Latin classics, notably Cicero and Vergil, he found his interest in legal subjects absolutely at an end. He was charmed by the literary power of the ancients, as he certainly was not by the logic and learning of the jurists, and though his father endeavored to discourage what he regarded as a sheer waste of time by burning the young enthusiast's precious Latin books, the love of the classics, once aroused, was never crushed out and the literary instinct remained dominant. The beginnings of the Renaissance spirit, which are so discernible in Dante, become in Petrarch the full expression of the new age. In the words of Professor Adams, "In him we clearly find, as controlling personal traits, all those specific features of the Renaissance which give it its distinguishing character as an intellectual revolution, and from their strong beginning in him they have never ceased among men. In the first place, he felt as no other man had done since the ancient days the beauty of nature and the pleasure of mere life, its sufficiency for itself; and he had also a sense of ability and power, and a self-confidence which led him to plan great things, and to hope for an immortality of fame in this world. In the second place, he had a most keen sense of the unity of past history, of the living bond of connection between himself and men of like sort in the ancient world. That world was for him no dead antiquity, but he lived and felt in it and with its poets and thinkers, as if they were his neighbors. His love for it amounted almost, if we may call it so, to an ecstatic enthusiasm. hardly understood by his own time, but it kindled in many others a similar feeling which has come down to us. The result is easily recognized in him as a genuine culture, the first of modern men in whom this can be found. . . . Finally, Petrarch first put the modern spirit into conscious opposition to the mediæval. The Renaissance meant rebellion and revolution. It meant a long and bitter struggle against the whole scholastic system, and all the follies and superstitions which flourished under its protection. Petrarch opened the attack along the whole line. Physicians, lawyers, astrologers, scholastic philosophers, the universities —all were enemies of the new learning, and so his enemies. And these attacks were not in set and formal polemics alone, his letters and almost all his writings were filled with them. It was the business of his life."[1]

In the latter part of his life Petrarch enjoyed the highest renown throughout Europe. The cities of Italy, especially, vied with one another in showering honors upon him. A decree of the Venetian senate affirmed that no Christian poet or philosopher could be compared with him. Arezzo, the town of his birth, awarded him a triumphal procession. Florence bought the estates once confiscated from his father and begged him to accept them as a meager gift to one "who for centuries had no equal and could scarcely find one in the ages to come." The climax came in 1341 when both the University of Paris and the Roman Senate invited him to present himself and receive the poet's crown, in revival of an old and all but forgotten ceremony of special honor. The invitation from Rome was accepted and the celebration attending the coronation was one of the most splendid of the age. In 1350 Petrarch became acquainted with Boccaccio and thenceforth there existed the warmest friendship between these two great exponents of Renaissance ideals and achievement. In 1369 he retired to Arquà, near Padua, where he died in 1374.

Besides his poems Petrarch wrote a great number of letters, some in Latin and some in Italian. Letter-writing was indeed a veritable passion with him; and he not only wrote freely but was careful to preserve copies of what he wrote. His prose correspondence has been classified in four divisions. The largest one comprises three hundred forty-seven letters, written between the years 1332 and 1362, and given the general title of *De Rebus Familiaribus*, because in them only topics presumably of everyday interest were discussed and without particular attention to style. The second group, the so-called *Epistolæ Variæ*, numbers about seventy. The third, the *Epistolæ de Rebus Senilibus* ("Letters of Old Age"), includes one hundred twenty-four letters written during the last twelve years of the poet's life. The fourth, comprising about twenty letters, was made up of epistles containing such sharp criticism of the papal régime at Avignon that the author thought it best to suppress the names of those to whom they were addressed. Their general designation, therefore, is *Epistolæ sine Titulo*. The following passages are taken from a letter found in the *Epistolæ Variæ*. It was written to a literary friend,

[1] George B. Adams, *Mediæval Civilization* (New York, 1904), pp. 375–377.

August 18, 1360, while Petrarch was at Milan, uncertain whither the political storms of the period would finally drive him.   In the portion which
precedes that given below the writer has been commenting on various
invitations which had reached him from friends in Padua, Florence,
and even beyond the Alps.   This gives him occasion to lament the
unsettled conditions of his times and to voice the longing of the scholar
for peace and quiet.   Thence he proceeds to speak of matters which
reveal in an interesting way his passionate love for the beauties of classical
literature and his sympathy with its dominant ideas.   Cicero was his
favorite Latin author; after him, Vergil and Ovid.   Greek literature,
unfortunately, it was impossible for him to know at first hand.   In spite
of a lifelong desire, and at least one determined effort (which is referred
to in the letter below), he never acquired even a rudimentary reading
knowledge of the Greek language.   At best he could only read fragments
of Homer, Plato, and Aristotle in extremely faulty Latin translations.[1]

Source—Franciscus Petrarca, *Epistolæ de Rebus Familiaribus et Variæ*
["Letters of Friendly Intercourse, and Miscellaneous Letters"],
edited by J. Fracassetti (Florence, 1869), Vol. III., pp. 364–371.
Adapted from translation in Merrick Whitcomb, *Source Book of
the Italian Renaissance* (Philadelphia, 1903), pp. 14–21 *passim*.

If you should ask me, in the midst of these opinions of my
friends, what I myself think of the matter, I can only reply that
I long for a place where solitude, leisure, repose, and silence
reign, however far from wealth and honors, power and favors.
But I confess I know not where to find it.   My own secluded
nook, where I have hoped not only to live, but even to die, has
lost all the advantages it once possessed, even that of safety.

**Petrarch's
longing for
peace and
seclusion**
I call to witness thirty or more volumes, which
I left there recently, thinking that no place
could be more secure, and which, a little later,
having escaped from the hands of robbers and returned, against

---

[1] "There was no apparatus for the study of Greek at that time.   Oral
instruction from Greek or Byzantine scholars was the only possible means
of access to the great writers of the past.   Such instruction was difficult to
secure, as Petrarch's efforts and failure prove."—Robinson and Rolfe,
Petrarch, p. 237.

all hope, to their master, seem yet to blanch and tremble and show upon their foreheads the troubled condition of the place whence they have escaped. Therefore I have lost all hope of revisiting this charming retreat, this longed-for country spot. Still, if the opportunity were offered me, I should seize it with both hands and hold it fast. I do not know whether I still possess a glimmer of hope, or am feigning it for self-deception, and to feed my soul's desire with empty expectation.

But I proceed, remembering that we had much conversation on this point last year, when we lived together in the same house, in this very city [Milan]; and that after having examined the matter most carefully, in so far as our light permitted, we came to the conclusion that while the affairs of Italy, and of Europe, remain in this condition, there is no place safer and better for my needs than Milan, nor any place that suits me so well. We made exception only of the city of Padua, whither I went **Drawbacks of** shortly after and whither I shall soon return; **even Milan** not that I may obliterate or diminish—that I **and Padua** should not wish—but that I may soften the regret which my absence causes the citizens of both places. I know not whether you have changed your opinion since that time; but for me I am convinced that to exchange the tumult of this great city and its annoyances for the annoyances of another city would bring me no advantage, perhaps some inconvenience, and beyond a doubt, much fatigue. Ah, if this tranquil solitude, which, in spite of all my seeking, I never find, as I have told you, should ever show itself on any side, you will hear, not that I have gone, but that I have flown, to it. . . .

In the succeeding paragraph of your letter you jest with much elegance, saying that I have been wounded by Cicero without having deserved it, on account of our too great intimacy.[1]

---

[1] This is a humorous allusion to the fact that Petrarch had recently received an injury from the fall of a heavy volume of Cicero's *Letters*.

"Because," you say, "those who are nearest to us most often injure us, and it is extremely rare that an Indian does an injury

Common indifference to people and events near at hand
to a Spaniard." True it is. It is on this account that in reading of the wars of the Athenians and Lacedaemonians, and in contemplating the troubles of our own people with our neighbors,
we are never struck with astonishment; still less so at the sight of the civil wars and domestic troubles which habit has made of so little account that concord itself would more easily cause surprise. But when we read that the king of Scythia has come to blows with the king of Egypt, and that Alexander of Macedonia has penetrated to the ends of India, we experience a sensation of astonishment which the reading of our histories, filled as they are with the deeds of Roman bravery in their distant expeditions, does not afford. You bring me consolation, in representing me as having been wounded by Cicero, to whom I am fondly attached, a thing that would probably never happen to me, at the hands of either Hippocrates [1] or Albumazar.[2] . .

You ask me to lend you the copy of Homer that was on sale at Padua, if, as you suppose, I have purchased it (since, you say, I have for a long time possessed another copy) so that our friend

A request for a copy of Homer
Leo [3] may translate it from Greek into Latin for your benefit and for the benefit of our other studious compatriots. I saw this book, but
neglected the opportunity of acquiring it, because it seemed inferior to my own. It can easily be had with the aid of the person to whom I owe my friendship with Leo; a letter from that source would be all-powerful in the matter, and I will myself write him.

If by chance the book escape us, which seems to be very unlikely, I will let you have mine. I have been always fond of this particular translation and of Greek literature in general,

[1] A renowned Greek physician of the fifth century B. C.
[2] A famous Arabian astronomer of the ninth century A. D.
[3] Leo Pilatus, a translator.

and if fortune had not frowned upon my beginnings, in the sad death of my excellent master, I should be perhaps to-day some-

Fondness for Greek literature
thing more than a Greek still at his alphabet. I approve with all my heart and strength your enterprise, for I regret and am indignant that an ancient translation, presumably the work of Cicero, the commencement of which Horace inserted in his *Ars Poetica*,[1] should have been lost to the Latin world, together with many other works. It angers me to see so much solicitude for the bad and so much neglect of the good. But what is to be done? We must be resigned. . . .

I wish to take this opportunity of warning you of one thing, lest later on I should regret having passed it over in silence. If, as you say, the translation is to be made literally in prose, listen for a moment to the opinion of St. Jerome as expressed in his preface to the book, *De Temporibus*, by Eusebius of Cæsarea, which he translated into Latin.[2] Here are the very words of this great man, well acquainted with these two languages, and indeed with many others, and of special fame for his art of translating:

Difficulty of translating works of literature
If any one, he says, *refuses to believe that transla-tion lessens the peculiar charm of the original, let him render Homer into Latin, word for word; I will say further, let him translate it into prose in his own tongue, and he will see a ridiculous array and the most eloquent of poets transformed into a stammerer.* I tell you this for your own good, while it is yet time, in order that so important a work may not prove useless. As for me, I wish the work to be done, whether

[1] Quintus Horatius Flaccus (65–8 B. C.), one of the literary lights of the Augustan Age, was a younger contemporary of Cicero. His *Ars Poetica* was a didactic poem setting forth the correct principles of poetry as an art.

[2] Eusebius, bishop of Cesaræa in Palestine, is noted chiefly as the author of an Ecclesiastical History which is in many ways our most important source of information on the early Christian Church. He lived about 250–339. St. Jerome was a great Church father of the later fourth century. His name is most commonly associated with the translation of the Bible from the original Hebrew and Greek into the Latin language. The resulting form of the Scriptures was the *Editio Vulgata* (the Edition Commonly Received), whence our English term "Vulgate."

well or ill. I am so famished for literature that just as he who is ravenously hungry is not inclined to quarrel with the cook's art, so I await with a lively impatience whatever dishes are to be set before my soul. And in truth, the morsel in which the same Leo, translating into Latin prose the beginning of Homer, has

Longing for the translation of Homer given me a foretaste of the whole work, although it confirms the sentiment of St. Jerome, does not displease me. It possesses, in fact, a secret charm, as certain viands, which have failed to take a moulded shape, although they are lacking in form, preserve nevertheless their taste and odor. May he continue with the aid of Heaven, and may he give us Homer, who has been lost to us!

In asking of me the volume of Plato which I have with me, and which escaped the fire at my transalpine country house, you give me proof of your ardor, and I shall hold this book at

A loan of a volume of Plato your disposal, whenever the time shall come. I wish to aid with all my power such noble enterprises. But beware lest it should be unbecoming to unite in one bundle these two great princes of Greece, lest the weight of these two spirits should overwhelm mortal shoulders. Let your messenger undertake, with God's aid, one of the two, and first him who has written many centuries before the other. Farewell.

82. Petrarch's Letter to Posterity

THE following is a letter of Petrarch addressed, by a curious whim, to Posterity. It gives an excellent idea of the poet's opinion of himself and reveals the sort of things that interested the typical man of culture in the early Renaissance period. It is supposed to have been written in the year 1370, when Petrarch had completed the sixty-sixth year of his life. The letter betrays a longing for individual fame which was common in classical times and during the Renaissance, but not in the Middle Ages.

Source—Franciscus Petrarca, *Epistolæ de Rebus Familiaribus et Variæ* ["Letters of Friendly Intercourse, and Miscellaneous Letters"], edited by J. Fracassetti (Florence, 1869), Vol. I., pp. 1–11. Translated in James H. Robinson and Henry W. Rolfe, *Petrarch, the First Modern Scholar and Man of Letters* (New York, 1898), pp. 59–76 *passim*.

Francis Petrarch, to Posterity, greeting:

It is possible that some word of me may have come to you, though even this is doubtful, since an insignificant and obscure name will scarcely penetrate far in either time or space. If, however, you should have heard of me, you may desire to know what manner of man I was, or what was the outcome of my labors, especially those of which some description or, at any rate, the bare titles may have reached you.

To begin, then, with myself. The utterances of men concerning me will differ widely, since in passing judgment almost every one is influenced not so much by truth as by preference, and good and evil report alike know no bounds. I was, in truth, a poor **Petrarch's** mortal like yourself, neither very exalted in my **early life** origin, nor, on the other hand, of the most humble birth, but belonging, as Augustus Cæsar says of himself, to an ancient family. As to my disposition, I was not naturally perverse or wanting in modesty, however the contagion of evil associations may have corrupted me.

My youth was gone before I realized it; I was carried away by the strength of manhood. But a riper age brought me to my senses and taught me by experience the truth I had long before read in books, that youth and pleasure are vanity—nay, that the Author of all ages and times permits us miserable mortals, puffed up with emptiness, thus to wander about, until finally, coming to a tardy consciousness of our sins, we shall learn to know ourselves.

In my prime I was blessed with a quick and active body, al- **Physical** though not exceptionally strong; and while I do **appearance** not lay claim to remarkable personal beauty, I was comely enough in my best days. I was possessed of a clear complexion, between light and dark, lively eyes, and for long years a keen vision, which, however, deserted me, contrary to my hopes, after I reached my sixtieth birthday, and forced me, to my great annoyance, to resort to glasses.[1] Although I had previously enjoyed perfect health, old age brought with it the usual array of discomforts.

My parents were honorable folk, Florentine in their origin, of medium fortune, or, I may as well admit it, in a condition verging upon poverty. They had been expelled from their native city,[2] and consequently I was born in exile, at Arezzo, in the year 1304 of this latter age, which begins with Christ's birth, July the 20th, on a Monday, at dawn. I have always possessed an extreme contempt for wealth; not that riches are not desirable in themselves, but because I hate the anxiety and care which are invariably associated with them. I certainly do not long to be able to give gorgeous banquets. I have, on the contrary, led a

Preference for plain and sensible living happier existence with plain living and ordinary fare than all the followers of Apicius,[3] with their elaborate dainties. So-called convivia, which are but vulgar bouts, sinning against sobriety and good manners, have always been repugnant to me. I have ever felt that it was irksome and profitless to invite others to such affairs, and not less so to be bidden to them myself. On the other hand, the pleasure of dining with one's friends is so great that nothing has ever given me more delight than their unexpected arrival, nor have I ever willingly sat down to table without a companion. Nothing displeases me more than display, for not only is it bad

---

[1] Eyeglasses were but beginning to come into use in Petrarch's day.

[2] Petrarch's father and Dante were banished from Florence upon the same day, January 27, 1302 [see p. 446].

[3] Marcus Gavius Apicius was a celebrated epicure of the time of Augustus and Tiberius. He was the author of a famous cook-book intended for the gratification of high-livers. Though worth a fortune, he was haunted by a fear of starving to death and eventually poisoned himself to escape such a fate. There was another Apicius in the third century who compiled a well-known collection of recipes for cooking, in ten books, entitled *De Re Coquinaria*. It is not quite clear which Apicius Petrarch had in mind.

in itself and opposed to humility, but it is troublesome and distracting.

In my familiar associations with kings and princes, and in my friendship with noble personages, my good fortune has been such as to excite envy. But it is the cruel fate of those who **Intimacy with** are growing old that they can commonly only **renowned men** weep for friends who have passed away. The greatest kings of this age have loved and courted me. They may know why; I certainly do not. With some of them I was on such terms that they seemed in a certain sense my guests rather than I theirs; their lofty position in no way embarrassing me, but, on the contrary, bringing with it many advantages. I fled, however, from many of those to whom I was greatly attached; and such was my innate longing for liberty that I studiously avoided those whose very name seemed incompatible with the freedom that I loved.

I possessed a well-balanced rather than a keen intellect—one prone to all kinds of good and wholesome study, but especially inclined to moral philosophy and the art of poetry. The latter, indeed, I neglected as time went on, and took delight in sacred literature. Finding in that a hidden sweetness which I had once esteemed but lightly, I came to regard the works of the poets as only amenities.

Among the many subjects that interested me, I dwelt especially upon antiquity, for our own age has always repelled me, **Admiration** so that, had it not been for the love of those **for antiquity** dear to me, I should have preferred to have been born in any other period than our own. In order to forget my own time, I have constantly striven to place myself in spirit in other ages, and consequently I delighted in history. The conflicting statements troubled me, but when in doubt I accepted what appeared most probable, or yielded to the authority of the writer.

My style, as many claimed, was clear and forcible; but to

me it seemed weak and obscure. In ordinary conversation with
friends, or with those about me, I never gave thought to my language, and I have always wondered that Augustus Cæsar should

**Attitude to-
ward liter-
ary style**

have taken such pains in this respect. When,
however, the subject itself, or the place or the
listener, seemed to demand it, I gave some attention to style, with what success I cannot pretend to say;
let them judge in whose presence I spoke. If only I have lived
well, it matters little to me how I talked. Mere elegance of
language can produce at best but an empty renown. . .

CHAPTER XXVII.

FORESHADOWINGS OF THE REFORMATION

83. The Reply of Wyclif to the Summons of Pope Urban VI. (1384)

THE fourteenth century was an era of religious decline in England, as indeed more or less generally throughout western Europe. The papacy was at its lowest ebb, unable to command either respect or obedience, except among the clergy and certain of the common people; bishops and abbots had grown wealthy and worldly and were often utterly neglectful of their religious obligations; and among the masses the services of worship had frequently become mere hollow formalities. There were still many good men in the Church, men who in an unpretentious way sought to do their duty faithfully; but of large numbers—possibly the majority—of both the higher and lower clergy this could not be said. The dissatisfaction of the people with industrial conditions which prompted the uprising of 1381 was accompanied by an almost equal discontent with the shortcomings of the selfish and avaricious clergy. It was harder, of course, to arouse men to an active hostility to the existing ecclesiastical system than to the industrial régime, because the Church still maintained a very close hold upon the sentiments and attachments of the average individual. Still, there were people here and there who were outspoken for reform, and chief among these was John Wyclif.

Wyclif was born in Yorkshire about 1320 and was educated at Oxford, where in time he became a leading teacher. He was one of those who saw clearly the evils of the times and did not lack the courage to speak out plainly against them. As early as 1366 he had denounced the claims of the papacy, in a pamphlet, *De Dominio Divino*, declaring that the pope ought to have no authority whatsoever over states and governments. This position he never yielded and it became one of the cardinal features of his teaching. He attacked the clergy for their wealth, their self-seeking, and their subservience to the pope, and hurled denunciation at the whole body of friars and vendors of indulgences with whom England was thronged. He even assailed the doctrines of the Church, particularly as to transubstantiation, the efficacy of confession to priests, and the nature of the sacraments. His teachings were very acceptable to large numbers of people who were disgusted with existing conditions, and hence he soon came to have a considerable body of followers, known as the Lollards, who, though not regularly organized into a sect, carried on in later times the work which Wyclif and his "poor priests" had begun.

In 1377 Pope Gregory XI. issued a bull in which he roundly condemned Wyclif and reproved the University of Oxford for not taking active steps to suppress the growing heresy; but it had little or no effect. In 1378 Gregory died and two popes were elected to succeed him—Clement VII. at Avignon and Urban VI. at Rome [see p. 389]. The Schism that resulted prevented further action for a time against Wyclif. In England, however, the uprising of 1381 aroused the government to the expediency of suppressing popular agitators, and in a church council at London, May 19, 1382, Wyclif's doctrines were formally condemned. In 1383 Oxford was compelled to banish all the Lollards from her walls and by the time of Wyclif's death in 1384 the new belief seemed to be pretty thoroughly suppressed. In reality it lived on by the more or less secret attachment of thousands of people to it, and became one of the great preparatory forces for the English Reformation a century and a half later. The document given below is a modernized version of a letter written by Wyclif to Pope Urban VI. in 1384 in response to a summons to appear at Rome to be tried for heresy. The letter was written in Latin and the English translation (given below) prepared by the writer's followers for distribution among Englishmen represents somewhat of an enlargement of the original document. When Wyclif wrote the letter he was in the last year of his life and was so disabled by paralysis that a journey to Rome was quite impossible.

Source—Text in Thomas Arnold, *Select English Works of John Wyclif* (Oxford, 1869), Vol. III., pp. 504–506. Adapted, with modernized spelling, in Guy Carleton Lee, *Source Book of English History* (New York, 1900), pp. 212–214.

I have joyfully to tell what I hold, to all true men that believe, and especially to the pope; for I suppose that if my faith be rightful and given of God, the pope will gladly confirm it; and if my faith be error, the pope will wisely amend it.

I suppose over this that the gospel of Christ be heart of the corps [body] of God's law; for I believe that Jesus Christ, that gave in His own person this gospel, is very God and very man, and by this heart passes all other laws.

I suppose over this that the pope be most obliged to the keeping of the gospel among all men that live here; for the pope is **The pope's high obligation** highest vicar that Christ has here in earth. For moreness of Christ's vicar is not measured by worldly moreness, but by this, that this vicar follows more Christ by virtuous living; for thus teacheth the gospel, that this is the sentence of Christ.

And of this gospel I take as believe, that Christ for time that He walked here, was most poor man of all, both in spirit and in having [possessions]; for Christ says that He had nought for to rest His head on. And Paul says that He was made needy for **Christ's earthly poverty** our love. And more poor might no man be, neither bodily nor in spirit. And thus Christ put from Him all manner of worldly lordship. For the gospel of John telleth that when they would have made Christ king, He fled and hid Him from them, for He would none such worldly highness.

And over this I take it as believe, that no man should follow the pope, nor no saint that now is in heaven, but in as much as he [the pope] follows Christ. For John and James erred when they **How far men ought to fol- low the pope** coveted worldly highness; and Peter and Paul sinned also when they denied and blasphemed in Christ; but men should not follow them in this, for then they went from Jesus Christ. And this I take as wholesome counsel, that the pope leave his worldly lordship to **The pope ex- horted to give up temporal authority** worldly lords, as Christ gave them,—and more speedily all his clerks [clergy] to do so. For thus did Christ, and taught thus His disciples, till the fiend [Satan] had blinded this world. And it seems to some men that clerks that dwell lastingly in this error against God's law, and flee to follow Christ in this, been open heretics, and their fautors [supporters] been partners.

And if I err in this sentence, I will meekly be amended [corrected], yea, by the death, if it be skilful [necessary], for that I hope were good to me. And if I might travel in mine own person, I would with good will go to the pope. But God has needed me to the contrary, and taught me more obedience to God than to men. And I suppose of our pope that he will not be Antichrist, and reverse Christ in this working, to the contrary of Christ's will; for if he summon against reason, by him or by any of his,

The pope should not demand what is contrary to the divine will and pursue this unskilful summoning, he is an open Antichrist. And merciful intent excused not Peter, that Christ should not clepe [call] him Satan; so blind intent and wicked counsel excuses not the pope here; but if he ask of true priests that they travel more than they may, he is not excused by reason of God, that he should not be Antichrist. For our belief teaches us that our blessed God suffers us not to be tempted more than we may; how should a man ask such service? And therefore pray we to God for our Pope Urban the Sixth, that his old [early] holy intent be not quenched by his enemies. And Christ, that may not lie, says that the enemies of a man been especially his home family; and this is sooth of men and fiends.

INDEX

ESSENTIALS IN MEDIÆVAL AND MODERN HISTORY

From Charlemagne to the Present Day. By SAMUEL BANNISTER HARDING, Ph.D., Professor of European History, Indiana University. In consultation with ALBERT BUSHNELL HART, LL.D., Professor of History, Harvard University

$1.50

THIS book is distinguished by the same vital pedagogical features which characterize the other volumes of the Essentials in History Series. It is intended for a year's work in secondary schools, and meets the requirements of the College Entrance Examination Board, and of the New York State Education Department.

¶ The difficulties usually encountered in treating mediæval and modern history are here overcome by an easy and satisfactory method. By this plan Italy, France, Germany, and England are taken up in turn as each becomes the central figure on the world's stage. About a third of the book is devoted to the period previous to the Reformation; another third to modern history from the Reformation to the French Revolution; and the remainder to the century and a quarter since the occurrence of that great event. These proportions give an opportunity to discuss the greatness of England, the unification of Italy, and of Germany, and the present organization of Europe under the control of the concert of powers, on the same plane as the Crusades, or the Thirty Years' War, or the age of Louis XIV.

¶ The three most difficult problems in mediæval history— the feudal state, the church, and the rivalry between the empire and the church—are here discussed with great clearness and brevity. The central idea of the book is the development of the principle of national independence in both politics and religion from the earlier condition of a world empire.

AMERICAN BOOK COMPANY

FISHER'S BRIEF HISTORY OF THE NATIONS

By GEORGE PARK FISHER, LL.D., Emeritus Professor
in Yale University

$1.50

THIS is an entirely independent work, written expressly
to meet the demand for a compact and acceptable text-
book on General History for secondary schools and lower
classes in colleges. Some of the distinctive qualities which will
commend this book to teachers and students are as follows :

¶ It narrates in fresh, vigorous, and attractive style the most
important facts of history in their due order and connection.
It explains the nature of historical evidence, and records only
well established judgments respecting persons and events. It
delineates the progress of peoples and nations in civilization
as well as the rise and succession of dynasties.

¶ It connects, in a single chain of narration, events related
to each other in the contemporary history of different nations
and countries. It is written from the standpoint of the
present, and incorporates the latest discoveries of historical
explorers and writers.

¶ It is illustrated by numerous colored maps, genealogical
tables, and artistic reproductions of architecture, sculpture,
painting, and portraits of celebrated men, representing every
period of the world's history.

FISHER'S OUTLINES OF UNIVERSAL HISTORY
Revised, $2.40

Also published in three parts, price, each, $1.00. Part I, Ancient History.
Part II, Mediaeval History. Part III, Modern History.

A NEW and revised edition of this standard work. Soon after the
publication of the first edition of this history the author was
honored by the University of Edinburgh with the degree of Doctor
of Laws, in recognition of his services in the cause of historical research.
In this edition the book is brought fully up to date in all particulars.

AMERICAN BOOK COMPANY

ESSENTIALS IN AMERICAN HISTORY

From the Discovery to the Present Day. By ALBERT BUSHNELL HART, LL.D., Professor of History, Harvard University

$1.50

PROFESSOR HART was a member of the Committee of Seven, and consequently is exceptionally qualified to supervise the preparation of a series of text-books which carry out the ideas of that Committee. The needs of secondary schools, and the entrance requirements to all colleges, are fully met by the Essentials in History Series.

¶ This volume reflects in an impressive manner the writer's broad grasp of the subject, his intimate knowledge of the relative importance of events, his keen insight into the cause and effect of each noteworthy occurrence, and his thorough familiarity with the most helpful pedagogical features—all of which make the work unusually well suited to students.

¶ The purpose of the book is to present an adequate description of all essential things in the upbuilding of the country, and to supplement this by good illustrations and maps. Political geography, being the background of all historical knowledge, is made a special topic, while the development of government, foreign relations, the diplomatic adjustment of controversies, and social and economic conditions have been duly emphasized.

¶ All sections of the Union, North, East, South, West, and Far West, have received fair treatment. Much attention is paid to the causes and results of our various wars, but only the most significant battles and campaigns have been described. The book aims to make distinct the character and public services of some great Americans, brief accounts of whose lives are given in special sections of the text. Towards the end a chapter sums up the services of America to mankind.

AMERICAN BOOK COMPANY

ESSENTIALS IN ENGLISH HISTORY

From the Earliest Records to the Present Day. By ALBERT
PERRY WALKER, A.M., Master in History, Eng-
lish High School, Boston. In consultation with ALBERT
BUSHNELL HART, LL.D., Professor of History,
Harvard University

$1.50

LIKE the other volumes of the Essentials in History Series,
this text-book is intended to form a year's work in
secondary schools, following out the recommendation
of the Committee of Seven, and meeting the requirements of
the College Entrance Examination Board, and of the New
York State Education Department. It contains the same
general features, the same pedagogic apparatus, and the same
topical method of treatment. The text is continuous, the
sectional headings being placed in the margin. The maps
and illustrations are worthy of special mention.

¶ The book is a model of good historical exposition, unusually clear in expression, logical and coherent in arrangement, and accurate in statement. The essential facts in the
development of the British Empire are vividly described, and
the relation of cause and effect is clearly brought out.

¶ The treatment begins with a brief survey of the whole
course of English history, deducing therefrom three general
movements: (1) the fusing of several races into the English people; (2) the solution by that people of two great
problems: free and democratic home government, and practical, enlightened government of foreign dependencies; and
(3) the extreme development of two great fields of industry,
commerce and manufacture. The narrative follows the
chronological order, and is full of matter which is as interesting as it is significant, ending with a masterly summary of
England's contribution to civilization.

AMERICAN BOOK COMPANY

ESSENTIALS IN ANCIENT HISTORY

From the Earliest Records to Charlemagne. By ARTHUR MAYER WOLFSON, Ph.D., First Assistant in History, DeWitt Clinton High School, New York. In consultation with ALBERT BUSHNELL HART, LL.D., Professor of History, Harvard University

$1.50

THIS volume belongs to the Essentials in History Series, which follows the plan recommended by the Committee of Seven, and adopted by the College Entrance Examination Board, and by the New York State Education Department. The pedagogic apparatus is amply sufficient for any secondary school.

¶ The essentials in ancient history are presented as a unit, beginning with the earliest civilization in the East, and ending with the establishment of the Western Empire by Charlemagne. More attention is paid to civilization than to mere constitutional development, the latter being brought out in the narrative, rather than as a series of separate episodes.

¶ A departure has been made from the time-honored method of carrying the subject down to the end of Greek political life before beginning the story of Rome. The history of the two civilizations is not entirely distinct; hence, it has seemed wise, after completing the account of the life and work of Alexander, to tell the story of the beginnings of Rome. Afterwards the history of the East is resumed, and carried on to the point where it merges into that of Rome. Should any teacher, however, prefer the old method of treating the two nations, he has only to take up Chapters XXIV and XXV before Chapters XVIII to XXIII. The Roman Empire, a very important but much neglected period of history, is brought out in its just proportions, and with reference to the events which had the greatest influence.

AMERICAN BOOK COMPANY

~K AND ROMAN
HISTORIES

M C. MOREY, Professor of History
al Science, University of Rochester

Each, $1.00

These books present a somewhat fuller course than that given in the author's single volume, Outlines of Ancient History. Each is written in a simple, interesting style, and is distinguished by the same pedagogical features, such as the topical method, progressive maps, etc.

¶ MOREY'S OUTLINES OF GREEK HISTORY, which is introduced by a brief sketch of the progress of civilization before the time of the Greeks among the Oriental peoples, pays greater attention to the civilization of ancient Greece than to its political history. The author has endeavored to illustrate by facts the most important and distinguishing traits of the Grecian character; to explain why the Greeks failed to develop a national state system, although successful to a considerable extent in developing free institutions and an organized city state; and to show the great advance made by the Greeks upon the previous culture of the Orient.

¶ MOREY'S OUTLINES OF ROMAN HISTORY gives the history of Rome to the revival of the empire by Charlemagne. Only those facts and events which illustrate the real character of the Roman people, which show the progressive development of Rome as a world power, and which explain the influence that Rome has exercised upon modern civilization, have been emphasized. The genius of the Romans for organization, which gives them their distinctive place in history, is kept prominently in mind, and the kingdom, the republic, and the empire are seen to be but successive stages in the growth of a policy to bring together and organize the various elements of the ancient world.

AMERICAN BOOK COMPANY

GRAY'S NEW MANUAL OF BOTANY—SEVENTH EDITION, ILLUSTRATED

Thoroughly revised and largely rewritten by BENJAMIN LINCOLN ROBINSON, Ph.D., Asa Gray Professor of Systematic Botany, and MERRITT LYNDON FERNALD, S.B., Assistant Professor of Botany, Harvard University, assisted by specialists in certain groups.

Regular edition. Cloth, 8vo, 926 pages $2.50
Tourist's edition.   Flexible leather, 12mo, 926 pages 3.00

Largely rewritten and rearranged, with its scope considerably widened. The nomenclature follows the code of international rules recently adopted in Europe. As now published, it presents in clear and well-ordered form the scattered results of diffuse publication, and treats its subject with due consideration for the results of the latest investigation.

AMES'S TEXT-BOOK OF GENERAL PHYSICS

For use in colleges.   By JOSEPH S. AMES, Ph.D., Professor of Physics and Director of the Physical Laboratory, Johns Hopkins University.

Cloth, 8vo, 768 pages, illustrated $3.50

A one year college course, stating the theory of the subject clearly and logically, and giving a concise summary of the experimental facts on which the science of physics is based.   Every important experiment and observation is mentioned and explained, and the few great principles of nature are given the prominence they deserve.

AMERICAN BOOK COMPANY

DESCRIPTIVE CATALOGUE OF HIGH SCHOOL AND COLLEGE TEXT-BOOKS

Published Complete and in Sections

WE issue a Catalogue of High School and College Text-Books, which we have tried to make as valuable and as useful to teachers as possible. In this catalogue are set forth briefly and clearly the scope and leading characteristics of each of our best text-books. In most cases there are also given testimonials from well-known teachers, which have been selected quite as much for their descriptive qualities as for their value as commendations.

¶ For the convenience of teachers this Catalogue is also published in separate sections treating of the various branches of study. These pamphlets are entitled : English, Mathematics, History and Political Science, Science, Modern Languages, Ancient Languages, and Philosophy and Education.

¶ In addition we have a single pamphlet devoted to Newest Books in every subject.

¶ Teachers seeking the newest and best books for their classes are invited to send for our Complete High School and College Catalogue, or for such sections as may be of greatest interest.

¶ Copies of our price lists, or of special circulars, in which these books are described at greater length than the space limitations of the catalogue permit, will be mailed to any address on request.

¶ All correspondence should be addressed to the nearest of the following offices of the company : New York, Cincinnati, Chicago, Boston, Atlanta, San Francisco.

AMERICAN BOOK COMPANY